Season's Greetings
FROM THE
WHITE HOUSE

Happy Birthday Sis —
8-4-2021

I came upon an after Christmas
Sale earlier this year and I one
of these for me and it turned
out to be a BOGO!!! I was
happy to be able to have
that one for you. It is so
well written by Mary Seeley,
a great Historian of The White House.
She lives in Florida! It is a neat
"Coffee Table" Book I think you'll enjoy

Love you & many
more Birthdays,

Imogene

Season's Greetings

FROM THE

WHITE HOUSE

MARY EVANS SEELEY

A PRESIDENTIAL CHRISTMAS
Tampa, Florida

To my husband, Ron, who had the vision
and who unselfishly helped make the book a reality.
To our children, who were an encouragement—
may you carry on the dream.

Published by A Presidential Christmas Corporation
Tampa, Florida
MLS42@aol.com
whitehouseholidays.com

ISBN 978-0-9909561-2-9

Designed by Bob Antler, Antler Designworks
Manufactured in the United States of America
10 9 8

Thomas William Jones was commissioned in January 2002 to paint *The South Portico at Christmas* as the new cover art for this book. Previously he had painted a series of White House State Rooms for President and Mrs. Reagan. In 1985 *The Blue Room at Christmas* was reproduced for the official holiday card and for the gift print given to the White House staff; in 1986 he was the first artist to depict *The East Room at Christmas* for an official Presidential card and gift print; in 1987 he did a painting of *The State Dining Room at Christmas*; in 1988, for the Reagans' last official Christmas card and gift print, he created *The North Entry Hall at Christmas*. The original 1988 painting is now a part of The Seeley Collection. The artist lives in Snohomish, Washington, with his wife, Carrie.

Frontispiece: **Créche in East Room, The White House** was selected by the President and Mrs. Kennedy for their official Christmas card in 1963 but was never sent. Less than 30 were personally signed by both the President and First Lady prior to their ill-fated trip to Dallas. This dual-signed Christmas card is among the rarest of Presidential Christmas memorabilia. HALLMARK CARDS

Contents

Foreword

Historians owe more to collectors than we usually recognize. Collectors are men and women of purpose and passion. They fall in love with a person or category or theme. They pursue and accumulate books, papers and artifacts–the memorabilia that symbolize and illuminate the objects of their affection. In doing so, they enrich the historical record and very often rescue evidence that might otherwise have vanished down the memory hole.

–Arthur M. Schlesinger, Jr.

This book began, as it should have, in Washington, D.C., many years ago. It was pushed into being, as it should have been, by an inveterate collector, my husband, Ron. It was written because it should have been written–but wasn't. If you can't understand how I ended up being the one to write it, you don't know what it's like to be married to an avid collector.

The first item he purchased on that medical convention trip to the nation's capital was a red velour presentation folder containing the portrait of George Washington. A gift from President and Mrs. Nixon to a White House employee, it eventually found its way into the political memorabilia shop where Ron found it. When he showed it to me that afternoon, he was excited; he was enthusiastic; his mood was contagious. Soon, I too, was learning everything I could about Presidential Christmas cards and gifts, and our quest began in earnest.

Along the way, we had the good fortune to meet Raleigh DeGeer Amyx of American Heritage Autographs and Collectibles. We were frankly overwhelmed by his careful preservation and beautiful presentation of American historical artifacts; his dedication to his work inspired us to continue our pursuit. Since then, we've acquired numerous one-of-a-kind Presidential Christmas-related items–one a letter dating back to James Madison–Christmas cards and gift prints, books and photographs signed by *many* other later Presidents–including the rare Créche Card signed by President and Mrs. Kennedy just days before the assassination–and Presidential gift items made of wood, pewter, sterling silver, leather, brass, glass and even yarn.

In time, the Seeley Collection gained us an invitation to the White House from its curator, the late Rex Scouten. He was especially interested in our early collection prior to President Eisenhower, and Ron and I were interested in learning from Mr. Scouten the history of many of our acquisitions. Our discussion of the facts and figures uncovered many discrepancies. Concerned about the accuracy of much of the information in circulation, Mr. Scouten stated: "Someone should write a book to set the record straight."

Ron was the one who knew I could write such a book; he already had me involved in this project when it still seemed like an impossible dream to me. It didn't take much persuasion, though, and with Mr. Scouten's endless assistance and Ron's enthusiasm, the book "to set the record straight" now exists–thousands of miles, hundreds of conversations and 3 1/2 years later.

Of invaluable research help were the greeting card companies that originally produced the Presidents' cards and gift prints; they also provided generous assistance in reproducing the art for this book. Jeannette Lee, consultant to Chairman Donald J. Hall at Hallmark, was a tremendous source of help after her 35 years of involvement in Presidential Christmas projects. She granted me the rare privilege of using the Hallmark Archives; Sharman Robertson, the Hallmark archivist, did the facts and figures work. At American Greetings, Barbara Hatala made the connections for me, including a memorable and informative luncheon with Harvey Levin, John Hernandis, Joe Cuffari, Chris Riddle, Paul Urban and the late Ed Pakish.

For the human interest stories behind the creative compositions, I interviewed the following artists and photographers: James Blake, David Drummond, Ray Ellis, William Gemmell, Mark Hampton, Chris Hankinson, Cindi Holt, Kay Jackson, Thomas W. Jones, Larassa Kabel, Kamil Kubik, Robert Laessig, Tim Allen Lawson, Edward Lehman, Adrian Martinez, Thomas McKnight, Barbara Ernst Prey, James Steinmeyer, Cecil Stoughton, Jamie Wyeth and Zhen-Huan Lu. I hope I have succeeded in passing along my greater appreciation of their work and my new respect for them as artists.

For first-hand historical information, I went straight to the source, where possible, and the generous offerings of personal anecdotes and memories of former First Family members greatly enhance this work. The high point of this project, for me, was interviewing 87-year-old John Coolidge in the very village where his father had been sworn in as President of the United States in the middle of an August night back in 1923. The biggest surprise was picking up my telephone and hearing the voice on the other end say, "Hello, this is Barbara Bush...." Not that I'll ever forget the unique privilege that was mine when Ron and I met President Ronald Reagan in his office, only to be followed by an interview with Mrs. Nancy Reagan as she graciously reminisced about Christmas in the White House. I am also indebted to Mrs. Laura Bush, Mrs. Betty Ford and Mrs. Rosalynn Carter for taking the time to talk with me, and I appreciate the cooperation from First Ladies Mrs. Lady Bird Johnson, Mrs. Hillary Rodham Clinton and Mrs. Melania Trump and from the children of Presidents, namely John Eisenhower, Mrs. Lynda Bird Johnson Robb and Mrs. Julie Nixon Eisenhower.

Invaluable details were supplied by Kay Holloway (Truman); Mary Jane McCaffree (Eisenhower); Bess Abell and Shirley James (Johnson); Helen Smith (Nixon); Maria Downs (Ford); Madeline Edwards and Melissa Montgomery (Carter); Linda Faulkner, Lisa Cavelier, Cathy Busch and Joanne Drake (Reagan); Laurie Firestone, Patti Presock, Quincy Hicks (G. Bush); Ann Stock and Anne McCoy (Clinton); and Andrea Ball and Alison Harden (G.W. Bush).

So many others have played major roles in making the book a reality. I am grateful for the meaningful contributions from Terry Adams, William Allman, Claudia Anderson, Peg Anderson-Lee, Russell Armentrout, Patricia Blair, Jim and Carole Bowers, Nelson Diaz, Ann Drexel, Claudia Dunne, Sara Eames, George Elsey, Mary Finch, Sanford Fox, Kate Henderson, Janice Ingersoll, Luanne Knox, Carolyn Malenick, B. Roland McElroy, Bob and Liz McEwen, Kellie McGuire, Betty Monkman, Ilona Nickels, Deidre Parkes, Lyn C. Probst, the late Joseph Riley, Chester Richardson, E. Ward Russell, Susan Sterner, Dan Stifter, Jude Tolley and Nelson Whitman. I deeply appreciate all the assistance so freely given by countless numbers of directors, archivists and audiovisual people at all the Presidential libraries, the Library of Congress and the National Archives.

I don't know how I can ever adequately thank Virginia Koenke Hunt, my editor, who showed respect for my research and helped to make the words flow; designer Bob Antler, whose creative talents are so evident in this work; Albert Yokum, a vital member of my team as print production coordinator, and Susan Stautberg, who, as president of MasterMedia Limited, believed in my project and brought it to life.

Above all, Ron and our children, Andrea, Michele, Todd and Mark, and their families, have been my support and strength. Each one encouraged me to be all I could be. When they needed me and I was elsewhere or preoccupied, they understood. Now, I have accomplished my impossible dream. I hope you will enjoy reading it as much as I have enjoyed writing it.

—Mary Evans Seeley

THE COOLIDGES
Beginning of a Tradition

President Calvin Coolidge issued the first official Christmas message to the American people in 1927. Written by his own hand on White House stationery, the statement appeared on Christmas Day in newspapers all across the country. The greeting came in response to numerous requests for the President to send a holiday greeting directly into the homes of America. While it took four years for Coolidge to honor these requests, every Chief Executive since, despite slightly differing ideologies, has delivered a Christmas message to the American people at a ceremony that is now a National Christmas Tree tradition.

1923: In the Beginning....

It all began in November 1923, when Lucretia Walker Hardy, the acting general director of the Community Center Department of the Public Schools of the District of Columbia, wrote to the President's secretary, C. Bascom Slemp, suggesting the erection of a Christmas tree on the south grounds of the White House. Such a location was to give the tree a national emphasis while the lighting of the tree by the President at a Christmas Eve ceremony would afford the local Washington community a holiday gathering in which all could participate. "The event which Christmas commemorates means more to the world as a whole than any other holiday that we observe," wrote Hardy. "The tree would be an outward evidence of the President's desire to give encouragement to the spirit of which it is symbolical."

Facing page: Artistic rendering of Calvin Coolidge's 1927 handwritten holiday message.

On December 4, Slemp denied Hardy the use of the White House grounds on Christmas Eve, because Mrs. Coolidge had already planned an event to which the public would be invited. Hardy finally agreed to erect the tree on the Ellipse and she invited the President to officially participate in the program. Thus was born the idea of the National Community Christmas Tree. To foster a national emphasis, Hardy suggested further that the tree be provided by the President's native state of Vermont; as to arranging the tree-lighting ceremony, Hardy offered the services of her department.

Shortly thereafter, the President received a letter from college president Paul D. Moody, who wrote: "Middlebury College counts it a privilege to send to you, from its forest preserve in the heart of the Green Mountains…a National Community Christmas tree. It is our hope that this Vermont tree, when electrically illuminated in Washington will contribute toward a spread of the true Christmas spirit throughout the nation." The 60-foot fir was accepted on December 18, hauled to the Ellipse, south of the Treasury Building, and erected by the Potomac Electric Power Company.

The installation of an electric button to enable the President to light the Community Christmas Tree from the Executive Office, it was calculated, would cost about $500. Lucretia Hardy sincerely hoped, therefore, that the President would be able to walk to the Ellipse on December 24 for the lighting. In view of the expense, he agreed to do so if his schedule permitted; the question of his delivering a Christmas message was not discussed.

National Festivities

On Christmas Eve 1923, the Coolidges participated in a series of celebrations. At 5:05 in the afternoon, after walking to the Ellipse, the President pressed, with his foot, the button that illuminated the 3,000 light bulbs on the first National Community Christmas Tree. With a fanfare of trumpets, this symbol of the spirit of Christmas was converted into a national emblem signifying that the celebration of Christmas had begun.

While President Coolidge began the National Christmas Tree tradition on this, his first Christmas in office, he made no speech at the ceremony. The program for the event included a choir from the Epiphany Church, accompanied by a "quartette" from the Marine Band, which led the crowd of thousands in Christmas carols. At 7 o'clock, the full band put on a concert of holiday music.

At 9 o'clock, from the home of the President and First Lady, 65 members of the First Congregational Church filed out singing "O, Come, All Ye Faithful," the first of its many carols. A reporter for the *Washington Post* described the scene:

From the steps of the White house there went forth last night a message of "peace on earth, goodwill to men." It was the message echoing down through the ages from the days of the three shepherds, and as it passed from the throats of a choir on the portico of the White House, it was echoed by the President and his family and thousands of citizens, all in harmony with the reecho in the hearts of the people of the nation and the rest of the world. It was the reverence of a Christian people giving at the seat of their government the expression of their praise for the "King of Kings" on the eve of the anniversary of his birth.

The writer estimated that the caroling at the White House drew nearly 10,000 people "who sought with their official leader, to voice their feelings on Christmas Eve.... So the Capital, so the nation, and so the world welcomed the advent of the 1923 Christmas."

The inspiration for the caroling had come to Grace Coolidge while listening to hymns at her church. The Sunday *Evening Star* printed the verses of the carols in the order in which they appeared on the program. It was suggested that the music be clipped and carried to the White House, along with a personal light to facilitate one's participation. Arrangements were made with the Chesapeake and Potomac Telephone Company to have station WCAP broadcast the program; it is likely that more than a million Americans listened in on this significant national event in Washington via radio.

First Family Festivities

The spirit of Christmas permeated the White House. The historic mansion was dressed with holly and mistletoe and other greens. Even the President's office was draped with boughs of holly. Contrary to newspaper reports that the Coolidges had never had a Christmas tree and that they would not have one this year either, an eight-foot Norway spruce was purchased for the Blue Room and a smaller one for the family quarters. Both were decorated by Mrs. Coolidge and sons John and Calvin.

Once John and Calvin, Jr., had arrived home for the holidays from Mercersburg Academy, Mrs. Coolidge made it a practice to keep her schedule free to prepare for a real homey New England family Christmas. The boys accompanied their father on a window-shopping excursion, but they especially enjoyed the close companionship of their mother. She had made the arrangements for a Christmas dance in their honor in the Blue Room. Having invited 60 boys, she took a turn to dance with each one.

While their first Christmas in the White House was a happy one, the tragic death the following July of 16-year-old Calvin, from staphylococcus septicemia, cast a shadow on the observance of the holiday the following

The family poses at the lily pond on the White House grounds. Mrs. Coolidge reported that the President was never the same after the death of their younger son, Calvin, Jr. (center), who died in the summer of 1924. LIBRARY OF CONGRESS

year. The devastated President said in his autobiography: "When he went, the power and the glory of the Presidency went with him. The ways of Providence are often beyond our understanding. It seemed to me that the world had need of the work it was probable he could do. I do not know why such a price was exacted for occupying the White House." Mrs. Coolidge noted that her husband was never the same after young Calvin's death.

1924: One Member Missing

As Christmas drew near, Mrs. Coolidge prepared herself for an avalanche of emotions. According to Ishbel Ross in *Grace Coolidge and Her Era,* the First Lady wrote: "I shall not be sad at that happy time of year. I found a quotation the other day which seems to express Calvin and something of what he is to me, one 'whose yesterdays look backward with a smile.' Always he seemed to be just ahead of me and I can see his smile."

Christmas cards arrived at the White House in record numbers—about 12,000 in fact. The *New York Times* reported that while the Coolidges did send Christmas cards and gifts, it was mostly to relatives and close friends. The President left all of the shopping to his wife and did not enter any of the stores during the holidays, as he had with both of his sons the previous year.

The tradition of the National Community Christmas Tree almost vanished as quickly as it appeared when the President informed the American Forestry Association (AFA) that he was against the cutting down of Christmas trees. To preserve the tradition, Ovid Butler, the AFA's executive secretary, presented to the President a 40-year-old, 35-foot living Norway spruce to be planted in Sherman Plaza between the statues of General Sherman and Alexander Hamilton. Intended to be used every year as the National Community Christmas Tree, it survived five Christmases before succumbing to the abuse of ladders, the weight of heavy ornaments and the intense heat of the lights.

On Christmas Eve President and Mrs. Coolidge attended the dual celebrations as in the first year. Receiving the living Christmas tree from the AFA, the President said, "I accept this tree and I will now light it for this occasion." Shortly after 8 o'clock the President illuminated the tree with its thousand brilliant red, green and amber lights. With as much significance as any other formal national ceremony, the lighting of the National Community Christmas Tree ushered in the observance of Christmas.

From Sherman Park, the First Family moved to the picturesque but seldom used North Portico, now brightly lighted for the vested choir of the First Congregational Church. John Coolidge, home at the time from Amherst College, recalled in a 1994 interview, at age 87: "I was given a coonskin coat for Christmas that year and wore it on Christmas Eve. That was quite a nice event. Mother was very musical. My father didn't know one note from another. If he did, he didn't admit it. In church, he never sang a hymn. My mother and I did, of course. I sang a great deal."

1925: *The Mission of Mercy*

By the year 1925, the lighting ceremony for the National Community Christmas Tree achieved national significance as the spirit of the holiday extended from Washington to all parts of the country. Congressman Hamilton Fish, Jr., from New York, speaking for the radio networks, expressed their hope that "the President would speak for a couple of minutes, simply wishing the children of America a Merry Christmas and a Happy New Year." The President's secretary, Everett Sanders, responded that the Chief Executive would not be making any remarks on Christmas Eve.

As the chimes on the Church of the Epiphany announced the prelude to the Eve of Christmas, President and Mrs. Coolidge made their way from

the White House to Sherman Park. At dusk, the Chief Executive humbly touched the switch that illuminated the living Norway spruce, a signal for community trees across the nation to be set aglow. Three hours after the ceremony at the tree, about 2,000 people were welcomed on the White House grounds by the First Family for the singing of carols, led, as in previous years,

Mrs. Grace Coolidge gives out toys at the Central Union Mission's Christmas party. STOCK MONTAGE

Thousands wait in line to meet President and Mrs. Coolidge at the New Year's Day reception. The First Lady's "hand got so swollen, the glove would have to be cut off."
UNDERWOOD & UNDERWOOD/
THE BETTMANN ARCHIVE

by the choir from the "President's Church." The message of Christmas sung from the front portico of the President's house was likewise broadcast by radio nationwide.

The spirit of Christmas that prevailed in the nation's capital that season was unprecedented. Enjoying the most prosperous Yuletide of the Coolidge Administration, Washingtonians appeared to be bent on a "mission of mercy." Never had the needs of the poor been met in so many ways. Mrs. Coolidge also participated in activities for them. She spent time holding and cuddling some of the 1,200 tots confined to the Children's Hospital. She assisted Santa Claus by giving out toys at Keith's Theater under the auspices of the Central Union Mission. At the Salvation Army hall, she joined in the religious service, made a brief speech and distributed baskets. Her compassionate caring for the needy would long be remembered in the hearts of Washington's poor.

While the country was geared to a lavish lifestyle, the President practiced and preached a message of thrift; to compensate for her husband's tight fist, the First Lady often gave little gifts to the staff. "What was austere and withdrawn in Calvin Coolidge was warm and gracious in his wife," wrote a reporter for the *New York Herald Tribune*. As husband and wife, they complemented each other.

For years the White House had held an official reception on New Year's Day for foreign dignitaries, national officials and ordinary citizens. "Silent Cal" had gained a reputation for the number of hands he could shake without suffering ill effects. Said John Coolidge: "My father had a pull-along handshake that didn't allow guests to linger and talk." On the first day of 1926, in the four and a half hours that the President and Mrs. Coolidge hosted the reception, between 3,000 and 4,000 people shook hands with them and received a smile and simple holiday greeting. "Mother would wear white gloves," her son remembered, "but still her hand got so swollen, the glove would have to be cut off."

1926: Carols Across the Country

Once again, on Christmas Eve, the President of a peaceful and prosperous nation set aglow the red, green and yellow lights of the National Community Christmas Tree. At that moment a flare illuminated the sky throughout Washington alerting Boy Scout buglers to sound the glad message of Christmas.

At 9 o'clock the choir of the First Congregational Church sang carols on the steps of the White House. A second celebration around the National Community Christmas Tree began at 10:30. An estimated 20 million people blended their voices with those of the 50-voice choir from the Central Congregational Church of Brooklyn, N. Y., in "seasonal fellowship and adoration." In Washington, the nationwide concert was carried by station WRC and sponsored by the *Evening Star*, which had issued a supplement containing all the words and music of the songs. President and Mrs. Coolidge, with John, gathered in front of the White House radio and joined the rest of the country in a reverent celebration that focused on the birth of Christ.

The generous outpouring of gifts and cards from all parts of the country reportedly touched the President in such a way that he gave a Christmas gift of a gold coin to each of the attachés and servants at the White House. Chief usher Ike Hoover, in *42 Years in the White House*, reported that despite "his reputation for being sphinx-like," the President went out of his way to know his employees personally. "It was one of his diversions to jest with them, and many is the time he saw fit to play jokes on them."

1927: The Handwritten Holiday Message

The following year, President Coolidge softened even more and finally replied to the many requests for a Christmas greeting from him. As usual, on Christmas Eve, he pressed the golden button that turned the stately spruce tree on the Ellipse into a conical pillar of 500 brilliant flashing lights and 2,000 reflecting jewels. The more elaborate lighting and decorations on the tree in 1927 were undertaken by the Electric League of Washington in cooperation with the General Electric Co. So as not to distract from the effectiveness of his Christmas Day message, the President addressed the crowd only as "Fellow Americans" and then lit the tree.

On Christmas morning, a short, simple, handwritten message from the Chief Executive appeared in every major newspaper. The *Evening Star* reported that the President was generally pleased with the wide circulation his message received and many favorable telegrams were sent in response.

THE WHITE HOUSE
WASHINGTON

December 25, 1927.

To the American People:-

Christmas is not a time or a season, but a state of mind. To cherish peace and good will, to be plenteous in mercy, is to have the real spirit of Christmas. If we think on these things, there will be born in us a Savior and over us will shine a star sending its gleam of hope to the world.

Calvin Coolidge

President Coolidge's handwritten holiday message to the nation. CALVIN COOLIDGE MEMORIAL FOUNDATION, INC.

Christmas Eve, 1927: the Coolidges at the National Community Christmas Tree.
UNDERWOOD & UNDERWOOD/THE BETTMANN ARCHIVE

On the fourth anniversary of his taking office, with his reelection virtually assured, Calvin Coolidge made the cryptic announcement, "I do not choose to run!" He had convinced himself that it was best for the country that he not seek another term, but return instead to the people. Ten years in office could possibly jeopardize the health and energy of both himself and his wife. "It costs a great deal to be President," he said. In an effort to prevent the nomination, President Coolidge instructed his secretary, Everett Sanders, to notify unpledged delegates at the convention not to vote for him. Heeding this advice, the Republicans gave their support to Secretary of Commerce Herbert Hoover, who was nominated on the first ballot.

1928: The President Speaks to the Nation

Christmas of 1928 was Calvin Coolidge's last one in office. In a show of support, the largest Christmas Eve crowd, ever, gathered at Sherman Square. Praised for his Christmas tree spirit, the President then stepped to the front and spoke briefly. With the nation listening by radio, he said: "In token of the good-will and happiness of the holiday season and as an expres-

Calvin Coolidge is thought to have used this General Electric Co. switch plate at the lighting of the National Community Christmas Tree. LYN C. PROBST

sion of the best wishes of the people of the United States toward a Community Christmas Tree, in behalf of the city of Washington, I now turn on the current which will illuminate this tree." At 8:05, under a full December moon, the President touched the button that transformed the tree from darkness into a burst of light.

This last Christmas at the White House was a happy one. Both President and Mrs. Coolidge appeared pleased about the prospects of returning to private life and regaining the freedom and privacy that had been denied them as the First Family. But it was also a poignant time. John, unable to leave his work in New Haven, Connecticut, was noticeably missing from the Yuletide celebration. To celebrate the Coolidges' first Christmas in the White House there had been two boys; this last year there were none. Death had claimed one and the world had prevented the other. The day after Christmas the President and Mrs. Coolidge left Washington for an extended vacation on Sapelo Island, off the coast of Georgia.

The Coolidge Christmas Legacy

The Coolidges' Christmas customs left an indelible mark on a White House Christmas. The tradition of lighting the National Community Christmas Tree initiated in 1923 has ushered in every Christmas since. A Christmas greeting by the President of the United States (or the Vice President on rare occasions) has been delivered to the American people every year since Coolidge's first handwritten message in 1927.

"Silent Cal" was not a sentimentalist, but in 1930, in his syndicated column *Calvin Coolidge Says*, he expressed these thoughts about the holiday: "For many generations Christmas has been joyously observed ... because on that day was born one who grew to be the only perfect man and became the Savior of the world. No other fact, no other influence in human experience has compared with the birth and life of Christ. Down through the ages he has borne the name of Master! He gained that everlasting title not by the use of any material force, but by demonstrating the moral and spiritual power of mankind.... Christmas holds its place in the hearts of men because they know that love is the greatest thing in the world. Christmas is celebrated in its true spirit only by those who make some sacrifice for the benefit of their fellow men."

A Merry Christmas
and a
Happy New Year
from Herbert Hoover

THE HOOVERS
Depression, Drought and a Natural Disaster

*H*erbert Hoover tried to find a solution for the Great Depression throughout most of his ill-fated term in office; punctuating much of the Hoover Administration was a devastating drought that affected a large portion of the country. These economic and personal disasters resulted in a disillusioned public and an eventual political defeat for the President.

Upon taking office, Hoover wrote to a friend: "I have no dread of the ordinary work of the Presidency. What I do fear is the result of an exaggerated idea the people have conceived of me. They have a conviction that I am some sort of superman, that no problem is beyond my capacity.... If some unprecedented calamity should come upon the nation ... I would be sacrificed to the unreasoning disappointment of a people who expected too much...." Prophetic words! When Herbert Hoover failed to become "the savior of the Depression," he lost the Presidency and invariably became, himself, a victim of that crisis.

1929: *Christmas During the Depression*
The Great Depression started slowly with the October stock market crash. By the middle of November, the crisis had worsened; by Christmas, the nation was feeling the need to cut back its holiday spending. Taking time

Facing page: President Hoover astride his horse, Billy, at his camp in Virginia's Shenandoah Valley. This photograph was one of many given as a Christmas gift to his staff. STOCK MONTAGE from the cares of the country to do some shopping, the President and First Lady, Lou Henry Hoover, visited various stores, including the most crowded "five and ten." The Chief Executive purchased dolls and toys to send to grandchildren Peggy Ann and Peter, who would be spending Christmas with their parents in California.

White House Prints

The First Lady was fond of old prints of Washington, particularly prints of the White House. Her secretary, Ruth Fesler, often shopped for her in secondhand book stores in Washington and New York. "I found in old books about Washington many lithographs and copies of etchings of the White House. It was an interesting project for me," she said, and it revealed a "sense of history that both President and Mrs. Hoover had about the White House." Their collection remained on display at the east end of the long corridor on the second floor of the White House.

One of the Hoover Christmas gifts in 1929 was this photograph of the White House. HERBERT HOOVER LIBRARY

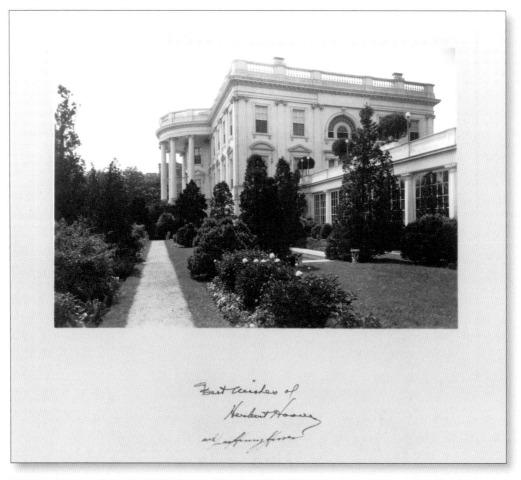

For Christmas, the President and Mrs. Hoover drew from this collection and gave their staff a reproduction of an etching of the South Portico; titled simply *The White House*, it was signed by the artist, M. Pierce. According to extensive lists compiled by Fesler, this etching was given to about 64 members of the Executive Office staff, the Medicine Ball Cabinet, White House aides, Secret Service agents and gardeners. A second etching of the North Portico of the White House by an unidentified artist was the gift selected for 75 employees detailed to the Executive Office. Engraved on the mat of this engraving was the greeting: "Best Wishes of Herbert Hoover and Lou Henry Hoover."

In addition to these gifts, 150 photographs of the South Lawn of the White House were ordered—some in gray, buff or green tones—and mounted on white stock. By Fesler's accounts, these photos, framed, cost $1.25 each and were presented to the White House police, clerks and horticultural employees. The President and First Lady gave two other photographs as staff gifts: one depicted the East Wing with the reflection pool in the foreground; the other showed the West Wing and its garden; each of these carried the message, "Best Wishes of Herbert Hoover and Lou Henry Hoover." To his personal staff the President also gave a photo of him on his horse, Billy, at Camp Hoover in the Shenandoah Valley. All in all, the First Family gave about 275 gift photographs to their staff for their first Christmas at the White House.

The Hoovers were certainly considerate of their employees, but there were times when the staff perceived that the President was less than cordial. Mrs. Hoover's maid, Lillian Rogers Parks, recalled how her coworkers viewed the First Family. In her book, *My Thirty Years Backstairs at the White House*, she said:

> *The servants couldn't get over the fact that the President, who had once been a great outdoor man, roughing it in the wilds, and a mining engineer, who was used to mixing with all classes of people, was completely aloof with the White House staff. He never spoke to them, and never paid the slightest bit of attention to anything they were doing. However, he was respected by everyone. They knew how busy he was. At Christmas, when the servants would have a party in the East Room, the President would simply walk in, say "Merry Christmas," and leave, and Mrs. Hoover would give us a little talk.*

Parks added that whenever an employee was ill, Mrs. Hoover would send a basket of food, flowers and a card. The First Lady was always there to step in for the President when he was reluctant to do so or preoccupied.

Tree Tradition Continues

Initiated during the Coolidge Administration, the tradition of lighting a National Community Christmas Tree was to be carried on by President Hoover. Preparations for the event had begun in March of 1929 with the planting of a new National Tree on Sherman Square to replace the previous one after it succumbed to the weight of heavy wiring and the heat of lighted bulbs. The new tree, a Norway spruce, was sent as a gift of the American Forestry Association from the Amawalk Nurseries in Amawalk, New York.

At the lighting ceremony on Christmas Eve, as the Marine Band struck up "Hail to the Chief," the President waved them to stop. Although he was not scheduled to speak, he delivered an impromptu greeting: "I want to have the privilege of wishing you all, and all the unseen audience, a merry Christmas and a prosperous New Year." Surrounded by a choir of junior high children, members of the President's Cabinet, Justices of the Supreme Court, members of Congress and District Commissioners, the President pushed the button to light the tree.

The Christmas Eve Fire

After the ceremony, President and Mrs. Hoover went back to the White House for Christmas Eve dinner with the families of their secretaries and aides. As the guests were finishing dessert, chief usher Ike Hoover discreetly notified the President that the White House was on fire! The blaze had been discovered by one of the White House police who had noticed smoke coming from the basement in the West Wing and had sounded the alarm at 8:09.

The President walked quickly to the scene of the fire—the Executive Office; in short order, though, he was forced to watch the fire from the roof of the Conservatory. Wearing a heavy blue topcoat and a black hat, he puffed nervously on a cigar. Secretary of War Pat Hurley ordered 150 soldiers from the Washington barracks to help the Metropolitan Police hold back the thousands of people who had gathered on the White House lawn and who were now trying to push forward for a closer look.

Meanwhile, the Christmas party inside continued. Although Mrs. Hoover was aware of the fire, she remained completely calm, never letting on that anything was amiss. The Marine Band continued playing Christmas carols at a volume calculated to drown out the sound of the arriving fire engines. Once the gifts were distributed, the party came to a quick close. Mrs. Hoover then escorted her guests out to the West Terrace, where in safety all could watch the fire fighters battle the third White House fire since 1814. The President's office finally succumbed to the fire and water, but not until the rescue of the most important documents, flags, rugs, and virtually all of the furnishings. His heavy desk could not be saved, but the secretarial

The President and Mrs. Hoover and numerous dignitaries at what was to be the last New Year's Day reception. With more than 6,300 guests filing through the White House, it was decided that the 129-year-old tradition was getting out of hand. AP/WIDE WORLD PHOTOS

The President and Mrs. Hoover

cordially reciprocate

your holiday greetings

1929 - 1930

offices, the Cabinet Room, the Press Room and the Main Lobby suffered no more than water and smoke damage. It was a night before Christmas the Hoovers would not soon forget.

The fire did not cancel the New Year's Day reception at the White House. One of the largest crowds since the Theodore Roosevelt Administration came to meet the popular President and Mrs. Hoover. The three-hour party was divided into two shifts. At 11 o'clock, the First Family greeted the Justices of the Supreme Court, members of Congress, the diplomatic corps, government officials and military officers. After lunch, the public, 6,300 strong, filed past the Chief Executive and First Lady. For obvious reasons, Hoover was the last President to receive guests on New Year's Day.

In response to the hundreds of cards and gifts that poured in for their first White House Christmas, the Hoovers acknowledged many with one of the 3,100 cards from Brewood Engraving. While all 3,100 bore the Presidential Seal, four different messages were printed: 850 read, "The

President and Mrs. Hoover cordially reciprocate your holiday greetings, 1929-1930"; 1,500 read, "The President thanks you for your holiday greeting, 1929-1930"; 350 read, "The President and Mrs. Hoover thank you for your holiday greetings, 1929-1930"; and 400 read "Mrs. Hoover thanks you for your holiday greeting, 1929-1930."

1930: *Gifts of Historic Wood*

The old roof of the White House that had sheltered Presidents for 100 years was replaced during the latter part of the Coolidge Administration. Dumped on a trash pile, the discarded wood was reclaimed by the Hoovers to be fashioned into the First Family's gifts to its staff in 1930. The final output came to 13 sets of bookends; 35 ashtrays; 9 large boxes; 43 long pen trays; 61 square trays; 27 paper cutters; 28 small round trays and 13 small boxes; a cane was made for the chief usher, and, for the social secretary, candlesticks. Enclosed with each gift was an original poem by Mrs. Hoover describing the historic wood:

Wood discarded from the rebuilding of the White House roof was used to make candlesticks, wooden boxes and paper knives. HERBERT HOOVER LIBRARY

Recollections of a Piece of Wood 1930

A pine-tree on the hills of Maryland–through many summers'
  heats and winters' snows,
Felled, carted, quartered, sawn, a metamorphosis within a week.
And then a century buried deep within the White House walls,–
  unseen, unsung, but one of myriads holding firm together
  the storied structure.
Until,–a new age came and replaced steel for wood.
Then months upon the dump-heap,–the dump cart actually
  arrived for one last ride,–
And then a rescue. Now here I rest upon your desk for a short
  space; until,–the wastebasket and the fire.
Then once again I'll go,–free smoke before free wind,–to touch
  again the hills of Maryland.

With each gift also was an engraved card with the Presidential Seal and the words, "The White House, Washington." The greeting read, "The President and Mrs. Hoover take Christmas pleasure in presenting this historic bit of pinewood with their greetings." In addition to the gifts of wood, about $650 worth of framed prints were distributed to White House aides and other employees.

On Christmas Eve, several hundred people braved the bitter cold to witness the simple but impressive tree-lighting ceremony and to hear the President's brief, 37-word address. Following the lighting, the First Family hurried back to the White House to join a party planned for their grandchildren and the children of the White House secretariat. Among the surprises, President and Mrs. Hoover gave a bright red fire truck to the three sons of George Ackerson, secretary to the President, as a remembrance of the previous Christmas when fire had broken out in the Executive Offices.

1931: *The Artists' Washington*

By 1931, Mrs. Hoover's print collection had expanded even more; for Christmas she had her favorite etchings and photographs reproduced as gifts for family, friends and staff. Among the prints were etchings by J.C. Claghorn of the

A red fire truck was given to the sons of Presidential secretary George Ackerson as a memento of the White House fire on Christmas Eve of 1929. HERBERT HOOVER LIBRARY

A Merry Christmas and a Happy New Year from Herbert Hoover

And from Lou Henry Hoover and Weegie and Pat.

1932-3

Dual photographs from the White House grounds: Herbert Hoover in the Rose Garden; Lou Henry Hoover, with pets Weegie and Pat, at the end of the Spanish reflection pool. HERBERT HOOVER LIBRARY

Washington Monument from South Portico, Arlington Memorial Amphitheater and *Mt. Vernon. The Capitol, March 4, 1929,* by Swann and the *Lincoln Memorial* by Cline were additional selections from which she chose her Christmas gifts. Some were framed, some were matted, and some were autographed. In addition, four photographs of the Washington Monument from different perspectives were matted, framed, signed and given as presents to the staff.

On Christmas Eve, President and Mrs. Hoover took their grandchildren, Peggy Ann and Peter, to the lighting ceremony in Sherman Square. At its conclusion, they all walked over to the tree for a closer look at the twinkling lights. Then they returned to the White House for a party with all the families of the White House secretariat and members of the President's personal and official household. The after-dinner program included the March

1932-33 Hoover reciprocal card.

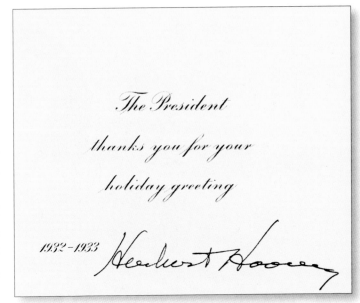

The President thanks you for your holiday greeting

1932–1933 Herbert Hoover

of the Wooden Soldiers, in which the entire group of 50 participated. The women carried candles in brass holders and the men rang tiny brass bells as together they marched to the music of the Marine Band, upstairs and down and all through the house, in search of Santa. Invariably, he would be found in the East Room, waiting to hand out gifts. Devised by Mrs. Hoover, this march was led by the President himself, who, in all likelihood, participated with utmost reluctance.

1932: *Personal Photographs*

For their gift in 1932, the Hoovers gave a leather folder that included a photograph of the President walking through the White House Rose Garden on his way to the Executive Office. Mrs. Hoover was photographed separately at the end of the Spanish reflection pool with two White House police dogs. First maid Maggie Rogers had brought the overindulged First Pets to Mrs. Hoover, and then hid behind the bushes while the photograph was taken. The remembrances were personally inscribed and autographed: "A Merry Christmas and a Happy New Year from Herbert Hoover and from Lou Henry Hoover and Weegie and Pat 1932–33."

A failed election behind them, President and Mrs. Hoover chose to go on a 10-day cruise aboard the *USS Sequoia* over the Christmas holidays. For the first time since the inception of the tree-lighting ceremony, the Vice President presided. In the White House, the 1929 total of 16 decorated trees had been reduced in 1932 to only one tall Norway spruce. Decorated under the supervision of Mrs. Hoover, the lone tree was placed in the East Room for visitors. With the Hoovers cruising the semitropical waters off Florida and Georgia, their domicile was dark and quiet.

Herbert Hoover, during his single term in office, had tried to bring the economy around with every progressive, corrective measure in his power, but his best efforts were just not enough. Now he was ready to lay aside the cares of his office and let it be known that for a time the President, an enthusiastic angler, had gone fishing.

Season's Greetings

AMERICA PAUSES AT THIS CHRISTMAS SEASON

TO EXTEND TO HER FRIENDS A GREETING OF GOOD WILL

AND GOOD CHEER. IT IS OUR PRIVILEGE TO JOIN

OUR VOICES IN THIS SINCERE GREETING TO ALL OUR

FRIENDS. MAY YOU HAVE A MERRY CHRISTMAS

AND MANY HAPPY YEARS IN WHICH TO ENJOY

PEACE ON EARTH GOOD WILL TOWARD MEN.

THE ROOSEVELTS
The Twelve Years of Christmases

Franklin and Eleanor Roosevelt loved Christmas: the scent of a fresh evergreen tree warmed by the fire of candles; the President's Christmas Eve ritual of reading and reciting from memory the Dickens classic *Christmas Carol*; the First Lady's gift buying for family, friends and the hundreds of people who made their life at the White House more enjoyable. Though half of the Christmases of the Roosevelts' 12-year tenure were seasoned by war, "There never was a Christmas in the White House while they were there that wasn't joyous," said their longtime housekeeper Henrietta Nesbitt in her *White House Diary*. "I never saw so much excitement and so much affection shown. I never knew people that loved Christmas the way the Roosevelts did."

"When Christmas is spent outside one's own home, particularly in government surroundings such as the White House," Mrs. Roosevelt explained in her *Christmas Book*, "you divide your Christmas in two parts. One covers your official obligations; the other, as far as possible, is the preservation of the home atmosphere and the home routine." Added Nesbitt, "Everyone in America knew what went on in the White House at Christmastime, because the Roosevelts wanted everyone to know and share in it, but only those inside knew the work that led up to it."

"It Is Better to Give...."

Eleanor Roosevelt enjoyed giving and believed she had "the right to give." In the December 1934 issue of *Home Companion* she wrote: "The real

Facing page: A patriotic card sent to card collector Franklin Delano Roosevelt during the war years. FRANKLIN D. ROOSEVELT LIBRARY

The East Room is decked out for the annual party for the staff and their children. AP/WIDE WORLD PHOTOS

spirit of Christmas is the joy of giving. We all of us enjoy what we receive, primarily because of the fact that behind each gift lies the loving thought of some individual. But for everyone the real thrill is the thrill of being able to give something no matter how small."

After one Christmas had passed, the First Lady was on to the next. Every January, with great foresight—and armed with the latest list of the White House employees and the names and ages of their children—she began shopping, collecting gifts as she went. Whenever she saw something on her travels, she would buy it. "That's for Christmas" she would say. "Just put it away," and into her "Christmas Closet" it would go. Her purchases: exquisitely fine needlework in Puerto Rico; furniture from a handicraft shop in West Virginia; pottery from a roadside stand in New England; baskets from a New York school for the blind; dollies from Tennessee mountaineers; woven rugs from Berea College, Kentucky, and pewter from her own Val-Kill shop at Hyde Park. Mrs. Roosevelt liked handmade objects and was attracted to anything that people enjoyed making. Wanting to share her travels with others, she did so by buying and giving gifts.

As Santa for the children of her staff, the First Lady purchased toys by the dozens from various manufacturers. As early as autumn, the gifts for the children were wrapped and staff Christmas cards containing cash were addressed. Mrs. Roosevelt was very careful to see that no one was overlooked and, to that end, relied heavily on the organization and planning of her staff. At first they were appalled at the amount of paper and ribbon it took to wrap the gifts; eventually they got used to buying in bulk. Final wrapping of the gifts would sometimes continue late into the night, but everything would invariably be ready for the White House staff party on the afternoon of Christmas Eve.

Mrs. Roosevelt started her first Christmas book in 1922; in this journal she had recorded the gifts she had given over the years to family, friends and those who had worked for the family. In 1935 the First Lady started on her second Christmas book. It contained hundreds of names and grew eventually to be two inches thick. To Presidential secretary Grace Tully, for instance, she gave $10 and stockings in 1935. In other years, the First Lady gave the secretary copies of her books, stamps, checks, and grapefruit and oranges. The 4 x 7-inch Christmas book sheets were alphabetized and kept systematically until Mrs. Roosevelt's death in 1962.

Holiday festivities for the White House staff and their families were usually held in the East Room on the afternoon of Christmas Eve. A 20-foot spruce from the New York State Conservation Commission was set up in the east window, between the portraits of George and Martha Washington. With the lighted tree decorated completely in white and silver, the toys for the children scattered under it, and "the tables fanning out on either side laden with the older people's gifts, the scene was festive and beautiful," recalled the First Lady. Each member of the staff was presented a gift of money and a cornucopia of candy. The police guards usually received a tie or a handkerchief, a fruitcake and candy. Children under 12 were given candy and a doll, a car or a stuffed animal from among the dozens that the First Lady had selected well in advance of the occasion.

The Family Celebration

Christmas was a three-day festival for the Roosevelt family, with four generations gathering at the Executive Mansion. The President's mother and half-sister-in-law joined them along with as many of the children and grandchildren as could make it for the activities stretching from Christmas Eve until the children's party the day after Christmas.

"Our Christmas tree was usually ready Christmas Eve, the older children helping to trim it," said Mrs. Roosevelt. "Franklin always directed the placing of every ornament or string of tinsel, even after he had polio, and never, as long as he lived, would he hear of our using anything but real candles." The fragrance of burning wax candles on a fresh evergreen was so reminiscent of the President's childhood at the family's home in Hyde Park, New York, that he insisted on real candles for the tree in the family quarters. "For all his advanced political theories," said the First Lady, "he clung to the old-fashioned traditions in many curious little ways." Eventually the *Washington Herald* reported that real wax candles were being used on the family tree because "the President will have none of these newfangled electric contraptions for lighting his family tree." That prompted a rise from an insurance company president who thought that the Chief Executive's proclamation during Fire Prevention Week was inconsistent with his tradition at Christmas.

A family Christmas gathering before the war: four generations of Roosevelts convene for a three-day Christmas festival. FRANKLIN D. ROOSEVELT LIBRARY

Marguerite (Missy) LeHand, the President's private secretary, tried to clarify the fact that there were *two* trees in the White House. The large one in the East Room where many people gathered was lighted with electric bulbs; wax candles were used only on the family's tree. She indicated that this had always been the family custom and that no one but the family gathered around it. Therefore, the Roosevelts believed they were entitled to carry on their family tradition. Furthermore, LeHand assured the insurance executive, no one would be "more careful in regard to fire prevention than the President."

On Christmas Eve, the President reveled in his annual rendering of the Charles Dickens holiday tale. Mrs. Roosevelt recalled the annual tradition: "I think the part he enjoyed most was the story of Fezziwig and the Christmas party. He always read that with relish," she wrote in *This I Remember*. "And of course having a great sense of the dramatic, he always put a great deal of drama into his reading of the parts about the ghosts. In fact, whenever he read anything aloud like this, he acted it out straight through, which was why he held the attention of the little children so well, even before they could understand the meaning of the words." After the reading, each member would file up to the President's bedroom to hang his or her stocking on the mantel. No ordinary stockings, each one was custom-stitched by Mrs. Roosevelt's maid, Lillian Rogers Parks. The First Lady would fill them late that night and be the first one up Christmas morning to put down the windows and light the fires before the pandemonium started. As soon as the grandchildren woke up, they woke everyone else up with their shouts of joy as they descended upon "Papa" at dawn. FDR was not ordinarily an early riser, but there was no escaping Christmas morning.

Gifts Galore From Val-Kill

The Forge was a part of the Val-Kill Industries that Eleanor Roosevelt and her partners established in 1934 with the idea of providing jobs for young men willing to learn the art of metal craft. The first of these, the Norwegian Arnold Berge, was trained in pewter-making by a Danish metal craftsman brought in for just that purpose. The products of this enterprise made their first appearance in April 1935 and were stamped with the Val-Kill trademark.

Over the years, The Forge continued to produce beautiful articles of pewter, brass, copper and iron. Although Mrs. Roosevelt purchased gifts of all kinds all through the year, she continued to rely heavily on The Forge for a variety of Christmas items, including matchboxes, bud vases, cheese knives, card cases, salad sets, salt containers, spoons and five-inch plates. She appreciated the craftsmanship of articles made at The Forge, visited the shop herself and paid retail prices for all her purchases. The First Lady, having established The Forge to provide jobs for others, was also one of its best customers.

1933: *The First Christmas*

On December 22, the Chief Executive invited his secretariat and all the members of his executive and social staffs into his office for a party. He presented each one a personally autographed copy of his book *Looking Forward*. The following day, President and Mrs. Roosevelt entertained the White House police force and their families in the East Room. At another reception later the same day they received the household servants, chauffeurs, maintenance men and their families.

The Chief Executive was deeply touched by the number of people who remembered him and his family with gifts and greetings during his first White House Christmas. The *New York Times* reported that on December 23 alone, 40,000 cards and letters were received, breaking all previous Christmas records. A special staff was assigned to handle the Christmas mail that amounted to approximately 300,000 greetings. According to Stephen Early, assistant secretary to the President, FDR did not send out Christmas

CHRISTMAS
1933

A MERRY CHRISTMAS
from
THE PRESIDENT
and MRS. ROOSEVELT

A MERRY CHRISTMAS
from
THE PRESIDENT AND MRS. ROOSEVELT

CHRISTMAS
1934

cards on a large scale, but the First Family did give cards with gifts to their personal friends and members of their family.

The Roosevelts' personal Christmas card was a 5 x 7-inch single-sided card with an attractive etching of the South Portico and reflection pool. Henrietta Nesbitt wrote in her diary that White House engraver A.B. Tolly prepared the lithograph by hand, lettered the words and had it reproduced by Brewood's on Crane paper.

A Tree-Lighting Speech

The official celebration of Christmas began on December 24, when the Chief Executive lit the National Community Christmas Tree in Sherman Square. More than 5,000 people formed a semicircle around the tall fir, which burst into a rainbow of colors and signaled the simultaneous lighting of thousands of other Christmas trees across the country. On the tenth anniversary of the lighting ceremony for the National Christmas Tree, President Roosevelt's greeting was broadcast to the nation. He delivered the longest tree ceremony speech to date and firmly established the practice as a holiday tradition, speaking directly and openly to his national audience.

For me and my family it is, I am sure, the happiest of Christmases. To the many thousands of you who have thought of me and have sent me greetings (and I hope all of you are hearing my voice) I want to tell you how profoundly grateful I am. If it were within my power so to do I would personally thank each and every one of you in every part of the land for your remembrances of me, but there are so many thousands of you that that happy task is impossible....

1934: Tree Lighting Ceremony Grows

The President gave more than 100 of his executive staff an appropriately autographed, dated copy of his book *On Our Way*. Mrs. Roosevelt ordered 400 Christmas cards and envelopes from Brewood Engraving to be enclosed with their gifts. A 2 3/8 x 3-inch photograph of the President and Mrs. Roosevelt seated on a leather sofa in front of the fireplace was inserted in a panel at the top of the single-sided card. The White House crest was stamped on the flap of the envelope.

Two New Trees and a New Location

To accommodate the ever increasing crowds attending the tree lighting, the ceremony was moved to Lafayette Park. A few weeks prior to Christmas, two Fraser firs from North Carolina were planted in the park. To minimize the effects of the intense heat of the bulbs, the 23-foot tree was to be alternated with the 30-foot tree as the National Community Christmas Tree. President Roosevelt always preferred the one located west of the monument of General Andrew Jackson because it was more visible from the North Portico of the White House.

About 10,000 people were on hand as the President officially opened the Christmas season by lighting the tree. As he pushed the button to transform the living tree into a blaze of color, there was a malfunction for a few seconds while he looked on, puzzled. Suddenly the light burst forth as the combined glee clubs of the Potomac Electric Power Company and the Chesapeake & Potomac Telephone Company launched into a program of Christmas carols. In his address, the President spoke of the courage and patriotism of Andrew Jackson.

1935: Val-Kill Productions

Products from The Forge first made their appearance in April 1935 and were stamped with the Val-Kill trademark. The Roosevelts gave a pewter matchbox cover crafted at The Forge to the 170 members of the executive staff. The cover had a small seal of the President's profile soldered on it and the words, "President Franklin D. Roosevelt, Hyde Park, N.Y." printed around it. FDR's initials were also engraved on the keepsake gift. The single-sided 3 1/2 x 5 1/2-inch card

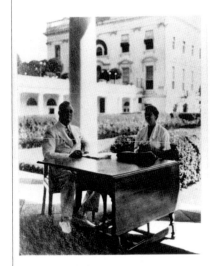

CHRISTMAS
1935

A Merry Christmas
from
The President
and Mrs. Roosevelt

FDR's gift to his staff in 1935 was a handcrafted pewter matchbox cover.

bore a black and white photograph of the President and Mrs. Roosevelt seated at a drop leaf table before the Executive Office. From Brewood Engravers, the First Lady ordered 400 cards with the White House crest on the envelopes. The President and Mrs. Roosevelt received more than 6,000 Christmas cards themselves that year.

1936: Scrooge at the Tree Lighting

From The Forge, the First Lady ordered 200 pewter paper knives for the President to give his staff. The rounded edge of the utensil bore a fac-simile of the Presidential Seal and below it, the initials of the President, all for a cost of $3 each. The card printed for the First Family by Brewood Engravers was marked with simplicity. In place of the photograph of previ-ous years was a small lithograph of a snowbound farm. The two red barns and two green trees provided a touch of color to the 3 x 4 card. The 600 cards carried an engraved greeting.

At the tree-lighting ceremony, the President told the 3,000 spectators and the untold numbers in his radio audience to keep the spirit of Christmas alive all through the year like the reformed Scrooge in Charles Dickens' classic. He said: "I have been reading the *Christmas Carol* to my family, in accordance with our old cus-tom. On this eve of Christmas I want to quote to you the pledge of old Scrooge when, after many vicissitudes, he had come to under-stand in his heart the great lesson and the great opportunity of Christmastide. 'I will honor Christmas in my heart and try to keep it all the year. I will live in the Past, the Present and the Future. The Spirits of all Three shall strive within me. I will not shut out the lessons that they teach.'"

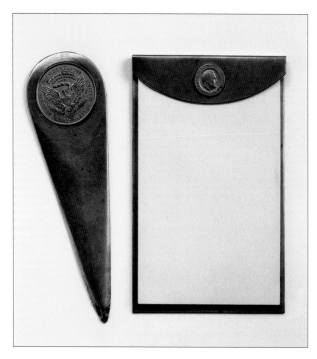

Staff gifts from The Forge: in 1936, a pewter paper knife; in 1937, a pewter desk pad.

The spirit of Christmas was reflected in the hearts and on the smiling faces of the throngs of people who flooded downtown Washington. Gone was the gloominess of the depression years. The *Evening Star* reported that never had "the Capital's stores been so busy as during the past week. All-time postal records have been shattered, attesting to an all-time volume of Christmas packages, letters and cards. The poor, the homeless and the needy have been remembered, fed and warmed."

CHRISTMAS 1936

A MERRY CHRISTMAS from THE PRESIDENT and MRS. ROOSEVELT

FRANKLIN D. ROOSEVELT LIBRARY

1937: Disintegration of Peace

With many people now aware of the Roosevelt family *Christmas Carol* tradition, Columbia Broadcasting System originated the idea of inviting the President to broadcast his family reading of the holiday classic. In October Sterling Fisher of CBS wrote a letter to the President's son James. "It seems to me," it read, "that this would have a very happy psychological effect in this country.... In a moment of wars and dread of wars, it would, throughout the world, emphasize kindliness, humanity and peace."

A prompt but negative answer came within two days from Stephen Early, secretary to the President. President Roosevelt's quotations from Dickens in his 1936 Christmas message would be the closest recitation of the story the public would ever hear.

President and Mrs. Roosevelt purchased 475 pewter articles from the Val-Kill shop for Christmas gifts. For the President, The Forge crafted 175 small pewter desk pads with the President's profile on the top for a special price of $1.25. The item also came in a larger size at $2.25 apiece. Only the year, 1937, distinguished the First Family's Christmas card from the previous year's card. The order came to 600 cards with the White House crest on the envelope.

"Many Are Weeping"

Peace in the world had begun to disintegrate. The situation in Europe and Asia was deteriorating rapidly.

On Christmas Eve, the President illuminated the living Christmas tree in Lafayette Square. In his greeting to the nation and to the 2,000 rain-soaked people in attendance, he called upon all Americans to forget all enmities and, in the Christian spirit of goodwill, to forgive everybody, as Christ had bestowed forgiveness upon Judas Iscariot. His message was taken almost in its entirety from New York newspaper columnist Heywood Broun's piece of the previous day.

On Christmas morning, a 35-year-old Rev. Peter Marshall, preaching his first sermon to a President, chose for his theme the same angel's song, "Peace on Earth, Goodwill Toward Men," that President Roosevelt had referred to in his Christmas greeting to the nation. The President heard Rev. Marshall call the song "the lost refrain." *The Washington Star* reported that Rev. Marshall went on to say that: "Christmas comes to mock us for our infidelity. It is Christmas Day in Spain—and machine guns rattle in the hills.... It is Christmas Day in China—and shrapnel is falling in the rice fields.... It is Christmas Day all over the world—and little children are being taught how to wear gas masks.... It is Christmas Day in Washington—and many are shivering, many are weeping. Peace on earth, goodwill toward men! Say the words over and over and you will be shocked at the hypocrisy of a world celebrating in solemn manner something it had not taken to heart."

1938: Lifting up Swords

From The Forge the President ordered 200 pewter paperweights for his office staff at a price of $1.25 each. For the third year, the Roosevelts' Christmas card remained the same except for the year, 1938. The small card met their needs and there appeared to be no reason to change.

On the day before Christmas Mrs. Roosevelt herself, accompanied by the press, went about the city giving the message of Christmas to 3,000 poor and needy people at five different charity programs. She told them, according to a *New York Times* account of the event, that "she realized as they did that 'love does not yet rule the world.'" To a group of 500 she said, "Many people thought Jesus of Nazareth a failure, but the mere fact that we still celebrate his birthday once a year and recall the ideas he lived for should give us courage."

All of 8,000 chilled souls braved an inclement Christmas Eve to see the Chief Executive push the button that illuminated the 20-foot fir into a rainbow of colors. In his mes-

The gift to the staff in 1938 was a pewter paperweight.

The First Lady helps Santa distribute gifts to underprivileged children at the Central Union Mission's annual party. UPI/THE BETTMANN ARCHIVE

sage, the President pledged to do whatever was in his power to bring about the day spoken of by the prophet Isaiah, when men "shall beat their swords into ploughshares and their spears into pruning hooks; when nation shall not lift up sword against nation, neither shall they learn war any more."

1939: A Shattered Hope for Peace

It was the year when Germany occupied Czechoslovakia and bombed Poland; Russia invaded Finland; Italy occupied Albania; France and Great Britain declared war on Germany. Hope for peace was shattered. On the eve of Christmas, Americans wondered if they would stay out of the conflict or if their Christmas too would be seasoned by war. Nevertheless, the Christmas of 1939 was celebrated as usual. The President made one more trip to The Forge and ordered 200 pewter letter holders at $1.25 each. On the front was the President's profile and beneath it, his initials. He also ordered ashtrays for his cabinet and close associates and had their initials put on them. With the outbreak of war and the resulting lack of raw materials, Arnold Berge was soon to close his pewter business. Consequently, the gifts FDR purchased from The Forge in 1939 were the last ones of this type he would give.

The ceremony for the lighting of the National Community Christmas

A Christmas 1939 staff gift from The Forge: a pewter letter holder.

Tree was returned to the Ellipse, where the annual tradition had begun in 1923. Concerned for the safety of the President, the Secret Service pushed for this move from Lafayette Park. The new location gave the nation's Christmas tree, a 36-foot red cedar from George Washington's estate in Virginia, greater visibility from all directions as well as affording the Chief Executive greater protection by its openness.

Joined by 17 members of his family and White House guests, President Franklin D. Roosevelt thanked God for "the interlude of Christmas" in a world "bowed down under the burden of suffering laid upon it by man's inhumanity to man." Speaking to the 8,000 shivering people who had come to the Ellipse to hear his Christmas message, the President called upon the warlike nations to read the Sermon on the Mount. "In these days of strife and sadness in many other lands," he said, "let us in this nation and in the other nations which still live at peace, forbear to give thanks not only for our good fortune in our peace. Let us rather pray that we may be given strength to live for others, to live more closely to the words of the Sermon on the Mount, and to pray that peoples in the nations which are at war may also read, learn and inwardly digest these deathless words."

1940: Europe at War

By Christmas, Nazi Germany had overrun most of Europe, Russia was still Hitler's partner in aggression, Japan occupied much of China, Great Britain suffered from constant air attacks, and the President of the United States felt the responsibility for preventing the enslavement of mankind as he entered his third term of office. Like many, the First Lady feared not only for humanity but also for the safety of her sons as they went off to war. In his foreword to Eleanor Roosevelt's *Christmas 1940,* Elliott Roosevelt wrote that his mother "believed that it was God's purpose that we should love and help our neighbors—an element of her faith that her own life exemplified with rare beauty.... I have known almost no one who could draw strength the way she did from her confident belief that some truths cannot be overcome by lies, that mankind will ultimately fight off every oppression, and that somehow we will achieve our Creator's purpose for us."

For Christmas 1940, FDR's Scotch terrier, Fala, was featured on this key chain.

Despite the gloom of the war and the uncertainty for the future, indicators revealed that holiday giving was greater than in any year in the past decade. As always, the First Lady bolstered the economy by ordering carton after carton of toys from Louis Marx & Company for the 200 children of the guards and servants who would be attending the White House Christmas party. The most popular toys ordered were the airplanes from the toy factory in Glendale, West Virginia.

The President was also most generous when it came to gift giving. His private secretary, Missy LeHand, ordered 212 Scottie key chains from Hammacher Schlemmer in New York for $1 each, including gift wrapping. Arrangements were made for any extras to be returned. In January, 15 of the sterling silver key chains were sent back for credit. The dog on the gift was a remembrance of Roosevelt's Scotch terrier, Fala. Devoted to his master, Fala soon became a prominent subject in photographs, cartoons and anecdotes. LeHand also ordered for the President silver money clips and silver key chains with a 25-cent coin from Cartier in New York. Costing $1.75 and $2.50, respectively, the gifts were personalized with the initials of each recipient. The President gave 42 initialed desk pads to members of his Cabinet and other close associates. The Christmas greeting card from The President and Mrs. Roosevelt remained the same as it had been in previous years and was titled "Christmas 1940."

Speaking informally to the crowd prior to the radio broadcast, the President stated that he and Mrs. Roosevelt would like to make the following year's ceremony "more homey" with a tree planted on the South Lawn; then he invited all the "good people in the District who come to this ceremony" to go to the White House in 1941 and he would deliver his Christmas greeting from the porch of the Executive Mansion. To the nation at large he said that we must "keep on striving for a better and happier world.... For most of us it can be a happy Christmas if by happiness we mean that we have done with doubts," the President concluded, "that we have set our hearts against fear, that we still believe in the golden rule for all mankind, that we intend to live more purely in the spirit of Christ, and that by our works, as well as our words, we will strive forward in faith and in hope and in love."

Describing the ceremony in the Christmas edition of the *Washington Post*, staff writer George Bookman wrote:

There is nothing in the Constitution of the United States, nothing in the Declaration of Independence, nothing in the Oath of Office of the President of the United States, about what took place last night on the browned turf of Washington's Ellipse, where President Roosevelt lit a Christmas tree and stood bareheaded listening to Christmas carols. Yet to 8,000 people who witnessed the ceremony and to millions more who heard it by radio, the brief, informal celebration gave new meaning to the democratic words, 'life, liberty and the pursuit of happiness.'

1941: War and a British Prime Minister

World events had cast their shadow over the holiday season, and Japan's December 7 attack on Pearl Harbor created an immediate state of emergency. For the next month, the United States was more preoccupied with mobilizing for war than preparing for Christmas. Nevertheless, the holiday was celebrated and the spirit of the season touched people like never before. There were indications that this may have been Washington's biggest Christmas. Department stores were filled with last-minute shoppers in search of gay and frivolous gifts. Train, bus and airport terminals were jammed with travelers, and post office receipts broke a 10-year record. Christmas lights twinkled in homes across the land and Christmas carols were sung wherever people gathered. Yet, in spite of it all, no one would be able to forget that America was at war.

For Christmas, 404 employees each received a 10 x 14-inch autographed photo of President and Mrs. Roosevelt. Taken on July 4 by George Skaddings of the Associated Press, the photograph was reproduced by Harris and Ewing for $50 a hundred. Bound copies of the President's campaign addresses were presented to members and ex-members of his Cabinet, administrative heads in the Executive Office, his immediate official family and a few friends, including Prime Minister Winston Churchill, the Crown Princess of Norway and Madame Chiang Kai-shek.

Tree Lighting Comes Home to the White House

Prime Minister Winston Churchill was the Roosevelts' houseguest in December of 1941. He had arrived secretly to discuss with the President the joint Allied operations in various theaters of the world. Together with American and British experts in strategy, the leaders of the world were working out a master plan for the war against the Axis.

Prior to the occasion, the President had selected two living Oriental spruce trees, each about 35 feet in height, to be planted just inside the grounds of the South Lawn. These were used alternatively as the National Tree for the next 13 years. On Christmas Eve, between 15,000 and 20,000

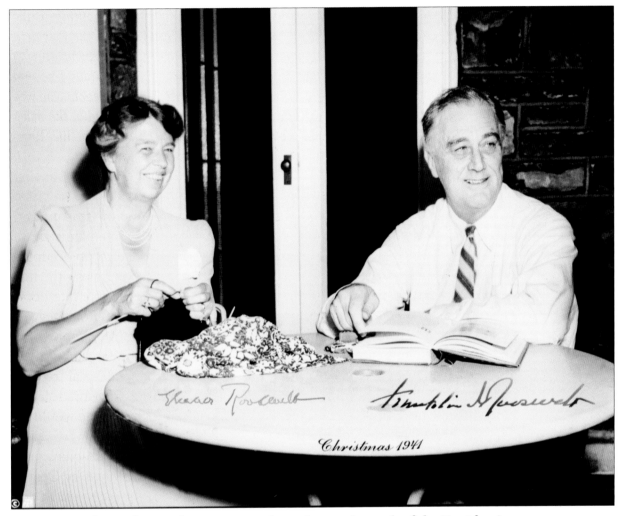

This photo of President and Mrs. Roosevelt on the south porch of the President's Hyde Park home was a Christmas gift to their staff in 1941. AP/WIDE WORLD PHOTO

people accepted the President's invitation of the previous year to come to the White House grounds for the ceremony.

As it turned out, just 17 days after Pearl Harbor, the two leaders of democracy delivered their Christmas messages from the South Portico of the White House. Their words were broadcast coast to coast to the American people and were transmitted to the rest of the world by short-wave radio. The realization that America was at war was unmistakable as both President Roosevelt and Prime Minister Churchill delivered messages plain in words and deep in conviction. From the President came an appeal for a preparation of American hearts and the proclamation of a day of prayer.

Winston Churchill expressed his pleasure at the privilege of being able to speak to the American people on Christmas Eve. He addressed them as

"Fellow workers in the cause of freedom." He continued:

> *Therefore we may cast aside, for this night at least, the cares and dangers which beset us, and make for the children an evening of happiness in a world of storm. Here then for one night only, each home throughout the English-speaking world should be a brightly lighted island of happiness and peace. Let the children have their night of fun and laughter–let the gifts of Father Christmas delight their play. Let us grownups share to the full in their unstained pleasures before we turn again to the stern tasks and formidable years that lie before us, resolved that by our sacrifice and daring these same children shall not be robbed of their inheritance or denied their right to live in a free and peaceful world....*

On Christmas Day, the President and Mrs. Roosevelt and their distinguished guest attended interdenominational services at the Foundry Methodist Church. On New Year's Day, Roosevelt and Churchill visited the tomb of George Washington at Mount Vernon, after worshipping at the same Christ Church in Alexandria, Virginia, that Washington had helped establish in 1773. The two leaders sat in the same white pew that the first President had used; together they prayed for the success of the Allied forces as soldiers marched past the windows, protecting their freedom to worship.

In her *Christmas Book*, Eleanor Roosevelt wrote, "I remember especially the Christmas that Mr. Churchill was with us after we were involved in World War II. After that year, the Christmases weren't so cheerful. My mother-in-law died in the autumn before that first war Christmas. The boys all went off to different war theaters. Their absence meant that we did what we could to cheer their families if they were with us, or we tried to get in touch with them by telephone if they were far away. We did more in those years for foreign people cut off from their homelands by war, but it was no longer the old-time Christmas and never was to be again." Unbeknown to Mrs. Roosevelt at the time was the fact that 1941 would also be the last time President Roosevelt pushed the button to light the National Christmas Tree. Over the next four years, due to the demands of war, the electric lights on the tree were to be eliminated.

1942: "Only Prayer Was Not Rationed"

By a joint resolution of Congress on December 26, 1941, the fourth Thursday of November became the legal holiday of Thanksgiving. On that first Thanksgiving, President Roosevelt joined with 250 government leaders, heads of the armed forces and friends in the East Room of the White House to participate in an unprecedented ceremony of song, scripture and prayer.

The 1942 gift to the staff was a black leather savings stamp album and a 25¢ war stamp with which to begin a collection that could be redeemed for a savings bond.

Broadcast to the nation, the 30-minute service began with the President reading a Thanksgiving proclamation and the 23rd Psalm. It was said that, at this critical time in history, "only prayer was not rationed." There was prayer for victory and peace, prayer for the President, prayer for the nation, prayer for all those in the service of the country and for the nation's Allies, prayer for those in mourning and a prayer of thanksgiving.

All during the year, the Treasury Department had been distributing United States savings stamps through retail stores to encourage the purchase of defense bonds and stamps. Supporting the defense drive, President and Mrs. Roosevelt's 1942 personal gift to their White House staff was a black leather savings stamp album. The Executive Office administrative staff, the Cabinet, family and close friends received a copy of the 1941 Christmas messages of Prime Minister Churchill and

FRANKLIN D. ROOSEVELT LIBRARY

1942

WITH

CHRISTMAS GREETINGS

AND OUR BEST WISHES

FOR A

HAPPIER NEW YEAR

THE PRESIDENT

AND

MRS. ROOSEVELT

President Roosevelt. One hundred copies were made at a cost of $2.50 each. The President's Christmas card was a departure from the design of the previous six years. The 1942 card included a photograph of the President and Mrs. Roosevelt seated at a drop leaf table with the Executive Office in the background.

President Roosevelt enjoyed sending Christmas cards as much as he enjoyed receiving them. For years he collected cards, not only the ones he considered interesting but also those that expressed the spirit of the times. His collection was kept in huge boxes and classified according to their historic value, with Missy LeHand in charge of its maintenance. *Life* magazine of January 1940 indicated that the collection numbered in excess of 3,000 pieces, including a series of patriotic cards that depicted Christmas in war.

A Tree Without Lights

In the Capital's second Christmas at war, even the lighting of the National Community Christmas Tree was affected by it. For the first time in the 19-year ceremony, the President did not pull the switch to illuminate the giant tree, but rather sounded chimes that were broadcast over nationwide radio. Because of wartime rationing, there were no electric lights on the tree; it was instead decorated with hundreds of ornaments donated by Washington schoolchildren. For the second year, Franklin Roosevelt delivered his Christmas message from the South Portico of the White House. A sparse crowd of 1,500 people gathered around the darkened tree to hear his solemn address.

This year, my friends, I am speaking on Christmas Eve not to this gathering at the White House only but to all of the citizens of our nation, to the men and women serving in our American armed forces and also to those who wear the uniforms of the other United Nations. I give you a message of cheer. I cannot say "Merry Christmas,"–for I think constantly of those thousands of soldiers and sailors who are in actual combat throughout the world–but I can express to you my thought that this is a happier Christmas than last year in the sense that the forces of darkness stand against us with less confidence in the success of their evil ways.

To you who toil in industry and in offices, toil for the common cause of helping to win the war, I send a message of cheer, that you can well continue to sacrifice without recrimination and with a look of Christmas cheer, a kindly spirit toward your fellow men. To you who serve in uniform I also send a message of cheer, that you are in the thoughts of your families, your friends at home, and that Christmas prayers follow you wherever you may be. To all Americans I say that loving your neighbor as we love ourselves is not enough, that we as a nation and as individuals will please God best by showing regard for the laws of God....

It is significant that tomorrow–Christmas Day–our plants and factories will be stilled. That is not true now of the other holidays we have long been accustomed to celebrate. On all other holidays work goes on, gladly, for the winning of the war.

So Christmas Day becomes the only holiday in all the year. I like to think that this is so because Christmas is a holy day. May all that it stands for live and grow through all the years.

The President's speech was followed by the singing of carols, during which a baby's cries could be heard from within the White House. One-year-old Christopher, the son of Lt. Franklin Roosevelt, Jr., was visiting without his father. Again this Christmas, none of the four Roosevelt sons would be home. Only three small stockings hung on the President's mantel.

1943: *The First Lady Saves the Tree*

In early December, while President Roosevelt was attending the Cairo and Teheran Conferences with Winston Churchill and Josef Stalin, the Board of Commissioners of the District of Columbia recommended that the National Community Christmas Tree be abandoned in an effort to conserve electricity and the resources of transportation. Commercial establishments had been asked to cut down on electric Christmas displays, and citizens were encouraged to curtail any unnecessary use of street cars, which were operated by electricity. Christmas shopping and the National Tree ceremony brought out the crowds and constituted a tremendous burden on the street car system. In the absence of the President, his secretary, William D. Hassett, accepted the recommendation of the Board of Commissioners.

It was Eleanor Roosevelt who interceded to save the 20-year tradition. She appealed to the board to spare the tree unless it was *absolutely* necessary to abolish the custom. Americans had sacrificed much, and the ceremony at the National Community Christmas Tree would usher in the only real holiday the country had left. Commissioner Guy Mason granted the First Lady's request. Conforming to war restrictions, however, electric lights would not be placed on the tree; instead schoolchildren were asked to make ornaments dedicated to a loved one serving in the armed forces.

Mrs. Roosevelt also informed the Commissioner that the President would not be attending the ceremony on the Ellipse, but would broadcast a holiday message to the troops. After spending 10 Christmases at the White House, the Roosevelts had decided to return to their family home, Springwood, in Hyde Park.

The domed magnifying glass paperweight.

1943

WITH CHRISTMAS GREETINGS

AND OUR BEST WISHES FOR A

HAPPIER NEW YEAR

THE PRESIDENT AND MRS. ROOSEVELT

FRANKLIN D. ROOSEVELT LIBRARY

In anticipation of going home, the Roosevelts' Christmas card included a photograph of them seated at a square, cloth-covered table in the yard at Val-Kill. With its photograph by Ralph Short of the *Poughkeepsie New Yorker*, the greeting card was made in two sizes; approximately 3 x 4 and 5 x 7.

On December 11, a Christmas tree from the President was shipped to Winston Churchill in Chequers, England. Back in October, FDR had decided he wanted to send the British Prime Minister such a gift from his tree farm. He then enlisted Grace Tully's services to be certain that the tree would arrive before Christmas, even if it had to be delivered by a bomber.

The President also instructed the Government Printing Office to put together a book of his three Inaugural Addresses. Costing $2.50 each, 100 copies of the gift book were given to members of his family, Cabinet, administrative assistants and foreign dignitaries.

On Thursday, December 23, the President received the White House executive staff in his office and gave each member a desk magnifying glass paperweight. The 300 gift paperweights had been purchased by Grace Tully from Belmont Advertising Specialties, in Bronx, New York, for 65 cents each. Recipient George Elsey remembered shaking hands with the President, being handed a gift by an aide and moving on through the line. "There were no extras such as food or entertainment," he said. "It was wartime." The

President stated that, in the interest of war conservation, his gifts would not be wrapped; he preferred that gifts to him from his friends and family would follow his example.

The Tree: No Lights, No President

The 21st annual National Community Christmas Tree ceremony was held on the South Lawn of the White House. Because of the President's absence, the crowd of 15,000 was able to get closer to the gaily decorated giant cedar and consequently found it to be more "homey" than in previous years. Among the 1,800 personalized children's decorations was a red ball with a white tag bearing the inscription, "William Hawk, killed in action." Another tag penned by a child simply read, "Dedicated to my daddy, Russell H. Brown, Lt. U.S.N.R." A green ball remembered "Charles Harris, Medical Corps, prisoner in Philippines." The inscriptions told a story of happier Christmases and the children's prayers for their loved ones at war. Despite wartime restrictions that prevented the lighting of the tree for the second year in a row, Harold Snyder of the District Recreation Department, who supervised the trimming of the tree, was quoted in the *Washington Star* as saying, "This is the most beautiful tree we have ever had."

The President delivered his Christmas message from his library in Hyde Park and it was extended to 30 minutes to enable him to report on the Cairo and Teheran Conferences. His remarks were carried by four radio networks, broadcast to the armed forces abroad and piped to the audience on the White House lawn by means of a special cable running out to the National Tree. The Chief Executive promised the nation and the world that they could expect peace with "certainty" even though "the cost may be high and the time long." He said that the United States, Great Britain, Soviet Russia and China all agreed to use force to maintain that peace "for as long as it may be necessary." He concluded with words of resolve, comfort and hope:

> The massive offensives which are in the making—both in Europe and the Far East—will require every ounce of energy and fortitude that we and our allies can summon on the fighting fronts and in all the workshops at home. As I have said before, you cannot order up a great attack on a Monday and demand that it be delivered on Saturday.
>
> Less than a month ago I flew in a big Army transport plane over the little town of Bethlehem, in Palestine. Tonight, on Christmas Eve, all men and women everywhere who love Christmas are thinking of that ancient town and of the star of faith that shone there more than nineteen centuries ago.
>
> American boys are fighting today in snow-covered mountains, in malarial jungles, and on blazing deserts. They are fighting on the far stretches of the

*sea and above the clouds, and the thing for which they struggle is best sym-
bolized by the message that came out of Bethlehem. On behalf of the
American people–your own people–I send this Christmas message to you
who are in our armed forces: In our hearts are prayers for you and for all
your comrades in arms who fight to rid the world of evil. We ask God's blessing upon you–upon your fathers and mothers, wives and children–all your
loved ones at home. We ask that the comfort of God's grace shall be granted
to those who are sick and wounded, and to those who are prisoners of war
in the hands of the enemy, waiting for the day when they will again be free.
And we ask that God receive and cherish those who have given their lives,
and that He keep them in honor and in the grateful memory of their countrymen forever.*

*God bless all of you who fight battles on this Christmas Eve. God bless us
all. Keep us strong in our faith that we fight for a better day for human kind–
here and everywhere.*

In his speech the President announced that General Dwight D.
Eisenhower would command the Anglo-American army. The Chief Executive
and Prime Minister Churchill had put control in the hands of "the soldier
who, in all history, has had the most experience in directing vast combined
land, sea and air operations." Fellow officers described the general as one
who worked long hours, expected the same of his associates and had the
capacity to grasp every detail of a campaign. Sharing his philosophy of war,
General Eisenhower once said: "You can't hit a home run by bunting. You
have to step up there and take your cut at the ball."

1944: Franklin Roosevelt's Last Christmas

Throughout 1944, there was never any question that ultimately victory
would come to the Allies. Rome, Paris and the Philippines, under General
Douglas MacArthur, had been liberated and victories were commonplace
throughout Europe and in the Pacific. In June, after the D-Day invasion of
Normandy, and as the landing craft began unloading American soldiers on
Omaha Beach, President Roosevelt read to the nation over the radio a prayer
that he had composed. By way of introduction, he said: "Last night, when I
spoke with you about the fall of Rome, I knew at that moment that troops of
the United States and our Allies were crossing the Channel in another and
greater operation. It has come to pass with success thus far. And so, in this
poignant hour, I ask you to join with me in prayer."

The text of the prayer had been read to Congress and printed in newspapers so that millions of Americans could read the words as the President
prayed. The Majority Leader, Senator Alben W. Barkley of Kentucky, said,

D-Day Prayer

by President Franklin D. Roosevelt from the White House · June 6, 1944

Last night, when I spoke with you about the fall of Rome, I knew at that moment that troops of the United States and our Allies were crossing the Channel in another and greater operation. It has come to pass with success thus far.

And so, in this poignant hour, I ask you to join with me in prayer:

Almighty God: our sons, pride of our Nation, this day have set upon a mighty endeavor, a struggle to preserve our Republic, our religion, and our civilization, and to set free a suffering humanity.

Lead them straight and true; give strength to their arms, stoutness to their hearts, steadfastness in their faith.

They will need Thy blessings. Their road will be long and hard. For the enemy is strong. He may hurl back our forces. Success may not come with rushing speed, but we shall return again and again; and we know that by Thy grace, and by the righteousness of our cause, our sons will triumph.

They will be sore tried, by night and by day, without rest—until the victory is won. The darkness will be rent by noise and flame. Men's souls will be shaken with the violences of war.

For these men are lately drawn from the ways of peace. They fight not for the lust of conquest. They fight to end conquest. They fight to liberate. They fight to let justice arise, and tolerance and good will among all Thy people. They yearn but for the end of battle, for their return to the haven of home.

Some will never return. Embrace these, Father, and receive them, thy heroic servants, into Thy kingdom.

And for us at home—fathers, mothers, children, wives, sisters and brothers of brave men overseas—whose thoughts and prayers are ever with them—help us, Almighty God, to rededicate ourselves in renewed faith in Thee in this hour of great sacrifice.

Many people have urged that I call the Nation into a single day of special prayer. But because the road is long and the desire is great, I ask that our people devote themselves in a continuance of prayer. As we rise to each new day, and again when each day is spent, let words of prayer be on our lips, invoking Thy help to our efforts.

Give us strength, too—strength in our daily tasks, to redouble the contributions we make in the physical and the material support of our armed forces.

And let our hearts be stout, to wait out the long travail, to bear sorrows that may come, to impart our courage unto our sons wheresoever they may be.

And, O Lord, give us faith. Give us faith in Thee; faith in our sons; faith in each other; faith in our united crusade. Let not the keenness of our spirit ever be dulled. Let not the impacts of temporary events, of temporal matters of but fleeting moment—let not these deter us in our unconquerable purpose.

With Thy blessing, we shall prevail over the unholy forces of our enemy. Help us to conquer the apostles of greed and racial arrogancies. Lead us to the saving of our country, and with our sister nations into a world unity that will spell a sure peace—a peace invulnerable to the schemings of unworthy men. And a peace that will let all men live in freedom, reaping the just rewards of their honest toil. Thy will be done, Almighty God. AMEN

Christmas · 1944 · from
F·D·R

A reproduction of The D-Day Prayer was the President's gift to his staff in 1944.

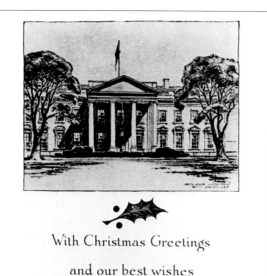

With Christmas Greetings

and our best wishes

for a

Happier Nineteen Forty-five

The President

and

Mrs. Roosevelt

"All we need or ought to do or can do is pray fervently and devoutly for the success of our troops and those of our allies."

In keeping with the solemnity of the fourth wartime Christmas, the President had copies made of his D-Day Prayer; imprinted at the top were the words "D-Day Prayer by Franklin D. Roosevelt from the White House–June 6, 1944." At the bottom of the engraved scroll were the words "Christmas 1944 from F.D.R." The President's prayer was printed in black, red and blue lettering, accented with gold. One of the 14 x 21-inch scrolls, along with the Roosevelts' personal Christmas card, was presented to each member of the executive office staff on December 21. At eleven o'clock, the 258-person office force gathered in the lobby and filed past President and Mrs. Roosevelt for a handshake and what would be their last Christmas remembrance from the Chief Executive. At four that afternoon, the household staff, numbering 440, including families, also shook hands with the President and First Lady. Each staff member received a gift of between $5 and $15; each child got a toy and candy.

As gifts for his friends, the President had his prayer printed by the U.S. Government Printing Office at $2.50 each. The handsome, 7 x 10-inch slip-cased book was designed with vellum-backed marble boards, black morocco lettering, gold gilt on the top edge; the other edges of the page were uncut. The edition was limited to 100 copies. This was the last of a series of Limited Edition Christmas gift books that the President had given since 1935.

The Christmas card of the family bore holiday greetings for a "Happier Nineteen Forty-five." Featured for the first time on the Roosevelts' card was an etching of the North Portico of the White House, flanked by two large trees. It was noted that this year the President also sent the card to a number of heads of state.

The year 1944 had been a grueling one for the President, and his election to a fourth term came only after an exhausting campaign. His health had been failing ever since the Cairo-Teheran conferences of a year earlier. Adolf Hitler's last-ditch attempt in mid-December to thwart the Allied armies in the Battle of the Bulge proved costly in human lives and ushered in a Christmas that was truly seasoned by war. For the second year in a row, the Roosevelts decided to spend Christmas at Hyde Park; hoping to get some much needed rest, their plans were not announced to the press. Leaving on the evening of the 23rd, they arrived home early Christmas Eve day.

From his library, the President delivered one of his most eloquent Christmas messages to the families and the fighting men and women around the world.

> *It is not easy to say "Merry Christmas" to you, my fellow Americans, in this time of destructive war. Nor can I say "Merry Christmas" lightly tonight to our armed forces at their battle stations all over the world—or to our Allies who fight by their side.... Our own thoughts go out to them, tonight and every night, in their distant places....*
>
> *On this Christmas Day, we cannot yet say when our victory will come. Our enemies still fight fanatically. They still have reserves of men and military power. But, they themselves know that they and their evil works are doomed. We may hasten the day of their doom if we here at home continue to do our full share. And we pray that that day may come soon. We pray that until then God will protect our gallant men and women in the uniforms of the United Nations—that He will receive into His infinite grace those who make their supreme sacrifice in the cause of righteousness and the cause of love of Him and His teachings.*
>
> *We pray that with victory will come a new day of peace on earth in which all the nations of the earth will join together for all time. That is the spirit of Christmas, the holy day. May that spirit live and grow throughout the world in all the years to come.*

The war had taken its toll on Franklin Delano Roosevelt. He had longed for an early and lasting peace and for the rebuilding of the world after the war. In February, he agreed to go to Yalta in the Russian Ukraine with the hope that it might strengthen his relationship with Marshal Stalin. The President felt the conference was successful but exhausting.

Still weary from the negotiations, FDR uncharacteristically chose to be seated as he delivered his Yalta report to both houses of Congress on March 1. After a weekend in Hyde Park, the President left on March 29 for Warm Springs, Georgia, and a longer rest. Confident that peace was at hand, the Chief Executive penned an addendum to an address he was about to give for the Jefferson Day dinners throughout the land. His final sentence was: "The only limit to our realization of tomorrow will be our doubts of today. Let us move forward with strong and active faith."

On April 12, 1945, President Roosevelt passed away in his sleep, never knowing how close the nation was to peace.

A Proclamation

THE ALLIED ARMIES, THROUGH SACRIFICE AND DEVOTION AND WITH GOD'S HELP, HAVE WRUNG FROM GERMANY A FINAL AND UNCONDITIONAL SURRENDER.

The western world has been freed of the evil forces which for five years and longer have imprisoned the bodies and broken the lives of millions upon millions of free-born men. They have violated their churches, destroyed their homes, corrupted their children, and murdered their loved ones. Our Armies of Liberation have restored freedom to these suffering peoples, whose spirit and will the oppressors could never enslave.

Much remains to be done. The victory won in the West must now be won in the East. The whole world must be cleansed of the evil from which half the world has been freed. United, the peace-loving nations have demonstrated in the West that their arms are stronger by far than the might of the dictators or the tyranny of military cliques that once called us soft and weak.

The power of our peoples to defend themselves against all enemies will be proved in the Pacific war as it has been proved in Europe.

For the triumph of spirit and of arms which we have won, and for its promise to the peoples everywhere who join us in the love of freedom, it is fitting that we, as a nation, give thanks to Almighty God, Who has strengthened us and given us the victory.

Now, therefore, I, Harry S. Truman, President of the United States of America, do hereby appoint Sunday, May 13, 1945, to be a day of prayer.

I call upon the people of the United States, whatever their faith, to unite in offering joyful thanks to God for the victory we have won and to pray that He will support us to the end of our present struggle and guide us into the ways of peace.

I also call upon my countrymen to dedicate this day of prayer to the memory of those who have given their lives to make possible our victory.

In witness whereof, I have hereunto set my hand and caused the seal of the United States of America to be affixed.

Washington, D.C., May 8, 1945

Harry Truman

THE TRUMANS
Home for the Holidays

arry S. Truman had been Vice President for only 83 days when news of FDR's death hit Washington; the man from Missouri was elevated to the Presidency suddenly and at a crucial time in history. The Trumans moved into the White House on May 7, 1945. The following day was both historic and memorable. Germany surrendered unconditionally to bring the war in Europe to an end, and the President celebrated his 61st birthday.

The jubilant Chief Executive announced the long-awaited surrender in a proclamation to the American people on May 8, which became known as V-E Day. Writing to his mother, he remarked, "Isn't that some birthday present?" The war in the Pacific ended three months later after the atomic bombing of Hiroshima on August 6 and of Nagasaki three days later. Japan surrendered, and peace was at last won after four wartime Christmases.

1945: A Christmas to Celebrate

The White House was adequately decorated in a festive and colorful manner. Evergreens and poinsettias added gaiety to the State Rooms and Great Hall. Cedar wreaths hung in the north windows complementing the two decorated Norway spruces that flanked the front door. Noticeably missing was the tinseled tree in the East Room, because the Trumans went home for the holidays to Independence, Missouri.

While it became a tradition for the First Family to go home for Christmas, the President always remained in Washington until after the staff

Facing page: V-E Day Proclamation, the Trumans' first Christmas gift to their staff.

Christmas party. Lillian Rogers Parks, a White House maid, said that the whole staff looked up to the President and Mrs. Truman. The genuine appreciation the Trumans felt toward their help seemed to come naturally. "You were just as important as anyone else, and you were treated with the respect of an equal," remarked the maid. She went on to say that the First Family never did anything for show. In fact, Mrs. Truman gave many gifts anonymously. The President also requested that each Christmas a needy white and a needy black family be singled out and supplied with cooked turkeys and gifts. Head butler Alonzo Fields was assigned to the detail of secretly helping the needy on behalf of the President.

Victory in Gifts and Tree Lights

For their first Christmas at the White House, President and Mrs. Truman gave the staff an embellished scroll of the V-E Day Proclamation bearing the signature of the new President. On December 22, the Commander-in-Chief sent season's greetings to the members of the armed forces. Thousands of them were awaiting discharge or furlough papers; others jammed transportation lines trying to get home for Christmas. To them all, he said: "On this Christmas Day I send a sincere and heartfelt greeting to you men and women of the United States Armed Forces who have brought us victory. I speak in behalf of a nation grateful for your service, your devotion and your sacrifice. We shall not forget the price you have paid...."

President Truman led the nation in celebrating its first peacetime Christmas in four years by lighting the hundreds of bulbs on the National Community Christmas Tree. Speaking in his gentle Missouri drawl, the President looked ahead with hope to a "long peace."

This is the Christmas that a war-weary world has prayed for through long and awful years. With peace come joy and gladness. The gloom of the war years fades as once more we light the National Community Christmas Tree.... Peace has its victories no less hard won than success at arms. We must not fail or falter. We must strive without ceasing to make real the prophecy of Isaiah: "They shall beat their swords into ploughshares and their spears into pruning hooks: nation shall not lift up sword against nation, neither shall they learn war any more."

Nearly 10,000 spectators had filed onto the White House grounds to watch the lighting ceremony—the first in four years. At the head of the line, Sgt. Eldwin Bell explained, "I have waited outside the gate since 2 p.m.—an hour and a half before opening time. We can't get home to Texas for our family Christmas tree so we thought we ought to attend Harry's party."

Two women fainted during the long, cold wait; after being revived and wrapped in blankets, they stayed through the whole event. Many shoppers arrived laden with packages that were forbidden on the grounds for security reasons. So anxious were they to see the whole ceremony, they simply parked their unmarked packages with a hasty plea, "Watch these for me, will you?" Needless to say, bedlam broke loose at the guardhouse as homebound shoppers sought to retrieve their holiday purchases.

Though snow, sleet and freezing rain were predicted on Christmas Eve, the President refused to take that night's train to join the First Lady, her mother, and the Trumans' daughter, Margaret, all of whom were already back in Missouri. He instead decided to fly back to Independence Christmas morning on his Presidential plane, the *Sacred Cow*, only to have bad weather ground all commercial planes in the area. The President, with every intention of being home for Christmas, waited until noon before he and his veteran pilot took off.

Daughter Margaret, in her *Bess W. Truman*, recalled: "It was one of the wildest flights of his life. The *New York Times*, the *Washington Post* and other guardians of the republic castigated the President for 'taking chances with his personal safety.' Bess' comments when he got to 219 North Delaware Street were not much more cordial.... 'So you have finally arrived,' Bess said. 'I guess you couldn't think of any more reasons to stay away. As far as I am concerned, you might as well have stayed in Washington.'"

To make matters worse, two days later the President was called back to Washington to deal with a crisis concerning the Moscow conference. Still upset with his wife over her cutting remarks, Truman sent her a curt letter via special delivery. The next day, after a change of heart, he called Margaret and asked her to intercept the letter and "burn it." He then composed a second letter in which he was more understanding; he apologized for exasperating her and asked for her continued support.

1946: Enter the TV Cameras

The *Sacred Cow* played a safer yet significant role in the Trumans' 1946 Christmas, as the backdrop for their Christmas gift to their White House staff. Waving and smiling broadly, the First Couple posed for a photograph

The 1946 gift print features Harry and Bess Truman boarding the President's private plane, the *Sacred Cow*. AP/WIDE WORLD PHOTOS

Below: Brewood Engravers designed 800 small enclosure cards for the First Family in 1946.

Christmas 1946

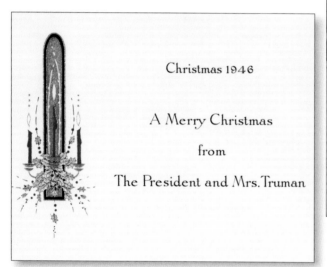

Christmas 1946

A Merry Christmas

from

The President and Mrs. Truman

before entering the plane. The White House ordered 1,000 copies of the black and white photograph at a cost of $402. On December 23, the President greeted 575 of his White House employees at an informal ceremony in his office and presented each an autographed photograph of himself and Mrs. Truman.

Before heading home to join the First Lady and Margaret, President Truman greeted the nation and a crowd of 10,000 at the lighting of the National Christmas Tree. For the first time in history, the ceremony was televised, though with both transmission and reception limited. He began with the message of Bethlehem:

If we as a nation, and the other nations of the world, will accept it, the star of faith will guide us into the place of peace as it did the shepherds on that day of Christ's birth long ago. I am sorry to say all is not harmony in the world today. We have found that it is easier for men to die together on the field of battle than it is for them to live together at home in peace. But those who died have died in vain if, in some measure, at least we shall not preserve for the peace that spiritual unity in which we won the war.

The problems facing the United Nations–the world's hope for peace–would overwhelm faint hearts. But as we continue to labor for an enduring peace through that great organization, we must remember that the world was not created in a day. We shall find strength and courage at this Christmas time because so brave a beginning had been made. So with faith and courage we shall work to hasten the day when the sword is replaced by the plowshare and nations do not "learn war any more".... We have made a good start toward peace in the world. Ahead of us lies the larger task of making the peace secure....

The illusion of peace weighed heavily on the President. In a letter to the Pope earlier in the year, Truman had also expressed his deep concern. "Although hostilities have ceased, peace has not yet been achieved.... We must employ every resource at our command to bring to this sadly troubled world an enduring peace and no peace can be permanent which is not based upon Christian principles."

1947: First Christmas in Washington

For their Christmas gift to the staff, the Trumans gave a maroon leatherette wallet bearing a gold-stamped Presidential Seal. Designed to hold identification cards, the 760 wallets were produced by Brown and Bigelow of St. Paul, Minnesota, at eight cents each. Because the gift itself carried the President's Christmas greeting, it was concluded that a separate Christmas card would be an unnecessary expense. For his Cabinet, President Truman ordered 40 black genuine leather identification billfolds, each with the White House pass in it, at a cost of 33 cents each. Each of 11

The President's 1947 gift to his employees was a leatherette wallet designed to hold identification cards.

billfolds was stamped with the recipient's title and the Presidential Seal in gilt. The remaining cases were printed with only the seal and were distributed as gifts throughout the year. A Christmas card from the President and Mrs. Truman was enclosed with their gift to the Cabinet. A.B. Tolley reportedly ordered only 100 Christmas cards from Brewood Engravers in 1947. It is uncertain who received the rest of the cards.

The Trumans had invited their whole family to the White House for the holidays and to attend Margaret's voice recital on December 22. In preparation, the President supervised the trimming of the tree, although he never participated in the work. Margaret recalled him just sitting there giving instructions: "You need more lights over here; you need more ornaments over there."

The Chief Executive continued in his gift-giving mood on Christmas Eve as he pledged U.S. aid abroad. Speaking on the 25th anniversary of the first National Community Christmas Tree, the President offered hope to those left desolate by war.

The great heart of the American people has been moved to compassion by the needs of those in other lands who are cold and hungry.... In extending aid to our less fortunate brothers we are developing in their hearts the return of "hope." Because of our efforts, the people of other lands see the advent of a new day in which they can lead lives free from the harrowing fear of starvation and want. With the return of hope to these peoples will come renewed faith–faith in the dignity of the individual and the brotherhood of man.

Chrismas dinner was at two o'clock in the family dining room. Margaret explained, in an article for *Family Weekly*, that her "Father wouldn't carve anything, and so we all had a good time when they set the turkey down in front of him. It turned out that the butler had carved the turkey and then put the skin back on. As soon as I realized what they had done, I looked at my father and said, 'I want some skin.' He said, 'You'll get what you are given.' He wasn't about to have that little ploy revealed."

The staff was dismissed after dinner. Before going, they readied the makings for sandwiches so the First Family could take care of themselves. In *Upstairs at the White House*, chief usher J.B. West added, "That's the way the entire Truman family was. They didn't want to be a bother to anybody on the staff, they asked for very little. They treated the staff with respect–respect for us personally, and respect for the work that we did."

1948: The President Beats the Odds
The election of 1948 marked one of the biggest upsets in political his-

This brown leather bookmark was the President's gift to his staff in 1948.

tory. The Republicans had gained control of the Congress in 1946. Odds were 20 to 1 that Republican Thomas E. Dewey would take the Presidency in a landslide vote, but Harry Truman rose to the challenge. Traveling 21,928 miles in his railroad car, the *Ferdinand Magellan*, the President took his family on a "whistle-stop campaign" across the heartland, where he attacked what he labeled "the do-nothing 80th Congress," calling it "the worst in my memory." When the American people went to the polls in November, they elected Truman to a full term.

Prior to Thanksgiving, severe structural problems in the White House necessitated renovation, forcing the victorious Trumans to move into Blair House across the street until its completion. "Doesn't that beat all!" joshed the President. "Here we've worked ourselves to death trying to stay in this jailhouse and they kick us out anyway!" It was well into December before the mansion was completely cleared out. Mrs. Truman placed on tables several odds and ends that would not be returning to the new White House, allowing the staff to select wonderful souvenirs from the move.

The Chief Executive's Christmas gift to his staff was a brown leather bookmark embossed with the Presidential Seal and his motto: "I would rather have peace in the world than be President." No separate gift card was given with the bookmark to the 740 employees at the White House. For his Cabinet, the President gave a paperweight with a bronze casting of the Presidential Seal on a wooden base. On the front of the plaque were the words: "Christmas Greetings From the President 1948." The back read: "This wood was part of the White House used in its reconstruction about 1817 and removed in 1948." Of the 45 paperweights made, only 16 were used as Christmas gifts in 1948.

Long-Distance Tree Lighting

President Truman offered season's greetings on Christmas Eve from his home in Independence. Despite his absence, some 2,100 Washingtonians gathered on the South Lawn of the White House to hear his broadcast speech and to be on hand when the switch thrown in Missouri lit up the National Community Christmas Tree in Washington. Celebrating "the great home festival" in the midst of his kinfolk, the President tried to reassure Americans that he was continuing to work for the cause of peace. He said:

The Christmas tree which we have just lighted in the South Grounds of the White House back in Washington symbolizes the family life of the Nation.

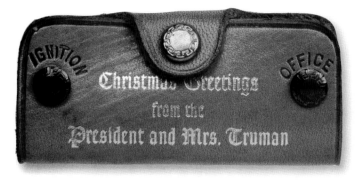

The 1949 staff gift was a leather key holder.

There are no ties like family ties. That is why I have made the journey back to Independence to celebrate this Christmas Day among the familiar scenes and associations of my old hometown.... I have been thinking of all these things here in my home on North Delaware Street in Independence. I am speaking to you from our living room. As I came up the street in the gathering dusk, I saw a hundred commonplace things that are hallowed to me on this Christmas Eve–hallowed because of their associations with the sanctuary of home....

We have had difficult problems, and that is why we can understand the problems of other peoples. Our own struggle fostered this feeling of goodwill. And goodwill, after all, is the very essence of Christmas; peace and friendship to men of goodwill.... I want to say once more, with all the emphasis that I can command, that I am working for peace. I shall continue to work for peace. What could be more appropriate than for all of us to dedicate ourselves to the cause of peace on this Holy Night?

1949: "Man From Independence"

The Trumans gave their staff a leather key holder. About 20 of the President's closest aides, secretaries and administrative assistants also received the wooden paperweight made the previous year, but the date was changed to 1949. The President's Christmas gift to his Cabinet was a bound book, *Selected Speeches and Statements on Foreign Affairs by Harry S. Truman.*

Once again the President left Washington before the lighting of the National Community Christmas Tree ceremony to go home for Christmas. Known as "the man from Independence," he enjoyed the informality of America's heartland and walking with and talking to family and friends. From his music room, the Chief Executive called upon the American people to "dedicate ourselves anew to the love of their fellowmen."

1950: Troops Back in Asia

In April 1949, the United States and 11 other nations signed the North Atlantic Treaty that provided for their collective defense against an aggressor. A little more than a year later, that treaty was tested when Communist forces from North Korea invaded South Korea. In June 1950, President Truman ordered American forces to protect South Korea's independence against Communist aggression. By the end of the year, Chinese Communist troops

Christmas Greetings 1950. HARRY S. TRUMAN LIBRARY

Christmas Greetings

♣ 1950 ♣

AS 1950 EBBS TO ITS CLOSE OUR HEARTS TURN ONCE MORE TO BETHLEHEM AND TO THE COMING OF A LITTLE CHILD, THE DIVINE INFANT, THAT BROUGHT LOVE TO a weary world. This is the season of love—the season wherein our thoughts are of the love of friends, the love of home, the love of children, the love of all those little half remembered things which, although they make up the best portion of our days, are too often forgotten in the distractions of troublous times.

❧ We need Christmas to bring us back to a due sense of spiritual values.

❧ And so at this blessed season we are thinking of those faithful members of the White House staff who, day in and day out, have so quietly and with such unobtrusive efficiency performed their tasks and by their continuous and often unnoticed labors, lightened our cares and added pleasure to our lives.

❧ May Christmas Day be a day of joy to each and every one.

❧ It is not possible for us personally to know all those to whom we owe so deep a debt of gratitude. But to each we send this heartfelt message of affection and appreciation.

❧ May the Star of Bethlehem, which came so mysteriously and lingered so briefly, shine in our hearts and light our way to joy and peace even as it directed the steps of the Wise Men to the Manger in the City of David in the long ago.

❧ And may we, too, hear the song which the Angel Choir sang on the night of the first Christmas: "Glory to God in the highest and on earth, peace, good will toward men."

Harry Truman

Bess W. Truman

had joined North Korea in the war. The Chief Executive knew that peace on earth would not last, but his goodwill toward the people of South Korea was a necessary part of his peacekeeping efforts.

His Christmas gift to his staff in 1950 reflected his goodwill and appreciation to those who faithfully and unobtrusively cared for his needs while he tended to the cares of the nation. *In Christmas Greetings 1950,* he reminded them that, "We need Christmas to bring us back to a due sense of spiritual values." The Government Printing Office produced 1,000 copies of the frameable keepsake. To his Cabinet and other close associates, the President gave a set of six crystal glasses engraved with the Presidential Coat of Arms.

With U.S. troops engaged in combat in Korea, the White House received thousands of letters from citizens and church organizations requesting that the President proclaim a national day of prayer. In his Christmas message, taped in Washington before he went to Missouri for Christmas, Truman responded by urging the American people to renew their faith in God. He called for prayer based upon righteousness. Due to an assassination attempt in November, security was tight and no one was permitted on the White House grounds. Outside the iron fence, a crowd of 3,000 heard the broadcast and listened to the Marine Band. President Truman spoke by tape from Washington, but lit the tree by remote control from Independence.

> *Many of us are fortunate enough to celebrate Christmas at our own fireside. But there are many others who are away from their homes and loved ones on this day. Thousands of our boys are on the cold and dreary battlefield of Korea. But all of us–at home, at war, wherever we may be–are within reach of God's love and power. We all can pray. We all should pray.... The Nation*

already is in the midst of a Crusade of Prayer. On the last Sunday of the old year, there will be special services devoted to a revival of faith. I call upon all of you to enlist in this common cause. I call upon you no matter what your spiritual allegiance.

We are all joined in the fight against the tyranny of Communism. Communism is godless. Democracy is the harvest of faith–faith in one's self, faith in one's neighbors, faith in God. Democracy's most powerful weapon is not a gun, tank, or bomb. It is faith–faith in the brotherhood and dignity of man under God.

No one knew whether this Christmas was to be one more postwar Christmas or the last Christmas before war. All across the nation, people of all faiths joined in prayer for peace.

1951: *Blair House Memento*

During the renovation of the White House, from November 1948 until March 1952, President and Mrs. Truman lived in Blair House. For their Christmas gift to their staff in 1951, the Chief Executive directed the Government Printing Office to produce 1,000 copies of a photograph of the Blair House taken by the Signal Corps. With a total cost of $90, the gift was given to the staff by the President on December 22 at his annual pre-Christmas reception. One of the recipients, M.O. Carter, was a White House electrician who, over time, became close to the President. Years later he wrote on the back of his Christmas gift, "He would come downstairs and eat bean soup with several of the boys. We all liked President Truman alot [sic]." To his Cabinet and close personal friends, the President gave 60 bound, limited editions of his opening address at the Conference on the Japanese Peace Treaty in San Francisco.

The 1951 gift print of Blair House. HARRY S. TRUMAN LIBRARY

From his home in Independence, on Christmas Eve 1951, the President recalled the year 1941 when our country was struggling in a war for survival. He said:

> Our hearts are saddened on this Christmas Eve by the suffering and the sacrifice of our brave men and women in Korea. We miss our boys and girls who are out there. They are protecting us, and all free men, from aggression. They are trying to prevent another world war. We honor them for the great job they are doing. We pray to the Prince of Peace for their success and safety.
>
> As we think of Korea, we should also think ... of another Christmas, 10 years ago, in 1941. That was just after Pearl Harbor, and the whole world was at war. Then almost every country, almost every home, was overshadowed by fear and sorrow.... Tonight we have a different goal, and a higher hope. Despite difficulties, the free nations of the world have drawn together solidly for a great purpose; not solely to defend themselves; not merely to win a bloody war if it should come; but for the purpose of creating a real peace— a peace that shall be a positive reality and not an empty hope; a just and lasting peace.
>
> When we look toward the battlefields of Korea, we see a conflict like no other in history. There the forces of the United Nations are fighting—not for territory, not for plunder, not to rule the lives of captive people. In Korea the free nations are proving, by deeds, that man is free and must remain free, that aggression must end, that nations must obey the law.

Americans on the front lines in Korea experienced snow and sleet, but a quiet Christmas, with only an occasional rumble of Communist artillery. Efforts were made to serve turkey, dressing, cranberry sauce, mixed nuts, pie and coffee to all the troops. Francis Cardinal Spellman celebrated Mass for 3,000 Marines on the eastern front. Santa Claus, dressed in red and white or khaki green, also paid a visit to the frozen front. While delegates talked of peace at Panmunjom, the soldiers in the midst of war turned their thoughts to home.

1952: Last Christmas in Office

When the President of the United States went to Independence for Christmas, scores of people went with him, including White House staff members, secretaries, Secret Service agents, military aides, his airplane crew, the press, and many others. Harry Truman had gone home for Christmas six of the eight years of his Presidency. Aware of the personal sacrifice of all those who accompanied him, he announced, early in December, "I'm staying at the White House this Christmas. It's my last Christmas as President and

The Trumans' last gift print was reproduced by the Government Printing Office.

Bess and I want to spend it in Washington." What he hadn't said was that, for a change, all his staff could spend the holiday with their own families.

The Trumans had moved back into the newly renovated White House in March. For Christmas they gave their staff a photograph of the historic mansion depicting the 1946 Truman Balcony. The Signal Corps shot the photograph and the Government Printing Office printed it. The gold Presidential Seal in the lower left corner accented their sentiment. The reproductions in black and white cost 50 cents each, and in color, $2, and were presented at the annual reception in the President's office. Mrs. Truman and Margaret broke tradition by being on hand to exchange holiday greetings with the 350 members of the executive staff and the crews of the *Sacred Cow* and the *Williamsburg,* the Presidential yacht.

For the first time in five years, the President appeared in person to light the National Community Christmas Tree on the White House lawn. To a crowd of several thousand watching from outside the iron fence, he said: "As we pray for our men and women in Korea, and all our service men and women wherever they are—let us also pray for our enemies. Let us pray that the spirit of God shall enter their lives and prevail in their lands. Let us pray for a fulfillment of the brotherhood of man. Through Jesus Christ the world will yet be a better and a fairer place. This faith sustains us today as it has sustained mankind for centuries past."

God appeared to answer the Americans' prayers in an unusual way. The Korean War did not end overnight, but it did cease for a day, as the enemy joined in the celebration. The cannons on Sniper Ridge were silent while Communist loudspeakers played Christmas carols, after announcing a cease fire until noon, "in observance of your Christmas." The enemy left toys, dolls and candy on the front lines, along with banners that read, "Merry Christmas." On the Western front, Allied watchers were stunned to see a decorated Christmas tree and numerous signs bearing holiday greetings in English.

In January 1953 "the man from Independence" went home for good. Harry Truman had become President as World War II was coming to a close, and left office in the last days of the Korean War. He faced crucial decisions in both crises but remained constant in his pursuit of peace. For a man who had tried to dodge the nomination for Vice President, the responsibility of the Presidency was heavy. He said of his sudden entry into office upon the death of FDR, "I felt like the moon, the stars, and all the planets had fallen on me." Almost eight years later, the departing President summed up his performance: "I have tried my best to give the nation everything I had in me."

PRESIDENT ABRAHAM LINCOLN
FROM A PHOTOGRAPH
BY ALEXANDER GARDNER
TAKEN NOVEMBER 15, 1863

BY

Dwight D. Eisenhower

CHRISTMAS 1953

THE EISENHOWERS
Art From a Painting President

*I*f ever a President took a personal interest in the gifts and cards that were sent from the White House, it was Dwight D. Eisenhower. Having had no formal training in painting, the President known as "Ike" allowed six of his own creations to be used as Christmas gifts to his staff during his administration. In a letter to Joyce C. Hall, president of Hallmark Cards, he wrote: "As you know I always hate to inflict 'art' on my friends and members of my staff, but Hallmark makes such a beautiful package job that I am, and I hope others are, distracted into the belief that the whole thing is a superior product."

While president of Columbia University, General Eisenhower began painting at the urging of New York painter Thomas E. Stephens. Interest had turned to fascination as Ike watched the artist work on a portrait of Mrs. Eisenhower. Before Stephens was finished, the General had borrowed paint, brushes and canvas from him and had begun his own portrait of Mamie, his wife. Thus was launched a new hobby for a man already in love with golf and fishing. Eisenhower always referred to his work not as art, but as "daubs, born of my love of color and in my pleasure in experimenting." Painting became a means of relaxation for him rather than an accomplishment. Consequently, the General gave his first painting to Stephens, who numbered it among his prized possessions. Having no deep attachment to his work, Eisenhower often created paintings that ended up as mementos for his personal friends or as thoughtful holiday gifts.

Facing page: Eisenhower's Abraham Lincoln, the 1953 gift print. HALLMARK CARDS

1953: *The Abe Lincoln Portrait*

When planning for their first White House Christmas, it seemed only natural to call on card expert Joyce C. Hall. The President had known the Hallmark chief executive since 1950, when Hall had been asked to serve on a committee to build the General's war trophies museum in Abilene, Kansas. That relationship grew over the years and resulted in a unique collection of Christmas cards unlike those of any other Presidential era. "Being an artist himself, Eisenhower was most challenging and imaginative to deal with," Hall said. "We felt strongly that he should use his own paintings on the cards, but he didn't think they were good enough. He had recently done a portrait of Abraham Lincoln which we thought was an excellent choice—a portrait of one President painted by another."

The President had begun work on the portrait of Lincoln while waiting for news of a Korean armistice. The Lincoln likeness was derived from an Alexander Gardner photograph of November 15, 1863. Hallmark reproduced the portrait and enclosed it in a white commemorative gift folder bearing the Presidential Seal. The President wrote to Hall: "Someone just showed me your reproduction of my laborious attempt to paint a portrait of Lincoln. I must say that if my work could only remotely approach the quality that is so evident in every part of your reproduction, the thing would be a real masterpiece. In fact ... I even like my head of Lincoln—except when I did it originally I did not realize I had allowed so much red to creep into the face tones. That was a mistake which one of these days I shall correct."

Of the 1,100 keepsake folders ordered that year, 516 were given to White House employees at the annual Christmas party in the East Room. Along with the gift print, each member of the staff received an official gift enclosure card with the words "Season's Greetings" engraved in gold.

In 1953, the list of Presidential Christmas card recipients was expanded significantly, with season's greetings going to American ambassadors abroad, foreign heads of state, government officials, members of the Cabinet and Congress. Thereafter, the Presidential greeting was to be the "official" White House Christmas card. In addition to the gift folder and gift enclosure card, Hallmark reproduced 1,100 official greeting cards for the Eisenhowers. The ivory white formal card for the year was designed with a blank embossed Presidential Seal and the words "Season's Greetings" engraved in gold. Inside, the black engraved message read, "The President and Mrs. Eisenhower extend their best wishes for Christmas and the New Year." A similar but less formal card was designed with embossed holly leaves and red berries. A simple engraved "Mamie and Ike," in Mamie's handwriting, was sent to 500 personal friends. The President wrote to Hall: "The Christmas cards are, of course, equally outstanding and both are completely appropri-

The 1953 official Presidential Christmas card. HALLMARK CARDS

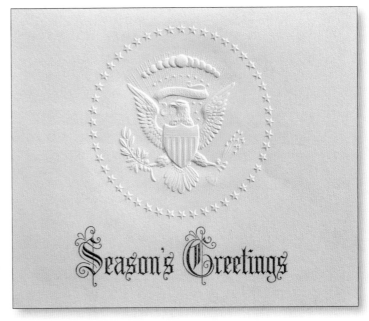

ate to the purpose for which we intend to use them."

Greeting the American people on Christmas Eve from inside the White House, the Chief Executive reached the nation by radio and television, and his words were carried around the world in 34 languages by Voice of America radio. While applauding the cessation of fighting in Korea, the Commander-in-Chief acknowledged that a cold war still existed. He said: "For us, this Christmas is truly a season of goodwill—and our first peaceful one since 1949. Our national and individual blessings are manifold. Our hopes are bright even though the world still stands divided in two antagonistic parts." Following his message, the President and Mrs. Eisenhower were driven to the South Lawn, where he set aglow the 1,500 red and green lights of the National Christmas Tree. Seven hundred invited guests crowded around the tree, while 3,500 watched the ceremony from outside the fence.

In those days, the cost for printing the gift folders and cards that were sent by the President came out of his personal account. On January 23, Ike expressed his appreciation to Joyce C. Hall: "Your bill was not only nominal, it was practically nonexistent. I have some inkling, at least, of the enormity of my obligation to you.... Incidentally, you will be pleased to know that the obvious excellence of your work in reproducing and mounting my *Lincoln* elicited far more compliments from my intimate friends than did my own effort." Enclosed was a check for $139.50.

1954: *The George Washington Portrait*

By February, the President was already thinking ahead to the next Christmas. His secretary, Thomas E. Stephens, contacted Hall for advice. Said Hall: "I doubt if there is anything he could do that would be as interesting as a series of Presidents and it also seems to me that he has put them in exactly the right order—Lincoln, Washington, Jefferson, and Theodore Roosevelt." He added, "If the President were willing to paint a series of these, the recipients would each have a priceless collection and the originals would be an exhibit worthy of a room in any gallery. Every good critic of art who

The 1954 official gift enclosure.
HALLMARK CARDS

Eisenhower's George Washington, the 1954 gift print. HALLMARK CARDS

saw the painting or the print has marveled at the President's ability as a portrait painter."

Hearing indirectly later in the year that the requests for the Lincoln print had exhausted the supply, Hall authorized a second printing to be forwarded to the President. In a thank you note to Hall he wrote: "I think you would be gratified, as I must confess I have been, by the flattering comments I have had throughout the year about the Lincoln. Recently, when

The 1954 personal embossed wreath Christmas card, complete with hand-applied nail polish on the red holly berries. HALLMARK CARDS *Below:* The 1954 personal gift enclosure card that turned out to be the first in a series of "Mamie Bangs" variations. HALLMARK CARDS

Chancellor Adenauer was here, I was astonished to hear him express a desire for one, and of course I was delighted to have a copy to give him."

In September, while on a fishing trip near Fraser, Colorado, the President had painted the portrait of George Washington from Gilbert Stuart's famed work. Hallmark reproduced the artwork in lithography and put the print in a folder with a blank embossed Presidential Seal. Some of the prints were marked "this edition is a limited edition of 950." Hallmark also shipped 350 without the words "limited edition." To accompany each Washington print, the President ordered 1,300 official gift enclosure cards, designed with the Presidential Seal and "Season's Greetings 1954" with a red border.

The gift print and enclosure card were distributed to 664 office associates, Secret Service agents, White House police force, chauffeurs, telephone operators and domestic employees. Gift folders were also hand-delivered to Cabinet members and government departments within Washington. Accompany-ing each was a greeting from the President: "Last Christmas time I had the audacity to send you a lithograph of a reputed 'portrait' I had done of President Lincoln. While my effort of this year is not even up to the woefully low standard of last year, I thought you might like a companion picture. It is a reproduction of a painting of President Washington which I have just completed."

The 1954 official Christmas card was a smooth, white greeting card with a blank embossed Presidential Seal; a gold, hot foil eagle; and a red, white and blue silk screen shield. The White House ordered 1,300 greeting cards. Hallmark also designed two personal cards for the Eisenhowers. While extremely pleased with the white blank embossed wreath card with a red bow and red berries, the President and First Lady never learned of the challenge those 400 personal cards posed for artists at Hallmark.

On the morning they were to be shipped, it was discovered that the red ink from the berries on one card would smear onto the next one. Artists armed with bottles of clear nail polish were quickly pressed into service to apply a dot of polish to each and every berry. Rendered smudge-proof, the cards were shipped that afternoon on TWA. That year also, a Hallmark artist designed a personal gift card for the First Lady's use. Meant to be an affectionate holiday greeting for close personal friends, the informal card caricatured her hairstyle and was identified by its clever trademark as the "Mamie Bangs" card. "Mrs. Eisenhower adored them," wrote her social secretary, Mary Jane McCaffree. "Please thank the artist for his originality," requested the First Lady.

On December 17, instead of on Christmas Eve, President Eisenhower lit the 70-foot National Christmas Tree to open a 21-day celebration of what was to be the first Pageant of Peace. Taking place in a large cross-shaped park on the Ellipse, the unprecedented event included musical presentations on a 40-foot stage, Protestant services, Catholic Masses, a nativity scene and a children's corner featuring Santa and eight reindeer from North Pole, New York. The inauguration of the Pageant of Peace provided Washington with one of the most successful civic celebrations in the city's history. More than 300,000 spectators visited the festival over several days, and millions witnessed it from around the world.

Having been confronted with the possibility of military action in Vietnam earlier in the year, the President focused on peace: "This year, even as two thousand years ago, when the Prince of Peace was born into the world, the drums of war are stilled. In their silence, after a whole generation of almost ceaseless beating, many people—already become fathers and mothers—enjoy the first peaceful Christmas they have known. So—mankind's unquenchable hope for peace burns brighter than for many years."

1955: "Distance in the Mountains"

An avid fisherman who especially enjoyed the excellent trout fishing near Fraser, Colorado, the President, in mid-September 1955, began a new painting, *St. Louis Creek, Byars Peak Ranch*. He had been working on it only a week when he suffered his first heart attack and was rushed to Fitzsimons Army Hospital in Denver. "The painting was to be his Christmas card that year," recalled Joyce C. Hall, "and he asked me to visit him to discuss it since he wasn't sure he could finish it in time. When I got to the hospital he had already started working on it again. Can anyone doubt what great therapy painting was for him?"

Eisenhower's St. Louis Creek, the 1955 gift print. HALLMARK CARDS

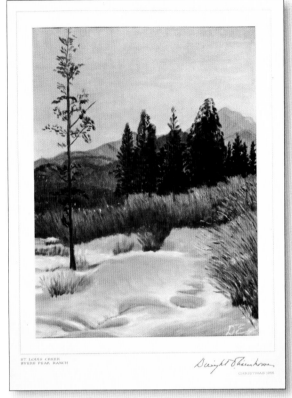

On November 3, Hallmark received the painting. The message of Hall to the President in his Denver White House was, "We all think it is exceptionally well done, and particularly like your treatment of snow and how well you achieved a feeling of distance in the mountains. These are hard things to do, and you should be very proud of your result. Our opinion is that it will reproduce very satisfactorily, and within a short time after size is determined we will send proofs to show you just how it will finish. We are greatly pleased with the news of your splendid improvement and will be praying for it to continue."

Even with the President's "never satisfied, always-critical eye," he was pleased with the results. He responded to Hall: "This year, perhaps because of my illness, I am more than ever grateful for some of the wonderful kindnesses shown to me by my friends. The assistance and cooperation of Hallmark, in producing—in a very limited space of time—the lithograph of the St. Louis Creek scene, is right on top of my list." The White House had ordered 1,500 prints.

The official greeting card kept the same design as the previous year's card with the exception of a blue silk screen background and gold foil stars to enhance the appearance of the 1,300 cards. Again Hallmark designed a card to extend "Christmas Greetings" to the First Family's personal friends. A second "Mamie Bangs" gift card was designed for Mrs. Eisenhower's personal use.

On December 16, President Eisenhower touched a telegraph key in the office of the president of Gettysburg College to light the 65-foot spruce on the Ellipse. Speaking from Gettysburg, the President's Christmas message took on more personal overtones than in previous years. He said: "For me, this particular Christmas has a very special meaning, and has brought to me, really, new understandings of people. During the past three months, my family and I have received literally thousands—tens of thousands of messages. Each of these has borne a sentence of good wishes and goodwill for

The 1955 official Presidential Christmas card.
HALLMARK CARDS

Below: The 1955 "Mamie Bangs" gift enclosure card. HALLMARK CARDS

health and happiness to us both. It has been heartwarming evidence that human understanding and human sympathy can surmount every obstacle—even those obstacles that some governments sometimes seem to raise in the attempt to divide us."

Having spent their first two Christmases in Augusta, Georgia, the President and First Lady decided to spend Christmas of 1955 at the White House. They were joined by their son, John, and three of his four children. John's wife, Barbara, remained in the hospital, having just given birth to the President's fourth grandchild.

1956: Photographic Gifts

In June the President underwent emergency surgery following an ileitis attack. Unable to spend much time painting, he decided to give the staff a portfolio of twin black and white pictures of himself and Mrs. Eisenhower. The President's photograph was taken by Willard Volz of Reni Photos at CBS at the beginning of the campaign for his second term in office. Mrs. Eisenhower's was a photograph of the Thomas E. Stephens painting of her in her pink 1953 inaugural gown.

The White House ordered 1,750 official gift enclosure cards along with the 1,750 gift portfolios, 200 of which were to be prepared blank so that a personal note could be added in longhand by the President and Mrs. Eisenhower. Just four days before Christmas, however, 175 of the blank folders were returned to Hallmark by air to add the engraving. The photographs to be inserted in the portfolio were likewise being returned by air from Rochester, New York. A wire to Joyce C. Hall from the White House queried whether it would be possible to make this change for the President; it went

THE EISENHOWER FARMS

The 1956 gift print: twin photographs of the President and First Lady. HALLMARK CARDS

Left: The 1956 personal Christmas card: the front door at the Eisenhowers' Gettysburg farm. HALLMARK CARDS

on to say that it would be all right if the order was shipped after Christmas. Also, an additional supply of 200 cards was needed.

Stating that "a Christmas card received after Christmas is about as effective as 'last year's bird nest,'" the Hallmark president assured the White House that his staff would see to it that the order was completed before Christmas. On the Saturday before Christmas, a number of Hallmark personnel arrived to help with the Presidential project. The folders to be engraved arrived from Washington, but the plane from Rochester, New York, carrying the photographs had been grounded due to bad weather, and there was no hope of getting them in time. At Hall's suggestion, photographs were taken of the portraits, providing negatives from which replacement photos could be made. Other "Hallmarkers" responded with equal enthusiasm and the deadline was met.

After learning from a trade magazine that the Eisenhowers had selected Castleton china with a wide gold band for use in the White House, Hallmark artist Bette Johnson designed their 1956 official card with this in mind. It portrayed a gold, hot foil eagle on the blank embossed Presidential Seal, against a gold litho background with embossed "Season's Greetings 1956" on the front. The White House ordered 1,900 of these along with another 800 personal cards depicting the front door at the Eisenhower Farms near Gettysburg, Pennsylvania. The farm, purchased in 1950 upon the Eisenhowers' return from Europe, became the First Family's weekend getaway. It also was the only permanent home the General and his wife had ever owned.

On December 20, President Eisenhower formally opened the Pageant of Peace by setting aglow the 5,000 lights and 4,000 decorations on the 67-foot spruce. The newly reelected Chief Executive extolled the spirit of Christmas in his remarks.

The 1957 personal gift enclosure card: Ike and Mamie on a golf cart. HALLMARK CARDS

Below: A Green Room photograph, the 1957 gift print. HALLMARK CARDS

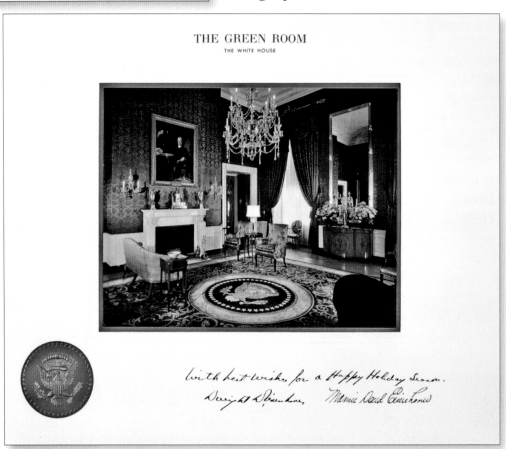

1957: The Green Room Photo

As their Christmas gift, the Eisenhowers chose to give their staff a color photo of the Green Room. An engraved message in the President's hand-writing under the picture eliminated the need for the official gift enclosure that year. The White House ordered 1,950 gift folders. Almost without exception, the White House would order the same number of official Christmas cards as they did gift folders, but in 1957 they ordered 2,500 cards. The official card shape also changed. Hallmark placed a blank embossed Presidential Seal and gold, hot foil eagle and stars on the oblong white card stock. The Eisenhowers sent 800 personal cards depicting in silver foil their house at the Eisenhower Farms.

The President's favorite sport was golf, and his pride and joy was the putting green on the South Lawn that had been a gift from the American Public Golf Association. In 1957 Hallmark designed a "Mamie Bangs" gift enclosure card depicting Ike and Mamie in a golf cart loaded down with packages and a Christmas tree. The 400 gift cards would have been useful to a First Family that gave many gifts. Chief usher J.B. West, in his *Upstairs at the White House*, said: "Mamie Eisenhower was personally a most thoughtful First Lady." Besides remembering her employees' birthdays with a cake and a card, she also selected something for everyone at Christmas.

At the annual ceremony at the Pageant of Peace in 1957, President Eisenhower warned the audience of 9,000 that sweat and toil, courage and self-sacrifice would be needed to achieve and sustain world peace.

1958: Deserted Barn

The Christmas staff gift for 1958 was a reproduction of *Deserted Barn*, a painting done by the Chief Executive at the Gettysburg farm the previous summer. A recipient of one of the 2,150 gift folders that year was Major Donald Glew, Jr., the Chief Executive's physician at Walter Reed Army Hospital. Later, in a letter to him, the President told the story behind the gift print.

As you well know, I have had no instruction in painting. I know nothing whatsoever about technique and in the course in mechanical drawing I pursued at West Point I was such a failure that I ran the risk of discharge. Actually my great interest is colors. They intrigue me and I try to indulge my bent in this direction by applying myself to attempt in oils, a representation of any scene or person I can think of. Frankly, I don't even know how to mix colors decently. Sometimes it is a real effort to achieve the approximate color and value I seek.

So far as my latest reproduction is concerned, I started it merely as an imaginative sketch. I wanted to see whether I could, from memory, project the straight lines to their approximately correct vanishing points—and do so without the aid of any model or drawing. In order to make the exercise of some interest to myself, I wanted also to represent desolation or hopelessness if this could be done in a structure. The other items of the composition were put in there merely incidentally, so I might judge my success in achieving the effect of relative distance and of color.

Once I had finished with this particular exercise, I was on the point of throwing it away when other members of the family asked me not to do so. Later I found that they had decided a reproduction would make a nice Christmas memento, but in the meantime I had given the painting away to a friend [Walter A. West]. So we had to get it back—and that is the way the project got underway despite all the imperfections I could easily see in the thing. After 1961 I am going to start taking lessons.

The 2,100 official Christmas cards for 1958 bore the traditional design of an embossed gold foil Presidential Seal with a field of blue silk screening placed on ivory white card stock. For the family's personal card, Hallmark

Eisenhower's *Deserted Barn*: the 1958 gift print. HALLMARK CARDS

WE WANTED TO PUT SOMETHING OF OURSELVES IN OUR CHRISTMAS CARD TO YOU....

MAMIE   IKE

MERRY CHRISTMAS

A 1958 contemporary card with an overlapping front and inside design. HALLMARK CARDS

Left: The 1958 personal card: a painting of the Eisenhower Museum in Abilene, Kansas. HALLMARK CARDS

framed a painting of the Eisenhower Museum in Abilene, Kansas, with a green wreath made of holly, red berries and a red bow. Mrs. Eisenhower ordered 300 of them and 200 of an informal contemporary card Hallmark had designed especially for the First Couple. A red original "Mamie Bangs" card completed the order for the First Family. Hallmark art director Jeannette Lee wrote of the relationship between her company and the Chief Executive: "We're so pleased to be doing cards for the President and Mrs. Eisenhower again this year. The most excitement we have around here is hearing the results of what they like."

A 99-foot Engelmann spruce from Montana served as the National Christmas Tree in 1958. Trimmed to a mere 79 feet, the stately spruce was decorated with 5,000 lights, 1,200 balls, 108 red bells and 60 three-foot candy canes. As he lit the tree, President Eisenhower made a pledge to the 7,500 present and to the millions in the television and radio audience. He said: "The United States is strong, and will remain strong, because that is the only way in today's world that the peace can be protected–but the United States will never use its strength to break the peace."

Above: Mount Eisenhower: the 1959 gift print. HALLMARK CARDS

Above left: The 1959 official Presidential Christmas card. HALLMARK CARDS

Participants that traveled the farthest for the Pageant of Peace were 14 reindeer and a caribou from north of the Arctic Circle. A Christmas gift to the nation from the Governor of Alaska, the herd traveled by plane, railroad, ship and truck to get to Washington, D.C. The biggest challenge of the long trip came when one of the reindeer became skittish and kicked open the door of the Alaskan Air National Guard plane at 2,000 feet. Despite the hair-raising incident, the animals arrived safely and retired to the zoo when the pageant was over.

1959: The Year of Mount Eisenhower

As their Christmas present in 1959 the White House staff received a reproduction of *Mount Eisenhower*, a painting of a tall rocky butte looming over Lake Louise with fir trees rising above the shore. At 9,390 feet, the mountain is located in Banff National Park in the Canadian Rockies, between Banff and Lake Louise, and was formerly called Castle Mountain. It was renamed on January 11, 1946, in appreciation of the leadership given to the Allied Forces in World War II by the Supreme Commander, General Dwight D. Eisenhower.

Sam Rayburn, longtime Speaker of the House, writing to the President in appreciation of his gift said, "I think the picture of the painting of Mount Eisenhower that you made is perfectly lovely. It will be framed and will find its way to the Memento Room of the Sam Rayburn Library in Bonham, Texas. Maybe you and I can do something sometime that people will remember us for, so I am putting a lot of you and me in the Library where it will be preserved always."

Hallmark printed 2,200 of the gift folders and 1,200 official gift enclosure cards. The 2,900 official Christmas cards took on a slightly different appearance with its red, white and blue silk screened borders. The Presidential Seal was also changed by Executive Order from 48 to 50 stars to reflect the recent addition of Alaska and Hawaii as states. The Eisenhowers' personal card featured a watercolor of the Little House at the farm, with a poem to describe it. For the First Lady's personal gift cards Hallmark turned out another "Mamie Bangs" creation using her favorite holly, red berries and bow to shape a hat.

Upon his return from a 19-day goodwill tour of 11 countries, the President spoke at the Pageant of Peace ceremonies on December 23 and said, "I wish that every American ... could see and hear what I have seen and what I have heard. The mutual understanding thereby created could in itself do much to dissolve the issues that plague the world."

1960: Church in Bavaria

Christmas of 1960 was the last one the Eisenhowers would spend in the White House. J.B. West recalled that Mrs. Eisenhower wanted this one "to be the most beautiful Christmas ever" and consequently "spread Christmas throughout the entire White House." Together with her social secretary, Mary Jane McCaffree, the First Lady scoured all of Washington's department stores for ideas and baubles. As elaborate as her 1960 preparations were, the 26 trees she had decorated in 1959 set a record that stood for many years.

On December 22, the President and First Lady gave their annual party for 1,000 members of the White House staff and employees. A reproduction of the President's painting *Church in Bavaria*, along with a gift enclosure card, was given to each person who had worked for them. Hallmark produced 2,225 gift folders and 1,200 official gift enclosure cards for the Eisenhowers' last Christmas in the White House.

Church in Bavaria was the sixth in the gallery of paintings the President shared with his White House staff. Over the years, he had created more than a hundred portraits of friends and family, landscapes, pastoral scenes and an occasional still life.

Between 1953 and 1960, the list of recipients of the official Christmas

Eisenhower's *Church in Bavaria*, the 1960 gift card.
HALLMARK CARDS

card from the President had almost tripled, growing from 1,100 to 3,100. The last official card featured a blank embossed Presidential Seal on a white card, with 50 gold, hot foil stars, placed on a wide band of red silk screen. For their personal card, Mrs. Eisenhower loved the watercolor of the South Portico and its two staircases leading into the White House, because that was the entrance she most often used. The White House ordered 500 of the watercolor cards along with 100 of the "Mamie Bangs" gift cards.

Joyce C. Hall and Dwight Eisenhower had a unique working relationship. In eight years, Hallmark produced a prodigious 38 different Christmas cards and gift prints for the President and First Lady. No previous administration, nor any since Eisenhower's, has sent such a variety of holiday greetings from the White House. "I like Ike" was more than a campaign slogan; it was the essence of Hall's appreciation for the famed General. "When you care enough to send the very best" was more than an advertising slogan for the President; it was the epitome of what he had come to rely on as an outlet for the products of his newfound passion for painting. Earle Chesney, Assistant to the Deputy Assistant to the President, captured their mutual admiration in an affectionate caricature.

On December 23, in his last Christmas message, Eisenhower called for a self-examination …"to test the sincerity of our own dedication to the ideals so beautifully expressed in the Christian ethic…. One of America's imperishable virtues is her pride in the national ideals proclaimed at her birth. When

The 1960 Official Christmas card.
HALLMARK CARDS

The 1960 personal card, a watercolor of the
South Portico. HALLMARK CARDS

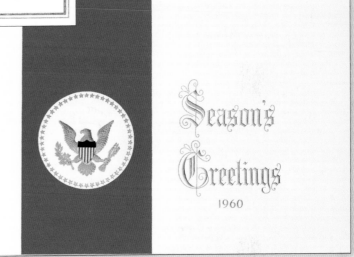

danger to them threatens, America will
fight for her spiritual heritage to the
expenditure of the last atom of her material wealth; she will put justice above life
itself. America will never cease in her
striving to remove the blemishes on her
own reflection...."

Together the President and First
Lady pressed the button that lit the thousands of colored lights on the 70-
foot Douglas fir tree from Oregon. More than 1,200 area citizens braved the
21-degree temperature to pay their respect to the President. When the
Marine Band finished the National Anthem, the Chief Executive walked to
the microphone and said, "For the last time as a part of this lovely ceremony, I wish you a merry Christmas and a very, very happy New Year—all of
you."

With our appreciation and best wishes for a happy Christmas

John F. Kennedy   Jacqueline Kennedy

1961

THE KENNEDYS
Art, History and Christmas

When John F. Kennedy came to the White House in 1961, First Lady Jacqueline Bouvier Kennedy was astonished by its lack of tradition. There was no sensof history; no reminders of the great Americans who had lived there in the past. She decided to take on the task of making the world-famous building "a showcase of American Art and History." With that goal in mind she embarked on an ambitious project to restore the White House rooms to their rightful place in history and to transform the Executive Mansion into an historic museum, a repository of period furniture and art that would reflect the history of the Presidency. Despite her husband's foreshortened administration, Mrs. Kennedy succeeded admirably in calling the nation's attention to the building's rich legacy.

1961: The White House Ducks

The American people have always been fascinated with the Kennedys. Volumes have been written and myriads of photographs have been taken of them. Consequently, when it came time to shop for a Christmas card idea, the subject matter had already been in the camera or the artwork was on the drawing board. It then became a simple matter of reproducing the image and gift wrapping it for the holidays.

For their first Christmas, the Kennedys gave their White House staff a photograph of the White House with Caroline's ducks in the fountain on the

Facing page: The Kennedys' first gift print to their staff in 1961. HALLMARK CARDS

The 1961 official Presidential Christmas card.

South Lawn. Chief usher J.B. West recalled, "With great glee, Mrs. Kennedy had me install a pen for the fluffy baby ducklings. Then as they grew, we acclimated them to the majestic fountain on the deep south lawn. But the ducks ate the tulips. And Charlie, the terrier, ate some of the ducks. And Caroline kept falling into the fountain, accompanied by great whoops from the tourists lined up at the fence." Before Caroline's ducks were transported to Rock Creek Park, Cecil Stoughton, the Presidents' personal photographer, recorded the familiar scene, including the fence that was put up not to keep the ducks in, but to keep Charlie out.

The photograph, taken in the spring, was given to General Ted Clifton, a military aide to the President, to pass on to the First Lady. The President and Mrs. Kennedy obviously appreciated having this memory recorded and chose to share it with their staff at Christmas. General Clifton, who had already been personally involved with Hallmark president Joyce C. Hall, asked if the card company would be willing to produce the gift print for the Kennedys. Hallmark agreed and placed the brilliantly colored photograph in a red folder, the front of which was embossed with a 50-star Presidential Seal.

The Christmas remembrance was presented to some 1,000 White House executive and military employees at an informal reception on December 13. Four-year-old Caroline Kennedy was the first of her family to arrive at the party, along with her four-year-old cousin, Stephen Smith. Oblivious to the guests, both children were intent on finding the children's tree in the Blue Room. For the first time, the tree was decorated around a theme—Tchaikovsky's *Nutcracker* ballet. To the delight of the children, the branches were laden with toy soldiers, sugar plum fairies, candy canes, lollipops, toy musical instruments, imitation mice, miniature toys and baskets of fruit.

The President and First Lady mingled and offered personal greetings to those who served them daily behind the scenes. Refreshments were served in both the State Dining Room and East Room. The Marine Band was set up in both rooms to play Christmas carols. A 68-voice choir from Howard University provided additional entertainment in the East Room.

Of special interest to all was the brief preview of the Red Room, which was being redecorated. Most of the French Empire red silk wall covering and furnishings had been donated by Secretary of the Treasury and Mrs. C. Douglas Dillon. A red and gold brocade Dolley Madison sofa and chair were grouped by the fireplace. A portrait of Thomas Jefferson hung over the mantel and a magnificent desk was placed between the two windows. While the room appeared to be complete, it was reportedly "far from finished."

Cards In; Telegrams Out

As for an official Christmas greeting card, the President had considered sending telegrams to the heads of governments around the world. Due to the high cost of transmission, though, it was agreed that the practice of sending Christmas cards should be continued. Hallmark designed a formal card, one very similar to the Eisenhower official card. On smooth white card stock with a wide green silk screen border, the Presidential Seal and the words "Season's Greetings 1961" were engraved, in gold. The sentiment read: "The President and Mrs. Kennedy wish you a Blessed Christmas and a Happy New Year."

Mrs. Kennedy's social secretary, Letitia Baldrige, ordered 800 of the official cards on December 13. As to the timing of the order, Jeannette Lee of Hallmark remarked, "When the President asks you to do something, you do it." Due to the various religions of the recipients, a New Year's greeting, without reference to Christmas, was ordered for 100 of the cards; 150 were designed to be personally signed by the President and Mrs. Kennedy. It was customary to sign cards to heads of state or the heads of government with whom there was a personal acquaintance.

By late November, the White House had not yet decided whether President Kennedy would participate at the Pageant of Peace ceremony, as every President had done since 1923. He did agree to speak, however, and the arrangements were set. Unfortunately, when the President's 73-year-old father, Joseph P. Kennedy, suffered a stroke, the First Family flew to Palm Beach to be with him. From Florida, the President proceeded with his plans to meet British Prime Minister Harold Macmillan in Bermuda. Representing the President at the Pageant of Peace on December 20 was Vice President Lyndon B. Johnson. He lit the 75-foot Washington State Douglas fir and delivered greetings to the approximately 4,000 people in attendance.

1962: The Red Room Painting

In little more than one year in the White House, Mrs. Kennedy and her Fine Arts Committee completed four rooms of her grand-scale restoration project. To stimulate the public's interest in the Executive Mansion, she also inspired the creation of the White House Historical Association. Its purpose was to research, produce and distribute educational materials of all kinds in

With our appreciation and best wishes for a happy Christmas 1962

Edward Lehman's Red Room painting was the 1962 gift print. HALLMARK CARDS

order to preserve the history of the White House and its occupants. In 1962, the organization's first book, *The White House, An Historical Guide*, was produced in conjunction with the National Geographic Society.

On Valentines Day, the First Lady invited the nation into the State Rooms of the White House via CBS television. Weeks in advance of the one-hour special, photographs of the rooms had been sent to the press. Barbara Barnes, home furnishings editor of the *Philadelphia Bulletin*, rejected the photographs and requested that she be allowed to send Edward Lehman, an advertising-illustrator artist, to sketch some renderings of the rooms. Permission was granted.

At the White House, Lehman was drawing his initial sketches in black and white when Mrs. Kennedy came in with fresh flowers for the room and said, "You must be Edward Lehman?" They talked briefly and established an instant rapport. She showed considerable interest in his work. "In art you create interest and feeling, an impression," said the artist. "You can't beat a photograph for detail, but seldom does a photo tell the warmth and create an impression an artist can make." Later, back in his studio, Lehman finished the drawing and delivered it to the newspaper.

On February 9, Lehman's sketches were published in the *Philadelphia Bulletin* and immediately caught the attention of Mrs. Kennedy. According to the artist, shortly thereafter, Mrs. Kennedy called to express her appreciation of his fine work. Assuming that the original sketches had been done in color, she asked if she might be able to obtain them, particularly the one of the Red Room. Lehman explained that due to the process of publishing the sketches in the newspaper, the originals would be of no value. Not wanting to disappoint Mrs. Kennedy, Lehman offered to return to the White House. When he did so, he painted a 20 x 30-inch watercolor of the Red Room, which, upon completion, was sent to the Executive Mansion. The task was sheer pleasure, he reported. "My first impression of the Red Room was love at first sight. My favorite color is red and I found it to be the most stimulating of all the rooms." Lehman later gave a watercolor of the Green Room also to Mrs. Kennedy.

The President and Mrs. Kennedy were so pleased with the results, there was little doubt that the painting of the Red Room would be reproduced by Hallmark and gift wrapped as the 1962 Christmas keepsake for their staff. The 15 x 17-inch gift prints were mounted in a red folder and facsimile signed by the President and First Lady. The 2,000 mementos were handed out at the annual staff Christmas party on December 12. As a special gift, the Kennedys also gave to the Cabinet and to members of their executive staff about 50 red leather-bound copies of the *The White House, An Historic Guide.*

The Chief Executive and First Lady gave gift prints of the Red Room for Christmas, and the artist gave the original to Mrs. Kennedy as a gift. On July 27, she sent him a thank you note. "You can't imagine how much I love the watercolors of the Red and Green Rooms, or how touched I am by your giving them," she wrote. "We are giving a picture of the Red Room one to all the people who work at the White House as a Christmas present this year. That shows you a little bit how much we treasure it. How I envy you being able to do that. I thought I would try to paint some rooms, but put it off as I couldn't face the disappointment I knew my efforts would give me. Now I don't have to bother! Thank you so very much." Lehman was surprised to hear the news but pleased to receive such a personal note from the First Lady. For a man who had never had an art lesson in his life, to be recognized by an art connoisseur such as Mrs. Kennedy was "a rare thrill."

A Cecil Stoughton photograph of a February sleigh ride on the White House lawn became the subject of the 1962 official Presidential Christmas card. HALLMARK CARDS

An Action Photograph Card

For their second official Christmas card the Kennedys chose a personal photograph of Mrs. Kennedy and the children taking a sleigh ride on the South Lawn of the White House. On February 13, after an unusual Washington snowfall, the First Lady had called for the sleigh and Caroline's pony, Macaroni, to be brought in from their farm in Glen Ora, Virginia, so she could take Caroline and her playmates sleighing. With Mrs. Kennedy at the reins, the one-horse open sleigh, complete with sleigh bells, traversed the grounds. After unhitching Macaroni, she took 14-month-old John John for a ride and then led the pony up to the outside of the Oval Office for a visit with the President.

Upon arriving that morning, CBS White House correspondent George Herman saw Mrs. Kennedy and the children enjoying the newly fallen snow. In violation of an agreement with press secretary Pierre Salinger that the media were not to disrupt the children's private lives by stealing photographs of them through the fence, Herman instructed cameraman Bruce Hoertel to film the sleigh ride. This CBS "exclusive," consequently, caused quite a disturbance among the press. Not subject to the privacy embargo, the Presidents' personal photographer, Cecil Stoughton, also recognized the photographic potential on that snowy day. With an artist's eye, he captured this unusual romp in the snow in classic Currier and Ives fashion. Salinger then released an official photograph of the sleigh ride to the press so all could cover the story.

Having herself once served as a fledgling photographer for the *Washington Times-Herald*, Mrs. Kennedy was pleased to have the picture of this "moment to remember." Later that year, she and the President decided to use the wintry picture for their official White House Christmas card. This informal setting was a great departure from their previous formal card, especially considering the fervency with which the Kennedys protected the children's privacy. Mrs. Kennedy did request that it be touched up a bit, however. Russell Armentrout, an airbrush artist, attested to the fact that the photograph was "airbrushed within an inch of its life." Whereas the original picture revealed tracks in the snow, cars and a horse trailer, the Christmas card did not.

The 1962 official Christmas card was produced by Hallmark with varied messages: 1,000 "Christmas Greetings and Best Wishes for a Happy New Year" with facsimile signatures; 700 "Christmas Greetings and Best Wishes for a Happy New Year" without a signature; 100 "With Best Wishes for a Happy New Year" with facsimile signatures; 50 "With Best Wishes for a Happy New Year" without signature; and 100 "Season's Greetings" with facsimile signature.

The White House made a token payment to Hallmark of $800 for the 1,950 Christmas cards and 2,000 gift folders. Hallmark's policy had always been to take extra special care of the President's Christmas order. Their production cost ran upward of $20,000 that year. Mrs. Kennedy expressed her appreciation to Joyce C. Hall in a note dated December 7. "The President and I are more than grateful for the magnificent job Hallmark did on our Christmas Staff present and on our official Christmas card. Both of them were technically difficult to execute, and the taste and skill with which they were done will be appreciated by everyone who receives them. Our deepest thanks to all of the people who worked on these projects and our best wishes to you and your family for the holiday season."

The Pageant of Peace was held on December 17 at 5 o'clock. As fate would have it, 1962 was the only year when President Kennedy would address the nation at Christmas. With indirect reference to the Cuban missile crisis a few weeks earlier, he said:

With the lighting of this tree, which is an old ceremony in Washington and one which has been among the most important responsibilities of a good many Presidents of the United States, we initiate, in a formal way, the Christmas Season.... It is the day when we remind ourselves that man can and must live in peace with his neighbors and that it is the peacemakers who are truly blessed.... We greet each other at Christmas with some special sense of the blessings of peace. This has been a year of peril when the peace has been sorely threatened. But it has been a year when peril was faced and when reason ruled. As a result, we may talk at this Christmas, just a little bit more confidently of peace on earth, goodwill to men. As a result, the hopes of the American people are perhaps a little higher. We have much yet to do. We still need to ask that God bless everyone. But yet I think we can enter this season of goodwill with more than usual joy in our hearts....

1963: Tragedy Changes Everything

Mrs. Kennedy began planning for the 1963 gift print as early as February. Pamela Turnure, Mrs. Kennedy's press secretary, sent the following letter to Lehman: "The staff present this past Christmas of the reproduction of your Red Room picture was such a success, that Mrs. Kennedy is thinking of continuing the series for future Christmas presents. You have already been more than generous but I wonder if you would possibly be able to come to Washington sometime late this Spring or Summer to do additional watercolors of the newly completed Blue Room and Green Room, which has new fabric on the walls?"

The Green Room Painting

In the middle of summer Lehman personally delivered the Green Room painting to the White House. Hallmark reproduced 2,300 gift prints for the Kennedys' Christmas present for their staff. A total of 2,000 were shipped and 100 were retained by Hallmark. The White House also wanted 200 prints without the greeting and without the folder. For whatever the apparent urgency, Hallmark art director Jeannette Lee sent a telegram to Pamela Turnure that the 2,000 Green Room fold-

Edward Lehman's Green Room painting was the Kennedys' 1963 gift print. Mrs. Kennedy gave it to the White House staff for Christmas after the President's death.

HALLMARK CARDS

200 prints without the facsimile had left Kansas City on November 22, the day of the assassination, and would arrive at Washington's Friendship Airport at 1:38 that afternoon.

The Blue Room for 1964

In the last week of August, Ed Lehman came to the White House at the request of Mrs. Kennedy. With him was the finished painting of the Blue Room that the First Lady intended to use for the 1964 Christmas gift. Pamela Turnure met Lehman and extended an invitation from the President and First Lady to spend Christmas in Virginia at the Kennedys' newly built home near Rattlesnake Mountain. They wanted Lehman, if he was interested, to paint the First Family around their Christmas tree. The prospect was exciting and Lehman agreed. The President arrived shortly and greeted the artist with comments of admiration for the newest painting. "The Blue Room is my favorite of the public rooms," the President said. The events of November, however, ended the possibilities for either a family portrait or a 1964 Christmas gift.

Despite her personal pain, Mrs. Kennedy decided to give the gift prints of the Green Room to the White House staff as planned. "I know it will have more meaning than ever at this particular time," wrote Nancy Tuckerman, Mrs. Kennedy's social secretary. In a White House memorandum that accompanied the gift, she told the employees:

Mrs. Kennedy has asked me to express her deep appreciation to The White House Staff for their faithfulness during the past three years. She is especially touched by your untiring devotion during the past two weeks and your loyalty at this sad time has been a great source of comfort to her. Unfortunately, circumstances prevent Mrs.

Edward Lehman's Blue Room painting was to have been the Kennedys' 1964 gift print—the third in a planned series of State Room Christmas gifts.

Kennedy from thanking each of you individually. However, it is with the warmest feelings that she gives each of you the painting of the Green Room, which was chosen by The President as this year's Christmas present. It is Mrs. Kennedy's hope that this will serve as a continual reminder of The President.

Following the assassination, in January 1964, Lehman received a copy of the Green Room painting with this handwritten note: "The President was the one who chose this picture to give to the White House staff this year. He loved it so much. Thank you for making him so proud of the Christmas present he would give to those who made his life so happy the past two years. With deep appreciation, Jacqueline Kennedy."

Mrs. Kennedy also decided to go ahead with a special gift she and the President had planned to give their executive staff for Christmas—reproductions of an engraving of W.H. Bartlett's painting, *The President's House, From Washington,* mounted on a handmade French mat. Each was dated and signed, "With deepest appreciation, John F. Kennedy, Jacqueline Kennedy." A favorite of the President, the engraving had hung in his office.

The Collectors' Cards

Unlike the gift folder that was distributed, the 1963 official Christmas card was never sent. The card, *Creche in East Room, The White House,* featured a color photo of a nativity scene. Beneath the gold embossed Presidential Seal appeared the engraved message "With our wishes for a Blessed Christmas and a Happy New Year" on 1,500 facsimile-signed; "With our wishes for a Blessed Christmas and a Happy New Year" on 700 without signature; "With best wishes for a Happy New Year" on 100 with facsimile signature; and "With best wishes for a Happy New Year" on 50 without signature. [The order for 750 cards without signature was placed with Hallmark on August 23, but only 500 were shipped in November. It is not known whether the White House later reduced the order or if 250 were held in reserve.]

In a letter dated November 14, Jeannette Lee informed Presidential aide General Clifton that "within the next day or two the five hundred blank cards you wanted will be shipped directly to you" pending notification of how to proceed with the billing. A separate order for 2,000 Green Room folders and 200 prints left Kansas City on November 22 and arrived in Washington only minutes after the President's death in Dallas. Obviously, having received the 500 blank Creche Christmas cards before departing for Texas, the President and Mrs. Kennedy had begun to sign them at their convenience through November 20. Jacqueline Kennedy signed in blue ink.

Crèche in East Room, The White House

A photograph of the creche in the East Room was the art for the 1963 official Presidential Christmas card that was never sent. Before departing for Dallas, the President and First Lady signed less than 30 of what were to become rare collector's items. HALLMARK CARDS

John Kennedy boldly signed in black ink. The next morning they flew to Texas, where they were to experience, according to Raleigh DeGeer Amyx, of American Heritage Autographs and Collectibles, an "unspeakable tragedy ... that negatively changed the history of the world." At the time, there was no official record of these authentically signed Christmas cards.

Amyx later offered an explanation. "This rendition of the 1963 Presidential Christmas card is the rarest known Christmas format ever signed by a President and First Lady.... These dual-signed Christmas cards were not located until 1985. Of the maximum 30 dual-signed cards, perhaps as many as half did not have the words imprinted 'Blessed Christmas.'" The remaining cards bore the sentiment "With Best Wishes for a Happy New Year." Once rediscovered, these rare cards "were quickly absorbed in other personal collections." The existence of these collectibles was unknown even by the Kennedy Library, he added.

The Jacqueline Kennedy Cards
Hallmark produced two other Kennedy Christmas cards in 1963.

Jacqueline Kennedy painted two watercolors, *The Journey of the Magi* and *Glad Tidings*, as art for Christmas cards. Proceeds from their sale went to build what was eventually to become Washington's Kennedy Center for the Performing Arts. HALLMARK CARDS

These were not *for* the Kennedys but were painted *by* Mrs. Kennedy and donated to help raise $30 million for the proposed performing arts center. Officials at the center had arranged for the First Lady's art to be produced on holiday cards and distributed by Hallmark. Their design had been discussed as early as June when Hallmark's art director Jeannette Lee and design stylist Alice Ann Biggerstaff met with the First Lady at Camp David.

Lee recalled, "Her hair was in a pony tail and her bare feet were in sandals. Mrs. Kennedy was picking up after her son, John, who was taking a nap. She couldn't have been more gracious or offered a warmer welcome. We talked about her painting for a couple of hours. Alice Ann showed her how to mix her paint, sponge the background and let it dry before she put ink on it. Mrs. Kennedy was delighted.

"At the time, she was pregnant with her third child, Patrick. It was late afternoon, and she suggested that we spend the night and have dinner with her," continued Lee. "When I mentioned that my belongings were at the hotel in Washington, the First Lady offered to send someone to get them. The cabin to which we were assigned was very beautiful and rustic. Mrs. Kennedy picked us up for dinner in an old stationwagon and drove us back to her house. Together we watched President Kennedy on television from her bedroom as he delivered a speech from Bonn, Germany. After dinner we talked about the difficulties she encountered redecorating the White House. We were completely charmed by her," said Lee. "Alice and I met with her as representatives from Hallmark. She didn't have to spend the whole evening with us, but she couldn't have been nicer. It was a remarkable day for us!"

Mrs. Kennedy, who had been painting since childhood, completed the two watercolors at Squaw Island on Cape Cod in July. As her personal interpretation of the true meaning of Christmas, one represented the three wise men on their way to Bethlehem and was entitled *The Journey of the Magi*. The other, *Glad Tidings*, depicted a golden-haired angel announcing the birth of Christ. Both works carry the initials "JBK" at the bottom.

These original tempera paintings are said to have been the first greeting cards ever designed for sale by a member of the First Family. Hallmark's Joyce C. Hall said of the project, "We are pleased to ... cooperate in this fashion with the National Cultural Center. Mrs. Kennedy's work is in excellent taste." The originals now reside at the Smithsonian Institution.

Shortly before the disaster in Dallas, Jacqueline Kennedy was asked to write a Christmas greeting as an introduction to a story about "Christmas at the White House" for the December 31 issue of *Look* magazine. In retrospect her message was insightful:

> An ancient tale tells us of the Christmas custom of burning a Yule log in every fireplace and of how, as the log was drawn from the forest, 'each wayfarer raised his hat as it passed, for he well knew that it was full of good promises, and that its flame would burn out old wrongs...'
>
> The lights of our trees and homes in this season still signal this most ancient promise of Christmas at the White House. But even though ... Even though the White House is often the center of national attention—a public building—during the Christmas season it is the home of an American family sharing in the anticipation of the joy of this festival. The world around us is a complicated and troubled place. But through Christmas, we keep unbroken contact with the simple message of the redemption and love that God sent into the world so many years ago. To many of us, Christmas has a deep religious significance. To all of us, it celebrates the most profound hopes for the comradeship of man.
>
> "Peace on earth, good will to men," the angels said. "Peace on earth goodwill to men," may we all repeat to our children and those we love, in villages and cities, this Christmas Eve, wherever men may gather."
>
> —Jacqueline Kennedy

With our warm wishes for a joyous Christmas
and a New Year full of happiness,

Lyndon B. Johnson   Lady Bird Johnson
                          December 1964

The 1964 gift print was a watercolor by American Greetings artist Robert Laessig.
AMERICAN GREETINGS

THE JOHNSONS
Presidential Plantings on Parchment

The tragedy that occurred in their beloved state of Texas on November 22, 1963, changed forever the lives of Lyndon and Lady Bird Johnson. One hour and 39 minutes after the death of John F. Kennedy, Lyndon Baines Johnson, aboard *Air Force One*, was sworn in as the 36th President. From that turmoil, through the transition, the ensuing days were filled with shock and sadness, but life had to go on. Protocol was followed to keep the White House on track, even when emotions would have led the primary figures to do otherwise.

1963: Last-Minute Arrangements

On November 27, Angier Biddle Duke, the Chief of Protocol at the State Department, sent a memorandum to the new President: "Unless you and Mrs. Johnson prefer not to do so this year, I recommend that you send holiday greeting cards to certain groups of top level government officials." He suggested that cards be sent to all foreign chiefs of state with whom the United States had relations, foreign ministers and heads of government that the President had met. He specifically mentioned the top ranking officials of delegations that had attended the Kennedy funeral. Walter Jenkins, LBJ's chief of staff, approved the recommendation on December 1 and notified Duke to forward the appropriate lists to the White House.

Hallmark had just finished shipping the remaining Kennedy Creche Christmas cards to the White House on November 22. Now, the card company was called upon again to produce an official Christmas card for a second President in the same year. The major difference was the emotional climate under which they worked to provide a card "for such a time as this." The simple official card was printed on textured white card stock with a blank embossed Presidential Seal and red silk screen band along the bottom.

Perhaps, when reflecting on a similarly late request from the Kennedys in 1961, designers at Hallmark decided to borrow the 1961 sentiment for the Johnsons' first card: "The President and Mrs. Johnson wish you a Blessed Christmas and a Happy New Year." A second message read: "The President and Mrs. Johnson extend Season's Greetings and Best Wishes for the New Year." Due to the devastating circumstances that caused its creation, the undated 1963 card was historically forgotten for 30 years. It was not until late in 1995 that Christmas card collector C.L. Arbelbide came upon it and, through the research of Claudia Anderson, senior archivist at the Lyndon B. Johnson Library, identified the red-bordered card as the first official Christmas greeting of President and Mrs. Johnson.

Dated December 16, 1963, a memo found at the LBJ Library listed the groups to whom the Christmas cards were sent. Included on the list were heads of state of foreign countries and a few other high officials whom the President had met, chiefs of mission in Washington, American ambassadors abroad, U.S. Senators and Representatives, Governors, the Supreme Court, the Cabinet and "Little Cabinet" members, and top officials of various independent government agencies. Newspaper clippings dated December 19, 1963, from the *Washington Post*, which pictured the Johnson card, and from the *New York Times* also confirmed the existence of the undated 1963 Christmas card.

Since the assassination, the Johnsons had received thousands of holiday messages from home and abroad. Acknowledgments were not ordinarily sent in response to every card or letter. Ivan Sinclair, an assistant in the Correspondence Office, requested that Walter Jenkins make some decision regarding Christmas cards, however. It would be most expedient, Sinclair suggested, to issue across-the-board acknowledgments rather than trying to be selective or pursuing missing addresses.

Forthwith, Sanford Fox of the White House Social Entertainment Office was instructed to ask Hallmark art director Jeannette Lee to design an appropriate card to express the President's appreciation. A complimentary card, smaller than the Christmas card, was made on textured white card stock with natural deckle enhanced by a small, blank embossed Presidential Seal and green silk screen border. The message read: "Thank you for your holiday greeting And best wishes For your happiness in the New Year," signed "The President and Mrs. Johnson." Approximately 30,000 of these Presidential thank you cards were mailed out after the first of the year.

The State Department approached President Johnson only five days after he entered office to learn his wishes about a holiday card. The Johnsons sent this simple greeting card for their first White House Christmas. HALLMARK CARDS

To mark the end of a month of official mourning for John F. Kennedy and the beginning of the Christmas holidays, a candlelight memorial service for the slain President was held at the Lincoln Memorial on December 22, just hours before the Pageant of Peace began. In his remarks at the memorial service, President Johnson said, "On this eve of Christmas, in this time of grief and unity, of sadness and continuity, let there be for all people in need the light of an era of new hope and time of new resolve. Let the light shine and let this Christmas be our thanksgiving and our dedication."

Moving later to the Ellipse for the Pageant of Peace ceremonies and the lighting of the 71-foot red spruce from West Virginia, the President spoke about the transition. "Tonight we come to the end of the season of great national sorrow, and the beginning of the season of great eternal joy. We mourn our great President, John F. Kennedy, but he would have us go on. While our spirits cannot be light, our hearts need not be heavy.... On this occasion one year ago, our beloved President John F. Kennedy reminded us that Christmas is the day when all of us dedicate our thoughts to others, when we are all reminded that mercy and compassion are the really enduring virtues, when all of us show, by small deeds and by large, that it is more blessed to give than to receive...."

Surprise Party

The following day, the President's simple suggestion for sharing was demonstrated by a kind of Texas hospitality characteristic of the new administration. About noon, the impetuous Lyndon Johnson decided he would invite members of Congress who were still in town to a 5 o'clock reception at the White House. Bess Abell, Mrs. Johnson's social secretary, exclaimed to the White House staff: "Hold on to your hat, President Johnson has just invited all of Congress and their wives over to the White House this afternoon ... What can we do?" Some White House staffers declared it just couldn't be done. But Lady Bird Johnson—who had been schooled over the years to

President and Mrs. Johnson, Lynda Bird (left) and Luci Baines in a family portrait they gave to close friends and employees for Christmas in 1963.
LYNDON B. JOHNSON LIBRARY

expect the unexpected from her husband—as well as those who had worked previously for the Johnsons, knew it could and would be done. One of them replied, "You just move ahead and do the impossible. He likes 'can do' people around him, and he expects you to do what he asks."

Immediately, the kitchen staff began making finger sandwiches and arranging cookies and fruitcake on trays. Concocting tubs of punch and making urns of coffee, the butlers enlisted reinforcements from other divisions of government to help. Gone was the black mourning crepe that had been draped over the doorways and around the chandeliers. The White House came alive as florists replaced crepe with holly, wreaths and fresh flowers. The Blue Room was transformed by the addition of a decorated 12-foot balsam fir from Vermont and a lighted nativity scene. With snow blowing outside, the fires crackling in every fireplace created the perfect setting for the most impromptu Christmas party in the history of the White House.

About 200 members of Congress battled the elements to come. Some had flown back from their homes to cast their vote on the crucial foreign aid bill before Congress, while others circled the skies above Washington in bad weather—landing too late to vote, but in time for the reception. The President and Mrs. Johnson received their guests in the Blue Room in full view of the National Christmas Tree. It was undoubtedly one of the happier moments for the new administration. Standing on a gold-cut velvet chair in the State Dining Room, the genial host greeted his guests with the colorful phrase, "You have labored through the vineyard and plowed through the snow."

The reception came off like a charm. The next morning, on December 24, the House of Representatives passed the foreign aid bill. By 9:30, the First Family was headed for Austin and Christmas at the ranch. On Christmas Day, 50 to 75 members of the press appeared at their doorstep to report to the world on the new First Family's holiday. Even though dinner was ready to be served, the President conducted a press tour of the house and gave all the reporters ash trays as gifts.

1964: The Willow Watercolor

By the middle of May 1964, Bess Abell was thinking ahead to Christmas. She inquired of Gen. C.V. Clifton about the possibility of his friend at Hallmark, Joyce C. Hall, making an offer to produce the card. "I am sure that Mr. Hall will be delighted to do the Christmas cards for us," replied Gen. Clifton.

American Greetings Corporation, in Cleveland, was also introduced into the Presidential Christmas card arena at this time. Abell received a letter from Raymond Nathan, of Ruder and Finn Incorporated, who affirmed that his client, American Greetings, "would be honored if they could have the privilege of supplying without charge, the greeting cards to be used by the President and Mrs. Johnson this year." In fact, Gen. Clifton confirmed that Ruder and Finn had tried on behalf of their client to "get the contract or part of it" for the previous three years. Irving I. Stone, president of American Greetings, had been a strong supporter of the administration and had contributed heavily to the Democratic National Campaign Committee. Cognizant of Hallmark's generosity over the past 11 years, Clifton suggested the situation be handled very delicately.

President Johnson decided to go with American Greetings Corporation. On July 9, Harry H. Stone, executive vice president of American Greetings, and Ed Pakish, his assistant manager of creative art, met at the White House with Mrs. Johnson's social secretary. Speaking for the First Lady, she suggested that the artwork somehow incorporate the mansion and its historical landscaping, specifically the commemorative trees planted by past Presidents. The Johnsons had lived in Washington since 1934 and had always appreciated the beautification project started by Thomas Jefferson in what had become known as the "President's Park."

The greatest challenge would be to get the right kind of artwork for Mrs. Johnson, who liked trees combined with softness. Of six artists submitting numerous samples, staff design consultant Robert H. Laessig seemed to have just the right touch. Having painted flowers for American Greetings for nearly 16 years, Laessig had won several national prizes for his work. Pakish now invited him to go to the White House to get inspiration for the task. Together they viewed the White House lawn from roof tops and every vantage point, taking pictures and making sketches of the landscape. Laessig believed that nature was only the beginning for his work. He refused to duplicate an object as seen by the eye. "Anyone can do that," he said. "I have to put in something of myself," he told the Cleveland *Plain Dealer*. "There has to be a mystery to what you see."

Among the three paintings Laessig produced for the President was a watercolor in which he created a Southwestern willow—the tree the Johnsons

The unique official Christmas card was a black and white version of the full-color gift print art (*see Page 100*). Though for many years a standard practice, 1964 marked the first time the President's Christmas art served double duty.

AMERICAN GREETINGS

would plant on the South Lawn later that fall—set against the backdrop of the White House. Exercising his artistic license, Laessig imagined it as a mighty oak, the way future Presidents would view it in later years. As a center of interest, the artist added two girls to represent the Johnson daughters, Lynda and Luci, and the two Johnson beagles, Him and Her. Mrs. Johnson suggested only minor adjustments to the "woebegone" tree on the right, but was very pleased with his realistic style and the softness of color. In Laessig's judgment, "it was not bad."

American Greetings reproduced 4,500 of the paintings on a 14 x 18-inch textured paper. The gift was presented in a folder with a blind embossed Presidential Seal on the cover and again inserted into a white envelope with cardboard stiffeners for protection. A red sateen ribbon and a large gold foil Presidential Seal completed the outer packaging. To accompany each print, Mrs. Johnson enclosed a personal message penned on parchment by Sanford Fox. In 1964 it read: "One of our happiest family times was the planting of two oaks—a Darlington and a willow—on the White House lawn in October, 1964. Beginning with Thomas Jefferson, thirty Presidential families have followed this tradition. At this season when friends and families occupy our thoughts, we hope—with this watercolor—your thoughts may turn to the passage from James Russell Lowell, 'Each year to ancient friendships add a ring, As to an oak....' "

By this time the White House staff had grown to about 1,500 and now included the White House Communications Agency, and the Bergstrom AFB and Marine helicopter pilots assigned to the White House and Camp David. The Social Office sent each guest a memorandum and card they could exchange for their gift print from the President and Mrs. Johnson at the annual Christmas party. What a surprise for each recipient of the commemorative print to find it gracing the December 28 cover of *Newsweek* as a backdrop for a portrait of Mrs. Johnson.

Lyndon Johnson was a giver of many kinds of gifts and gadgets. "No matter how much planning ahead we do," Mrs. Johnson wrote in her *White House Diary*, "about five or six days before Christmas, Lyndon gets frantic, thinking about all the things he wants to do for all the people he loves, and heaping work on all those around him, and issuing orders, 'Recheck the names! Plan gifts! Get it done!' I know this results in many midnight hours for secretaries, merchants, picture framers, parcel post deliverers—and me. But after more than thiry years I, at least, should know what to expect." Among the gifts the Johnsons gave to about 200 of their executive staff was a framed French-matted engraving by Robert Cruikshank entitled *The President's Levee of All Creation Going to the White House*. The cherished gift was personalized, signed and dated by the President and First Lady.

For their second official Christmas card, President and Mrs. Johnson chose a small black and white rendering of Laessig's painting of the willow oak. The Christmas card was designed with different messages. "With our wishes for a joyous Christmas and a Happy New Year" appeared on 2,904 facsimile-signed cards and 225 unsigned cards. "Season's Greetings and best wishes for the New Year" was ordered for 175 cards without a signature. The President continued to acknowledge those who had sent him a holiday greeting; 25,003 prints of the card designed by Laessig carried the message "Thank you for your holiday greeting and best wishes for happiness in the New Year."

Janice Ingersoll, who had worked in the Social Entertainment Office since the Eisenhower Administration, was the keeper of the Christmas card list. Said Bess Abell: "As far as I was concerned, Jan was a miracle person.... She knew who was married, divorced or had moved away, and she knew how to get anyone's address. After the President had given his input, she put the Christmas card list together."

All of the staff at American Greetings—artists, writers, lithographers, production people and management—had taken great pride in being able to design and produce the 1964 official Christmas card and gift print for the President of the United States. At a special White House ceremony, the executive vice president, Harry H. Stone, design consultant Robert Laessig and art director Ed Pakish presented the original painting for the gift print to the First Lady upstairs in the living quarters at the White House. Mrs. Johnson had liked the painting so much, Mr. Pakish said, that she wanted it for the ranch in Texas.

On December 18, when the President flipped the switch to light the National Christmas Tree, the 5,000 red and white lights gleamed in the night. The beautifully shaped 72-foot white spruce from New York's Adirondacks was surrounded by 53 other trees, each representing a state or territory. Extending best wishes, President Johnson addressed the crowd of 7,000 and spoke optimistically of peace: "At this Christmas season of 1964, we can think of broader and brighter horizons than any who have lived before these times. For there is rising in the sky of the age a new star—the star of peace...."

On December 23, President Johnson also sent Christmas greetings to the American troops in Southeast Asia:

You who carry freedom's banner in Vietnam are engaged in a war that is undeclared—yet tragically real. It is a war of terror where the aggressor moves in the secret shadows of the nights. Murder and kidnapping and deception are his tools. Subversion and conquest are his goals.... But your sacrifices are known and honored in American towns and cities more familiar to you, for you are meeting your country's commitment to a world of justice....

1965: The White House in Winter

By May, work had already begun on the 1965 Christmas gift print. Continuing the theme of Presidential plantings, Robert Laessig chose to focus on the Jefferson mounds on the South Lawn of the White House. When John Adams moved into the mansion in 1800, it reportedly was surrounded by barren land strewn with rubbish. Thomas Jefferson moved in the following year and developed a landscape plan that included tree-covered mounds on the South Lawn to provide privacy. Each new family that occupied the White House left its own mark on the landscape, and the barren expanse eventually became a "President's Park."

Having visited the White House only in the spring and summer, Laessig had to imagine the two tree-covered mounds as a winter scene. He confessed, "I never even thought about the history. I was more concerned about getting the trees and landscaping right." Given photographs of the dogs, he figured that they were important and added people taking them for a walk. When Mrs. Johnson received the nostalgic watercolor, she wrote him, "The President and I appreciate your lovely Christmas greeting. Seeing your card made me wonder if you had drawn family and home into the background of your Christmas scene."

Each gift print of Laessig's paintings for the First Family was accompanied by a parchment scroll—the only way to learn about the Presidential plantings. In 1965, it stated: "First to develop a plan for landscaping of the White House was our third President Thomas Jefferson. In his attempt to make the terrain of the South Lawn more interesting, he directed the placement of the two tree-covered mounds which slope gracefully toward the center of the President's Park. This winter scene of the White House is

Artist Robert Laessig focused on the Jefferson mound on the South Lawn in winter for the 1965 Christmas card and gift print. AMERICAN GREETINGS

viewed from the East Mound." American Greetings produced 2,760 gift prints of the nostalgic *Winter at the White House* scene. Because of a high percentage of spoilage in production plus a request for all additional prints to be sent to the White House in January 1966, there were no prints held in reserve that year. The 950 White House employees were presented their gift at a staff Christmas party on December 17. A second engraving, entitled *Washington From the President's House* by W. H. Bartlett, framed with a French mat, was given to 200 of the executive White House staff.

Winter at the White House was also used as the 1965 official Christmas card. American Greetings printed it with different messages. "With our wishes for a Joyous Christmas and a Happy New Year" appeared on 2,000 facsimile signed cards and 200 unsigned cards. "Season's Greetings and Best Wishes for the New Year" was ordered for 200 unsigned cards. "Thank you for your holiday greeting and best wishes for happiness in the New Year" appeared on 27,800 facsimile signed reciprocating cards.

On December 17, President Johnson illuminated the 6,250 lights on the Nation's Tree, an 85-foot blue spruce donated by the White Mountain Apaches of Arizona. The crowd of several thousand listened to the President's words:

> As in other Christmas seasons in the past, our celebration this year is tempered by the absence of brave men from their homes and from their loved ones. We would not have it so. We have not sought the combat in which they are engaged. We have hungered for not one foot of another's territory, nor for the life of a single adversary. Our sons patrol the hills of Vietnam at this hour because we have learned that though men cry "Peace, peace," there is no peace to be gained ever by yielding to aggression. That lesson has been learned by a hundred generations. The guarantors of peace on earth have been those prepared to make sacrifices in its behalf.

The Johnsons' 1966 Christmas card featured the American elm planted by President Woodrow Wilson in 1913. AMERICAN GREETINGS

1966: The North Portico

A night view of the North Portico of the White House would be the third in a series of Laessig watercolors of Presidential plantings. The 1966 selection depicted the tall American elm planted by President Wilson in 1913. The accompanying parchment read: "Tall and graceful, with fan-shaped crowns of finely subdividing branches, the American elm has long been favored as an ornamental, stately shade tree. A few days before Christmas 1913, President Woodrow Wilson took a moment from the affairs of State to plant this symbol of peace and serenity which today shades the North Portico of the White House."

A total of 3,000 prints were lithographed in six different colors on high-quality text paper and enclosed in a folder embossed with the Presidential Seal. The gifts were presented to the White House staff at a party on December 15. The executive staff also received a French matted engraving, *President's House* by August Kollner.

The official Christmas card kept the same design as the gift print. American Greetings printed a total of 2,400 of the cards with Christmas as well as nonsectarian verses, as had been requested in the past. The administration discontinued the large order for thank you cards of previous years.

Early in the afternoon of the 15th, the East Room was the scene of a holiday reception for 125 recuperating Vietnam veterans from five Washington hospitals. Serving as hostesses were the Johnsons' daughter Lynda Bird; Muriel Humphrey, wife of Vice President Hubert Humphrey; and the wives of the Cabinet. President Johnson, who stopped by to salute the men, some on stretchers and many on crutches, said that "no guests had ever been more welcome in the White House.... I hope you have a good Christmas," he told them, "You deserve it more than anyone I know."

Rounding out his busy schedule that day, the Chief Executive ushered in the Christmas season at the ceremony for the Pageant of Peace. The 65-foot red fir from California's Sierra Nevada Mountains blazed in the glory of its 2,500 red and yellow lights. Speaking on the 175th anniversary of the Bill of Rights, the President greeted the American people in a somber tone.

> *Exactly 175 years ago today America sent another light into the world. That light—and that promise—was America's Bill of Rights. Few documents in all the history of freedom have ever so illuminated the paths of men. Today, the light of that great charter guides us yet.... I know, as you know, that we face an uncertain future.... Here at home, in our own land, more than 20 million Negroes still yearn for the rights and the dignity that the rest of us take for granted..... In Vietnam, the tide of battle has turned. No one can say just how long that war will last. But we can say that aggression has been blunted, and that peace, with honor, will surely follow. The months ahead will not be easy ones. They will require great sacrifice, patience, understanding and tolerance from each of us....*

1967: The Blue Room Tree

Much planning and forethought went into Christmas when the Johnsons lived in the Executive Mansion. This was especially so in 1967 with daughter Lynda Bird's wedding scheduled for December 9. That year the First Lady decided to depart from Presidential plantings and suggested an interior painting of the Christmas tree that traditionally graced the Blue Room. As he had done each year, Robert Laessig prepared several rough drafts of scenes appropriate for the gift print and official card. Mrs. Johnson finally settled on the Christmas Tree in the Blue Room for both the gift print and Christmas card. She also requested that the artist complete a winter scene she particularly liked and used that print as a special Christmas gift.

The White House ordered 2,600 official Christmas cards and 3,000 lithographs of the Blue Room. The accompanying parchment message read: "The first White House Christmas tree was introduced in 1889 by President Benjamin Harrison, a custom he asked 'be followed by every family in the land.' It is the hope of the President and Mrs. Johnson that the lights which blaze on this tree and the trees throughout our nation rekindle the ancient promise of the Christmas season, 'Peace on earth, goodwill to men.'" The print and scroll were enclosed in a blue envelope and secured with a gold ribbon and Presidential Seal. Executive staff members again received the French matted engraving Mrs. Johnson had selected for them. This year it was *The President's House, Washington,* by English artist H. Brown.

Because of Lynda Bird's wedding, Christmas came early to the White House in 1967. Decorators, florists and technicians mixed bridal white with Christmas reds and greens, turning the historic mansion into a winter wedding wonderland.

Artist Robert Laessig's Blue Room card and gift print painting showcased the official White House Christmas tree in 1967. AMERICAN GREETINGS

"The Christmas decorating is done so exquisitely here that I try to fill the house with people who would enjoy it," the First Lady was quoted in the *Washington Post*. Of particular interest to all who visited that year was the 30-piece, 18th-century antique Baroque creche, valued at $25,000, that was presented to the White House by Mr. and Mrs. Charles W. Engelhard, Jr., of Far Hills, New Jersey. Mrs. Johnson received it at a ceremony on December 15.

Later that day, President Johnson greeted the 4,500 attending the 44th annual lighting of the National Christmas Tree, a 70-foot balsam fir from Vermont's Green Mountain National Forest. He referred in his message to the military activities in Southeast Asia. "Today, a young soldier, in the prime of his life, was killed in the central highlands of Vietnam.... Half a million brave American men—who love their country and are willing to die for their land—will be celebrating Christmas in a strange land, surrounded by the weapons of war.... A part of every American heart will be with them."

Christmas 1967 was the first one in seven years that the Johnsons spent at the White House. "I know that my husband prefers to be in Texas," the First Lady said, "but the 'family council' decided that this time they would gather in the White House." The family had increased by two: the President's first grandchild, 6-month-old Patrick Lyndon Nugent, and Lynda's new husband, Chuck Robb.

1968: *The White House in Spring*

As early as May 1967 Bess Abell was already suggesting to American Greetings an idea for the following year's Christmas print. She related that Mrs. Johnson would like to have a spring or summer scene encompassing the South Lawn looking beyond to the monuments, with the color and the species of the flowers as true to life as possible. It was the view enjoyed by the First Lady from her second floor bedroom window on the south side of the house. Robert Laessig came to Washington in the spring and drew several sketches. Again the artist was able to so please the First Family that they chose two scenes, one for the Christmas print and the other for their official card, something they had not done previously.

The 1968 Christmas print was a nostalgic springtime view from the South Portico of the White House. The First Lady recalled that, "this beautiful setting in the midst of the rushing city" provided her with "a constant serenity." In an article in the December 1968 issue of *McCalls*, she further said, "Calm has followed crisis on so many occasions.... In any season, this view, frosted with the luminous glow surrounding the Jefferson Memorial and Washington Monument across the Ellipse at evening, always restores a sense of peace and proportion in turbulent times."

The White House ordered 3,680 Christmas prints of the watercolor. The parchment scroll that accompanied the gift to the White House staff, associates and friends read: "We have loved sharing the history and beauty

Washington from the South Portico was Mrs. Johnson's favorite view, especially in the springtime. It became the subject of the 1968 gift print. AMERICAN GREETINGS

For their last official Christmas card, the Johnsons chose another Robert Laessig winter view of the South Portico. AMERICAN GREETINGS

of the White House these past five years. One of the memories we carry with us is the view from the South Portico, across the grounds to those great white memorials that rise between the White House and the Potomac River. The Washington Monument symbolizes the pride and steadfast faith of the American people in the principles of the founders of our nation. The Jefferson Memorial commemorates our strength in the democratic ideals. May this season refresh our spirit and devotion to the eternal goal of peace on earth, goodwill to men." The White House Executive staff received the last of the French matted engraving series, *Mill's Colossal Equestrian Statue of General Andrew Jackson*, signed and personalized for each recipient.

For their official Christmas card, President and Mrs. Johnson chose a winter scene by Robert Laessig depicting the South Portico of the White House as seen through the branches of a snow-laden fir tree. The Christmas verse on 2,300 of them read: "With our wishes for a joyous Christmas and a Happy New Year." Another 300 were printed with the nonsectarian sentiment "Season's Greetings and Best Wishes For the New Year." As in the past, the card was sent to some 1,500 dignitaries at home and abroad.

As chief stylist of American Greetings, Robert Laessig experienced great satisfaction from designing seven different images for Christmas gift prints and official cards for the President and First Lady. No other artist has had that distinction. Reflecting on this honor, he said humbly, "I'm pleased that I was chosen to do it, but so much depended on where you were at the time. I wasn't always satisfied with my paintings, but I painted to try to please the First Lady." To express his appreciation for that privilege, the "posy painter" sent Mrs. Johnson an original painting of wildflowers.

At his last lighting ceremony of the National Christmas Tree on December 16, President Johnson spoke indirectly of the War on Povery with which he had kicked off his full term in office; its last two years had been painfully punctuated by urban unrest and rioting. He said, "We have had to preserve a dream; to work day and night to close the gap between promise and reality, so that all would have equal opportunity to fulfill the talents that God granted them; and to do so in an environment which protected the rights of all, including the right to expect that the law will be obeyed by everyone among us. We cannot say that we have triumphed in this endeavor. But we have begun—at long last."

A Second Surprise Party

At the last minute before the family's last Christmas Eve in the White House, Mrs. Johnson decided to throw a party. With the Johnsons' short-notice first Christmas party now a faded memory, Mrs. Johnson said of this one: "Never was a party at the White House put together so quickly and informally! I made most of the calls myself. By 4, all the fires were burning, and the spirit of Christmas and real joy was as strong as I have ever felt it." She invited longtime Washington friends, their children and grandchildren.

After the guests left, the Johnsons adjourned to the Yellow Oval Room in the family's quarters. There, hanging on the mantel, were personalized Christmas stockings, each illustrating important events in their lives. The symbols on the President's stocking included the Presidential flag, a scroll listing his public offices, a shape of Texas, a picture of the LBJ ranch, his horse Old Blue, *Air Force One*, the National Christmas Tree, the dove of peace and his dogs, Him and Yuki. "My sentimental Lynda had put small gifts for Christmas morning in all of them," Mrs. Johnson said.

The party came at the end of what the First Lady described as "this most awful year." Yet some good things had happened as well during 1968. Unemployment was at a 15-year low; the captured crew of the *Pueblo* had returned home; and three astronauts had circled the moon. While both sons-in-law were in Vietnam that holiday, both were safe and spent the day together near Da Nang. By telephone the First Family talked with Charles Robb of the Marine Corps and Patrick Nugent of the Air Force.

"Christmas of 1968 was a particular time of joy for us," according to Mrs. Johnson. "There was a special feeling of closeness to family and friends, and reflections on jobs done with heart and hope along with expectations about the time to come. We were looking forward to going home to the ranch with its fields of wildflowers to renew us—and for Lyndon to start afresh. He eagerly looked forward to having time for family and self and, perhaps, to teaching again and helping young people prepare for their future. That Christmas, our last in the White House and in Washington, was a glorious chapter in our lives that was drawing to a close. So many changes had taken place while we lived there. Truly, we counted our blessings."

THE NIXONS
White House as Open House

Before we came to the White House, our friends always looked to us to see what surprises we were going to give them at Christmas, with our decorations, our 'open house' party. We've always tried to make Christmas special and different. At the White House we enjoy giving surprises, too," admitted Mrs. Nixon in a *House and Garden* interview. "Because we want to share the house with as many people as possible, we've started a tradition of candlelight tours." Among other special surprises Richard and Pat Nixon shared with the nation at Christmas were the rare and authentic acquisitions for the State Rooms, the televised specials of holiday festivities and decorations, the exterior lighting of the White House, and the first-ever Christmas gingerbread house. At Christmas, the Nixons, more than any previous First Family, allowed their private home to become the most public house in America.

Candles and TV Cameras

Their first Christmas in the White House, President and Mrs. Nixon began candlelight tours of the mansion. With so many people visiting the nation's capital at Christmastime, the Open House offered an opportunity to enjoy the President's house as well. Chandeliers were dimmed, fires were set ablaze in the fireplaces and music was played throughout the house. The First Lady recalled that from their private quarters, they'd "hear people

Facing page: Gilbert Stuart's George Washington, the first in a series of Nixon portraits of Presidents, was the gift print for 1969. HALLMARK CARDS

Julie Nixon Eisenhower plays tour guide for CBS-TV's Charles Kuralt and Marya McLaughlin and the rest of the nation on the Christmas Eve 1971 special, "Christmas at the White House." NIXON PRESIDENTIAL MATERIALS PROJECT/NATIONAL ARCHIVES

breaking into song ... that's so nice, to know they are enjoying it," she told a *House and Garden* writer. "I suppose of all the places we've spent Christmas, the White House must be our favorite," the First Lady continued. "To be in this historical house with the memories of all the other families who've been here means so much—and to realize that we, in our way, are making a moment of history, too."

While becoming a popular Nixon tradition, the candlelight tours could be enjoyed only by those able to travel to Washington. For the rest of the nation there were the TV specials. "Christmas at the White House" aired on Christmas Eve in 1969 and featured an interview of Mrs. Nixon and daughter Tricia by *Time* magazine reporter Bonnie Angelo. Mrs. Nixon discussed family traditions and White House decorations, reminisced about Christmases past and, like all Americans, hoped for true "peace on earth." Shortly before Christmas of 1971, NBC aired "December 6, 1971: A Day in the Presidency," with correspondent John Chancellor as commentator. On Christmas Eve, Charles Kuralt and CBS television crews, escorted by the Nixons' daughter Julie Nixon Eisenhower, went where tourists can't—to the family quarters—for a candid visit with the President and the rest of the family. When Kuralt asked about a favorite Christmas, the Chief Executive replied, "Christmas is always a rich and a happy day.... For me, it's a time of children, a time of family, a time of music and a time of wonderful Christmas decorations."

The First Lady's Agenda

While the President's early months in office were devoted to restoring peace to the Far East and bringing American troops back home, Mrs. Nixon quietly went about a major restoration project at the White House. With a million and a half tourists visiting the mansion each year, and with countless millions looking in by way of television, she felt a responsibility to keep the house in perfect condition for the "guests." Many areas had simply been worn out since Mrs. Kennedy's renovation in 1962. "Dick and I want this to be the most beautiful house in America," she informed newly appointed White House curator Clement E. Conger, according to the *Providence Sunday Journal.* Together, the First Lady and her curator embarked on a "campaign that would restore the White House to its golden age, the first quarter of the 19th century."

Mrs. Nixon acquired things for the White House that others had not. Gilbert Stuart's portraits of George Washington and Dolley Madison were two paintings that were rescued when the British burned the White House in 1814. Dolley, wife of President James Madison, refused to flee until she was certain that the canvas bearing Washington's portrait had been removed for safekeeping. Her own portrait was also snatched from the flames, though without fanfare.

During the Nixon Administration, Conger located the portrait of Dolley Madison in the basement of the Pennsylvania Academy of Fine Arts. So thrilled was Mrs. Nixon that she persuaded the Academy's board to loan it to the White House. In 100 years the Academy had never permitted any piece to go on loan outside Philadelphia. Conger pointed out that "Dolley Madison saved George Washington and Pat Nixon saved Dolley."

Of the 14 First Lady original portraits that were missing when the Nixons moved to the White House, seven were acquired during their administration, as well as six original portraits of former Presidents. Many American paintings and sculpture pieces, nine period chandeliers, 13 period rugs, three gilded beechwood chairs from the Monroe era and several pieces of Duncan Phyfe furniture were all added during the Nixon years. Conger noted that the 10 pieces of the Monroe furniture found in the basement of the Philadelphia Museum was "the greatest retrieval of White House furniture in the history of the White House."

According to the *Providence Sunday Journal*, White House historian William Seale noted that "The Nixon era was the greatest single period of collecting in White House history. The great collection of White House Americana today is the long shadow of Mrs. Nixon. The impulse, the idea and the energy were hers."

1969: First President Graces a First Christmas

An admirer of his great predecessors, President Nixon was presented with the idea of giving a reproduction of a Presidential portrait to the staff for Christmas. The first year it was Gilbert Stuart's famous portrait of George Washington. The portrait was photographed by *National Geographic* and sent to Hallmark, which produced 3,500 mementos for the President. Hallmark framed the colored print with a linenlike mat on which a small gold plaque bore the words: "George Washington by Gilbert Stuart, The White House Collection from The President and Mrs. Nixon, Christmas 1969." The keepsake portrait was enclosed in a red velour folder with the blank embossed Presidential Coat of Arms on the front. A parchment frontispiece with gold lettering described the painting and protected the portrait. It noted, "The White House Collection's portrait of George Washington hangs in the President's Oval Office. It is a replica by Gilbert Stuart of his 'Athenaeum' portrait, the best known likeness of our first President. It was painted in 1796, the last year of Washington's Administration." The gift was signed, "With our best wishes, The President and Mrs. Nixon At Christmas 1969."

For their official Christmas card, the Nixons used a blank embossed engraving of a south view of the White House, a design submitted by James Hamil of Hallmark. The elegant creation was enhanced by a red and gold lithographed border. Of the 40,000 cards printed by Hallmark, 37,000 were sent to members of Congress, government officials, governors, foreign ambassadors, heads of state, business executives and friends.

Before the first guest arrived for the first Nixon Christmas party, the White House, under Mrs.

The 1969 Christmas card featured a south view of the White House.
HALLMARK CARDS

Nixon's personal supervision, had been dressed in all of its holiday finery. More notably decorated than in previous years was the Great Hall, where the main White House tree was a 19-foot fir covered with huge ornate ornaments representing each state's flower.

The most spectacular sight was the gilded chandelier in the State Dining Room, laden with holly and red electrified candles and an enormous red bow. Gone were the portraits of Daniel Webster and Martin Van Buren to make room for the two holly-filled gilded wall sconces taken out of storage and returned to their original position adjoining the six other matching sconces in the room. In the State Dining Room a first-ever, three-foot, 45-pound gingerbread house was on display. Created by White House assistant chef Hans Raffert, it would be followed for each of the next Christmases by a different Hansel and Gretel confectionery castle.

For the first time in 25 years, green wreaths and red candles were hung in the 16 windows facing Pennsylvania Avenue. "We love to decorate; you can't overdo at Christmas," Mrs. Nixon was quoted in an *Evening Star* account of her first White House tour for the press. Some who viewed the decorations described them as "the most colorful in many years."

On December 16, the President was scheduled to speak at the Pageant of Peace on the Ellipse. Prior to his arrival, park police had arrested eight adults and one juvenile for disorderly conduct. In contrast to the 65-foot Norway spruce donated by the town of Glen Falls, New York, the hecklers had brought their own tree, decorated it with soft drink cans and tin foil peace emblems. After the President began his remarks, the group of 50 to 200 hecklers, mostly students from the D.C. Moratorium Committee to End the War in Vietnam, shouted "Peace Now" and "Stop the War." A few unfurled Viet Cong flags, while others lined the fence separating them from the ceremony. Their chants required the President to raise his voice as he delivered his remarks to the crowd of several thousand and expressed hope for "peace for all people in the years to come." Other than that, he appeared unperturbed by their demonstration over the war he had inherited with the Presidency; he spoke of a bygone time when the nation was not at war.

> ... *Above everything else in this Christmas season, as we open this Pageant of Peace and as we light this nation's Christmas tree, our wish, our prayer, is for peace, the kind of peace that we can live with, the kind of peace that we can be proud of, the kind of peace that exists not just for now but that gives a chance for our children also to live in peace.... There is an old saying about Christmas trees.... May a Christmas tree be as sturdy as faith, as high as hope, as wide as love. And I could add, may a Christmas tree, our Christmas tree, be as beautiful as peace.*

The heckling continued intermittently throughout the President's remarks, but when he lit the National Tree, the jeers were drowned out by the joy of the rest of the crowd.

1970: The Jefferson Portrait and a New China Room

On November 25, Mrs. Nixon pushed a button that illuminated the exterior of the White House and transformed it into a monument within a city of monuments. Formerly only a lighted chandelier in the North Portico was visible to the approximately 35,000 cars that passed the White House each day. Speaking to more than 1,000 staff and their families, President Nixon said, "The lighting of the White House is being given as a gift to the nation. Once the White House is lighted at night it will be seen by millions of Americans as a symbol...." In actuality, the "gift" came from funds left over from the Republican Inaugural Committee.

Completed by Christmas on the inside of the house was the China Room with its new acquisitions of Presidential porcelain, hand-woven carpet and an English chandelier. The most striking surprise was the creation of a new ground floor "Map Room" reception area—where FDR had kept his war maps. The rare American Chippendale furniture and Heriz rug donated by private citizens were in place well before the holidays.

The Thomas Jefferson portrait by Rembrandt Peale was the Nixons' choice for their Christmas gift to their staff in 1970. Hallmark reproduced 4,000 of the gift print, which was enclosed in a green velour folder. The parchment page protecting the Presidential portrait described it as follows: "Rembrandt Peale's portrait of Thomas Jefferson hangs in the Blue Room of the White House. The painting was done from life in 1800, one year before he became President. It has been called 'the true Jefferson—the man, the statesman, and the serene human being.'" The greeting read: "With our best wishes, The President and Mrs. Nixon At Christmas 1970."

For the Nixons' official Christmas card, Hallmark was asked to create a design featuring the North Portico of the White House. Hallmark spokesperson Sally Guyton, who coordinated the project, said: "The card we created is a gold embossed representation of the portico, set off by a green embossed foil wreath on a green silk-screen background. The engraving is very close to the real thing. The famous chandelier on the portico is authentic. The number of windows, their size, and the spacing, are all accurate." Hallmark printed 45,000 Christmas cards for the Nixons in 1970.

In the East Wing corridor where visitors began their tour of the White House, two special cases displaying past and present Christmas cards of the President of the United States formed part of Mrs. Nixon's Christmas decor. The first included cards from Presidents Hoover, Roosevelt, Truman,

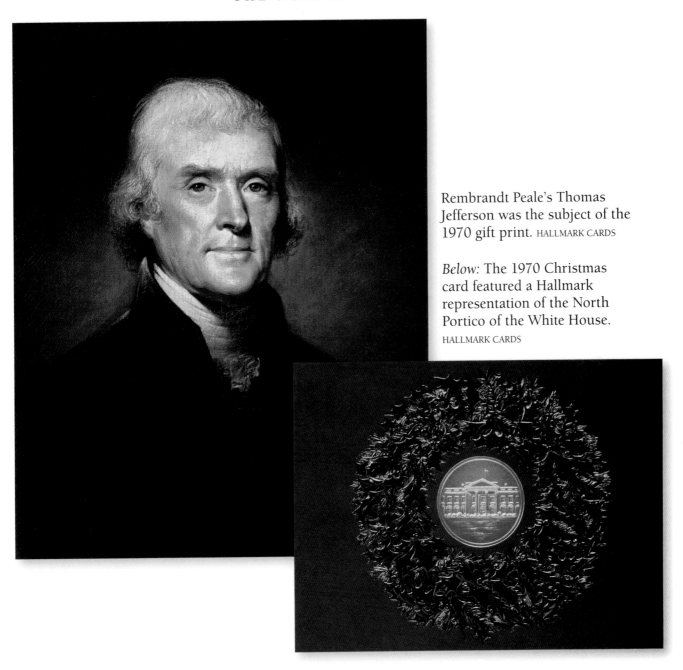

Rembrandt Peale's Thomas Jefferson was the subject of the 1970 gift print. HALLMARK CARDS

Below: The 1970 Christmas card featured a Hallmark representation of the North Portico of the White House. HALLMARK CARDS

Eisenhower, Kennedy, Johnson and Nixon; a card from Prime Minister Churchill to President Truman; and three Christmas cards received by Rutherford B. Hayes during his 1877–81 Presidency. The second case featured Presidential Christmas ornaments representing each of these administrations. Also on display was the 1866 edition of Dickens' *A Christmas Carol* read by President Roosevelt to his family every Christmas Eve; a red fire engine given as a Christmas gift by President Hoover to the sons of his secretary as a memento of the fire that shortened his 1929 Christmas Eve dinner party; the Eisenhower grandchildren's script for a "Children's Pageant of the Birth of Christ"; and the large doll house made for Fanny Hayes, daughter of Rutherford B. Hayes, by White House carpenters for her first Christmas in the White House.

While the National Christmas Tree ceremony on December 16 was dampened by rain, the spirit of Christmas prevailed as the President expressed, to a live audience of about 1,000 and a television audience of millions, his high hopes for peace in the world.

On Christmas Eve the President said, "Let us put aside what divides us and rediscover what unites us—concern for one another, love of liberty and justice, pride in our own diversity. Let us resolve to work together."

Acting upon his concern for the national family, President Nixon personally delivered season's greetings to the residents of the Washington Home for Incurables on Christmas Eve. The surprise visit was the first ever by a President. The patients were deeply touched by his gentleness and his unhurried chats, and were thrilled to shake his hand. Though speechless that night, many of them would for the rest of their lives talk about their Christmas Eve visit from the President, who was, in turn, inspired by their courage and optimism.

1971: *The Lincoln Portrait and New Red and Green Rooms*

Yuletide visitors were in for a surprise as the Red and the Green Rooms were open to the public just in time for the holiday open house at the White House. "The rooms are so full of beauty they just need a little dressing up for Christmas. I love the aroma of fresh flowers and plants—pines, firs, and spruce," Mrs. Nixon told *House and Garden*. "It was my idea to have lots of things in pots that can be watered easily. Potted miniature ivy makes marvelous garlands across the mantels, and the greenery helps to hide the pots holding the poinsettias. Red and white poinsettias all through turned out to be a great success." For the First Lady it was a constant challenge to beautify the house, which she described as "so full of history and now aglow with the magic and spirit of Christmas."

For Christmas, President and Mrs. Nixon gave members of the White House staff a reproduction of George Healy's 1869 portrait of Abraham Lincoln, the Civil War President for whom Richard Nixon had a special regard. Enclosed in a royal blue velour cover, the portrait was described as follows: "George P.A. Healy's portrait of Abraham Lincoln hangs in the State Dining Room of the White House. Lincoln sat for Healy in 1864 as one of the subjects in 'The Peacemakers,' a painting which also included Lincoln's military advisors, General Grant, Admiral Porter, and General Sherman. The portrait shown here, painted in 1869, is one of four based on the likeness of

George P.A. Healy's Abraham Lincoln was the subject of the 1971 gift print. HALLMARK CARDS

Below: N.C. Wyeth painted *Building the First White House* for a patriotic poster for the Pennsylvania Railroad. Depicting George Washington and architect James Hoban inspecting the uncompleted building, it became the art for the Nixons' official Christmas card in 1971. HALLMARK CARDS

Lincoln as depicted in 'The Peacemakers.'" The greetings read: "With our best wishes, The President and Mrs. Nixon At Christmas 1971."

The Nixons' official Christmas card was a reproduction of a painting N.C. Wyeth did for a patriotic poster for the Pennsylvania Railroad in 1930. The company originally planned a series of 12 historical posters to identify that railroad with national growth, but only four were completed. Poster No. 4 was called *Building the First White House* and depicted George Washington and the architect James Hoban inspecting the uncompleted building. The White House ordered 50,000 cards in 1971.

With President Nixon in Key Biscayne, Florida, preparing for talks with British Prime Minister Edward Heath, Vice President Spiro Agnew pushed the button to light the National Christmas Tree on December 16.

1972: Theodore Roosevelt and the Blue Room

"Change that works" was the slogan used to sum up the President's first term in office. The cold war had diminished. There were 25,200 troops in Vietnam as compared to a half million when Richard Nixon had entered office. Mrs. Nixon's major refurbishing of the state rooms had been completed with the opening of the Blue Room. It was there that the First Lady chose to place the 1972 White House Christmas tree, a 20-foot Noble fir from Washington State.

Apparently thrilled with the prospect of having their state tree displayed in the White House, an unidentified party in Tacoma requested that it be returned after Christmas. Just the thought of such a task brought out social secretary Lucy Winchester's sense of humor. She said, "Unfortunately, the tree—like the Social Secretary—is a dried up, shattered wreck after Christmas. Neither one of us could be sent to Tacoma, as both of us are carried out in vacuum cleaner bags after the festivities."

For their 1972 Christmas gift folder to their staff, President and Mrs. Nixon chose the portrait of Theodore Roosevelt by John Singer Sargent. Nixon greatly admired the former President and created the Roosevelt Room in the West Wing of the White House in his honor.

The description of the portrait as recorded on the parchment page of the gift folder read: "Theodore Roosevelt posed on a White House stairway for this 1903 portrait by John Singer Sargent. The painting now hangs in the Red Room and is one of the finest Presidential portraits in The White House Collection. Roosevelt preferred it. In 1918 he wrote, 'I care even more for the Sargent, which seems to me to have a singular quality, a blend of both the spiritual and the heroic.'" Hallmark prepared 5,000 of the keepsakes for the White House. In addition to the gift print, the Nixons also gave their household staff a 2 x 3-inch marble paperweight on which is adhered a brass seal of the President of the United States in red, white and blue. Beneath it was a small brass plate bearing the names Richard Nixon and Patricia Nixon in script and "Christmas 1972" in block letters. Mrs. Nixon gave a chatelaine pin to the women on her staff and Dion cuff links to the men.

For their official Christmas card, the President and First Lady reproduced an 1839 etching of the White House by English artist William Henry Bartlett. *View From the Tiber*, as it was called, depicted the lush foliage on the south grounds of the White House with Tiber Creek in the foreground. Filled in during the 1880's, the creek today runs under Constitution Avenue.

The 1972 gift print was John Singer Sargent's Theodore Roosevelt.
HALLMARK CARDS

Below: In 1839, English artist William Henry Bartlett created the White House etching *View From the Tiber*. The Nixons selected it for their 1972 official card.
HALLMARK CARDS

This painting was one that was acquired during the Nixon Administration and hung in the Oval Office. Hallmark framed the card with a green and antique gold hot foil border and produced 60,000 for the Nixons.

The lighting of the National Christmas Tree was held on December 14, amidst a chilly rain but heated controversy. Due to legal action against the National Park Service, the Christmas star that had traditionally adorned the top of the National Tree was to be substituted with a newly designed emblem. An even greater controversy had been brewing over the presence of the nativity scene at the pageant. It, however, was allowed to stay. In the absence of President Nixon, Vice President Spiro Agnew again brought Christmas greetings from the President.

1973: Old-Fashioned Christmas Saves Energy

In the throes of a national energy crisis, a Monroe Christmas was the theme for Christmas 1973. James Monroe, who had served as President from 1817 to 1825, had already influenced the Nixon White House in a number of ways. Many of the original pieces of furniture of the Monroe era, for instance, had been returned to their rightful place. The Monroe furniture in the Cross Hall had been a recent acquisition and added to the history and authenticity of the mansion. Because Monroe and his staff had used vermeil for their White House, the modern decorations included lots of natural greens and pine cones, accented by shiny gold.

In keeping with the Monroe Christmas theme, the President and Mrs. Nixon decided to give a reproduction of President James Monroe by Samuel F.B. Morse as their Christmas gift to their staff in 1973. *National Geographic* photographed the portrait and Hallmark placed it in a white velour folder. The description included with the gift print read: "This portrait of James Monroe, fifth President of the United States, was painted in the White House by Samuel F.B. Morse in 1819. Born in Virginia in 1758, Monroe served in the American Revolution and later became a United States Senator, U.S. Minister to France, Governor of Virginia, and U.S. Secretary of State. He was elected President in 1816. The portrait hangs in the Green Room of the White House." The sentiment on the keepsake was the following: "With our best wishes, The President and Mrs. Nixon At Christmas 1973."

The official card for that year was a reproduction of a 19th century view of the *President's House*, a painting by the German artist August Kollner. Hallmark framed the print with a gold antique hot foil border against a red silk-screened border. The black engraved message below a blank embossed Presidential Seal read: "With all best wishes for a Merry Christmas and a Happy New Year, The President and Mrs. Nixon." The 60,000 cards were sent to heads of state, American and foreign diplomats, government officials, friends and close supporters of the First Family.

The 50th anniversary of the lighting of the National Christmas Tree was held on December 14. What might have been slated as a major celebration was unusual in many ways. For the first time in 20 years, the committee had reverted to using a live tree, a 42-foot Colorado blue spruce grown in Pennsylvania and presented by the National Arborist Society. Planted on the Ellipse, the 40-year-old tree was expected to live another 150 years. Due to

James Monroe, the fifth President, as painted by Samuel F.B. Morse, was the subject of the 1973 gift print. HALLMARK CARDS

Below: The official Christmas card for 1973 featured the White House as depicted by the German painter August Kollner. The 19th century view from Lafayette Park shows the bronze statue of Thomas Jefferson placed on the north lawn by President James Polk in 1847. HALLMARK CARDS

the energy crisis, a drastic energy reduction of 81.9 percent over the previous year would be achieved by the use of one electric light on the tree and four spotlights on it from the ground. The surrounding 57 smaller trees would have no lights at all.

Another difference from Christmases past was that the traditional nativity scene would be eliminated from the Pageant of Peace due to a U.S.

Court of Appeals ruling stating that it constituted "excessive entanglement" of the government in religion and violated the First Amendment. The controversy, lodged by five plaintiffs, had been in the courts for four years. A lower court decision ruled the nativity scene could stay, but a higher one ruled it had to go. As a result of many protests, a private organization was granted a permit to erect a nativity scene near but not on the Pageant of Peace complex.

To many the most significant difference was the fact that this would be the first Christmas in 12 years that the United States would not have troops committed in a military conflict around the world. The Vietnam War had concluded. In his Christmas message to the nation on the 50th anniversary of the lighting of the National Community Christmas Tree, President Nixon reflected on the affairs of the nation as he shared from his heart.

> *... This year Christmas will be different in terms of lights, perhaps, all across America. Instead of having many lights on the tree as you will see over there in a few moments, there will be only one on it, the star at the top, and the other lights you see will simply be the glitter from the ground lights which are around the tree. And in a way, I suppose one could say with only one light on the tree, this will be a very dreary Christmas, but we know that isn't true, because the spirit of Christmas is not measured by the number of lights on a tree. The spirit of Christmas is measured by the love that each of us has in his heart for his family, for his friends, for his fellow Americans and for people all over the world. And this year, while we have a problem, ... the problem of energy.... This year we will drive a little slower. This year the thermostats will be a little lower. This year every American perhaps will sacrifice a little, but no one will suffer.*

One young man who rejoiced at the lighting of the lone star on the tree was 9-year-old Scott Stewart of Middlefield, Ohio. Writing to the President after the ceremony, he said, "Dear President Nixon; My Dad made the star on your Christmas Tree. We were afraid you wouldn't light it, But you did! I told all the kids in my room my Dad made the star but they wouldn't believe me. A lady from the paper came and took our picture. She wrote about how my Dad made the star. I thought you would like to see it. We love you and Mrs. Nixon too. Have a happy Christmas. Your friend, Scott Stewart. P.S. Hope Santa brings you a nice present.

Without a doubt, the one present Richard Nixon would have liked to have received never came. While he had brought peace to the world, there was no peace on Capitol Hill. Several Nixon loyalists had broken into the Democratic National Headquarters at the Watergate complex in an attempt to discover the Democratic campaign strategy, and Nixon was implicated in efforts to cover up the scandal. Impeachment was the talk of the time. Even during Christmas, the President's lawyers worked long hours to defend their client against a myriad of charges involving "Watergate." As it turned out, this would be his last Christmas message to the nation. At his first tree ceremony, he had to talk above the shouts of hecklers: "Peace Now—Stop the War." At his last ceremony, sections of the audience waved signs, "God loves America, God loves Nixon." When his message was finished, they chanted, "We want Nixon" and "We want the President."

A Somber Christmas

For Richard Nixon, Christmas 1973 was a time of family. It was a somber occasion, daughter Julie Nixon Eisenhower said: "All of us in the family were discouraged and frankly overwhelmed by the repeated blows of Watergate." She recalled: "My father made several Christmas phone calls ... to the small- and big-town heroes and heroines across the country. As my parents and their guests enjoyed a turkey dinner in the Red Room, my father became nostalgic." He talked about the kindness of one of his Duke University law professors who had invited him and another student to his home for Christmas because they couldn't afford to return to their own homes for the holidays. "The conversation became more nostalgic," the daughter said, "especially about his foreign policy triumphs—the trip to China, the meetings with Mao and Brezhnev, the conversations with Golda Meir at the time of the Yom Kippur War and the military alert."

"As I look back," the President said, "while it has been a rough game, it has been worth it. I might not want to do it again, but I would not have missed it.... I know I have lived for a purpose, and I have at least in part achieved it. You must live your life for something more important than your life alone. One who has never lost himself in a cause bigger than himself has missed one of life's mountaintop experiences. Only by losing yourself in this way can you really find yourself."

In his last message to the American people as President, Richard Nixon said, "We think sometimes when things don't go the right way, when we suffer a defeat, that all has ended. Not true. It is only a beginning, always. Greatness comes when you are really tested, when you take some knocks, some disappointments, when sadness comes. Because only if you have been in the deepest valley can you ever know how magnificent it is to be on the highest mountain. Always give your best. Never get discouraged, never be petty. Always remember, others may hate you, but those that hate you don't win unless you hate them, and then you destroy yourself."

NEW ENGLAND SNOW SCENE

GEORGE DURRIE (1820-1863)

Wishing you a Joyous Christmas and a Happy New Year
THE PRESIDENT AND MRS. FORD
1974

THE FORDS
An Old-Fashioned Christmas

President and Mrs. Gerald Ford brought to the White House an informality that reflected their unique style and personality. Prior to Richard Nixon's resignation, Betty Ford was quoted in *U.S. News and World Report*, "If I go there, I'm going to make it fun. I couldn't stand to live there unless it were happy, free and open. Because we are that kind of people and we're not going to change." And they didn't. The ambiance of the Ford White House was warm and folksy, simple and low-key. Mrs. Ford described it as kind of "down-home-like." Especially at Christmas, the First Lady was able to define her independence and leave the distinctive mark of an old-fashioned Christmas on the White House, a tradition the Ford family had always enjoyed.

Gerald Ford had served in the House of Representatives since the Truman days. Mrs. Ford said, "My husband was so dedicated to this country, having first visited Washington as an Eagle Scout, that his devotion rubbed off on me. My desire throughout the time we served in the White House was to present an American feeling." She insisted that every event have a theme and portray American arts and crafts, American antiques and artists.

1974: A Patchwork Theme

Preparing for Christmas would be a challenge for any administration that had just come into being at the end of summer. Despite the turmoil of Watergate, plus the trauma of major surgery within her first few months in the White House, Mrs. Ford's outlook was courageous. She said, "Having been in Washington for 25 years, I had the advantage of being at the White House for quite a few Christmases. I had seen how others had served the President and First Lady. I knew a lot of people and felt a part of the whole thing." In addition to being an insider, she added, "I had a very good staff and I leaned on them."

In fact, the topic of Christmas didn't even surface until November, recalled Mrs. Ford's press secretary, Sheila Weidenfeld, in her book *First Lady's Lady*. The Johnsons and the Kennedys had taken their holiday decorations with them. The Nixons' tree ornaments were available, but they were not Mrs. Ford's style. She preferred handmade ornaments or ones that had a sentimental attachment. Her idea of a Christmas tree was that it "should be warm and personal and familial, even if it is 19 1/2 feet tall and stands in the middle of the White House." In her enthusiasm, she actually considered using decorations made by everyone who wished to do so. When the reality of the moment sunk in, Weidenfeld said, they decided to compromise and asked specific groups to participate in the project to make ornaments for the White House tree.

Coordinating with Washington florist William Dove, Mrs. Ford chose a patchwork theme for the mansion. Patchwork ornaments were made by the Blue Ridge Cottage Industries in North Carolina, the Quilters Workshop in New York and the Farm Women's Cooperative Market in Bethesda, Maryland. The 19 1/2-foot concolor fir that had been coincidentally selected the previous year from the Fords' home state of Michigan was swagged with blue moiré lined with calico. The base was accented with a prize-winning patchwork quilt and fabric-wrapped packages.

Mrs. Ford's "old-fashioned handmade theme" emphasized thrift and simplicity amidst a recession-time holiday; choosing a piece of lace that had sentimental value, she decorated an ornament created for her. Daughter Susan, using scraps from her sewing basket, also made ornaments for the White House tree. High prices "affect my budget and everyone else's," the First Lady said, and encouraged families across America to save money by getting together to make their own Christmas ornaments from scraps. She even offered a White House how-to pamphlet on patchwork Christmas tree ornaments. While it was intended that these hand-crafted ornaments would be more economical than the ostentatious decorations of previous years, Mrs. Ford was surprised when she received the bill, according to a *Washington Post* account. "Patching up the White House tree" was simple but costly after paying the craftspeople for their labor. It was, however, an investment the First Lady was happy to make, because it created work for many senior citizens.

Mrs. Ford's personality and thinking were also reflected in the kind of

An 1831 engraving of the White House, after a drawing by English artist H. Brown, was used on the 1974 official Presidential card. HALLMARK CARDS

gifts she chose. "When I think of Christmas, I always think of snow," she said. "For years our family has spent time together between Christmas and New Years in the mountains of Colorado." The Fords admired the beautiful prints in the White House collection of snow scenes in America. In 1974, they chose George Durrie's *New England Snow Scene* as the First Family's Christmas gift print to their staff. While it was a departure from the formal portraits of previous Presidents, the 19th-century Durrie represented the folksy atmosphere of the Ford White House. This particular painting hung on the second floor of the White House and had been acquired for the mansion during the Nixon Administration. Hallmark Cards reproduced 5,000 of the Christmas gift print.

Before Gerald Ford had become President, the Fords customarily had sent a family photograph as their Christmas card. This tradition, however, was now complicated by the fact that the family was too scattered to take a picture. Also, concerned that such an informal card would not be appropriate for foreign dignitaries, the President and Mrs. Ford asked Hallmark to reproduce an engraving entitled *The President's House, Washington* for their official 1974 Christmas card. Hallmark printed the lithograph on clearform silk, edged with a gold bronzed line and green lithographed border. A notation on the back said: "The pastoral atmosphere of the nation's capital in the early 19th century is shown in 'The President's House, Washington.' This engraving published in 1831 depicting a French style garden was made by Fenner Sears and Company, London, after a drawing by the English artist, H. Brown." On the inside was a blank embossed Presidential Seal. The green engraved message read: "With best wishes from our family for a Merry Christmas and a Happy New Year, The President and Mrs. Ford." The White House ordered 50,000 Christmas cards, which were personally paid for by the President.

On December 17, the President participated in the lighting of the National Christmas Tree. Sharing the platform with the University of

Michigan Chorus, he greeted those present: "My fellow Michiganders, my fellow Americans ... I would like to share with you my personal list of Christmas wishes. At the top of my list are peace, economic well-being for all, and a caring climate that will permit everyone to achieve the fullest potential of their human gifts. And I wish this nation a strong future out of a very proud past. And I wish everyone of us the realization of love and belonging...."

Mindful of the economy, social activities at the White House that Christmas were limited, but those that were held were warm and cheerful, just as Mrs. Ford had planned. "It had occurred to me that while the White House looked so beautiful during the holidays it would be an ideal time to entertain the Congress with a great black-tie gathering." The Fords hosted the first annual Christmas Ball in years for their Cabinet and members of Congress. The gala event, held after the lighting of the National Christmas Tree, was one that dispensed with protocol and included both sides of the aisle. "It was healthy for us all," said the First Lady. "I had in mind to bring everyone together for food and dancing in an effort to lighten up the spirit. I think the country was in need of that because we had gone through a very traumatic and difficult time."

Addressing the crowd, President Ford compared himself to the White House tree. "That tree and I have a lot in common. Neither one of us expected to be in the White House a few months ago. Both of us were a little green, both of us were put on a pedestal," he said. "And I'd like to add this as a postscript—we've both been trimmed a little lately." Many of the 900 guests were friends that the President had served with for a quarter of a century. "We live here but my heart is really up there," said the President referring to members of Congress who came to help him celebrate his first Christmas in the White House. One guest, according to *U.S. News and World Report*, described the reunion as "warm and genial—like a party in a private house, not a formal function in an official residence."

The First Family, believing that "A family that skis together stays together," then left for Vail, Colorado, as was their Christmas custom. Invariably their holiday gifts revolved around their favorite sport. Even after he had become President, though, the Gerald Ford who had always been proud of his thrifty habits continued to encourage his children to go careful with money. I'm "still a Ford," he was quoted in the Sunday *Globe Democrat*, "and not a Lincoln and don't go overboard on gifts." Having always enjoyed a more casual Christmas, the Fords were able to set an example for a country brought, earlier in the year, to the brink of impeachment and whose economy had been stymied by war. A time of healing and rebuilding was needed before the country could move forward.

1975: A Colonial Christmas

Mrs. Ford recalled, "I loved Christmas of 1975, when we were preparing for the Bicentennial of our country. It was a very exciting time. The preparation for that got underway early in the year. We had been to Williamsburg for Christmas several times. I was so impressed with the trees and candles and the beauty of Williamsburg at Christmas. I figured we could get a lot of help from the people there and that is the way it turned out."

Advised by the staff of the Colonial Williamsburg Foundation, the Fords opted for another old-fashioned Christmas. Their second Christmas tree, an 18-foot Douglas fir from New York, was decorated with 3,000 ornaments reminiscent of those used in early American homes. Reflecting her personal preference for natural and hand-crafted ornaments, which she had used on her family's trees for many years, Mrs. Ford chose an early American theme for the eve of America's Bicentennial. The Williamsburg advisers suggested such ornaments as "corn dollies," pine cone angels, felt and wooden animals, crocheted snowflakes, paper cutouts, baskets filled with dried flowers, gingerbread cookies and garlands of popcorn, cranberries and red peppers. All the decorations were constructed from easily accessible and inexpensive materials. Natural materials such as peanuts, acorns, pine cones, dried fruits and flowers replaced the sequins and glitter to preserve a theme steeped in tradition and heritage. The task of "taking out the tinsel" was left to 75 professional florists who had volunteered to help decorate the White House for Christmas.

For their Christmas gift to their White House staff as well as for their official greeting card, the President and Mrs. Ford chose another George H. Durrie snow painting, one entitled *Farmyard in Winter*. Durrie, growing up in New Haven, Connecticut, shunned the crowded city life in favor of the solitude of rural America, which became the setting for his best works. Many of his paintings were reproduced as lithographs by Currier and Ives.

In 1971, the Richard King Mellon Foundation gifted Durrie's original oil painting of *Farmyard in Winter*, done in 1858, to the White House as part of Mrs. Nixon's restoration project. She had it hung in the Green Room. The Fords liked Durrie's work in

Mrs. Ford chose an old-fashioned Christmas as the theme for the White House tree on the eve of the American Bicentennial. GERALD R. FORD LIBRARY

A second George H. Durrie painting, *Farmyard in Winter*, graced the 1975 official Christmas card and gift print.
HALLMARK CARDS

general and asked Hallmark to reproduce this snow-covered Connecticut farmyard for both their Christmas gift and card. The First Family ordered 5,000 of the keepsakes and presented them to their White House staff. The Fords mailed 35,000 Christmas cards bearing Durrie's *Farmyard in Winter* painting and framed it with a red hot foil border.

In preparation for America's Bicentennial, the Pageant of Peace in 1975 was inspired by Colonial America. The National Christmas Tree was decorated with 4,600 red, white and blue ornaments and illuminated by 12,000 low-watt minibulbs. A specially designed four-foot gold and green replica of the Liberty Bell, donated by the General Electric Company, was placed atop the 45-foot Colorado blue spruce. The National Tree was surrounded by 13 smaller trees representing the 13 colonies. The 44 other trees representing states and territories were placed in a row leading up to it.

With the mercury plummeting, President Ford ushered in the holiday season on December 18 by switching on the tree's lights. About 7,500 chilled people were on hand to hear his Christmas message and watch the performance of Colonial Williamsburg Dancers and the Mount Vernon Fife and Drum Corps. Members of the Colonial Congress were characterized by actors portraying Benjamin Franklin, Thomas Jefferson, John Adams and Richard Henry Lee. Against this backdrop, the President greeted the American people:

> *In our 200 years, we Americans have always honored the spiritual testament of 2,000 years ago. We embrace the spirit of the Prince of Peace so that we might find peace in our own hearts and in our own land, and hopefully in the world as well.... Yes, we have endured economic difficulties, but our Nation and we in the American family can now look forward to a more prosperous new year. And on this eve of our Bicentennial year, liberty and justice still burn brightly as guiding stars of our Nation.*

1976: The Bicentennial Christmas

The "natural look" of flowers and evergreens was the main emphasis of decorations used by President and Mrs. Ford their last Christmas in the White House. The 20-foot balsam fir from Black River Falls, Wisconsin, was decorated with more than 2,500 handmade flowers, including the state flowers of all 50 states. The flowers, crafted by garden clubs, art classes and senior citizens across the nation, were made of silk, felt, beads, shells, ribbon, seeds, bamboo, cornhusks, metal, porcelain and glass. Baby's-breath and small baskets of dried flowers hung on the tree along with tiny white lights. A nosegay of flowers topped the tree. Dolls, quilts, pillows, stuffed animals, a hand-carved dove and other gifts sent to the White House to commemorate the Bicentennial were arranged under the tree. Unveiling it to the press, Mrs. Ford said that the inspiration for the decorations was in "the spirit of love that is Christmas." To express this, she hung two turtledoves on the tree to set the mood.

That mood changed dramatically, though, at the party for Washington diplomats' children, many in native costume, as they marched around the tree to the music of the Army's Brass Band. Awed by the toys and decorations, their initial polite restraint was soon dissolved by the antics of Big Bird and his "Sesame Street" friends. Santa Claus only added to the children's wild excitement. According to one report, "Thomas Jefferson and James Madison rocked in their frames–the Christmas tree in the Blue Room teetered–Santa Claus wiped his brow and staggered back– The children's invasion of the White House was over for another year."

Appropriately chosen for the First Family's Bicentennial Christmas gift to the staff at the White House was a reproduction of Ferdinand Richardt's painting *Philadelphia in 1858*, which hung in the Green Room. White House curator Clem Conger tells an incredible story of how the painting came home to the Executive Mansion. Richardt, an artist from Denmark, sketched the Philadelphia scene while he was in America painting Niagara Falls, for which he became quite famous. Moving on to London, he apparently finished the painting there and signed it "Reichardt," as his name was spelled in England. In 1863, he held an exhibition in his studio in which New York and Philadelphia street scenes were on display. The Philadelphia scene was purchased, probably by Saler Jung, who had extensive holdings in Hyderabad, India, as well as a museum that he gave to the city of Hyderabad.

It was in Hyderabad that Albert Nesle, a New York antiques dealer involved in liquidating the estate of Saler Jung, noticed it at one of the auctions. In a letter to Conger, he wrote:

It looked interesting to me. The steeple, the architecture of the building in the *background, the people, made me to believe it to be of Colonial America, or somewhere in England. The canvas was in shocking condition. Anyway, I purchased it for $7 and had it shipped to New York with my shipment of many things. Upon its arrival, I showed it to one or two of my friends, especially a man named Jack Treleaven of Needham's. We discussed the possibility of restoring it, but we thought it too expensive, and I subsequently sold it to Kennedy [Galleries, Inc., in New York] for a very modest figure. It was later illustrated in the "Antique Magazine" and a few months later was considered a great discovery. Anyhow, Mr. Conger, now you have it and that is the story. I feel I have done a nice thing by rescuing it from the junk pile.*

Thus it was that this piece of American history, also known as *Independence Hall in Philadelphia*, became known as "the greatest bargain in American paintings in the history of the world," according to Conger. Mr. and Mrs. Joseph Levine later purchased it and gave it to the White House in memory of the late John F. Kennedy. Hallmark reproduced the painting and published 5,000 folders for the Fords' 1976 Christmas gift.

President and Mrs. Ford liked the work of George Durrie. For their third Christmas card, they chose a third snow painting, entitled *Going to*

Philadelphia in 1858, a painting once purchased for $7, was reproduced as the 1976 gift print. HALLMARK CARDS

Wishing you a Joyous Christmas and a Happy New Year
THE PRESIDENT AND MRS. FORD
1976

Going to Church, a third George H. Durrie painting, was featured on the 1976 official Presidential Christmas card. HALLMARK CARDS

Church. On the back of the card is the following description. "In his classic painting 'Going to Church,' George Durrie (1820–1863) beautifully captured the mood of winter in his native Connecticut. Reproductions of this work were widely circulated, making it a familiar scene to nineteenth century Americans." The original painting was presented to the White House in 1963 by collector George Frelinghuysen. The Fords sent out 35,000 Christmas cards that year.

On December 16, no less than 10,000 people witnessed the annual lighting of the 1976 National Christmas Tree. It was the last ceremony for President Ford and the last for the 44-year-old Colorado spruce that had served as the nation's tree since 1973. Having lost most of its bottom branches, the tree would have looked scrawny without a "transplant" of 50 healthy branches wired on to the barren trunk and covered with ornaments.

The focus of the ceremony, however, was the Bicentennial. The President said: "As our Bicentennial year comes to a close, it is especially appropriate to gather once more around the traditional symbol of family ties and friendly reunions, our Nation's Christmas Tree. In doing so, we combine our year-long celebration of historical events with a personal rededication to timeless values."

Looking back over their last year, Mrs. Ford said, "It was such a wonderful, historically exciting kind of period. It was very demanding, but very interesting. The Bicentennial year was tremendously busy. I always said it was like having a revolving door with one head of state going out, while the next one was coming in. I never expected to meet so many important figures, but they all wanted to pay their respects to our country. Each one was a buildup to the Queen's visit, which was the icing on the cake. Historically, it was a great privilege to represent America during its Bicentennial!"

THE CARTERS
The President's House

resident and Mrs. Carter were "Sunday painters" who appreciated American art. Jimmy Carter first became interested in art history as an education officer in the Navy. In time, he and his wife, Rosalynn, studied the great masterpieces together, "not to become experts," she explained, "but for enjoyment." When they moved into the mansion of the Governor of Georgia, they found in it a wonderful collection of Federal period furniture. Taking up residence in the White House, the Carters realized their marvelous opportunity to surround themselves not only with the furniture of former Presidents but also with great works of art. The task of selecting art for their personal residence was one Mrs. Carter compared to Christmas. "Here were all these great paintings and you could pick any you wanted," she was quoted in the *New York Times Magazine*. The Carters' preference was American impressionist.

Remarked White House curator Clement E. Conger: "The Carters knew more about American furniture and American art than any other First Family in the twentieth century." During the Carter Administration a great many pieces were added to the White House collection, 150 of which were acquired on loan. To share their love of art and the honor of living at 1600 Pennsylvania Avenue, the Carters' Christmas card each year while there presented a painting of the President's House.

Facing page: The First Family poses in front of the White House tree. Its ornaments were handmade by retarded adults and children from across the country. JIMMY CARTER LIBRARY

The White House · Christmas 1977

Harvey Moriarty's *The President's House* was the art used on the 1977 Christmas card and gift print. HALLMARK CARDS

1977: *South Portico Drawing*

"As a friend of two of my sons," Mrs. Carter later said, "Harvey Moriarty was in and out of the Governor's Mansion often when my husband was Governor of Georgia. I thought Harvey was very talented, and I have one of his paintings in my dining room. When you are at the White House," she continued, "you get so busy doing so many things that when it got close to Christmas, Harvey was just there. We asked him to draw us a picture of the White House for our Christmas card. We let him do whatever he wanted. He came up with a pen and ink detail drawing of the South Portico, and I was very pleased, because that's the view of the White House most people in our country associate with."

Hallmark reproduced the image in sepia and lithographed it on ivory paper with a deckled edge. The engraved message read: "With best wishes from our family for a Merry Christmas and a Happy New Year. The President and Mrs. Carter." Early on, Paul Sullivan, executive director of the Democratic National Committee (DNC), suggested to the President that he send Christmas cards to the 1976 campaign workers and donors not only because it would be a good way to show appreciation for their past efforts but also because it could solicit support for his current programs and the 1980 campaign. The advice was received favorably and the strategy was adopted. The Carter White House ordered 60,000 Christmas cards—more than any previous administration had ever ordered—and sent the bill to the DNC. Hallmark also produced for the Carters 5,000 gift prints, which featured the same Moriarty drawing. The sepia memento was titled: "The White House - 1977." Facsimile signatures of the President and First Lady appeared below the inscription.

In preparation for 11 straight days of holiday entertaining, the President's House was dressed with all the usual trappings of Christmas, but not to the lavish extent of previous administrations. The Carters' style consisted of simple ornaments handmade by retarded children and adults all across the country. The 2,500 ornaments adorning the Blue Room's 20-foot Noble fir from Washington State varied in size, material and design, and according to the skill of their makers. Mrs. Carter explained in a *Washington Post* story, "We wanted to show that retarded citizens have talents, and we recognize their right to develop them fully." The First Lady sent each person a certificate recognizing his or her contribution to the First Family's first White House Christmas.

The modest decorations in the President's House were consistent with the Chief Executive's approach toward conserving energy and halting inflation. Following in the steps of Franklin Roosevelt and Harry Truman, President Carter also called upon the nation to set aside a National Day of Prayer, encouraging the people to pray for world peace and for guidance for themselves and their leaders. The day of prayer, December 15, coincided with the opening of the Pageant of Peace. The President addressed the nation and spoke of, among other things, his American family theme: "... I hope that we'll make every effort during this Christmas season not only to bring our immediate family together but to look at the family of all humankind, so that we not any longer cherish a commitment toward animosity or the retention of enemies but that we forgive one another and indeed, form a worldwide family where every human being on Earth is our brother or our sister...." With the help of daughter Amy, the President lit the live, newly transplanted 30-foot Colorado blue spruce and its 2,000 low-wattage green lights.

After a full schedule of holiday entertaining, the President and Mrs. Carter returned to Plains, Georgia, for a quiet Christmas. While the tourists had long since departed, now hundreds of farmers descended on the President's hometown to protest low farm prices. His only word, however, was a warm wish to all Americans on Christmas Eve. "Our country has been especially blessed throughout our history," he said. "In this season of hope we seek, as individuals and as a nation, to serve as instruments to bring the ancient promises of peace and goodwill closer to fulfillment for all the peoples of the earth...."

When Mrs. Carter came upon a hand-colored wood engraving of the White House, it became the first of the historic White House scenes to adorn the Carters' official Christmas cards and gift prints. AMERICAN GREETINGS

1978: Carriages at the North Portico

On January 26, just weeks after the tree-lighting ceremony, the tree that had served as the 1977 National Christmas Tree was knocked down, twice in the same day, by brutal winds. Having been ripped out of the frozen ground by its roots, it was not expected to live and ended its days as a yule log. After a National Park Service search of 2,000 miles of back roads north of Washington, D.C., a "perfect" 26-foot Colorado blue spruce was found quite by chance in the front yard of the York, Pennsylvania, residence of Mr. and Mrs. William E. Myers. The National Park Service purchased the tree and moved it to the Ellipse, where it served as the National Christmas Tree until Christmas of 2012.

In the summer, while redecorating the third floor solarium, Mrs. Carter began exploring ways to furnish it. "It was really exciting for us to wander through the White House warehouse where all the unused furniture and paintings are kept. We brought in Harry Truman's desk for one of our sons; a table that Mary Lincoln had bought; and John F. Kennedy's bed," she said. Then she discovered a hand-colored wood engraving of a photograph of the Executive Mansion by L.E. Walker that had originally appeared in *Harper's*

Weekly in 1877. It portrayed guests arriving at the North Portico of the White House in horse-drawn carriages. Becoming aware of a number of other historic White House scenes, the First Lady decided to continue to depict the President's House on the Carters' official Christmas card.

A change in vendor was made, however. American Greetings Corporation, with its "union label," was selected to reproduce the print Mrs. Carter had selected. Because the original engraving lacked the color she thought would reproduce appropriately, American Greetings artists were instructed to enhance the color before final printing.

A woman for details, Mrs. Carter also noticed that "her flowery script didn't match the precise, minutely executed pen of her husband. She addressed the apparent different look, asking him to redo his name to better match the look of the inside of the card," a spokesperson for American Greetings noted. No year appeared on the card, only the Presidential Seal and the Carters' greeting: "With best wishes from our family for a happy holiday season."

The initial White House order was for 60,000 Christmas cards and 5,100 Christmas gift prints. By mid-September, there was a new request for a second run of another 40,000 cards, a total increase of 67 percent over the previous year. Much effort, meanwhile, was being put into the compiling of an accurate master Christmas card list and purging the list of duplications and address errors. Volunteers were enlisted to address, stuff and stamp. The Christmas card project became a major undertaking at the President's House. Volunteers included some men, but mostly women, from various clubs in the Washington area. The White House Correspondence Office sent representatives to speak with organizations as they were setting their schedules for the coming year. Christmas card volunteers represented nearby Andrews Air Force Base; Fort Meade, Maryland; Fort Myer in Arlington, Virginia; the Minnesota State Society; former Eastern Airlines stewardesses; B'nai B'rith, and various Democratic Clubs.

To complement her 1877 card, the First Lady decided also to decorate the White House with holiday memorabilia from a century of Christmases. To adorn the 20-foot Veitchii fir from New York State, the Margaret Woodbury Strong Museum of Rochester, New York, loaned 2,500 antique dolls, toys and furniture from their collection, even sending along seven museum staff members to create a Victorian nostalgia in the Executive Mansion, according to *Antique Monthly*. In place of the traditional gingerbread house, a 42-inch Victorian doll house and about 40 other large toys were arranged along the base of the tree in the Blue Room.

Simplicity was the keynote of the second Carter Christmas. Red candles, pine cones and evergreens enhanced the mantels. Pink and white cyclamen and small undecorated cedar trees stood in the crosshall. The creche in the East Room was positioned in the window so that the draperies could be pulled during other functions. Joy Billington of the *Washington Star* wrote that it seemed to harken "back to less troubled times ... when china dolls wore lace and rocking horses had manes and tails of real horsehair, when halls were decked with boughs of holly, when first families lived more like other families and plastic hadn't been invented."

Mrs. Carter admitted that living in the White House was a humbling privilege for her family. "At first you are awed by being there and then after a busy day you sit down to eat dinner off the plate of a former President. Sometimes, you'd think, I can't believe this is happening to me. It was all very exciting. But also the White House was a haven for our family. Amy was little, Chip lived there, as did Jeff and his wife. Whenever the First Family went out in public, there were always people who wanted your photograph or your autograph because we were the family of the President," she continued. "But the times we really treasured were the times we could be home upstairs in the White House and just be normal people. We had lots of stories to share because Jimmy always made us feel that we were a part of what he was doing. It really drew our family close together."

With a new live Colorado blue spruce serving as the National Christmas Tree, President Carter spoke at the Pageant of Peace ceremonies on December 14, having just announced that he had decided to recognize mainland China and was working to bring about peace between Israel and Egypt. Addressing a crowd of about 10,000, the President expressed his hope that these two ancient enemies could "turn their energies and talents away from war and death ... to building, instead of preparing to destroy."

When asked what the Carters wanted most for Christmas, the First Lady replied, according to *U.S. News and World Report*, "A Mideast peace settlement. You especially hope for peace in the world at Christmastime, but this year it's more significant than ever."

1979: South View of 1860 White House

The year 1979 was full of challenges—the Iran crisis, the hostage crisis and the continuing energy crisis to name but a few. To some members of the White House staff, even the Christmas card project proved a challenge. Anticipating the need to mail twice as many Christmas cards as in the previous year, there was a recommendation made for the creation of a separate Christmas card management team to alleviate the tremendous burden on the Correspondence Office.

Evaluation of the whole Christmas card project was necessary due to the "tight financial position" taken by the DNC with regard to the bill. An

The historic print selected for the 1979 gift print and official Christmas card is Lefevre J. Cranstone's *The President's House, Washington.* AMERICAN GREETINGS

investigation was even made as to whether Presidential Christmas cards justified the use of appropriated funds. Because they did not, however, and were regarded as the personal expense of the person sending them, the DNC finally approved the purchase of the 105,000 Christmas cards.

Mrs. Carter chose Lefevre J. Cranstone's 1860 watercolor of the south view of the White House as the art for the 1979 Christmas card. Titled *The President's House, Washington,* the painting had been a gift to the White House from Wilmarth Lewis that had hung in the Lincoln Bedroom. The greeting from the Carters read: "With best wishes from our family for a happy holiday season." Five thousand gift prints were also ordered for the First Family's Christmas present to their staff. American Greetings provided an extra 2,000 prints for the Carters' personal use.

The crisis with Iran in late November resulted in one of the most critical challenges to the Carter Presidency. After the transfer of American allegiance from the Shah of Iran to the Ayatollah Ruhollah Khomeini in his rise to power, Khomeini's followers had unexpectedly attacked the U.S. Embassy in Iran on November 4 and took the 50 Americans there hostage. Aides to the President suggested that the Chief Executive consider canceling all holiday festivities, but, according to a *U.S. News and World Report* account, he countered with the statement that "canceling Christmas would be giving the Iranians more power over events here than they ought to have."

The halls of the Executive Mansion were decked for Christmas against a subdued national backdrop. Fine arts students from the Corcoran School of Art, inspired by the folk art of the American Colonial period, crafted 500 ornaments, including rocking horses, angels, ships, fruit and birds. Students from the Ceramic Department created such objects as ballet slippers, a tiny grand piano, a teddy bear, a ski boot and duffel bag—all displayed under Plexiglas at the base of the 18-foot Douglas fir from West Virginia. A reporter for the *New York Times* described them as the most "avant-garde decorations ever to grace the White House." While unveiling them to the press, Mrs.

Carter said, "It's a special time of the year. Christmas is still Jesus' birthday—a time to come together, to count your blessings and to pray for the hostages," reported *U.S. News and World Report*. A highlight of the holidays in 1979 was the State Dinner held for British Prime Minister Margaret Thatcher.

Since November 4, the hostage crisis was on everyone's mind—especially the President's, as he came to speak at the lighting of the National Christmas Tree on December 13. He said:

> ... *I think it would be appropriate for all those in this audience and for all those listening to my voice or watching on television to pause just a few seconds in a silent prayer that American hostages will come home safe and come home soon—if you'd please join me just for a moment. [Pause for silent prayer.] Thank you very much.*
>
> *Nineteen seventy-nine has not been a bad year. Many good things have happened to us individually and have also happened to our Nation. Not far from here, on the north side of the White House, we saw a remarkable ceremony, headed by a Jew, the leader of Israel, a Moslem, the President of Egypt, and myself, a Christian, the President of our country, signing a treaty of peace. This peace treaty was a historic development, and it was compatible with the commitment that we feel so deeply in the religious season now upon us.... We've seen divisions among people because of religious beliefs. The recent events in Iran are an unfortunate example of that misguided application of belief in God. But I know that all Americans feel very deeply that the relationships between ourselves and the Moslem believers in the world of Islam is one of respect and care and brotherhood and goodwill and love.*
>
> *So, we do have disappointments; we do have suffering; we do have divisions; we often have war. But in the midst of pain, we can still remember what Christmas is—a time of joy, a time of light, a time of warmth, a time of families, and a time of peace.*

Amy Carter threw the switch to light the National Christmas Tree. Only the Star of Hope on the top and the blue lights on the 50 Christmas trees around the periphery lit up—one small tree for each hostage. The President announced that the rest of the lights would be turned on when the hostages came home.

There had been no warning that the National Christmas Tree would not be lit. Mrs. Carter said, "We had talked it over and Jimmy decided it was the right thing to do!" The audience was touched by the President's dramatic gesture to identify with the hostage crisis. One father remarked, "It makes it more meaningful to see a darkened tree. It symbolizes the suffering of the hostages." Another in the audience of 7,500 said, "I thought it was super. It was a warm effort to signify the hostages' plight." After a moment of silence, the crowd broke into applause, reported the *Washington Post*. The decision of the President marked the second time since World War II that the National Christmas Tree had not been lit during the Christmas season. War restrictions had prevented the use of electricity for the lights on the tree from 1942 to 1944. In 1973, due to the energy crisis, only the star at the top and four spotlights from the ground were lit.

Concern over the hostages in Iran changed the Carters' plans for Christmas. As the First Lady would later explain, "We always went home for Christmas except the one year when the hostages had just been taken. That year we had Christmas at Camp David. We thought any day the hostages would be coming home. My husband didn't want to be too far from the White House. The whole family came and it was really wonderful."

Two days after Christmas, the peace among nations had eroded as Russia invaded Afghanistan; by the following December, reports of Soviet aggression against Poland posed an additional threat to "peace on earth." At home, inflation, recession and unemployment caused a disillusioned electorate to speak their mind in November. The economy and foreign affairs dealt President Carter a decisive blow in his bid for reelection. Sarah Booth Conroy of the *Washington Post* concluded that "even in the times of sadness to the occupants of the White House—when elections have been lost, or scandals threatened resignations, the Christmas celebration goes on, with only a bit of poignancy for the Spirit of White House Christmases Never-to-Be." While it was difficult to project a Merry Christmas, Mrs. Carter was determined to make their last Christmas in the White House a memorable one.

1980: *The Andrew Jackson White House*

Planning actually began as the decorations came down from the previous Christmas, remarked Gretchen Posten. "We decided that this year would be our romantic, old-fashioned Christmas," the First Lady's social secretary is quoted in the *Washington Post*. "Mrs. Carter has been especially interested in adding to the White House's painting collection. So all year, she's kept her eye out to pick out the painting to use on the Christmas card." The First Lady finally chose a romantic 19th century painting of *The President's House*. In the foreground the unknown artist placed Sunday sailors and straw-hatted fishermen in boats on the serene, but smelly, Tiber Creek. What now flows through a channel under Constitution Avenue was then known to be a "home for dead cats." On a knoll in the background was the White House as it appeared in the days of Andrew Jackson.

The President's House is a mid 19th century painting by an unknown artist which is part of the permanent collection of The White House and hangs in the Oval Office of the President

The President's House

The 1980 gift print and Christmas card. AMERICAN GREETINGS

On the back of the card, American Greetings printed a description of the artwork. "This romantic mid 19th century painting of the President's House was executed by an unknown artist after a drawing of the White House by the English artist William H. Bartlett. Bartlett first visited North America in 1836 and steel engravings based on his drawings began appearing in 1837. These engravings were published in England, Germany, France and the United States. They were immensely popular and served as the source for oil paintings and watercolors by many American and European artists. The origin of *The President's House* is unknown." The painting was given to the White House in 1967 by Mr. and Mrs. Hawley S. Simpson. President Carter enjoyed it so much, he chose it to hang in the Oval Office.

The cards were printed by American Greetings Corporation, whose artists began working on the design in the spring and who carefully inspected each card individually. Shortly after receiving the envelopes, 1,000 volunteers began addressing the record number of 120,000 Christmas cards. The message, "With best wishes from our family for a happy holiday season," was intended to be a holiday greeting to those on their official list, as well as a political thank you and good-bye to those who had supported and worked on their 1980 and 1976 campaigns. Mrs. Carter later recalled all the people, all around the country, who campaigned so hard for the President. "It was such a warm, wonderful feeling to have people help you. They would do just about anything for you. We really tried to thank them as we went along, but we also realized how important it was for someone to receive a letter or a Christmas card from the White House. It meant so much to people and we were happy to be able to send it."

The romantic, old-fashioned theme was carried throughout the Executive Mansion. The fantasy of ecru lace and old rose pink was found in the velvet and moiré bows on the wreaths and in the ornaments on the tree. Louis Nichole, a craftsman and interior designer from Hartford, Connecticut, coordinated the Victorian-style decorations. The tree was covered with reproductions of 19th century dolls with porcelain heads; parasols; miniature hats and fans; balls decorated with tapestry and lace; baby's-breath; tassels and 1,000 miniature lights. Under the tree, Nichole and his family re-created a Victorian street scene with their handmade Victorian houses and toys. "I always thought our Christmas decorations were the best in the White House. It was always so beautiful," Mrs. Carter said.

As a real change of pace, President and Mrs. Carter offered snow and Southern hospitality on the South Lawn of the White House to some 4,000 White House staff members, military personnel, Secret Service agents and their families. Using snow made for the occasion, there was a snowman-making contest that was judged by the President himself, with prizes for the winners. A special ice rink was constructed for a performance by Olympic skater Peggy Fleming and a skating snowman. Carolers from churches and schools sang as the White House staffers munched on hot dogs and popcorn and drank hot chocolate and cider. The evening was special, but "the end was spectacular," recalled Gretchen Poston, referring to the final, huge fireworks "Christmas card saying 'Merry Christmas, Jimmy and Rosalynn.'"

White House employees each received one of the 7,000 gift prints of *The President's House* that had been ordered in 1980. Some staffers received, in addition, a leather-bound copy of the President's book *Why Not the Best?*, which he had written on the campaign trail in 1976. As a special parting gift of appreciation in December 1980, the Carters gave a print of Howard Watson's painting of the White House to their staff, senior administration officials and Carter friends. Each print was inscribed and signed by the President and the First Lady.

The last Christmas at the White House was a melancholy time for the Carters. Their social obligations for the season brought them face-to-face with folks they had come to know over the past four years. The First Family took time out to be photographed with each one who had worked for them. President Carter spent his days preparing the last budget he would submit to Congress, while, according to one official, "a kind of aimlessness" set in on those who no longer found it necessary to plan beyond the next month. It was disappointing to the President that the hostages had not yet been released; it was disenchanting to contemplate his future as a former President. In his remarks at the lighting of the National Christmas Tree on December 18, he alluded to both.

> *... Last year, we had a very sober Christmas, and we all were hoping that there would be an early release of the American hostages. And along with that we prayed that their lives would be spared, that they would stay in touch with all Americans who love them, and that we would not be forced to give up either our hope or our faith in God.... Our American hostages have not yet come home. But most of our prayers have been answered. They have stayed in touch with their families. So far as we know, they are safe and their lives have been spared....*

This reproduction of Howard Watson's painting was a special parting gift to the staff, senior administration officials and friends. JIMMY CARTER LIBRARY

Thanks for your friendship and support!
With our best wishes,

Jimmy Carter   Rosalynn Carter

President and Mrs. Carter and daughter Amy look on as the National Christmas Tree of 1980 is lighted for only 417 seconds in recognition of the Americans being held hostage in Iran.

JIMMY CARTER LIBRARY

Last weekend the families of the American hostages met here in Washington to have a briefing by the State Department officials, including the Secretary of State, about the status of the negotiations for their release and to receive the information that we have about how those hostages are getting along. I asked the families of the hostages whether or not they wanted all the lights on the Christmas tree to be lit tonight, or whether they wanted us to light just the Star of Hope on top of the tree and then all Americans to pray that the hostages would come home.... The hostage families asked me to do this year the same thing we did last year. And that is just to light the Star of Hope and to hold the other lights unlit until the hostages come home. And they also asked me to ask all Americans to continue to pray for the lives and safety of our hostages and for their early return to freedom....

For a second straight year the National Christmas Tree remained darkened pending the return of the 50 American hostages. Special recognition was paid to the hostages by the National Association of Broadcasters, who lit the tree for 417 seconds, one second of light for each day in captivity. Christmas came and went. Finally, on the morning of January 20, Inauguration Day, the Carter White House got word that the hostages would be released after 444 days in captivity and put on a plane to leave Tehran. The plane sat on the runway, however, until Ronald Reagan had been sworn in as President of the United States. At noon, the new President got the official word that the plane carrying the hostages was no longer in Iranian air space and that they were on their way to Germany. Jimmy Carter was on his way to Georgia. It was not until then, on January 20, that the National Christmas Tree was fully lighted. Altogether it was a bittersweet day for the former President.

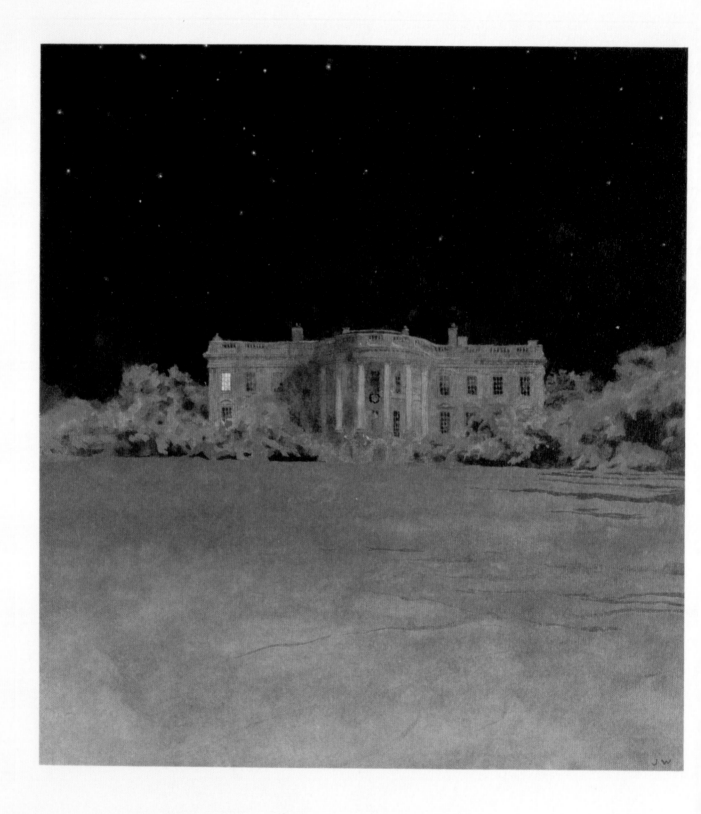

THE REAGANS
Years of Young Artists

Christmas in Illinois, where both Ronald and Nancy Reagan grew up, was a sharp contrast to their Christmases in Washington. In his autobiography, *An American Life*, the President recalls that his family never had a really fancy Christmas. His father, a salesman, struggled to provide for his family, especially during the Depression. When the family couldn't afford a Christmas tree, his mother would decorate a table or make a cardboard fireplace out of a packing box. "Those Christmases when we didn't have much money ... our home radiated with a love and a warmth that meant a lot more to me than packages wrapped in colored paper," said Reagan. While young Reagan learned the value of hard work from his father, it was the faith of his mother that kept the family going during the disappointments of life. She raised her son to believe that God had a plan for everyone and that even the most disheartening setbacks were part of that plan. In the end everything would work out for the best.

As President, Ronald Reagan was to draw upon the faith of his mother when, in an address to the nation on December 23, 1981, he shared some thoughts about Christmas: "Like the shepherds and wise men of that first Christmas, we Americans have always tried to follow a higher light, a star, if you will. At lonely campfire vigils along the frontier, in the darkest days of

Facing page: The Reagans commissioned a number of young artists to produce art for their official Christmas cards and gift prints. The first, *Christmas Eve at the White House*, was painted by Jamie Wyeth. HALLMARK CARDS the Great Depression, through war and peace, the twin beacons of faith and freedom have brightened the American sky. At times our footsteps may have faltered, but trusting in God's help, we've never lost our way."

The future First Lady, formally named Anne Frances Robbins, was born into a world of change. Her father left shortly after her birth. Her actress mother took Nancy, as she was called, with her from theater to theater, until deciding it would be better for the child to live with her sister. When her mother remarried, Nancy suddenly had a father, a brother, a home in Chicago and a new last name, Davis. "I was indoctrinated early to love Christmas," she said, fondly remembering the old-fashioned tree decorated with all the ornaments she and her brother had made in school. Little Nancy would stay awake Christmas Eve listening for the sound of reindeer on the roof and waited anxiously to see if she had received what she had requested in her letter to Santa.

As First Lady, Nancy Reagan was much less dependent on Santa. "Christmas at the White House was truly magical," she recalled. "We worked out a theme and it was so much fun. The huge tree in the Blue Room was very beautiful and the trees in the East Room looked like they were standing in snow with tiny white lights on them. I remember going in there with the family alone to look at the decorations right after they were finished. Everything was just beautiful. I loved Christmas at the White House even though it was a very busy time."

1981: A Jamie Wyeth White House

To share the aura of the White House at Christmas, the Reagans decided to invite young artists to paint scenes of the Executive Mansion for their Christmas cards. "I thought that people would want to see the different rooms in the White House and that's what we did," explained the First Lady. To introduce the series, social secretary Muffie Brandon recommended the young artist Jamie Wyeth, whose grandfather, N.C. Wyeth, had provided the artwork for one of the Nixons' official Christmas cards.

Jamie Wyeth came to Washington in September to get inspired. "I was given free rein to do whatever I wanted, which was very nice," he said. As he wandered around the White House, he saw that it was more than a people's museum; it was a President's home. "We tend to forget that the First Family actually lives here. They prepare for Christmas, late at night, just like everyone else," he explained. He decided to try something instructive and different—to symbolize by a single light that this is Christmas Eve at the President's House. "I literally went down and sat on the lawn of the White House and began to paint. A large part was done right there, because I don't work from photographs," he said. "I drove down to Washington a couple other days and painted some more and the rest was done back at my farm."

Evoking his powers of imagination, Wyeth sketched the White House under a blanket of snow and, with the magic of his brush, cast a spell of indigo. Using a mixed medium on a toned board, he revealed the mystery of night through the star-studded sky and his single White House light. When he took his work to the White House for the unveiling, the President and Mrs. Reagan both came into the Red Room to see it. The First Lady got the message. It looked, she said, like "everyone else had gone to bed and I was still up in my dressing room wrapping presents and doing all those things you do the night before Christmas. I loved it!"

Entitled *Christmas Eve at the White House*, the Wyeth work required eight color separations and was reproduced by Hallmark. The artist was most pleased with the rich color of the finished product. "Jeannette Lee was wonderful to work with; Hallmark did a terrific job," he said of the company and its veteran consultant. The White House ordered 65,000 cards, slightly more than half of what the Carter Administration had sent the previous year. The engraved message in deep blue script read: "The President and Mrs. Reagan extend to you their best wishes for a joyous Christmas and a peaceful New Year." A blank embossed Presidential Seal appeared above the message, the year 1981 below it. A commemorative postage stamp honoring James Hoban, the architect of the White House and the subject of N.C. Wyeth's 1971 card, was used on the Reagans' first Christmas greeting.

The Reagans' gift to their staff was a keepsake version of Jamie Wyeth's artwork for the Christmas card. A simple enclosure read, "With special holiday wishes, The President and Mrs. Reagan 1981." Mrs. Reagan also gave her East Wing staff a silver-framed photograph with the engraved message: "Merry Christmas 1981, Nancy Reagan." In addition, signed photographs were given to the resident domestic staff. As holiday party favors, the White House ordered 5,000 four-inch brass tree ornaments with the inscription "Merry Christmas, The White House 1981."

The holiday season was ushered in by the first snowfall of the winter. Mrs. Reagan's old-fashioned American Christmas decor reflected the nostalgia of a simpler life, with wreaths in windows, boughs of holly, magnolia leaves, and red and white poinsettias decking the halls of the White House. The 19-foot Fraser fir in the Blue Room was decorated with 200 ornaments by eight craftspeople who had been selected by the director of the Museum of American Folk Art. They had created animals from tin, fabric and wood; some were painted with sponges dipped in color; others arrived with hand-painted faces. The White House menagerie roaming the branches of the tree represented the animals that spoke at midnight and shared the stable with the Christ child. Inspired by Edward Hicks' *The Peaceable Kingdom*, where beast of the field and farm came together in friendship, Muffie Brandon planned the display. At the very top, a nearly two-foot angel Gabriel watched over the flock.

International Posturing Hits the Front Pages

Events of the President's first year in office put a damper on the peaceful holiday mood. Only 70 days after his inauguration, Reagan had received a gunshot wound in an assassination attempt. When, shortly before the holidays, rumors surfaced that a Libyan hit squad had been sent to assassinate the President and other officials, the threat was taken seriously. As a precautionary measure, Ronald Reagan did not appear at the Pageant of Peace and the lighting of the National Christmas Tree on December 17. Instead he remained in the East Room and, by remote control before an audience of 25 children, lit the living Colorado blue spruce on the Ellipse—the same tree that had served in this capacity since 1978. In his televised speech, the Chief Executive alluded only briefly to the international crisis and opted to talk of Christmas traditions and how peace could be achieved. He said: "I know there are some who celebrate this day, the Christmas Day, as the birthday of a great teacher and philosopher. To others of us, he is more than that; he is also divine. But to all of us, he taught us the way that we could have peace on Earth and goodwill to men, and that is if we would do unto others as we would have others do unto us."

Unfortunately, for security reasons, Ronald Reagan was never to attend a tree-lighting ceremony in person. For the eight years of his administration, the Secret Service kept him at least one block from the tree and the crowds.

Disturbing news from Poland also interrupted the mood of Christmas at the White House in 1981. In what was supposed to be a Christmas speech to the nation on December 23, the President sent a strong message to the Soviets condemning their action in Poland and suggesting a way for Americans to make a personal statement. "Yesterday," he said, "I met ... with Romuald Spasowski, the distinguished former Polish ambassador who has sought asylum in our country in protest for the suppression of his native land.... Ambassador Spasowski requested that on Christmas Eve a lighted candle will burn in the White House window as a small but certain beacon of our solidarity with the Polish people. I urge all of you to do the same tomorrow night, on Christmas Eve, as a personal statement of your commitment to the steps we're taking to support the brave people of Poland in their time of troubles."

On Christmas Eve, the candle flickering in the window of the North Portico stood as a symbol of solidarity with the Polish people in their time of crisis. Confined to the White House on Christmas Day because strict security measures would have interfered with the worship of others, the First Family did not attend church services. Instead, they spent their first Christmas in the Executive Mansion quietly among family and friends.

1982: A James Steinmeyer Red Room

For their second official Christmas card, the Reagans continued their idea of commissioning a young American artist to showcase the White House. After seeing his work in *House and Garden* magazine, Mrs. Reagan selected James Steinmeyer, an illustrator noted for his interior renderings, to do the Red Room. The First Lady later admitted her particular fondness of

The Red Room was the subject of illustrator James Steinmeyer's 1982 official Christmas card and gift print for the Reagans. GIBSON GREETING CARDS that room. It was where she and Soviet leader Mikhail Gorbachev's wife, Raisa, would have coffee and talk; where the Soviet Foreign Minister Andrei Gromyko asked her, "Does your husband believe in peace or war?" "Peace," she said. "You're sure?" "Yes, I'm sure," the First Lady answered. "Well, then, you whisper peace in his ear every night," he instructed her. "I certainly will, and I'll also whisper it in your ear too!" she replied.

Steinmeyer painted in his studio from detailed photographs he had taken of the overall room and its furnishings. Focusing on the fireplace, he meticulously documented the periphery, then added a holiday touch by placing evergreens and pomegranates on the mantel along with magnolia leaves in vases. At a Christmas open house in December, he finally met the Reagans, and the First Lady told him how pleased she and the President were with his warm rendering of the subject. Said Steinmeyer, "The Red Room is a pretty room and the decorative Empire furniture was fun to paint." Reimbursed for his work, the artist gave the painting to the White House. A press release noted that Steinmeyer's gouaches were reminiscent of early 19th century watercolors that reproduced every object in the room in detail while conveying fully the sense of light and shadow.

For the first time, Gibson Greeting Cards, Inc., reproduced the official Presidential Christmas card. That was quite a coup for Gibson, which is just one quarter the size of Hallmark. While printing the Presidential card doesn't enhance a company's finances, "It is nice to be able to say the President uses our card," admitted Ward Cavanaugh, chief financial officer of Gibson. "That puts us in pretty good company," he was quoted in the *Wall Street Journal*.

The White House ordered 65,000 cards and 6,000 gift prints in 1982. These keepsakes were accompanied by an enclosure card bearing the message: "With all best wishes for a joyous Christmas and a peaceful New Year from the President and Mrs. Reagan 1982."

Because in 1981 the White House Historical Society had begun offering for sale to the public a White House Christmas ornament (a Christmas angel in '81 and a dove of peace in '82), there was no need for the Reagans to duplicate the effort as a holiday party favor. Mrs. Reagan did give the press a home-made, red-wrapped present—Monkey Bread, a traditional family favorite at Christmas dinner.

The Reagans kept the theme of a simple old-fashioned American Christmas. Dominating the house were red and green decorations with accents of white. Because of the First Lady's deep involvement with the war against drugs, she enlisted volunteers from Second Genesis, a local rehabilitation center, to help make 2,000 silver and gold metallic ornaments, wrap 100 pounds of California walnuts in lace and trim the White House Christmas tree. The group began working October 29 in the Executive Office

Building. Sidney Shankman, executive director of Second Genesis, wrote Mrs. Reagan to thank her for giving these young people the opportunity to assist her. They were delighted and in awe of having been asked. He said, "Our kids, once they graduate from the program, will not have easy lives. But those who worked with you last Friday will carry with them always the memory that the very gracious First Lady of the Land took time to show them her concern and her love."

Unfortunately, the tree in the First Family's private quarters was lacking its usual nostalgic decorations. "By mistake all our ornaments were sent to storage," Mrs. Reagan lamented in a *Washington Home* article. "I'd have to go through everything to find them, and I'm not in California." A sentimentalist, she had always treasured the decorations her children made in school, as her own mother did. "One year they both did a green cut-out star with silver pasted on it that said 'Merry Christmas, Mom.' They made clay stars too. I kept those things for years. One of the clay ornaments finally broke, but I would keep getting it out, and they would tease me and say, 'Oh, Mom, you don't want to put that on the tree again.'"

The year 1982 also saw the launching of "Christmas in Washington," a TV special bringing the American people into the White House at Christmas as well as providing the First Family a vehicle to communicate their Christmas wishes directly to the nation. Underwritten by NBC, such a holiday musical extravaganza had long been a dream of George Stevens, Jr., founding director of the American Film Institute. Mrs. Reagan showed the taping crew of NBC the White House Christmas tree and gave a history of Christmases in the house for her segment of the special. Then President Reagan talked to a group of children about the real meaning of Christmas and told one of his favorite stories, "One Solitary Life," a piece about Jesus. Said the President:

> *He never wrote a book. He never held office. He never owned a home. He never had a family. He never went to college. He never put his foot inside a big city. He never did any of the things that usually accompany greatness.... Nineteen wide centuries have come and gone, and today He is the centerpiece of much of the human race. All the armies that have ever marched; all the navies that ever were built; all the parliaments that ever sat; all the kings that ever reigned, put together, have not affected the life of man upon the earth as powerfully as this One Solitary Life.*

On December 16, at the lighting of the National Christmas Tree with its 1,500 green, gold and white bulbs, the President made a plea for *all* Americans in the spirit of charity to reach out to others; for neighbor to help neighbor, for employed to help the unemployed, for the fortunate to remember the less fortunate. "They are not statistics, they are people" who have a need, said the President. He was delivering his speech from the Rose Garden of the White House to the crowd at the Pageant of Peace on the Ellipse as well as to the nation at large.

Unemployment had been a troublesome issue for the Reagan Administration. With 12 million Americans out of work, the President looked forward to signing a gas-tax bill to provide more than 320,000 jobs but denounced the temporary "make work" programs that suited the pork barrel needs of Congress. While growing up in Dixon, Illinois, he had seen how ordinary people had solved the problems of their community.

"Whether it was my mother bringing a meal to a family that was down on its luck, my dad canvassing the county in search of work for the jobless, or a group of neighbors getting together to help rebuild a farmer's barn lost in a fire," the President recalls in his autobiography, *An American Life*, "I witnessed how people helping one another could be a far more effective means of solving a community's problem than government giveaway programs." His memories of the Great Depression were too personal and too vivid for him not to show empathy with the plight of the unemployed. He admitted, "I prayed a lot during this period, not only for the country and the people who were out of work, but for help and guidance in doing the right thing."

1983: A Mark Hampton Green Room

Planning for the 1983 official Christmas card began with a search for a watercolorist to paint the Green Room. Shelia Tate, the First Lady's press secretary, said, "It's very difficult to find artists who do such detailed work in watercolor. The Reagans are fond of that style." In the end, five artists were asked to submit samples. Mrs. Reagan chose Mark Hampton's style from a preliminary watercolor of the room. While the First Family had not met Hampton, he was well known as a New York interior decorator, and he had refurbished much of the official residence of Vice President and Mrs. Bush.

Painting from sittings in the Green Room and from photographs, Hampton captured the fine detail of the French crystal chandelier and the Duncan Phyfe secretary. The 1767 portrait of Benjamin Franklin by David Martin was clearly discernible over the fireplace. Holiday greens, red candles, flowers and a wreath in the window added a touch of Christmas. Hampton summed it up: "The Green Room, because of its color, its paintings and its furniture, is one of the most loved of the White House drawing rooms. Furthermore, the Green Room Christmas card served as a pendant to the Red Room Christmas card; that their colors relate to Christmas is obvious." Titled *Green Room at the White House*, the original watercolor was repro-

A watercolor of the Green Room by Mark Hampton became the art for the Reagans' 1983 gift print and official Christmas card.
HALLMARK CARDS

duced by Hallmark, which printed 100,000 Christmas cards and 7,500 gift prints.

Addressing the cards for President and Mrs. Reagan was a diverse group of approximately 20 men and 380 women who had volunteered at the Office of Presidential Inquiry. Beginning in November, as reported in a *Los Angeles Times* story by Betty Cuniberti, the "pen-pushers"—as they were affectionately described by the director of volunteers, Joan DeCain—addressed envelopes at an average rate of 30 per hour and 150 per day. Many, using their best penmanship, addressed more than 700 each. Nothing left the White House unless neatly presented. Explains DeCain: "I like it done right. We have a firm policy. Everything is spelled out. We use black ink, and we don't abbreviate the states." A volunteer would choose a favorite pen from a half dozen types and insert a darkly lined "cheat sheet" into an envelope to avoid a downhill slant. A list of the 50 states was taped in front of each volunteer, just in case the brain shut down in the middle of *Mississippi.*

The Republican National Committee picked up the tab for the President's stamps and cards, but duplication was still a concern. "A computer isn't good enough for me. We find we are more accurate," declared DeCain in explaining why volunteers checked names by hand against ZIP codes. Volunteers also stamp the envelopes. "We hand-place the stamps with moisteners, but some of the old-timers lick," admitted the director. Professional calligrapher Kathlyn Peake addressed the envelopes to members of the Senate, the House of Representatives, the Supreme Court and the past Presidents. Her work is a form of art. She managed about 20 an hour. That was a lot of work with no recognition from the VIP, because it was probable that such mail was opened by a staff member who discarded the envelope. "You can only hope that whoever sees it might appreciate it," said Peake.

At the 1983 Pageant of Peace ceremony on December 15, President Reagan was assisted by seven-year-old Amy Benham of Westport, Wash-

"I wish so much to help President Reagan turn on those Christmas lights," wrote seven-year-old Amy Benham to the Make a Wish Foundation. At the Pageant of Peace in 1983, her wish came true.
RONALD REAGAN LIBRARY

ington. A victim of Hodgkin's disease, Amy had written a letter to the National Make a Wish Foundation to explain her dream. She wrote, "Dear Make a Wish, The Christmas tree that lights up for our country must be seen all the way to heaven. I wish so much to help President Reagan turn on those Christmas lights. In my school we learned only about Presidint Washington and Presidint Lincoln. I would like to meet our now Presidint because he is the one that we trust now. He isn't done but I trust him because he loves Jesus just like I do. Love Amy."

Before the lighting of the National Christmas Tree from the South Portico of the White House, President Reagan drew again from the "One Solitary Life" story he liked so well and then introduced Amy, declaring that very shortly "the whole world will know that Amy Benham lit up the skies, sending America's love, hope, and joy all the way to heaven and making the angels sing." Amy's wish came true when 3,600 clear and magenta lights came to life.

On Christmas Eve, in a radio address to the nation, Reagan spoke of the Christmas of 1776, the country's first year as a nation. He said: "The image of George Washington kneeling in prayer in the snow is one of the most famous in American history. He personified a people who knew it was not enough to depend on their own courage and goodness; they must also seek help from God, their Father and Preserver."

1984: A Jamie Wyeth North Portico

For the fourth Christmas at the White House, the Reagans invited Jamie Wyeth back to create an image for a second official Christmas card. Having had such a pleasant experience working with Mrs. Reagan in 1981, Wyeth agreed to paint again if he could do something out of sequence. Capturing the essence of a room did not personally interest him. "She was very open to any interpretation I would do," he recalled.

Wyeth returned to Washington during the fall to get inspired for Christmas. Contemplating the task, he thought, "The White House has so much history. It is a remarkable building, but I have already painted the

Jamie Wyeth's second painting for a Reagan official Christmas card and gift print was this 1984 *Christmas Morning at the White House*. HALLMARK CARDS

With special holiday wishes
The President and Mrs. Reagan
1984

whole house. This time I want it to be more of an intimate interpretation." As he wandered around, he noticed the squirrels. "President Reagan even fed them while I was with him. He kept a bag of acorns right in his office," he observed. Right then and there, he knew he had found that intimate moment; he had his inspiration. When finished, Wyeth had created, in oils, a peaceful view of the North Portico blanketed by newly fallen snow. An American flag unfurled gently in the breeze over the residence of the President. Garlands covered the chains of the lantern, while Christmas trees flanked the front door and wreaths hung in the windows. Only a lone squirrel had left its calling card—little paw prints winding through the fresh snow at dawn.

Nancy Reagan loved it! It reminded her of their weekends at Camp David. "My husband and I would go up every weekend we could. He would gather up nuts for the squirrels at the White House and put them in front of the door by the Oval Office. The squirrels began to know the nuts would be there and they would come every Monday. One weekend—there weren't any nuts—I don't know what happened. The squirrels came to the door of the oval room and they were very upset—very upset and they made their feelings known," she recalled.

After a successful bid for reelection in 1984, the Reagans had need for more Christmas cards and gift prints to appropriately thank people. Hallmark reproduced approximately 125,000 cards and 7,000 gift prints at cost. Both of the original works painted by Jamie Wyeth for the Reagan

Christmas cards were loaned to the White House during the President's term of office. They were later returned to the personal collection of the artist.

The nativity scene, which had been part of the federally sponsored Pageant of Peace until 1973, returned to the Ellipse on December 11 for the first time in 12 years. At the South Portico of the White House, President Reagan spoke of the meaning of the nativity in his remarks at the Lighting of the National Christmas Tree on December 13.

1985: A Thomas William Jones Blue Room

Thomas William Jones was chosen to paint the Reagans' Christmas card in 1985. Lloyd M. Taggart, a member of the President's Committee for Arts and Humanities, had viewed Jones' work at an invitational "Artists in America" exhibition in Denver, Colorado, and made a presentation to the White House on his behalf. The Reagans liked what they saw and asked the artist to paint the Blue Room as part of their series of cards of the White House at Christmas.

The artist first came to the White House in June 1985. For three days he studied photographs taken of Christmas and sketched several scenes of the oval room. His thoughtful approach was to choose a portion of the mantel or a window with a wreath that suggested the Blue Room, but which would not be overwhelmed by the Executive Mansion's tree. White House curator Rex Scouten showed Jones' sketches to the First Lady, who really wanted a panorama of the room. "I loved the Blue Room," she said. It was the only State Room she refurbished by adding furniture that had been kept in storage. It was also the room where she and the President received guests at Christmas and after State Dinners.

As Scouten's trips to the private quarters became more

Thomas William Jones created *The Blue Room at Christmas* for the Reagans' 1985 official Christmas card and gift print, little suspecting that this was to lead to a four-year engagement.
HALLMARK CARDS

frequent, Jones' painting became more encompassing. Together they agreed to a rendering of the room that included the fireplace, two windows and a table, all adorned with simple decorations to capture the holiday spirit, but which would balance Christmas with the character of the room. "It was very interesting listening to the staff excitement about how things are decorated at Christmas and the magic that the White House takes on," said Jones. "It's a very special and exciting time and the spirit and the enthusiasm of the project very rapidly caught up with me."

Jones spent about two months on the painting trying to get every detail right. While he normally employed a looser, freer flowing movement in his paintings than was required for this illustration, his main goal was to please the First Lady. Behind closed doors, the artist rearranged furniture to simplify the composition. He softened edges and utilized underpainting to build textures and suggest detail in areas like the rug and on the wall while actually softening the overall effect.

Was the First Lady pleased? "She was very pleased," he said. "It was a challenge, really, to please a lot of people. I think I did that and I pleased myself," he added. "It's a nice opportunity to do something like this and have the appreciation given to your art." Hallmark reproduced 125,000 Christmas cards and 8,000 gift prints of *The Blue Room at Christmas*. The Republican National Committee paid $27,000 for the printing and mailing.

Having returned from an historic first summit meeting with Soviet leader Mikhail Gorbachev in late November, President Reagan came to light the 1,200 red and gold bulbs on the National Christmas Tree on December 11 with renewed hope for a lasting peace in a nuclear age. At the Geneva summit, the two most powerful men in the world had come together to establish a personal working relationship with each other. Proceeding to that end, Reagan invited Gorbachev to Washington for a future summit meeting. Speaking from the South Portico of the White House to an audience of 12,500 on the Ellipse, the Chief Executive gave "thanks for an America abundantly blessed, for a nation united, free and at peace."

NBC's 1985 "Christmas in Washington" on December 15 focused on children. The First Lady's taped White House segment included a feature on the annual Christmas party for the children of foreign diplomats. The President, with an apology to NBC News correspondent Tom Brokaw, read a contemporary news account of the event in Bethlehem 1,985 years earlier. He quoted:

"And there were in the same country shepherds abiding in the field, keeping watch over their flocks by night. And, lo, the Angel of the Lord came unto them, and the glory of the Lord shone round them; and they were sore afraid.

And the Angel said unto them, Fear not; for, behold, I bring you good tidings of great joy, which shall be to all people. For unto you is born this day in the city of David a Savior, which is Christ the Lord."

So it's appropriate that in the Christmas season we honor the little children. Like the Savior, who first appeared in this world a helpless infant, our children, in their vulnerability, innocence, and trust, carry the light of the world in their hearts.

1986: The Jones East Room

Within a week after the Reagans' 1985 Christmas card was revealed to the press, Thomas William Jones was asked to paint the 1986 image. He would be honored to offer his talent to the Reagans for their next card, and he agreed on the condition that he be allowed the freedom to simplify the composition and interpret his own emotions toward the subject.

As in the previous year, Rex Scouten was to be the liaison. "Rex was very cordial to me from the beginning and we developed a friendship," Jones said. When the artist returned to the White House that Christmas, Scouten laid out the plan for the next three years! Mrs. Reagan wanted to make an historical statement by showcasing the East Room, the State Dining Room and the North Entry Hall. None of these had ever been the subject of a Presidential card before. Jones was given a complete vote of confidence; he was free to paint his own impressions of the rooms.

When Tom Jones and his wife, Carrie, walked into the East Room, it looked like a winter wonderland—eight trees covered with tiny white lights, tinsel and a synthetic product called "Real Snow." The mantels were nicely decorated with turn-of-the-century dolls engaged in winter activities. The artist's first impression of Christmas at the White House was collected in a quiet moment and stored in the recesses of his mind. Said Jones, "I don't try to duplicate what's there; I try to duplicate my emotional impression. I seek

NBC News correspondent Tom Brokaw and singer Pat Boone are joined on stage by President and Mrs. Reagan for the network's "Christmas in Washington" extravaganza.

RONALD REAGAN LIBRARY

The Thomas William Jones 1986 card and gift print art: *The East Room at Christmas.* HALLMARK CARDS

to put on paper what is in my mind. If a branch is too geometric, I paint it the way I want it to be, rather than the way it is. I take a lot of liberties in my painting, but most are very subtle."

The East Room at Christmas was a study of visual simplicity. With a progression of movement, Jones captured the reflection of the room in the mirror, the children playing on the mantel, the crackling fire and the snow-covered trees. Through his use of light and shadow, he directed the viewer's attention to Gilbert Stuart's painting of George Washington—the focal point of the painting and the entire East Room as well. Jones was thoroughly pleased with his watercolor. He later admitted that it was his favorite of the four cards he designed for the White House. Hallmark reproduced 125,000 Christmas cards and 7,200 gift prints for the Reagans' fifth Christmas at the White House.

President Reagan delivered his 1986 Christmas message for the lighting of the National Christmas Tree on December 10 from the Diplomatic Reception Room of the White House. On hand to throw the switch was eight-year-old Byron Whyte, of Prince Georges County, Maryland, with "Big Brother" Francis Hutton. Saluting that program, the President said, "the greatest gift we can give each other is the gift of ourselves."

1987: The Jones State Dining Room

Thomas William Jones returned to the White House during the Christmas of 1986 to sketch preliminary studies of the State Dining Room and the North Entry Hall. The decorations carried the same traditional feeling from year to year, so it was possible to plan the composition of the Christmas cards for the next two years on that visit. For 1987, he painted *The State Dining Room at Christmas.* The fireplace and the painting of Lincoln were draped with boughs of evergreen and red bows. A single poinsettia flanked by brass candelabra adorned the mantel.

To offer a choice, Jones made two preliminary studies of the room. One was an angled view of Lincoln from an opened door; the second focused

The State Dining Room at Christmas was the Thomas William Jones art for the Reagans' 1987 official Christmas card and gift print.
HALLMARK CARDS

straight ahead on the portrait. The Reagans chose the latter, which concerned the artist, because everything was so symmetrical. By incorporating lights and diagonal shadows, however, he worked the opposing elements together to create spontaneity and direction. To simplify the composition, the artist decided to remove the dining room table from the image; when he related that to Scouten, the curator literally had the table moved while the artist painted.

Because Jones likes the elusiveness that watercolor gives his work, he is one of the few artists using it as his primary medium. In the State Dining Room, he was challenged by the hard edges in the architecture. Like an oil painter, he used underpainting to create tonal qualities in the rug and softened the paneling behind Healy's portrait of Abraham Lincoln. Hallmark reproduced 6,600 gift prints and 125,000 Christmas cards of *The State Dining Room*.

The Pageant of Peace was held earlier than usual in 1987 because of a previously scheduled summit meeting with Soviet leader Mikhail Gorbachev and a State Dinner for him and Mrs. Gorbachev. Speaking from the South Balcony of the White House, the President shared his hopes for the summit with the 12,500 people who had gathered on the Ellipse. He said:

Two hours ago, General Secretary Gorbachev's plane touched down on American soil.... He and I will meet in hopes of promoting peace for our peoples and all the people of the Earth. I hope the General Secretary is watching this on TV. I'd like him to see what we're celebrating, because for us, Christmas celebrates the cause of peace on Earth, goodwill toward men. Peace on Earth, goodwill toward men–I cannot think of a better spirit in which to begin the meetings of the next several days. As a small reminder of that spirit, the Star of Peace atop the National Christmas Tree will be lit day and night during the time our Soviet guests are here. And as we look out from

Soviet General Secretary Mikhail Gorbachev and his wife, Raisa, are honored guests of President and Mrs. Reagan at a State Dinner at the White House on December 8, 1987. RONALD REAGAN LIBRARY

the White House during our discussions, let the star remind us why we've gathered and what we seek.

In Luke, chapter 10, verse 5, we read: "Peace be to this house." That blessing is most appropriate over the next several days.

The following day President Reagan and General Secretary Gorbachev took a giant step toward peace by signing an historic treaty that would hopefully eliminate an entire class of nuclear weapons. In the years that followed, Reagan's policy of "peace through strength" led to the demise of the Soviet empire and the end of the cold war.

1988: The Jones North Entry Hall

The Reagans' final White House Christmas card art was titled *North Entry Hall at Christmas*; like the three before it, it was designed by Thomas William Jones. The unique view from the Cross Hall, through garland-draped marble columns, focused on a circa 1795 gilded mirror above a pier table purchased by President James Monroe in 1817. The mirror and table were to the west of the Blue Room entrance, and a portrait of President Gerald Ford hung to the right of the mirror. The artist did not want anything to distract from the furniture; consequently, he made the portrait barely visible through the columns and added hurricane lamps and poinsettias.

Hallmark reproduced 125,000 of the cards with the sentiment: "The President and Mrs. Reagan extend to you warm wishes that your holidays and the coming year will be filled with happiness and peace." For the staff, 7,000 gift prints were prepared. T.W. Jones received no remuneration for his labor, but he said, "just the honor of being asked is payment enough." Besides being able to keep his original paintings, Jones met some wonderful people while working with the White House. "The staff was more than gracious and very thoughtful of my every need," he recalled. "It was an experience my wife and I will never forget."

On December 15, President Reagan spoke for the last time at the light-

With warmest wishes for the holidays.
The President and Mrs. Reagan

1988

Thomas William Jones painted *The North Entry at Christmas* for the Reagans' last official Christmas card and gift print. HALLMARK CARDS

ing of the National Christmas Tree at the Pageant of Peace ceremony. From the South Balcony of the White House he addressed the crowd of 12,000 on the Ellipse and extended his final official holiday wishes to the nation. In his speech, he discussed the freedoms Americans often take for granted.

Celebrating Christmas for the last time with the White House staff was bittersweet. "I've always thought of the Presidency as an institution of which Presidents are granted only temporary custody; now my custody was coming to an end and the hardest part was having to say good-bye to those who had helped me carry out my responsibilities and had always been there to help us in difficult personal times," Reagan remarked. Over time, this core of people had become family. It was difficult to express appreciation for the sac-

Despite the works of contemporary young artists on their Christmas cards and gift prints, the Reagans had a preference for an old-fashioned American tree–this their last one in the White House in 1988.

RONALD REAGAN LIBRARY

rifices they had made on behalf of the First Family. Yet at the same time, the Reagans were looking forward to moving back to California. For a few days over Christmas they were going to live in their new home.

Reflecting on his going home, President Reagan said, "During the eight years we lived in the White House, it became a real *home* because Nancy worked to make it that way. I never stopped missing California; I've often said that a Californian (even one transplanted from the Midwest like me) who has to live someplace else lives in a perpetual state of homesickness. California, I like to say, isn't a place, it's a way of life."

In a Christmas message released by his press secretary on December 19, the President wrote: "As we come home with gladness to family and friends this Christmas, let us also remember our neighbors who cannot go home themselves. Our compassion and concern this Christmas and all year long will mean much to the hospitalized, the homeless, the convalescent, the orphaned–and will surely lead us on our way to the joy and peace of Bethlehem and the Christ Child Who bids us come. For it is only in finding and living the eternal meaning of the Nativity that we can be truly happy, truly at peace, truly home."

Ronald Reagan was a man who unashamedly lived his faith. In his farewell address to the nation on January 11, 1989, he read a quote that his mother had written in her Bible: "You can be too big for God to use, but you can never be too small." His mother, who lived by faith and who died with Alzheimer's, would have been proud of her son. His wife of more than 40 years acknowledged: "He has a very deep faith that comes through in practically every speech he gave." In her *Memoirs,* the First Lady attested to the fact that there is no secret to Ronald Reagan. "He is exactly the man he appears to be," she said. "The Ronald Reagan you see in public is the same Ronald Reagan I live with."

With best wishes for all the joy and peace of Christmas.

The President and Mrs. Bush
1989

THE GEORGE BUSHES
The First Family of "Firsts"

Ever since "Poppy" Bush met Barbara Pierce at a Christmas party in December 1941, they had celebrated life together. After 44 years of marriage, raising five children, losing a sixth to leukemia and moving 29 times, George and Barbara Bush relocated, with much fanfare, to 1600 Pennsylvania Avenue. They especially enjoyed celebrating Christmas at the White House with family and friends and the thousands of visitors who came each year to enjoy the beautiful Christmas sights and sounds with them. In so doing, this First Family established four "firsts" in the cards they selected and sent: the first holiday card done by a White House staff artist; the first card to showcase the Oval Office; the first card to reveal the family quarters at Christmas, and the first card depicting activities on the White House lawn during the lighting of the National Christmas Tree.

1989: First Card by a White House Staffer

To capture the mood of the festive White House for their official Christmas card, Mrs. Bush was encouraged to choose an insider, one who had celebrated many Christmases in the mansion. Director of graphics William Gemmell had, over the years, drawn various images for White House invitations and programs but had never been asked to draw the Presidential Christmas card. Mrs. Bush thought it "would be fun to have someone who had worked so long in the White House and who loved it so much to paint our card."

Facing page: The Bushes' first Christmas gift print. HALLMARK CARDS

Coming on the heels of the Reagan Christmas card series by accomplished American painters, Gemmell felt a lot of pressure. "I was scared to death," he said, "but you do the best you can." Previously he had done the Truman Balcony in black and white, from which he now designed two variations. Using the mixed media of watercolor and acrylic, he sought in both to capture the warmth of the Christmas tree in the Blue Room as viewed through the windows from the South Lawn. Exterior Christmas decorations punctuated the familiar scene, but also incorporated was the Bushes' exclusive, personal entrance into the house, the door leading into the Diplomatic Reception Room. "When the deadline came at the end of May," Gemmell said, "I just had to hand it in and walk away." The title, *Celebrating Christmas at the President's House*, was Mrs. Gemmell's contribution.

Mrs. Bush showed both of Gemmell's paintings of the South Portico to Hallmark representatives. She told them the President liked the version with more snow, while she preferred the one with less snow. To break the tie, Hallmark was asked to take both and reduce them to the appropriate size and pick one. Hallmark's Jeannette Lee, by now a retired consultant, said, "We did the one with more snow because he [the President] told us to." Mrs. Bush was thrilled nonetheless. "Bill did a wonderful job. We loved it, because that's the way you think of the White House."

Hallmark reproduced 150,000 of these official Christmas cards for the First Family in 1989. The inside greeting read: "The President and Mrs. Bush extend their warmest wishes that Christmas and the New Year will hold much happiness and peace for you and those you love." The same image was used for 7,500 gift prints. The executive staff and Cabinet members also received a personalized copy of two books: *The Inaugural Addresses, 1789–1989* and *The American Presidents* (The American Bicentennial Presidential Inaugural Edition).

A Story Book Theme
Not only was Mrs. Bush pleased with their Christmas greetings but also with the holiday decorations of the Executive Mansion. In her *Memoirs*, she wrote: "Planning had begun from almost the minute we moved in.... We settled on a Story Book theme, which seemed appropriate to my interest in reading. Down in the bowels of the first floor the flower shop worked all year under the direction of chief floral designer Nancy Clarke. Often when I would drop by I would see figures appearing that looked like Aladdin with smoke coming out of his magic lamp, Babar and Miss Rumphius, a favorite of mine by author Barbara Cooney." Other characters were Mary Poppins, the Mad Hatter, the Tin Man, the Little Lame Prince, Pinocchio, and the Pokey Little Puppy. Books, tied with red bows, became gifts under the tree.

"Bad weather gave us one of the very nicest experiences we had in George's four years as President—watching the Christmas decorations go up," remarked Mrs. Bush. The 18-foot Fraser fir from Spartansburg, Pennsylvania, was decorated in the Blue Room with literary characters that emphasized the importance of reading to children. White House elves also decorated the family tree in the Yellow Oval Room. It was covered with tiny white lights, decorations the family had gathered over the years and edible gingerbread cookie decorations made by the Bushes' beloved housekeeper, Paula Rendon. Of all the perks that come with living in the White House, "one of the greatest is to come home to find your Christmas tree all decorated," said a delighted Mrs. Bush.

Returning home one Saturday evening, the Bushes walked in on the staff and volunteers engaged in a "snowball fight" following the application of artificial snow to the 17 trees in the front entrance. The First Lady was quick to add that she and the President "didn't partake in the activity. The whole house was full of snow. We wouldn't have missed this weekend for anything." As a special treat, President and Mrs. Bush invited the volunteers upstairs to see their family tree and the magnificent 50-piece needlepoint creche that members of St. Martin's Church in Houston had made for them.

Many parties were held in the upcoming days. Among them was the innovation of "eclectic" receptions that became a tradition of the Bush Administration. Staff members mingled with Cabinet members, the Supreme Court, the Secret Service, the press and friends of the First Family. The Bushes entertained the household staff at a special party so they could get to know the spouses and children of those who worked so hard to maintain the house and make them happy.

Another activity that delighted the First Lady was attending a party for tiny tots at northwest D.C.'s Central Union Mission, a shelter for the homeless and needy. After giving out Christmas bags, the First Lady was to read the Christmas story from the Gospel of Luke. Looking over her very young audience, she quickly switched from storyreader to storyteller, giving it her own personal touch, reported the *Washington Post*. "This is a good story," she began. "So good it lasted almost 2,000 years. Who knows the name of the baby?" "What did the shepherds see in the sky? A star? That's right! Where did they go?" she asked. "Bethlehem," a tiny voice answered. "You've heard this story before, haven't you?" she said.

Amidst the celebration of Christmas, the President faced unbelievable changes on foreign fronts. On December 20, he sent troops into Panama to protect the thousands of American families living there during the ouster of dictator Manuel Noriega. Romania's Communist president, Nicolae Ceausescu, had fled his country, only later to be captured and executed.

From the Soviet Union, President Mikhail Gorbachev announced the collapse of Communism in Eastern Europe.

"The Hammer and the Chisel"

There was reason to celebrate when George Bush came to the end of his first year as President. In his speech at the lighting of the National Christmas Tree, he said:

This is the Christmas that we've awaited for 50 years. And across Europe, East and West, 1989 is ending, bright with the prospect of a far better Christmastime than Europe has ever known—a far better future than the world dared to imagine. And 50 winters have come and gone since darkness closed over Europe in 1939—50 years. But last month ... the wall in Berlin came tumbling down ... And today—there's a new sound at the wall. New sound rings out—not the hammer and sickle but the hammer and the chisel. The glad sound you hear is not only the bells of Christmas but also the bells of freedom.

1990: Oval Office in the Spotlight

It was the President's idea to feature the Oval Office on the holiday card. Built in 1909 for President Taft and opened up to look out over the Rose Garden by President Roosevelt in 1934, the office had been decorated by each new President according to his own personal taste.

New York interior designer Mark Hampton had worked previously with the Bushes on the renovation and decoration of their official residence. In the never-ending task of maintaining the Executive Mansion, Mrs. Bush brought in Hampton to redecorate the President's office and freshen up a few rooms. Hampton told *Town & Country* that the Chief Executive was "very vocal about what he likes. President Bush wanted a new rug—blue with a gold seal. I recovered some chairs for his office, too; they were made for the White House in 1818 and had been in and out of storage over the years." Hampton installed curtains in a shade of blue the President preferred and changed the sofas to a more traditional style. When done, the designer presented the President with a watercolor of the room, which also included the traditional Christmas tree—decorated with Paula's cookies.

For their second official card and gift, President and Mrs. Bush asked Hampton to create a more formal rendering of the Oval Office. The "Sunday painter," as he described himself, sent the Bushes a preliminary sketch. The First Lady said, "He sent the most *marvelous* painting for us to approve and there in the middle was Millie! George felt, and I did too, that when you send greetings to Kings and Queens, you don't need the dog in the picture. So he

The Bushes commissioned Mark Hampton to create a watercolor of the Oval Office for their 1990 gift print. The Presidential card "veteran" had previously done a painting of the Green Room for the Reagans' 1983 official Christmas card and gift print.
HALLMARK CARDS

With our warmest wishes for a blessed Christmas and a peaceful new year.

The President and Mrs. Bush

1990

painted another, and I have both of his sketches—for the official card and the unofficial card." Said Hampton: "It was a great thrill and an honor, especially to someone who has been doing watercolors for 50 years."

Hallmark made 153,000 copies of *The Oval Office, The White House* for the Bushes' official 1990 greeting card and also printed 7,000 gift folders. The President gave members of the Cabinet and executive staff personalized copies of *The Americans: The Democratic Experience* from Daniel Boorstin's trilogy.

The 18 1/2-foot Fraser fir in the Blue Room was laden with ornaments in keeping with the year's Nutcracker theme. On a press tour of the 47 Christmas trees and holiday decorations, Mrs. Bush pointed out some of the 45 porcelain dancers from Tchaikovsky's ballet, 50 pairs of ballet slippers and the hundreds of velvet balls and glass ornaments dating back to the Eisenhower Administration. Then, with a twinkle in her eye, she took the press—and her staff—totally by surprise by inviting the reporters for a quick peek at the family's quarters. As described in the *Washington Post*, the only stipulation was that they had to be up and out in 15 minutes, before the arrival of the President's luncheon guests.

UPI correspondent Helen Thomas called the tour a "first" in her many years of White House reporting. ABC correspondent Ann Compton, who had never been beyond the public floors, witnessed a homey suite of rooms filled with stuffed animals, holiday mementos, the 1989 needlepoint creche and many oversized Christmas stockings for the Bush grandchildren. Centered in the window overlooking the Truman Balcony was a 16-foot Fraser fir loaded with family ornaments.

Threat of Persian Gulf War

Christmas 1990 was a time of uncertainty. The line in the sand had been drawn. With American troops already dispatched to the Persian Gulf, the whole world watched and waited. Hovering on the brink of war, President George Bush kept alive the spirit of peace and goodwill. At the lighting of the National Christmas Tree on December 13, he called on all Americans to make their particular contributions as lights in a dark world:

> We're determined that our nation will become a constellation of hope made up of thousands of separate Points of Light, people helping those in need across our land. People like the more than 100 representatives of daily Points of Light here tonight.... And following the lead of these Points of Light, let all of us echo that beautiful carol, "O, Little Town of Bethlehem" and like that long-ago star, let us shine in all "dark streets" and to all people in the "deep and dreamless sleep" of loneliness and despair.

For 300,000 American servicemen and women, Christmas in the desert was without lights, tinsel and trees, Christmas carols and church programs; without family and friends, spouses and spirits. Soldiers stationed in the sand of Saudi Arabia faced a possible attack from Iraq. On duty in an Islamic country where only secular songs are permitted, where non-Islamic religious services are forbidden, where bareheaded women are culturally offensive and alcohol is illegal, they found little reason to be jolly. Therefore, many found solace in the President's Christmas message broadcast to American troops on Christmas Day.

> We're in the Gulf because the world must not reward aggression, because our vital interests are at stake, and because of the brutality and danger of Saddam Hussein. We're there backed by 12 United Nations resolutions and the forces of 25 other countries.... Today at the White House and all across America, candles burn in remembrance of you and all our troops across the country and around the world. There is no way Americans can forget the contribution you are making to world peace and to our country. Whenever we see Old Glory snapping in the breeze, we think of you. Whenever we hear

the inspirational words of "The Star-Spangled Banner," we think of you. And whenever we enjoy the boundless opportunities of a free country, we think of you....

1991: A First View of Family Quarters

War arrived and then the peace. Kuwait was liberated. In March President and Mrs. Bush visited the freed nation as guests of the Kuwaiti government. "The gratitude toward the United States was overwhelming," said the First Lady. Slowly but surely the troops began to return home.

When it came time to plan the 1991 Christmas card, Mrs. Bush remembered her friend Kamil Kubik, an artist who had been a victim of oppression in his native Czechoslovakia, who had escaped Communism in 1948 and ended up in New York in 1962. It was there in his art gallery on Madison Avenue that Barbara Bush, wife of the then Ambassador to the United Nations, found him and his work. In 1991 she invited him to the White House to create the image of a family Christmas. Set up in the Yellow Oval Room on the second floor with photographs from previous Christmases, the impressionistic artist painted for two days. He remembers it as an "incredible experience to be in that elegant room, surrounded by magnificent American paintings."

Kamil Kubik depicted the Bushes as "First a Family" that loved to be surrounded by their "grands." With all the clan assembled, Christmas morning was a time of great excitement and much commotion. In *The Family Tree, Upstairs at the White House*, the artist portrayed a scene of the

With our warmest wishes for all the joys of Christmas and peace in the new year.

The President and Mrs. Bush
1991

The Family Tree, Upstairs at the White House, by Kamil Kubik, was the art for the Bushes' 1991 gift print.

opened presents and the toys scattered around the family's living area. It was the first time the private quarters had been featured on an official Christmas card. Mrs. Bush reported that she really "loved that card!"

Hallmark reproduced 160,000 of Kubik's pastel for the Presidential card. For the White House staff and others there were 5,000 gift prints made. A subsequent Daniel Boorstin book, *The Americans: The National Experience*, was given to the President's top staff.

Inspired by Mrs. Bush's enjoyment of the art, a Needlepoint Christmas was the theme for decorations at the White House in 1991. The Blue Room's 18 1/2-foot Noble fir was laden with 1,200 needlepoint ornaments based on 106 patterns, mostly by the talented Nancy Clarke, who organized the entire project. Under the tree, an electric train ran through an 82-piece, turn-of-the-century, snow-covered needlepoint village. Along the west wall was a display of Noah's Ark, made of wood, featuring 44 pairs of three-dimensional needlepoint animals plus Noah's family. In the south window rested the needlepoint creche given to the Bushes in 1989, which had spawned the theme. Referring to the 150,000 hours of work logged by 600 volunteers since the project's inception in March of 1990, Mrs. Bush said: "We never dreamed it would be this beautiful. I believe this was our prettiest Christmas of all."

Hostages Back Home

Christmas 1991 was very special. Five newly freed Americans were standing on the platform with the President at the lighting of the National Christmas Tree on December 12. They had spent the previous Christmas chained and blindfolded as hostages in Lebanon. This Christmas the President was welcoming them home as heroes. He said:

> *This is a very special night.... And on behalf of our loving country I say, finally, to Terry Anderson, to Tom Sutherland, Joseph Cicippio and Alann Steen and Jesse Turner, and the others not here: Welcome home.... And when Terry and Tom and Joseph and Alann and Jesse light our Nation's tree tonight, that act will be a reminder of what they and their companions, living and gone, have already done to light our Nation's soul. God bless these five men, this wonderful country...*

When Terry Anderson, who had been held the longest—2,455 days—flipped the switch to light the tree, nothing happened! The President tried; again nothing happened. Despite having been tested five times by park engineers, the switch malfunctioned. The 38-foot blue spruce remained in darkness 28 seconds longer than planned. Then, in patriotic red, white and blue, the lights burst forth for the 12,000 people attending. While the engineers

Terry Anderson (center) flips the switch to light the 1991 National Christmas Tree while President Bush and Alann Steen wait through a momentary electrical malfunction. Anderson, Steen and three other Americans were enjoying their first Christmas at home after being held hostage in Lebanon for a varying number of years. GEORGE BUSH PRESIDENTIAL MATERIALS PROJECT

were mortified, the hostages were just glad to be home.

Kamil Kubik was there, on the Ellipse, his easel set up to record this historic evening on canvas. He viewed the panorama of tiers of red, white and blue lights on the National Tree, multicolored flags on each of the state trees, and white snow on the boughs of the tree on the South Lawn. The artist seized the opportunity to create a picture of a warmly lit Presidential home contrasted against an indigo sky. He later said, "I didn't do it with any idea in mind, I just liked the scene and activity at Christmas."

1992: The National Christmas Tree on Canvas

The Bushes were thrilled with Kubik's impression of the National Christmas Tree and asked to use it for their official card—the first time the tree was the subject of a White House card. Even though the artist had previously met and painted for four American Presidents, he described the chance to have his work used in this way as "an incredible honor." Having just become an American citizen in 1992, the immigrant from Czechoslovakia said, "During World War II, I escaped from the Communists and found refuge in the American army. Without America, I don't think the civilized world would be today. The President, as Commander-in-Chief ... is the Guardian Angel. For me to be able to do something for the President, I would drop everything at any time."

Hallmark had incorporated 8,500 reproductions of the Kubik painting into a commemorative folder. The greeting card company also reproduced 185,000 official Christmas cards for the First Family with the same image. Once again the executive staff and Cabinet received a Daniel Boorstin book, this time the last in the trilogy, *The Americans: The Colonial Experience.*

*Wishing you all the blessings of Christmas
and happiness in the new year.
The President and Mrs. Bush
1992*

The 1992 Christmas gift print. *The National Christmas Tree* by Kamil Kubik.
HALLMARK CARDS

Champion Cherry Picker Rider

For 12 consecutive years, as the Vice President's wife and then as First Lady, Barbara Bush had been the one to ride to the top of the National Christmas Tree and hang the star. She first did the honors in 1981 when Nancy Reagan couldn't make it. On her last cherry picker ride, the First Lady kidded, "I'm going to be in the *Guinness Book of Records*. No one else will ever be able to say that, partially because I was greedy and wouldn't let Marilyn [Quayle] do it—not that she asked! But I had my mind made up that that was going to be *my* treat." For her enthusiastic support of the Pageant of Peace, James Ridenour, director of the National Park Service, presented her with a special Park Service citation. Mrs. Bush had become as much of a tradition as the star itself.

The election of November 1992 brought a bittersweet ending to the Bush Administration. When Mrs. Bush conducted her tour of White House decorations for the press, the official Christmas card and gift print were on display. In keeping with the theme of Gift Givers, 86 dolls had been dressed, by Nancy Clarke's floral shop elves, in authentic costumes of gift givers as

Barbara Bush took a record-setting total of 12 cherry picker rides to top the National Christmas Tree. GEORGE BUSH PRESIDENTIAL MATERIALS PROJECT

they had evolved through the centuries from the Magi to Santa Claus. Unlike 1990, when Mrs. Bush had generously given reporters a rare peek at the family's tree, in 1992 the press appeared more interested in Somalia than Santas, more curious about the President's spirits than the First Lady's remarks. Not interested in holding a press conference, Mrs. Bush wished them a Merry Christmas, according to the *Washington Post* account, and left the room.

"To the Children"

The President's remarks at the lighting of the National Christmas Tree on December 10 were short and to the point. Despite the dismal rain, about 7,000 people came out to wish him well. He said:

> ... *Barbara and I want to dedicate this Christmas tree to the children of America, for they are more than our future; they are our present. And they remind us that we must love one another in order to achieve peace. We must love one another. Our prayers are with them and the ones they cherish.... May I simply say, let us think of the children of Somalia, too, the children everywhere who live in fear and want. Our prayers are with them, and may their families be safe and the sporadic fighting over there end soon.*

George and Barbara Bush celebrated Christmas in the White House one last time. Each reception and party took on greater meaning. Their children and grandchildren came for one last visit. Over the four years the White House had become their home. They had enjoyed the "snowball fights" in the entry hall, listening to the carolers, talking to the visitors and watching in their pajamas the guests who had come to dance. "As someone blessed with the extraordinary privilege of living here," the First Lady remarked in an article in *American Home*, "it was a bit surprising that this house so quickly became our home ... the White House must be many things to many people: repository of much of our history, seat of government, public museum and, of course, private residence. This wonderful place fills each of these roles magnificently."

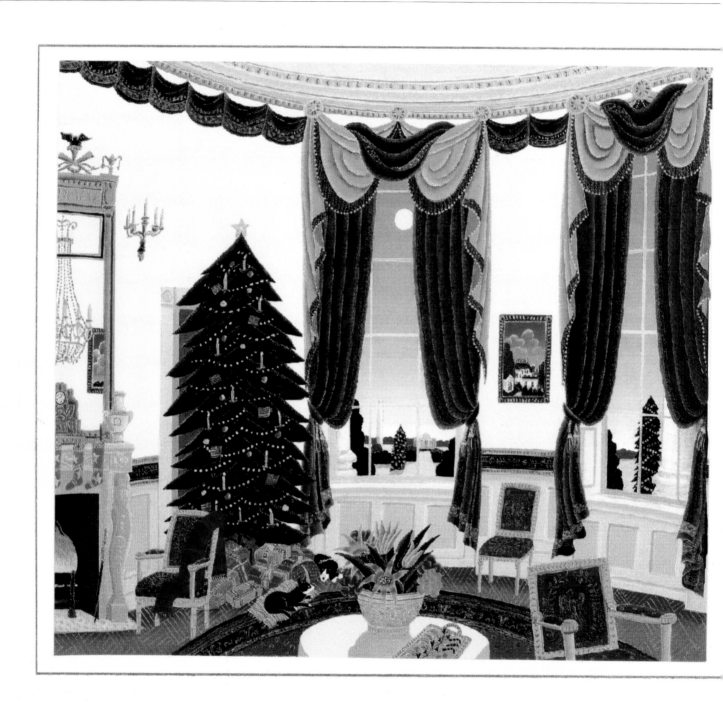

THE WHITE HOUSE, The Blue Room, 1995

THE CLINTONS
A Contemporary Christmas

oing shopping at the malls, walking around and watching people always was a big part of Christmas for Bill Clinton, Hillary Rodham Clinton and their daughter, Chelsea—but one tradition not easily carried out as a First Family of the land. Though the Clintons were all "pretty crazy ... about celebrating Christmas," according to the First Lady, the new President's ambitious agenda for the country absorbed most of their attention. They were not prepared for the reality of having to have plans fully under way by May for the official Christmas card, decorating the White House, scheduling entertainment, staging holiday receptions and ordering gifts. Head usher Gary Walters informed Mrs. Clinton of the procedure. "Being the type who's relieved if my tree is up and decorated by Christmas Eve, I was shocked to hear this," she was quoted in the *Washington Times*. Myriads of decisions and responsibilities fell upon her office. Even though planning for mistletoe and holly began during cherry blossom time, the task of choosing the design for the official Christmas card was to present an unexpected challenge for the new administration.

1993: Finally, It's a Photograph
Mrs. Clinton originally wanted to portray the exterior of the White House on the first Clinton Christmas card, said Anne McCoy, deputy social secretary. In June a White House staff artist was asked to do a painting of the South Portico. After it had been completed, as fate would have it, Hallmark

Facing page: The Fantasy Blue Room of Thomas McKnight was the art for the 1995 official Presidential Christmas card. AMERICAN GREETINGS consultant Jeannette Lee was at the White House to offer her service and expertise on producing the upcoming Presidential Christmas card. Having worked on them for 35 years, she pointed out that the artwork bore a striking resemblance to the 1989 Bush official card, thus saving the new administration from a potentially disastrous political embarrassment.

In August, with the design unsettled, Mrs. Clinton's social office commissioned Washington illustrator Susan Davis to submit a prototype for the card. She chose to paint the Truman Balcony. While the social office staff was initially pleased, the artist was asked to add Socks or a snowman, or both, to make the painting more personal. Of the several choices she offered, none seemed to capture the essence Mrs. Clinton wanted. Davis was then asked to paint the North Portico, and she produced a night scene of the White House in the snow. "I thought it was very peaceful, very gentle and beautiful," declared the artist. "It had a sweet feeling and represented the youthfulness and hope of the family in the White House." Davis was told that "Mrs. Clinton loved it."

With the First Lady having posed for photographs in *Vogue*, however, the First Family decided they would instead use a photograph. Finally, on Veterans Day, New York photographer Neal Slavin took several shots, including a casual one of the North Portico with trees decorated with Christmas folk art. Deciding to use a more stately setting, the State Dining Room became the backdrop for the photograph. The florist shop decorated the mantel and brought in a tree laden with American crafts ornaments. A feeling of warmth emanated from the fire in the fireplace, from the amber glow of the sconces on the wall and from the artfully positioned bright photographer's lights. The Clintons, posing under a pensive portrait of Abraham Lincoln, had finally found the design for their first official Christmas card.

Neel Lattimore, deputy press secretary for Mrs. Clinton, explained to the *Washington Post*, "We started getting ready for Christmas last summer and a lot of things had a lot of incarnations." Although the Clintons' official Christmas card had undergone a metamorphosis like none other, Mrs. Clinton was pleased with the final product. "We love this room and we love the portrait of Lincoln," she said. "Most people who get this card will never get to come to the State Dining Room." Also, while Hallmark had produced at least one Presidential Christmas card for every administration since Eisenhower's, the President's staff chose to engage American Greetings to reproduce the official 1993 Christmas card.

John Barker, American Greetings manager of investor relations, said, "We have a history of working with Democratic administrations." That, along with the fact that Milton Wolfe was a longtime member of the American Greetings' board as well as a friend of President Clinton, may have figured

The 1993 Clinton Christmas card.
AMERICAN GREETINGS

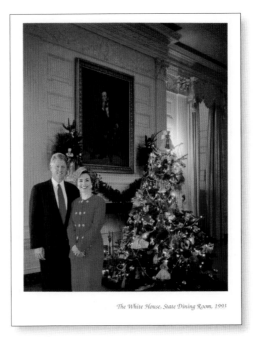

The White House, State Dining Room, 1993

into the administration's choice for a card company.

Chris Riddle, creative director at American Greetings, called on a number of the tricks of his trade to enhance the degree of warmth and the inclusiveness Mrs. Clinton had requested. "We worked very closely with the White House and with Neal Slavin, shipping things daily by jet to get approval. We wanted to make sure the skin tones stayed healthy and that we kept every detail in the Lincoln portrait. It was exciting for us," he recalled. The cards bore a blind embossed Presidential Seal on the inside with an ecumenical message: "Our family wishes you and yours a joyful holiday season and a new year blessed with health, happiness and peace." Eventually, 250,000 cards were produced along with 10,000 keepsake gift prints bearing the same image.

The American Greetings plant in Corbin, Kentucky, handled the initial printing of the artwork on the cards; workers at the Kentucky Bardstown plant embossed the Presidential Seal. In Arkansas, workers at the Osceola plant supplied 300,000 "basic but elegant" envelopes to the President's Christmas package. Paid for by the Democratic National Committee, the cards were printed on recycled paper; the back carried the logos of American Greetings and the teamsters union.

Tight security measures at the Kentucky plants assured the secrecy the White House required, including individual hand inspection, counting and locking up cards at the end of every work session. In an effort to deliver the season's greetings to the Executive Mansion by the first week in December, the cards were printed over Thanksgiving weekend. Having the White House as a customer meant more pressure for plant workers, but most of them probably would have agreed with American Greetings chairman Morry Weiss. "It's been a pleasure to work with the White House in the creation of the first Christmas card of the Clinton Administration," he said. "We are honored to have lent our creative expertise to the Clintons in communicating their holiday greetings." Whatever honor had gone to the volunteers who in previous years had prepared First Family cards for mailing ended, however, as the Democratic National Committee hired a bulk mailer to address, stuff and seal the envelopes. With time being of the essence, technology was the solution.

American Crafts Ornaments

Amidst what was described as a "tour de force of American creativity" that enhanced the Clinton White House, the First Lady declared, in the Cleveland *Plain Dealer*, "In looking for a theme that would tie together what we cared about and the kind of fun we wanted to have at Christmas, it seemed to us that highlighting American crafts would be a way to really show what is best about America and also have a beautiful Christmas filled with lots of the symbols of the season." Her staff solicited 70 of the nation's top craft artists to contribute their best work for the White House's permanent display. Hundreds of other artists were asked to design ornaments, primarily angels and musical instruments, to decorate the 22 Christmas trees. In describing the ornaments, the First Lady said, "Some are quite elegant and rather magnificent. Some are funky and down to earth. They run the whole gamut. I like them all." The decorations also included a quilted tree skirt made of 57 patches representing each of the states and territories.

To Anne Gowen of the *Washington Times*, "It was a little disconcerting to see folk art in the very formal White House rooms, a blue gift bag-shaped glass below the portrait of Nancy Reagan, for example, or an assortment of wood balls under the portrait of John F. Kennedy." Defending the Year of the Craft theme, social secretary Ann Stock said, "They might not seem to fit into what seems very traditional, but they really do." Other visitors liked the contrast. One commented, "It certainly puts a different spin on the 18th century White House." Chief White House floral designer Nancy Clarke, who planned the transformation with Stock, called the look "contemporary," saying, "It's a cheerier, happier look for the White House. It's a younger look" for a young First Family.

For Christmas, members of the White House staff received a commemorative gift print of the photographic portrait of the Clintons taken in the State Dining Room. The President also gave leather bookmarks in various colors. Each carried the Presidential Seal, the President's signature, and the words "The White House, 1993." The gift was enclosed in a paper envelope bearing a message from the Chief Executive.

The Clintons' contemporary Christmas was also reflected at the Pageant of Peace ceremony on December 9, with a fiber-optically illuminated sphere perched on the living Colorado blue spruce that had served as the National Christmas Tree since 1978. A shivering crowd of about 9,000 listened to the President, who called on Americans "to bring more peace to the streets, the homes and hearts of our own people, and especially our children."

Presidential Pandemonium

A big part of a Clinton Christmas is going to the malls to shop. Mrs. Clinton is a year-round shopper who admits, "I squirrel things away that people would like." Before assuming the Presidency, Mr. Clinton would go out on Christmas Eve and shop for about six hours with friends, all of whom were trying to figure out what to buy their wives for Christmas. When he expressed concern about how, as President, he would accomplish his shopping, the First Lady told him: "We're going to do it. I don't quite know how yet, but we are." When the Clintons finally took time off for last-minute Christmas shopping in a Georgetown mall, their short visit caused pandemonium and brought surprised shoppers to the balconies. Consequently, the President spent only 30 minutes in only one store, but did manage to fill two shopping bags with gifts selected by all the family. "It still was a lot of fun, so we'll probably figure out ways for us to shop," said Mrs. Clinton as she jokingly hinted at a disguise. "Groucho Marx glasses or something? We'll have to work on that," she told *USA Today's* Katy Kelly.

Admitted Ann Stock, the Clinton staff learned a lot that first year about how to prepare for Christmas at the White House. At a logistical debriefing in January, Mrs. Clinton and her staff evaluated what worked and what needed refining. One thing was sure—their approach for the second year would be very different from the first one.

1994: Enchanted Red Room

After personally being a part of the first Clinton Christmas card, the First Lady decided that with the second Presidential card she wanted "to highlight the house and the feeling that the house has during Christmas, which really is magical," according to *USA Today*. Mrs. Clinton was partial to the popular, contemporary Thomas F. McKnight, a romantic figurative artist known in the art world for his boldly colorful silkscreens. Before coming to Washington, the Clintons had acquired a serigraph print of McKnight's *Constitution*, which was used as the official image for the historic document's Bicentennial. It was included in "our idiosyncratic little collection of stuff that we have accumulated over the years," said Mrs. Clinton. McKnight's print hangs in the White House solarium, which serves as the Clintons' living room. According to *Greenwich Time*, the First Lady said to her press secretary, Lisa Caputo: "We just love Thomas McKnight. We'd love to have him do our Christmas card."

McKnight met the Clintons at a reception in the White House in October 1993. Ann Stock showed him around the State Rooms and commissioned him to paint the 1994 official Christmas card. The artist returned to the White House during Christmas of 1993 and took lots of photographs

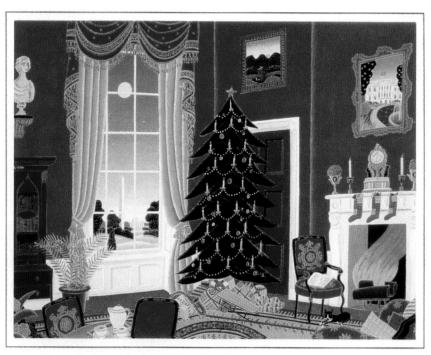

THE WHITE HOUSE, THE RED ROOM, 1994

Our family wishes you and yours a joyful holiday season
and a new year blessed with health, happiness, and peace

Bill Clinton   Hillary Rodham Clinton

McKnight's Red Room was the art for the 1994 gift print. AMERICAN GREETINGS

from which to paint. Back in his studio in Palm Beach, visions of Christmas did not come naturally, as he admitted to the *Palm Beach Daily News*: "You're not exactly inspired to do Christmas scenes in Florida." Eventually, though, he painted fantasy interiors of both the Red Room and Blue Room on canvas in casein, a milk protein/water-based pigment that produces a velvety matte finish. In March he sent transparencies of his images to the White House to await approval. Because the Blue Room was on the agenda to be renovated, the Clintons chose McKnight's sensuous silkscreen of the Red Room decked out in Clintonian Christmas finery. The First Lady, exclaimed Ann Stock, was "immediately drawn to it because of its warmth. This was exactly as he painted it. She required no changes to be made. She loved it!"

Inspired by Henri Matisse's *Red Studio*, McKnight had given the Red Room an enchanted, almost humorous look, a marked departure from the traditionally formal Red Room scene of the Kennedy and Reagan Christmas cards. In keeping with his recognizable style, the artist brought the Washington and Jefferson monuments in full view of one looking out a Red Room window. His light source was a dreamy moon, the icon of his work. Wrote McKnight in his *Voyage to Paradise*: "I attempt to evoke with color, form and imagination the essence of a place or thing without so much regard for historical accuracy."

Consequently, McKnight removed 19th century paintings from the walls of the Red Room and added personal images that were not a part of the room. Above the door, he portrayed himself and his wife's dog, Shadow, gazing over the rolling hills of Middletown, where he had attended Wesleyan University in the 1960's. "The view is actually from a classroom window on the Wesleyan campus," he told the *Litchfield County Times*. Above the fireplace he rendered a fanciful picture of the White House. Traditionally, there had never been a Christmas tree in the Red Room until the artist superimposed one along with other images that were sentimental to the First Family. On the mantel, McKnight hung three stockings designed with American flags; under the gracefully decorated tree he placed a new saxophone for the President and a sled for Chelsea; under the chair he caught the Clinton cat napping; on the table he placed a tea set for the tea-loving Mrs. Clinton and books in keeping with the family's avid reading habits.

While some suggest that McKnight's inspiration easily could have come from the children's book *Good Night Moon* by Margaret Brown, the artist had never seen the work before doing the painting. "I must have read *Good Night Moon* 10,000 times," admitted the First Lady, who, for *USA Today*, described the card as "magical."

American Greetings, according to chairman Morry Weiss, produced 250,000 Presidential holiday cards and 15,000 gift prints. Again, the Democratic National Committee paid for printing the Presidential cards on recycled paper and for mailing them out. The envelopes, made at the American Greetings plant in Osceola, Arkansas, were addressed by computer, stuffed by machine and stamped by meter. For the first time, those who didn't make the mailing list could view a color graphic of the card by computer at the Internet home page http://www.whitehouse.gov.

The Twelve Days of Christmas

At about the same time the White House Christmas card was being unveiled, the Blue Room tree, an 18-foot Missouri-grown Colorado blue spruce, arrived from Clinton County. The theme of the decorations was the Twelve Days of Christmas, which, according to Mrs. Clinton, is one of the family's favorite carols. "It's one that traditionally for our family we sing and act out—which is something we will not do in public—for the benefit of everyone's sensibility.... This will be a wonderful Christmas, although a little bittersweet, because my father won't be here and my husband's mother won't be here either."

On December 7, with springlike temperatures, more than 9,000 people gathered for the lighting of the National Christmas Tree. Scott Bowles of the *Washington Post* wrote: "The event is quintessential Washington: White House Staff members and Secret Service officers elbow to elbow; traffic snarls that turn the mall into a parking lot; stand still lines (everyone attending has to pass through metal detectors and submit bags for police searches); and better views from homes across the country than at the scene. But ... it is one of the few Washington spectacles that draws out the local crowd." President Clinton called the National Christmas Tree "a symbol of the enduring values in our lives."

The Clintons enjoyed their second White House Christmas with friends, helping those in need and going to church—all the traditions important to the President and his family. Mrs. Clinton added: "I would love for the Christmas season to enter into the heart of every American and for the Spirit of Christmas and the Christmas story to be a part of how we treat one another and feel about ourselves. And really the root of the Christmas story is love and hope, and that to me is the greatest gift that anyone can give."

1995: *Fantasy Blue Room*

With the defeat of the administration's health care bill, the First Lady diverted her energy from reform to the renovation of the Blue Room, a project made public in February of 1995. As far back as 1990 the Committee for the Preservation of the White House had concluded that the Blue Room had become unpresidentially frayed and recommended that it be renovated. In 1994, the oval room's carpet, which had been woven in Peking around 1850 for a French palace, was pronounced beyond repair. The First Lady observed that the entire room had become "a little bit tired" since its restoration in 1972. Following a long period of research and planning, work on the room began as soon as the 1994 Christmas tree was removed. Mrs. Clinton determined that the color would be a stronger blue than it had been in 23 years.

The new Blue Room was showcased on the Clintons' Christmas card in 1995. The First Family requested that Thomas McKnight again provide an artistic image for their official card. Despite the honor such an assignment held, the artist had mixed feelings about a repeat performance. "It takes a lot of work to get it right. It has to be fairly accurate. A lot of my work is fantasy and it comes right out of my head," he told the *Palm Beach Daily News*. The previous year, to give the Clintons a choice of either the Red Room or the Blue Room for their holiday card, McKnight had painted a more formal Blue

The 1995 National Christmas Tree. NATIONAL PARK SERVICE

Room scene that wasn't used. This second time, the artist did a more cozy one.

Comfortable in the fanciful setting was the First Cat, Socks, snuggling under a blanket below a Christmas tree decorated with miniature American flags. Socks' apparent White House guest was Mrs. McKnight's dog, Shadow, who had also appeared in a painting in the 1994 rendering of the Red Room. The curious painting between the windows was a substitute for the portrait of President James Madison that normally hangs in the room. The artist does not duplicate existing paintings but instead creates new ones. In this case, he painted the view of his neighbor's backyard in Litchfield, Connecticut. "It's my own fantasy," claimed McKnight. The backyard scene even included the historic Sheldon's Tavern where George Washington was said to have stayed. "I put this image in the painting because I love New England, and Litchfield is a beautiful old New England town. What could be more reflective of America?" queried the artist in the *Litchfield County Times*. He also admitted that he truncated the distance between the fireplace and the window in order to get both of the windows in the rendering. The Blue Room actually has three windows overlooking the Washington Monument, which he skewed to highlight a dreamy trademark full moon.

American Greetings' Chris Riddle said, "It was very important to Mrs. Clinton that everything in the Blue Room be exact in color and design. On our trip to Washington, D.C., we toured the Blue Room with the artist, and received actual samples of the drapery from the office archives to compare with our color proofs." Quality control continued at the American Greetings plant in Corbin, Kentucky. "Everyone works their hardest to make sure it's the best it can be," said third-shift press operator Eddie Hubbard in *Expressions*. In the same publication, Maureen Stratton, director of marketing/public relations and trade relations for American Greetings, said: "We are contributing to a historical event. Presidential Christmas cards become part of our nation's archives. This makes American Greetings part of our country's official history."

American Greetings reproduced 300,000 official cards and 15,000 gift prints for the President and First Lady. McKnight's full-color image was "tipped on" to the front of an off-white folder with a natural deckle edge. The card was enhanced by a gold hot-stamped border and a blind embossed Presidential Seal.

"The Night Before Christmas"

McKnight's original painting of the Blue Room was displayed in the Blue Room along with an 18 1/2-foot Fraser fir from Ashe County, North Carolina. The official theme for the Clintons' third White House Christmas was "The Night Before Christmas." Said Ann Stock, "The selection was a personal one. The President has read the Clement Moore poem to his daughter every Christmas since she was born." Awaiting the Clintons upon their return from a five-day European trip were 32 Christmas trees, all decorated with hand-crafted ornaments, and a gingerbread house fashioned after the First Lady's childhood home.

Speaking at the lighting of the National Christmas Tree on December 6, President Clinton asked the American people to join him "to be peacemakers. For just as many nations around the world and so many children around the world cry for peace, so do we need peace here at home in our toughest neighborhoods, where there are children, so many children who deserve to have their childhood and their future free and peaceful."

1996: Magical Green Room

For 1996 and the third year in a row, Thomas McKnight was asked to design the Clintons' Christmas card. Explained press secretary Neel Lattimore, "They like his style. He represented the rooms in a classic, but festive, whimsical and magical way." With the Red Room and Blue Room already done, Mrs. Clinton asked that the famed artist complete the trio with his inimitable rendition of the Green Room. She also suggested that the work include three stockings hanging at the fireplace, her tea service on the table, and the First Cat, Socks. Because of the favorable reception received by Mrs. McKnight's dog in his two previous paintings, according to McKnight, the First Lady even welcomed Shadow's return appearance in the composition.

Socks, initially resting in a winged chair, was depicted with a feline profile that caused quite a stir. McKnight received a call from a staff member on *Air Force One* requesting that the animal's snout be corrected. "I worked from a PR photo that was sent from the White House. Because I'm more of a dog person," said McKnight, "I gather that the staff thought I had extended the nose too much and made Socks look like a fox." By that time, unfortunately, the artwork had already been sent to the printer, and the nose job had to be completed by American Greetings on a computer.

True to his style, the artist added fantasy to the historically correct room. His version of the portrait of Benjamin Franklin that actually hangs over the Green Room mantel appears in the art. The painting above the doorway is McKnight's original view of the White House from the South Lawn. Over the china cabinet is a painting of the artist's backyard in Litchfield,

Thomas McKnight's painting of the Magical Green Room was the art for the 1996 official Presidential Christmas card.
AMERICAN GREETINGS

THE WHITE HOUSE, The Green Room, 1996

Connecticut—meant to symbolize all the rest of the country. To position the fireplace and the two windows on the same canvas, while also bringing the Washington Monument into view, the artist admits to having skewed the perspective rather drastically. Comparing this Green Room likeness to his previous two Christmas paintings, he commented that there was not too much he could do differently. "Painting-wise," he said, "I think this is a better work than the others. Personally, it was more of a challenge for me because green is a hard color to work with, especially when you also have the green tree."

To ensure historical accuracy, American Greetings produced the card using fabric swatches of the draperies and furniture the administration had given them. Lattimore later praised the veteran American Greetings staff for their expertise and diligence in designing, printing and inspecting the 300,000 Green Room cards in a timely manner.

1997: *White House Nocturne*

A nocturnal scene on a postcard caught the eye of Mrs. Clinton during the summer of 1997 as she and her staff once again prepared for the holiday season. Entranced with the idea of a White House nocturne at Christmas, the First Lady requested that the painting's artist, Kay Jackson of nearby Georgetown, be commissioned to paint the South Portico at night for the Clintons' next Christmas card. Consequently, in September, Mrs. Clinton's social secretary, Capricia Marshall, approached Jackson to make the arrangements.

Unaccustomed to doing commissions, Jackson found the project a bit of a "mental mind stretch." Traditionally, she reported, "artists made their living from commissions. Twentieth century artists are different in that we do not create art specifically for patrons anymore. We create them for ourselves

White House Nocturne, South Lawn 1997 by Kay Jackson served as art for the Clintons' Christmas card and gift print.
AMERICAN GREETINGS

and hopefully for the grander conscience of the world."

With an October deadline looming and given the fact of the large audience in waiting, achieving the proper focus on the project became an intriguing mind game for the local artist. Though preferring to work in several art forms simultaneously, Jackson focused on just one work for three weeks.

"It was enough for me to only paint this painting. I didn't have time to get excited or worry about messing up," she recalled. "I just did it. In retrospect, it worked out great."

The part she most enjoyed was sitting on the South Lawn carefully studying the American icon. "You can't get that feeling from a painting or photograph. The White House is such an elegant building," she said.

Back in her studio, Jackson worked from her sketches and photographs as well as archive photographs of the White House in winter. Her artistic response in oil on canvas was to engulf the Executive Mansion in twilight through applying 10 layers of glazes. With each glaze likened to a transparent veil in a different shade of blue, she created an abstract reflection of the President's House in the snow.

"I love color," said Jackson. "Doing a nocturne was my opportunity to render a poetic interpretation that wasn't really there." Characteristic of her trademark, the artist stamped gold leaf into the paint making up the windows to give the building both light and life. It was this particular technique that won her the Clintons' acclaim.

Were they pleased? "President and Mrs. Clinton were so positive," Jackson said after she and her husband met the First Family at a White House Christmas party. "I could tell they really liked the painting. Their response was so genuine. It was a thrilling experience and an honor to be selected." Beyond the honor of being commissioned to paint for the First Family, Jackson had earned the distinction of being the first woman to have created the art used on an official Christmas card.

Titled *White House Nocturne, South Lawn 1997*, the painting was reproduced by American Greetings on the Clintons' 300,000 Christmas cards as well as on the gift prints to their staff. The message read, "Our family wishes you and yours a beautiful holiday season filled with the warmth of friends and loved ones, and with the promise of a happy new year."

The holiday season opened on December 4 at the lighting of the National Christmas tree. Rain, unfortunately, caused the President to limit his remarks to a mere 140 words, making it the shortest tree-lighting speech since the days of Herbert Hoover. The White House, meanwhile, was decorated around the theme of Santa's Workshop. Harking back to memories of daughter Chelsea's Christmas morning delight in opening all her presents, the Clintons chose to portray the holiday through the eyes of a child.

The Clintons' closing statement in their 1997 White House holiday visitor booklet looked to the future with these words: "Through a child's eyes, the holidays are a time of wonder, promise and hope. As we approach a new millennium, let them so remind us of our blessings as a nation and our ability to realize dreams of every one of our nation's children. May you and yours have a blessed holiday and a healthy and prosperous New Year."

1998: State Dining Room

The year 1998 proved to be anything but blessed and prosperous for Bill and Hillary Clinton. It was a year made tumultuous by revelation of a sex scandal involving the President and a former White House intern. The road to impeachment began on January 17 when the Chief Executive, as he later testified, "knowingly provided evasive and misleading answers" about the relationship. After an investigation by an independent counsel, the House of Representatives Judiciary Committee was to bring four articles of impeachment against the President.

Meanwhile, the White House wished to convey the appearance of business as usual in matters of holiday tradition. After 1997's depiction of light shimmering from snow on the South Lawn at night, the 1998 card would go back inside the White House for an interior setting. Instead of the imaginative feel of several of their previous interior cards, the newest one would convey solid realism.

The Clintons frequently vacationed at Martha's Vineyard, the Massachusetts island home of artist Ray Ellis, but it was through his series of three books on the coasts of America, with text written by veteran CBS newsman Walter Cronkite, that Mrs. Clinton found the painter. With a fondness for his impressionistic seascapes, the First Lady instructed her social secretary, Capricia Marshall, to contact him.

"Any time anybody gets a call from the White House, they immediately

Ray Ellis' stately State Dining Room was the 1998 Presidential Christmas art. AMERICAN GREETINGS

THE WHITE HOUSE, The State Dining Room, 1998

think someone is playing a joke on them," quipped the 77-year-old artist. "When I realized, however, that it was the White House calling and they wanted me to do their Christmas card, I considered that this was quite an honor." Ellis' first inquiry was about time constraints, as it was already late September and he was leaving for Europe on October 15. Hearing mid-October, he matter-of-factly replied, "The only way I could possibly do that is if I fly to Washington tomorrow and begin my preliminary planning and sketching of what I would like to do."

Ray Ellis arrived at the White House on September 29. The President and Mrs. Clinton wanted him to do a painting of the State Dining Room, which was in the process of being redecorated. On that day, consequently, the room was totally empty, except for George P.A. Healy's portrait of Abraham Lincoln over the mantel and the 1902 chandelier dating back to Theodore Roosevelt. Concerned over how he would create an image from this challenging situation, Ellis shot numerous photos of the room and of the furniture that had been removed. He also made note of the White House china. The next day he received swatches of the new draperies and carpet.

"Not only was it not an easy task," Ellis confided, "it was one of the biggest challenges I have ever faced. Repainting the painting of Lincoln was one of the toughest parts." After several ideas proved too cumbersome, the artist had to decide, in short order, to showcase a dignified State Dining Room in readiness for a holiday dinner. Complete with floral arrangements, the tables were set formally with the Wilson china.

Awash in warm shades of gold and cream, the watercolor portrayed a holiday setting with fresh evergreen boughs draped above the painting of Abraham Lincoln. A fire blazing in the hearth stood in stark contrast to the chill of the December snow outside. Within two days Ellis sent a sketch to the White House. Upon approval, this prolific artist brought all his years of skill and experience to bear as he completed the watercolor within a day. He received final approval two days before leaving for Europe.

Upon his return, Ellis ironed out production details with American Greetings who, for the sixth straight year, was selected to reproduce the official Presidential Christmas card and gift print. Said Chris Riddle, the company's creative director: "Mr. Ellis has captured the beauty and the elegance of the newly decorated State Dining Room." Embossed with a Presidential Seal, the inside of the card read, "May peace and joy be yours at the holiday season and throughout the new year." The card bore the facsimile signatures of Bill Clinton and Hillary Rodham Clinton. According to the *Palm Beach Post*, about 300,000 of these cards were printed for the President and 200,000 separate Vice President cards were printed for Al Gore. As usual, the Democratic National Committee was to foot the bill for the cards and postage.

It wasn't until the unveiling of the original painting in December that Ellis finally had the opportunity to meet Mrs. Clinton. "She was very gracious and introduced me to the press, who were curious as to how I had been selected. Mrs. Clinton told them about how she and the President had become familiar with my paintings through my books and that I had been recommended by a number of museums, which was very nice," Ellis said. He recalled having met the President in Martha's Vineyard three years earlier. The President had told Ellis at that time how much he loved the artist's paintings.

The official card appeared in almost every newspaper in the United States. Ellis found the publicity of having painted such high-profile art for the President to be "priceless." Said he: "You couldn't buy that kind of publicity. It proves that if you live long enough, good things happen to you." When asked to donate the painting to the White House collection, Ray Ellis was most happy to oblige.

Holiday Cheer Dampened by Legal Turmoil

On a day when it was unseasonably warm outside, Mrs. Clinton brought the press inside for a tour of the White House holiday décor. Admitting that the "look" was a departure from the traditional reds and greens used in the past, she said: "This year we decided to do something a little different to create this kind of silver, gold and crystal 'Winter Wonderland.'" In the introduction to the holiday brochure, the Clintons had written, "We have so many fond memories of Chelsea's first winters. Through her eyes we relived the pleasure of playing in the first snowfall, the silver glint of skate blades on a frozen pond, breathless sled rides down a glistening slope and lopsided snowmen with carrots for noses, destined to melt in the morning sun."

Craftspeople from around the country had created their unique images of winter that brought cheer throughout the public areas. From the Silent Night Tree Farm in Endeavor, Wisconsin, came the 18 1/2-foot Blue Room balsam fir that was now bedecked with 230 snowmen and 271 mitten-and-hat ornaments, and sparkling with 2,700 lights. New York confectionary artist Colette Peters designed the mantelpieces. A polar bear Christmas scene adorned the mantel in the Red Room, and an edible ice palace and ice garden stole the show in the Green Room.

It would take more than wintry holiday decorations to keep the residents of the White House cool, for things were heating up on Capitol Hill. The House was headed shortly for a vote on impeaching the President. On December 18 Mrs. Clinton said to reporters: "In this holiday season, as we celebrate Christmas and Hanukkah and Ramadan—and at the time for reflection and reconciliation among people—we in our country ought to practice reconciliation and we ought to bring our country together.... There are so many important issues for us to address. I would hope that we as a nation would turn our attention to what we can do together, what we can do positively, how we can build each other up. So I hope that this holiday season is a very happy and blessed one for everyone."

When the press corps gathered at the White House for its annual Christmas party, they found a lot of changes. The usual cadre of 700 credentialed journalists was joined by many more who had never before attended a press conference. The traditionally extravagant holiday feast had been replaced by cookies, according to Marian Burros of the *New York Times*. The lavish entertainment of years past had been moved from the State Rooms to a tent on the South Lawn. Gone, too, was an opportunity to mingle and get photographed with the President and First Lady. Laid up with a bad back, Mrs. Clinton was not able to attend at all. The President appeared, but briefly, to make a short speech. Frank Sesno, Washington bureau chief of CNN, said, "I always had thought it was a terrible imposition to force the President and First Lady to smile in photographs with journalists who are their avowed enemies. This year particularly, I would think it was too much to bear."

On December 19, in an historic vote, and for only the second time in United States history, the House of Representatives impeached an elected President. The two charges against Bill Clinton that passed were perjury to a federal grand jury and obstructing the administration of justice in a sexual harassment case. The House recommended that the Senate convict and remove him from office.

Within three hours of having been impeached, President Bill Clinton, with Mrs. Clinton by his side, appeared in the Rose Garden to make a statement. Blaming his impeachment on the "politics of personal destruction," he said, "We must get rid of the poisonous venom of excessive partisanship, obsessive animosity and uncontrolled anger." Accepting the responsibility "for what I did wrong in my personal life," he vowed to remain in office "until the last hour of the last day of my term." Scores of Democratic members of the House applauded the resolve of their leader. Vice President Al Gore called it "the saddest day."

The following February, failing to get the two-thirds majority of 67 required for conviction, the Senate acquitted the President of the charges in the two articles passed by the House. Standing alone in the Rose Garden, he said, "I want to say again to the American people how profoundly sorry I am for what I said and did to trigger these events and the great burden they have imposed on the Congress and on the American people...." He concluded, "This can be and must be a time of reconciliation and renewal for America."

1999: "An American Treasure"

In early October, the White House called Ray Ellis to ask if he would again paint the Christmas card art. The artist replied, "I would love to do it, but I would like to have the opportunity of doing what I want. Since I am accustomed to doing landscapes, I wish to paint an outdoor snow scene." It was agreed that he would focus on the North Portico; he left for Washington the next day. The staff at the White House was most accommodating.

"By this time, I knew the people and it got to be like old home week," he recalled. At the White House, he got right to work, planning and sketching, taking note of the details in the windows and the lantern. Careful planning went into his sketches as he removed leaves from the trees, placed on the ground a blanket of snow—which is rare in Washington—and added three people entering the warmly lit Executive Mansion on a snowy night. En route to Europe aboard *Air Force One,* the First Lady approved Ellis' sketch as rendered. He executed the final painting and sent it to the White House within days. "Mrs. Clinton just loved it," he was told. The artist liked it too, as the landscape was more his style.

American Greetings reproduced the image on white card stock. The greeting from the President and Mrs. Clinton read: "Our family wishes you and yours a blessed holiday season filled with treasured memories of past traditions and joy and peace in the new millennium. The card bore facsimile signatures of Bill Clinton and Hillary Rodham Clinton along with a blank embossed Presidential Seal. The gift print bore the same image and greeting.

The 1999 holiday theme, "Holiday Treasures at the White House," focused on America's tradition-steeped past. For the Blue Room tree, craftspeople created candlesticks, Windsor chairs and hooked rugs. Doll makers

In 1999 Ray Ellis rendered a view of the North Portico for the official Christmas card.
AMERICAN GREETINGS

THE WHITE HOUSE, AN AMERICAN TREASURE
North Portico, 1999

fashioned the likes of Benjamin Franklin, Sacagawea and Amelia Earhart. Mantel tops and tables were filled with models of historic sites that, through a program called Save America's Treasures, were being preserved for future generations. On the eve of the new millennium, it seemed appropriate to honor the rich traditions that had made America great.

Mrs. Clinton chose to scale back her duties as First Lady, for the most part, and opted not to take on any major new responsibilities for the year 2000. Preparing for the future, the Clintons purchased a new home in suburban New York, where they planned to relocate after the President left office.

The President attended the December 8 lighting of the National Christmas tree ceremony alone; his wife was in New York campaigning for the Senate seat soon to be vacated by the honorable Daniel P. Moynihan. The President was assisted by two scouts, Caitlin Fong and Chris Alvarez, who pulled the switch lighting up the 75,000 bulbs on a tree full of poinsettia ornaments. Singer Wayne Newton headed the lineup of performers.

On Christmas Day President Clinton made the announcement of a $900,000 grant to America's homeless. The Christmas gift came from the Department of Housing and Urban Development to help provide housing, job training, mental health services and drug treatment to an estimated 245,000 people. "Here at home, we're reaching out to the poorest among us—to those who do not yet share in America's growing prosperity," said the President. The announcement was timed to coincide with the season of giving. The President and First Lady spent a quiet day at the White House with daughter Chelsea and other family members.

In his annual Christmas message to the nation, the President looked forward. He said: "Today, as the world stands at the dawn of a new millennium, His [Jesus'] timeless message of God's enduring and unconditional love for each and every person continues to strengthen and inspire us. During this blessed season and the Jubilee Year it inaugurates, let us share the gift of God's love by giving of ourselves and by sharing generously with those in need. Let us reach out to those who are different from us, yet one in the human family, by living the profound and universal lesson Jesus taught us: that we are to love our neighbors as ourselves. Let us, like Jesus, become true peacemakers, bringing the gifts of peace to our homes, our schools, our communities, and our nation."

200th Birthday of the White House

With the dawning of the new millennium came also the 200th anniversary of the White House. Its first occupant, President John Adams, arrived on November 1, 1800. After spending the night in an unfinished building, he penned to his wife these words, which were later engraved in the marble mantel of the State Dining Room: "I pray Heaven to bestow the best blessings on this house, and on all that shall hereafter inhabit it. May none but honest and wise men ever rule under this roof!" On November 1, 2000, to mark that historic event and begin a month-long celebration of the building's 200th anniversary, a reenactment of the second President's arrival at the Executive Mansion was staged.

President and Mrs. Clinton invited all the living former Presidents and First Ladies to celebrate this historic anniversary at a commemoration dinner on November 9. Sharing the President's table were George and Barbara Bush, Jimmy and Rosalynn Carter, Gerald and Betty Ford and Lady Bird Johnson. Ronald and Nancy Reagan were unable to attend. Never in 200 years had this many former Presidents and First Ladies gathered in the East Room of the White House for dinner. The first time two former Presidents had dined together in the White House was when John Adams invited Thomas Jefferson to join him after the 1800 election but before the results were in. It was December before Jefferson was declared the winner. In November 2000 the nation and candidates also awaited the results of an election whose outcome was not decided until the following month.

2000: "Holiday Reflections"

For their final holiday card, the Clintons had planned on an artist's rendering of the crèche in the East Room. When this didn't work out, Mrs. Clinton's staff went back to their friend, Ray Ellis, who was more than happy to help them for the third year in a row. In October, on his trip to Washington for his preparation work, he recalled that the First Family was away. Walking the grounds, the artist took photographs and made sketches looking into various rooms, including the Oval Office. When the President's secretary, Betty Currie, recognized the artist, she brought him inside, escorted him into the Oval Office and invited him to make himself comfortable. Taking a seat behind the President's desk, he asked Mrs. Currie to capture the moment on film—one he will never forget.

Back on Martha's Vineyard, Ellis finished the sketches and sent them to the White House for approval. Mrs. Clinton liked what he had done but expressed the idea that it would be nice to do something that people hadn't seen—such as her family's living room on the second floor. Always the accommodating artist, Ellis proceeded to give the Yellow Oval Room a bright and cheery ambience, complete with a full view of the Washington Monument. He decorated the room for Christmas with a tree and colored lights, presents and poinsettias. The First Lady asked if he would add First Cat Socks and First Dog Buddy to the painting. He did, and she was very pleased.

Unveiling the watercolor for the press in December, Mrs. Clinton stated, "This is where we have our personal tree. That's why we saved our own for last." To which the 79-year-old artist amusingly added, "That's the closest I'll ever get to the Lincoln Bedroom."

The greeting on the Clintons' last official card was nostalgic: "With warm and treasured memories of our special time in the White House, our family sends you and yours our heartfelt wishes for a joyous holiday season and a new year filled with peace and good will." They again bore the facsimile signatures of Bill Clinton and Hillary Rodham Clinton. The more than 400,000 cards were designed at American Greetings world headquarters in Cleveland, Ohio, printed at the company's plant in Corbin, Kentucky, and completed at its facility in nearby Bardstown. Chairman Morry Weiss said, "We are very pleased to have provided the President with his holiday cards for the past eight years."

"Holiday Reflections" was the theme for Christmas decorations in 2000. With Mrs. Clinton campaigning for the Senate seat in New York, for 2000 she chose to showcase the most memorable decorations from the previous seven holidays the Clintons had spent in the White House.

"This year is setting up to be a nostalgic time," the First Lady admitted. Her decision sent White House Chief Florist Nancy Clarke to storage to pick out the best of the best. Back came the grapevine angels and several craft items from 1993; the Christopher Radko ballet scene from 1996; a confectionary mantel piece from 1998, re-created fresh by cake artist Colette Peters; Robert Isabell's cone-shaped topiary trees from 1999, as well as other ornaments of historical significance. Volunteers came in to fluff up bows, iron ribbons, recycle pine cones and choose from among the 10,000 ornaments the

For the Clintons' last official Presidential Christmas card, Ray Ellis depicted the First Family's private quarters.
AMERICAN GREETINGS

THE YELLOW OVAL ROOM, FIRST FAMILY RESIDENCE
The White House 2000

Clintons had received over the past years.

"There will be a lot of Christmas remembering going on in the coming days," Mrs. Clinton told reporters at the press preview. When asked what advice she had for the next First Lady, she replied, "There is no instruction book.... She should do whatever is best for her and her family and not feel she has to do what everybody else did."

The nation had neither a President-elect nor a First Lady-designate for more than a month after the most melodramatic Presidential election in history. It was not until December 13, a long 37 days after the deciding Florida votes had been cast—and counted and recounted and counted again—that George W. Bush was declared the winner. The United States would have a President-elect, finally, before Christmas. On December 20, outgoing President Bill Clinton and Senator-elect Hillary Clinton welcomed their successors to the White House. The business of transition had begun yet again.

In his final days as President, Bill Clinton openly enjoyed the glory of his wife's election to the U.S. Senate. Quietly, he was working to tighten regulations on a number of controversial issues and weighing numerous pardons to grant. The First Family spent Christmas at the White House and New Year's Eve weekend at Camp David, with the President's brother recording the festivities on film.

The President delivered his final Yuletide greeting on Christmas Day. "As Hillary, Chelsea and I enjoy our last Christmas in the White House," he said, "we extend best wishes to all for a wonderful celebration and for peace and happiness in the years to come."

THE GEORGE W. BUSHES
Christmas in a New Kind of World

*J*ust nine months into the Presidency of George W. Bush, on September 11, 2001, the United States of America came under attack by terrorists the President described as "enemies of freedom." Of the four commercial airliners commandeered that bright, beautiful morning, two crashed into and took down the Twin Towers of the World Trade Center in New York; one inflicted heavy damage when it flew into the Pentagon in Washington; the fourth, diverted from its destination by passengers, crashed in a field in rural Pennsylvania. Some 3,000 people died in the attacks of that day, but the nation's sudden awareness of its vulnerability was to bring about more dramatic changes than just about anyone could have imagined. Reluctantly Americans accepted the necessity for heightened security in public places. One of the nation's most highly visible landmarks, obviously, was the White House.

America was at war! On September 13, until further notice, the White House suspended public tours. Also withdrawn was the previously open invitation to the traditional holiday tours that once drew an estimated 5,500 people a day. In response to criticism, White House Press Secretary Ari Fleischer said, "A time-honored tradition has to change in a time of war." Not since the Gulf War in 1991 had the White House been closed to the public.

"Laura and I regret that the public tours aren't going on, particularly

Facing page: The First Lady and President Bush pose before the Blue Room tree for their annual official Christmas photo. This one was taken in 2003.
WHITE HOUSE PHOTO BY ERIC DRAPER

during the Christmas holiday season," the President commented on November 21. "I know a lot of Americans look forward to touring the White House during this period of time, but we're in extraordinary times," he continued. "Evil knows no holiday; evil doesn't welcome Thanksgiving or Christmas season, and in these extraordinary times, we're taking extraordinary measures."

This announcement came on the heels of restrictions for attendance at the lighting of the National Christmas Tree, the closing of the Capitol to regular tours and the closing of the Reagan National Airport. The operation of the U.S. Congress was also impeded because of the discovery of anthrax-contaminated mail destined for the Capitol. These security-driven changes left many people saddened and angry. To make matters worse, tourism to Washington, D.C., had declined as well as revenue and jobs. It was as if a terrorist Grinch truly had stolen Christmas as far as the nation's capital was concerned.

2001: A White House Interior by an Artist with Washington Roots

Long before the events of September 11, First Lady Laura Bush had begun to prepare for her family's first Christmas in the White House. In March she enlisted the help of Hallmark Cards and Adrian Martinez. A classically trained artist, Martinez worked as the exhibit designer for the Kimball Art Museum in Fort Worth, Texas, before he started to paint full-time. It was while he was living in Texas that Mrs. Bush came to know of his work. One of his major paintings, *Approaching Storm*, was placed on loan in the Texas Governor's Mansion, where the Bushes fell in love with and purchased it. Now the painting "hangs above the fireplace at the ranch," Mrs. Bush said. "I think he is a painterly painter, and I have always really liked his work. So, since I love his work and he now lives nearby in Pennsylvania, we asked him to do the painting."

When Martinez first learned that Mrs. Bush was interested in having him paint the art for the holiday card, the artist thought the White House would reproduce one of his existing paintings. Instead, Mrs. Bush's Chief of Staff, Andrea Ball, informed the representational painter that he would need to come to Washington to get an idea for original art that would be of or about the White House. "That is when I really began to sweat the big drop," admitted Martinez.

As a child growing up in a neighborhood only seven blocks from the White House, Adrian Martinez was very familiar with the President's House even though he had never actually been inside. "I must have walked past it ten thousand times," he said. "I was a walking kid." What remained with him over the years were memories of large, black cars going in and out through the imposing iron gates. The coming and going was always a fascinating mystery to him.

Also located in Washington was the National Gallery of Art and the various museums that made up the Smithsonian Institution. These repositories of art and culture were places in which the young Martinez developed an early love for art, to the extent that he considered them a second home. "I came to know them like the back of my hand," he said. After college, before moving to Texas, he was privileged to work at one of the art museums of the Smithsonian. Early in 2001, with the prospect of creating a Christmas work for the President's family, his art was bringing him full circle, back to the White House.

Martinez visited the Executive Mansion for the first time on March 21. He was taken on an extensive tour of the public as well as private rooms; with the President away, the tour also included the Oval Office. "The White House staff wanted me to see everything during my research and development time," he said. Shooting at least a hundred photographs, Martinez reported that he "went looking for the details of an intimate microcosm that would imply the whole." Doing a painting of a State Room in all its grandeur was beyond his experience. "Illustration," he said, "is just a catalog of information, while art reflects the emotional significance of its subject." His goal was to find a subject with depth that evoked an emotional response in him.

"He almost wept when I met him in the White House," Mrs. Bush recalled. "He was here in this beautiful house to do the Christmas card. We walked around and looked at various sites. I really didn't give him any guidelines." Over lunch the First Lady expressed total confidence in his ability. "That was one of the things that was so inspiring to me," Martinez said. "She was looking forward to what I would do, without influencing me or giving me specific instructions." Drawing on Mrs. Bush's air of confidence in him, the artist's misgivings began to dissolve.

Martinez took home with him that day a stack of previous official Christmas cards for reference purposes. The cards confused him, though. "These were mostly done in watercolors and pastels. I don't do this!" he told his wife, Leah. "I paint with oils."

"Obviously, the First Lady chose you because she wants you to do something different," she replied. Contemplating all the information he had been given, Martinez was captivated by an elegantly decorated corridor in the Bushes' private residence. He made a couple of sketches and sent them to the White House.

On May 18, when Martinez returned to 1600 Pennsylvania Avenue for further collaboration, he learned that the colors for the holiday decorations would be white, gold and silver. To incorporate these colors into the painting, Martinez asked that packages be wrapped in gold and silver paper and tied with some of the extraordinary ribbon from the White House. The artist felt that these reflective surfaces would be a perfect complement to his painting, adding color as well as compositional lines.

The artwork Martinez created for the Bushes' first Christmas card was a serene setting inside the Second Floor Corridor. The composition included a Chinese porcelain lamp carefully reduced to feature a section of the 1908 Mary Cassatt painting *Young Mother and Two Children*. The artist then removed all the objects on the Chinese Chippendale side table, which he flanked with a reproduction of an English Regency chair. A gilded wooden eagle sconce was expanded five times to give balance to the Cassatt work on the wall. Martinez admitted to adjusting the colors of the walls, the wainscoting and the carpet. The addition of packages, he felt, caused one's eye to move from the light to the floor to the eagle to the painting. "It became a balancing act of color, size, temperature and movement," he said.

The result was a representation of character: "the power and the strength of the First Family, of this country and of our times," he noted. "In the painting, I tried to convey a serene, contemplative, reflective self-confidence. To me, that is power—real power." The finished work gave him "a great sense of accomplishment."

"I was thrilled when we got the painting," Mrs. Bush said. "I wanted an elegant card. I didn't realize just how elegant it would be. Adrian really did a beautiful job. We were very, very happy with it." In July, the artist and his wife and son, Sebastian, were invited to the White House. While Leah and Sebastian were given a personal tour, Martinez met with Mrs. Bush, her Chief of Staff and Hallmark's seasonal cards executives Dan Stifter and Peg Anderson-Lee. The artist was concerned about the reproduction process of his oil painting, but he found the Hallmark people to be in complete agreement with him on the potential direction for the card.

The President asked to meet the Martinez family before their departure. Relaxing after a game of horseshoes with his previous guests, the President expressed sincere appreciation to the artist for his paintings. Martinez, recalling this as one of the greatest moments in his life, described it as "a great gift for which I will always be grateful! Sharing this experience with my family—the three of us together—was just perfect," he said. "It's not only my story, it's theirs too."

All the while, Martinez was forcing himself to block out the days of his less than affluent boyhood, the memories of being on the outside, looking in. Never in his youth could he have imagined being on the inside, looking out. Recalling the first time a White House staff car took him through the

A White House interior by Adrian Martinez featured a painting within a painting for the Bushes' first Presidential card in 2001.

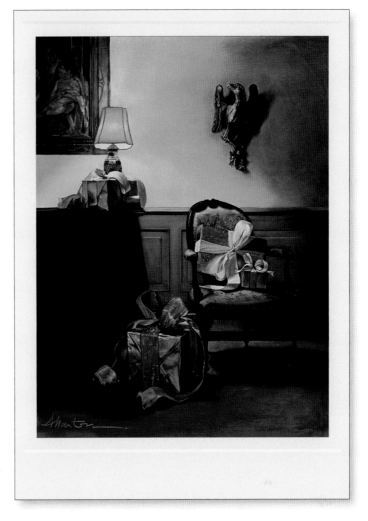

imposing iron gates, he said: "No longer was it a mystery; I, myself, was the passenger, and it was a very emotional experience." Having been treated with such respect and kindness, he would never be the same, he admitted.

Hallmark Returns to the Presidential Card Arena

After a break of eight years, Hallmark would once again have the privilege of producing the official Christmas card for the President. The company had produced at least one holiday card for every administration since Eisenhower, with the exception of Clinton. The new Bush card would be their 34th one. The Republican National Committee paid for these cards, which, as usual, were sent to family, friends, government officials, ambassadors, heads of state, and political supporters.

Capable of printing 12 million cards a week, Hallmark's plant in Lawrence, Kansas, was chosen as the site for this important job. The elegant card stock was manufactured at the Fox River Paper Company in Appleton, Wisconsin. According to Peg Anderson-Lee, the art was reproduced on a nonporous stock with a high-gloss coating to duplicate the exact effect of the painting and to hold all of the detail. This was then "tip-toned" onto a porous stock surrounded by a debossed border. The ecru-colored paper with its felt-textured finish gave the appearance of hand-made paper. Hallmark spokesperson Deidre Parkes said, "The paper complements the painting on the card very well."

The 2001 Christmas card distinguished itself from all previous Presidential Christmas cards in that it was the first to include a Bible verse.

Despite the fact that the cards were already at the printer by September 11, the insert had not been printed. After hearing the chaplain at Camp David teach from Psalm 27 on September 16, the First Lady was moved to use it in place of her original selection of scripture.

Psalm 27:3 says, "Though a host should encamp against me, My heart shall not fear; Though war shall rise against me, in this I will be confident." Two other verses from Psalm 27 were incorporated in the holiday greeting: verse 8, "Thy face, Lord, do I seek"; and verse 13, "I believe that I shall see the goodness of the Lord in the land of the living!" In an interview with CNN's Larry King, Mrs. Bush explained, "We saw a handful of people commit a horrible crime, but at the same time we saw hundreds and thousands of people do good things. And that's what I really think happened on September 11."

Interviewed by *Newsweek*'s Howard Fineman and Martha Brant, both President and Mrs. Bush agreed that their faith is what has given them the strength to go on under the circumstances. The Chief Executive said, "My attitude about threats is, if it's the Lord's will...." The First Lady confided, "I really am not that afraid ... if something happens, it happens. I think both of us have a little bit of an attitude that ... this is our life now and we can deal with it." The President added that prayer has meant a lot to them. It was important before September 11 and even more since the attack. "There's a lot of people praying for me, and I feel it," he said.

The Bushes' holiday greeting was one of peace and goodwill. It read: "May happiness be yours during this season of goodwill and may the New Year bring peace on Earth. 2001." The sentiment was hand-lettered by the White House calligrapher. Mrs. Bush preferred that the President's and her signatures would appear at the bottom of the card, while a gold-foil Presidential Seal adorned the top. The card measured 5 5/8 x 8 inches.

"The circumstances leading to this year's holiday season made this card more important to get just right," said Dan Stifter. "It took considerable time to create nuances that made the image and the verse work well together—and the end results are perfect." Hallmark printed 870,000 official greeting cards for the President and First Lady as well as 4,500 large gift prints, which bore the same image. "Best wishes for a joyous holiday season. 2001" appeared at the bottom of the print along with an embossed Presidential Seal and facsimile signed signatures. The matching gift print was enclosed in a 13 1/4 x 17-inch presentation folder.

Hallmark also produced holiday cards for Dick and Lynne Cheney. The Vice President's card featured an embossed Vice Presidential Seal on white card stock. The message on the inside read: "In this holiday season and in the time ahead may we walk in the path of righteousness and know God's

Facsimile signatures of the President and First Lady complete the insert to the 2001 card. HALLMARK CARDS

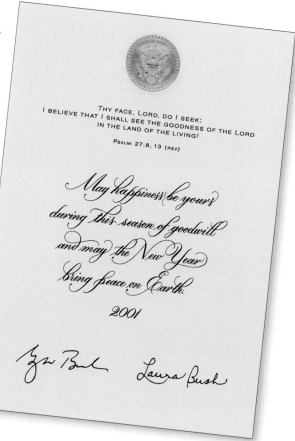

THY FACE, LORD, DO I SEEK:
I BELIEVE THAT I SHALL SEE THE GOODNESS OF THE LORD IN THE LAND OF THE LIVING!
PSALM: 27:8, 13 (RSV)

May happiness be yours during this season of goodwill and may the New Year bring peace on Earth.

2001

love." Peg Anderson-Lee said, "It's an honor to be involved with the creation of the greeting cards being sent from the top two officials of our government. We are proud of the end products—and to be part of the process."

"Home for the Holidays"

In the spring, with the Presidential card under way, the First Lady began to focus on the White House decorations and chose the theme "Home for the Holidays." President and Mrs. Bush stated later in their holiday program, "Because this year's holiday season follows a national tragedy, both *home* and *family* have a special meaning to all Americans. Gatherings of friends and family can be a tremendous source of strength and reassurance during this time."

Mrs. Bush chose a monochromatic white color scheme for its elegance and simplicity. White House Chief Florist Nancy Clarke said, "The First Lady knew exactly what she wanted. She had a vision; she chose the color scheme. This is totally, totally hers." When the planning finally gave way to execution, 49 freshly cut fragrant trees, dusted with new-fallen faux snow, transformed the White House into a magical wintry wonderland. The myriad of miniature white lights illuminating the crystal icicles, snowflakes and tinsel on clusters of snow trees created a stunning reflection of light in the polished floors of the Executive Mansion.

Adding a sense of history, replicas of 16 private homes of past Presidents graced the snow-covered mantels and pier tables in the public rooms. The White House carpenters, plumbers, electricians and ushers built each of the 12 to 18-inch-high homesteads from original house plans.

"I love the idea of miniature houses," Mrs. Bush told an audience in the White House Visitor Center. "They look like dollhouses to little girls—and big girls—and that was a special part of my Christmas. I remember getting a doll-

A replica of the home of President Rutherford B. Hayes was but one of many Presidential homes that graced the mantels and pier tables of the grandly decorated White House. WHITE HOUSE PHOTO BY TINA HAGER

house when I was four. Santa gave me a dollhouse.... It was my favorite toy, a favorite thing to play with." In addition to the fact that her father built houses and that she and the President had just built a new home, the First Lady thought that "Home for the Holidays" would be a fun theme.

In the Blue Room, the magnificent 18-foot, snow-clad concolor fir provided by the Bowersox Family of Middleburg, Pennsylvania, was decked out with an additional 181 stately ornaments in varying shades of white. In keeping with the theme, artists from the 50 states and the District of Columbia created one-of-a-kind little replicas of historic houses that paid homage to each artist's region. Among the favorites were a unique paper perspective of North Carolina's Biltmore Mansion and a folded paper rendition of the Twin Towers by a teacher and her students. Another favorite was a pair of tiny leather cowboy boots, each bearing the image of a 400-year-old mission in Nogalas, Arizona; these had been fashioned by an 86-year-old artisan. More than 6,100 white lights illuminated the crystal icicles and snowflakes, the gold and silver glass balls, and white glass pinecones. Forty-eight boxes of tinsel added the final touch. "It's such a beautiful, beautiful house to decorate," Mrs. Bush confided to Larry King. "And certainly the trees—the reflection of the lights of these trees in the marble floors makes this room look so magical."

The mantel in the President's Oval Office was decorated with garlands and pinecones. A nine-foot Christmas tree near the door was covered with glittery paper snowflakes in various shapes and sizes that had been made by third-graders from schools on military bases in the metropolitan Washington area. The tree was also decorated with cookies baked daily by the White House Pastry Chef for guests who visited the President's office. The centerpiece of the Oval Office was a new rug, a $60,800 Christmas gift from private funds donated through the White House Historical Association. Made by Edward Fields Inc., the rug featured a design created by the President and First Lady that incorporated the Presidential Seal centered on a cream background. Pale gold rays extend from the center of the rug to a border of laurel leaves, which is separated by eight blue stars. According to the President, these single stars reminded him of his "Lone Star" state of Texas.

White House Open, But for Invited Guests Only

With the White House dressed for Christmas, the Bushes hosted 22 holiday parties, entertaining almost every evening and hosting several receptions during the day. The Executive Mansion was opened only to prescreened, invited guests, including attendees of the annual special tours. The first of the evening holiday events was the Congressional Ball. Members of Congress also brought their families to a reception in their honor. Congress, as their Christmas gift to the President, passed an education reform bill that the Chief Executive gladly received. The Secret Service and their families came for a reception, as did White House staff members and certain members of the military, law enforcement and fire fighter organizations.

Although the White House had been officially closed to the public since September 13, the Bushes made every effort to work within the given limitations to showcase their beautifully decorated home. Expressing regret to the media, the First Lady said, "I'm sorry about that. I think our responsibility—the President's and mine as the current residents—is to err on the side of caution and safety for everyone who lives and works here."

Reporters and photographers were treated to a special holiday tour on December 3. The First Lady encouraged them to publicize the decorations as much as possible.

The following day, Barbara Walters of ABC-TV conducted an interview and toured the White House with President and Mrs. Bush. On December 18, the First Lady welcomed CNN's Larry King for an hour-long interview and tour. Fox News Channel likewise recorded a Christmas special featuring the First Lady with Jim Angle, senior White House correspondent. Airing seven times from the 22nd to the 25th of December, the show gave a glimpse

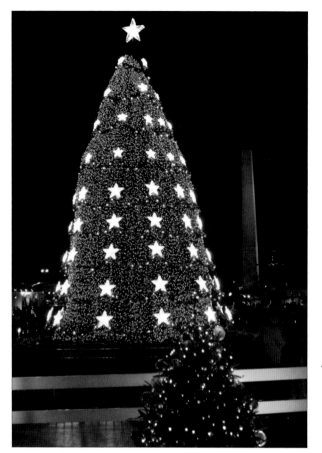

The 2001 National Christmas Tree on the Ellipse. PAGEANT OF PEACE

of past White House Christmases, including a look by this book's author at rare Presidential cards.

In addition, the cameras of ABC's *Good Morning, America* went into the pastry shop with Chef Mesnier and ABC Guest Chef Emeril Lagasse to prepare the President's favorite dessert, Christmas Cherry Trifle. Press Secretary Noelia Rodriguez appeared on the *CBS Morning Show*, and Deputy Press Secretary Ashleigh Adams conducted a holiday tour for C-SPAN. White House Chief Usher Gary Walters confirmed to Fox News' Jim Angle that because the White House granted more access to the networks in 2001, "many more people than ever before had an opportunity to see the White House decorations."

"Why did you close the White House to the public when you expect us to live a normal life?" queried Barbara Walters of the President in her interview for ABC. He replied, "We urged the Secret Service to be more open-minded, but they convinced us that the security risk is such that we cannot jeopardize the lives of others…. It is hard to have normalcy when you know the White House is a target," he continued. "… I hope people understand this. This is a decision that we wish wasn't made." Expressing optimism that his strong anti-terrorism effort would make a difference in the future, he added, "You know, I hope next year, when we do the job that people want us to do, that tours will be back and more and more Americans can come and see it." Said Mrs. Bush: "I am really glad you're doing this tour, because then people can see how beautiful it [the house] is."

Before they sat down for the formal interview, President and Mrs. Bush took Barbara Walters on a tour of the White House in all its Christmas finery. They also invited her up to the residence to see their personal tree decorated with sentimental family ornaments: a baseball reminiscent of the President's part ownership of the Texas Rangers prior to becoming Governor of Texas; a picture of Barney; a tattered construction paper card with a photograph of their twin daughters, Barbara and Jenna, when they were

2 1/2 years old; plus several ornaments the girls had made in school. Also on display was one of the family's holiday favorites, a Mexican crèche in clay. The librarian in Laura Bush always had a collection of their favorite Christmas books on the coffee table.

Susan Kelliher Ungaro's interview of the First Lady for *Family Circle* magazine revealed other family traditions. The First Lady admitted, "We have ornaments that belonged to my grandmother and ornaments that were mine when I was a little girl. And because Barbara and Jenna were born on November 25, a lot of their baby gifts were Christmas ornaments—'baby's first Christmas'—that they love to put on the tree." She added, "We also have all the ornaments that the White House Historical Association sells as part of their fund-raising."

The National Tree in Red, White and Blue

The 2001 National Christmas Tree reflected "the wonderful patriotism ... that burns so intensely in the hearts and minds of all Americans," declared General Electric designer Kathy Presciano. More than 100,000 blue and white lights decorated the Colorado blue spruce that had been planted on the Ellipse in 1978. Red garland and oversize luminescent star ornaments adorned the branches of the 40-foot tree.

Vice President Dick Cheney's wife, Lynne, and two of their grand-daughters helped Peter F. Nostrand, chairman of the Pageant of Peace, place a red and white star atop the tree. In the pageant's program book, he stated, "Peace can be very fragile. We have to work hard to achieve it, to sustain it—to spread it. May we use this night and this season to renew our commitment to spreading peace and goodwill to all people—everywhere."

Presiding over a more subdued than spirited tree-lighting ceremony on December 6, President Bush said, "We once again celebrate the season of hope and the season of joy." Speaking from behind protective glass, he called it a "time of conflict and challenge ... a time of testing, with American troops far from home.... This is a year we will not forget those who lost loved ones in the attacks on September the 11th and on the battlefield. They will remain in our prayers," he said. In dedication to those who died, Mrs. Bush lit the National Christmas Tree. She was assisted by Leon Patterson and Faith Elseth, both of whom had lost their fathers on September 11 in the attack on the Pentagon.

Because of tightened security, admission was initially limited to those with tickets issued by the Administration or Congress. After much protest, the Secret Service relented and allowed 2,700 tickets to be distributed through the National Park Service. Park police and Secret Service agents searched all bags entering the Ellipse. Despite the necessity of such measures, more than 5,000 people attended the ceremony. Andrew De Millo of the *Washington Post* wrote, "Last night's lighting of the National Christmas tree wasn't just another holiday event: It was a sign of normalcy and tradition in a year that has been anything but normal and traditional."

A Flurry of "Alternative" Activities

In an effort to make up for the suspension of public holiday tours, the White House Visitor Center became a substitute destination. Its display consisted of a 12-foot snow-covered tree complete with icicles, snowflakes and tinsel; a festive arrangement of poinsettias; an extensive exhibit of photographs depicting the current White House decorations, and a virtual tour on computer. Three 12 to 18-inch replicas of homes of Presidents Hoover, Truman and Eisenhower were set up nearby. The Home & Garden Television video, with a greeting and farewell by Mrs. Bush, provided an insight into the activities of transforming the most famous house in America into a holiday showplace.

The exhibit's opening ceremony took place on December 9. While thanking the Bushes for their input into the last-minute decision to allow the public onto the Ellipse for the tree-lighting ceremony, District of Columbia Mayor Anthony A. Williams boasted of the city's "more than 400 holiday activities, special promotions and discounted hotels, restaurants and tours." When former First Lady Barbara Bush came to the microphone, she commented, "Mr. Mayor, I'd like very much to stay in one of your cut-rate hotels, but I have relatives here." Reflecting on her own four Christmases in the White House, she added, "Our memories are extraordinary, but it never has looked more beautiful than it looks today."

Laura Bush spoke about the "Home for the Holidays" theme she had chosen the previous summer. "When we picked it, we had no idea what a deep meaning home would have for all of us this Christmas," she said. "We didn't know, of course, at the time, that there would be a lot of people who won't be home for the holidays or who will be missing a loved one for the holidays—either because they lost somebody on September 11th or because their loved one is a member of the United States military, someone who is defending our country right now overseas." She encouraged Americans to continue the generosity and compassion they had shown for others after the terrorist attack.

The First Lady touched many hearts during the holiday season. In the December 18 issue of *Family Circle*, she offered a special holiday message of hope to all Americans. It read:

This year the holiday season holds a special meaning for Americans around the world. The terrorist attacks of September 11 were designed to tear at the fabric of our nation's confidence and spirit. They failed. Instead, Americans of diverse backgrounds are united as never before. We stand shoulder to shoulder behind a flag that stands for freedom, honor and pride.

As we welcome the holiday season, let us reflect on life's true treasures: the smile of a child, the embrace of a family member, the memory of loved ones, faith in the goodness of others. Let us also pray for peace and understanding among our neighbors near and far. May God bless you and your family during this season of goodwill, and may tranquility fill your days in the New Year.

The annual lighting of the national menorah took place on the evening of December 9 on the Ellipse. After riding up in a cherry picker to light the 30-foot-high candelabra, Deputy Secretary of Defense Paul D. Wolfowitz called it "a symbol of hope against violence and oppression." He said, "We can see this victory over the darkness of evil dawning today in Afghanistan." The traditional program of Hanukkah songs included "God Bless America" and "Oseh Shalom," the Jewish prayer for peace.

The following evening, to mark the second night of Hanukkah, President and Mrs. Bush held the first-ever Hanukkah reception in the White House. They made further history when in the East Wing Foyer of the White House a candle was lit on a menorah, this being a 100-year-old menorah lamp borrowed from the Jewish Museum in New York. In his remarks the President said, "America and Israel have been through much together. This year we have grieved together. But as we watch the lighting of this second candle of Hanukkah, we're reminded of the ancient story of Israel's courage and of the power of faith to make the darkness bright."

Earlier that day, the President set aside the duties of his office to enjoy the magic of Christmas during a White House Christmas story hour in the East Room. His special guests were 50 first-graders, their teachers and principal from Hoffman-Boston Elementary School in Arlington, Virginia, near the Pentagon. Many of the children had been on the

President Bush looks on as a Hanukkah menorah candle is lit by the child of a White House staff member in the East Wing Foyer. WHITE HOUSE PHOTO BY ERIC DRAPER school's playground on September 11 when a terrorist-controlled plane flew into the Pentagon. One of the casualties was the husband of the school's principal.

Welcoming the group to the White House, the President explained, "This is not really our house. Mrs. Bush and I will live here only for a period of time. This is the people's house." The President then put on his glasses and read Clement Moore's famous "Night Before Christmas" poem. After he had finished, he asked the First Lady—a former librarian—to read one of her favorite books, *If You Take a Mouse to the Movies* by Laura Joffe Numeroff. She enthusiastically drew the children into the story with numerous questions as she read.

A week later at the White House, the President gave gifts to Muslim children celebrating the holiday of Eid. "This season is meant to be a time of rejoicing as well as a time of generosity," he said. "I'm proud that our country, during Eid, is helping the people of Afghanistan. And I am proud that the children of America, through America's fund for Afghan Children, are giving food and clothes and toys to the children of Afghanistan."

To respond to numerous Americans who had wished the First Family a happy holiday on the occasion of their first Christmas in the White House, the Bushes ordered a reciprocal holiday card in December. The one-sided card was designed with the Presidential Seal, a twig of holly and the following message: "Your kindness adds to our holiday enjoyment. May the New Year bring health and happiness to you and those you love." The Government Printing Office ordered more than 200,000 cards from Bethesda Engravers. While orders of this size are not unusual for this company, extra precautions were necessitated by fear of the anthrax virus. George Ward, president of Bethesda Engravers, said, "We put a lot of security in the place. I don't want anybody picking up a Presidential envelope and putting something nasty in it."

President Bush, in his weekly radio message on December 22, urged all Americans to spend Christmas "appreciating more than ever the things that matter most—our families, our friends and our faith. We count our blessings, and we remember all those who feel loss, separation and need. For the families that lost a loved one on September 11 or in the fighting in Afghanistan, this will be the first Christmas without a husband or a wife, or a father or a mother, or son or daughter. Our nation shares their grief. Many thousands of our fighting men and women will spend Christmas far from home, accepting hardship and danger to protect us all. We are grateful to every military family for the sacrifice they are making for America. We owe them much...." He concluded with the words: "The year now ending saw a few acts of terrible evil. It also saw many more acts of courage and kindness and love.

These reflect the great hope of Christmas—a light shines in the darkness, and the darkness shall not overcome it."

Christmas at Camp David and Back Home on the Ranch

The First Family spent the holidays at the Camp David retreat in Maryland. They were joined by the First Lady's mother, Jenna Welsh; the President's parents, George H.W. and Barbara Bush; and the President's siblings and their families. On Christmas Eve, the Bushes enjoyed their traditional Tex-Mex dinner and attended Christmas Eve services at the Camp David chapel. The President telephoned nine men and women in the U.S. military to thank them for their service to their country and extend his best wishes for the holiday. He also gave his holiday greetings to the families of the military staff permanently assigned to Camp David.

Amidst the joys of opening presents, relaxing and feasting on a turkey dinner complete with pumpkin and pecan pies, the President delivered his Christmas Day radio message from Camp David. The next day President and Mrs. Bush flew to their Texas ranch with their daughters for the rest of their holiday. While the war on terrorism was never completely out of mind, the family did find joy in their festivities.

Laura Bush described their first Christmas at the White House as one of special poignancy. "It was a wonderful Christmas; the White House looked absolutely beautiful," she said. "But knowing how many families were suffering—either they had lost someone on September 11th or they had a loved one overseas—made it a really bittersweet holiday for us," she admitted. "Though it was a joyous season, it was a sad time as well."

The President and Mrs. Bush did all that they could to generate the Christmas spirit in Washington and among the American people. They started early and planned thoroughly. The result was an incredibly beautiful home decorated for the holidays. Working in concert with the media, George and Laura Bush exposed more people than ever before to a White House Christmas.

2002: A Grand Piano in the Grand Foyer

The country was still unsettled by the events of the previous September 11 when Mrs. Bush began to prepare for the First Family's second Christmas in the White House. "I knew about the artist Zhen-Huan Lu, who had done some painting for friends of mine," she said. "He was born in China and became an American citizen seven years ago." She especially liked his style, which combined European realism, French impressionism and traditional Chinese painting. In March, her Chief of Staff, Andrea Ball, called to ask him if he would paint the art for the 2002 Christmas card. At first the artist

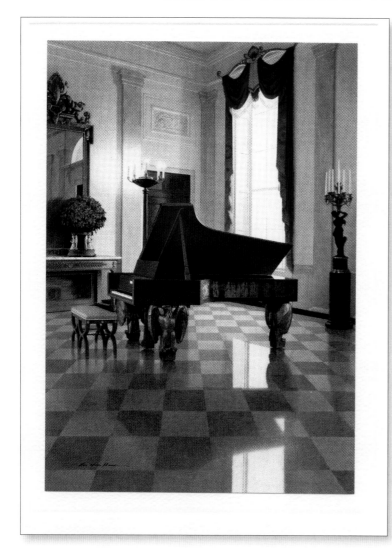

Zhen-Huan Lu's painting of a 1938 Steinway grand piano in the Grand Foyer was the art for the 2002 Presidential card and gift print.
HALLMARK CARDS

thought he was dreaming. "Of course I will," he exclaimed. "This is special not only for me, but for all Chinese artists living in America."

On April 10, Zhen-Huan Lu flew from his home in Kennesaw, Georgia, for a tour of the White House. He noted the special forces stationed on the building's roof and the use of dogs to sniff even the vehicle the White House had sent to pick him up at the airport. Security remained very tight.

Andrea Ball welcomed the artist to the White House and introduced him to key personnel: Chief Florist Nancy Clarke explained the holiday theme and what the decorations would look like; Chief Usher Gary Walters assigned him an usher to accompany him throughout the day. Zhen-Huan Lu asked specifically to see samples of previous Presidential Christmas cards. Fully informed, he set out to find a unique subject. Within the house and out in the gardens he snapped two hundred photos while waiting for inspiration to strike.

In the afternoon, Mrs. Bush caught up with the artist in the gardens. They enjoyed a warm visit and shared thoughts about the card. Her only directive was that the illustration be vertical in orientation and painted in oil. His quest for the perfect subject continued as he made sketches of the Library and the Red Room.

It was in the Grand Foyer that Zhen-Huan Lu first saw the beautiful antique Steinway piano. Before photographing it, he asked if the piano could be moved in front of the corner window to give him a backlight for his subject. Visualizing the distinctive shape of the piano against the light reflected off the marble floor, he knew this was it. The scene, he thought, evoked a "very romantic feeling and would be beautiful to paint." The artist's subsequent black and white sketches revealed his talent for capturing beauty along with simplicity. When Mrs. Bush saw them, she agreed that this was what she wanted.

Back in his studio in Georgia, Zhen-Huan Lu sketched with meticulous detail the 1938 concert grand piano and its Honduran mahogany case decorated with gold leaf vignettes of American dance. "I liked the eagles that made up the piano legs because they symbolized the spirit and patriotism of this country, especially after 9/11," he said. Keeping the White House updated by digital images, he experimented with various scenes and angles until there was agreement on the composition's elements. A portion of the gilded pier table and the elaborately carved English mirror above it were added to create an airy sense of depth and height while showcasing the holiday poinsettias. Their color beautifully complemented the red of the drapes framing the window behind the piano.

Zhen-Huan Lu skillfully applied layer after layer of rich color to his 30 by 40-inch canvas to make the final work as perfect as possible. He reveled in the experience and was completely happy with the result. So was Mrs. Bush, and the finished painting was sent to Hallmark for color separation.

On September 20, the various parties met at the White House, including the artist, with valid fears that the layers of very precise color would be difficult to reproduce. Dan Stifter, Hallmark's Vice President–Seasonal Cards, acknowledged that, "everything has its own challenges.... It all depends upon the artist. We will do whatever they would like us to do to make their work exactly as they want it." Proof sets of the painting were then shipped back and forth between Hallmark and the artist, who requested color corrections until he was satisfied with Hallmark's reproduction. Ultimately, the artist was thoroughly pleased. He remarked, "They were very nice to me and did a terrific job!" His painting was reproduced on the 5 3/8 x 7 1/2-inch card as a tip-on on elegant ecru stock and surrounded by a debossed border.

The 2002 Bush Christmas card was entitled "1938 Steinway Piano in the Grand Foyer, The White House 2002." The practice of including a Scripture verse in their Christmas card had become a Bush tradition. For 2002, they chose Psalm 100, verse 5: "For the Lord is good; His mercy is everlasting; and his truth endureth to all generations." Andrea Ball explained that all through the year the First Lady collected favorite verses. When the decision had to be made for the Christmas card, she would review them and make a selection. The signatures of George Bush and Laura Bush were facsimiles, but the greeting was genuine, "May love and peace fill your heart and

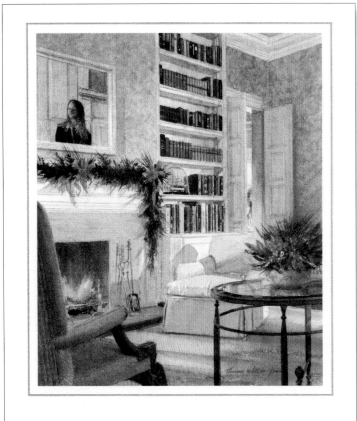

Titled "The Library at Christmas, The Vice President's House 2002," the art for Dick and Lynne Cheney's 2002 Vice Presidential card was painted by Thomas William Jones, the artist who did four Presidential cards for the Reagans. In addition to a 1790 quotation by George Washington, the greeting expressed "Best wishes to you and your family in this holiday season and throughout the year ahead." HALLMARK CARDS

home during this holiday season and throughout the new year. 2002."

The number of people who received a 2002 Presidential Christmas card reached an all-time record of 1.15 million, a significant jump from the quantity sent in 2001. The Christmas card list of the First Family was recreated anew every year and included heads of state, American ambassadors abroad, members of Congress, the President's Cabinet, the Republican National Committee, the state Republican parties, supporters, volunteers and friends. Paid for by the Republican National Committee, the cards were addressed, stuffed, adorned with a 37-cent stamp and sent from a mail house in Austin, Texas, bearing a postmark borrowed from Crawford, Texas.

Members of the press met Zhen-Huan Lu and his family on December 5 at the White House for the unveiling of his painting. They kept him busy signing the card, which he had just seen for the first time that day, and answering questions concerning how he was chosen for this American honor.

From Poverty to the President's House

The youngest of 12 children, Zhen-Huan Lu was born into poverty in Shanghai, China. Six of his siblings died young as a result of malnutrition and disease. During the Great Cultural Revolution, schools were closed for eight years. Too small to compete as an athlete and unable to sing, he chose art. At 14, he picked up a paintbrush and the course of the rest of his life fell into place. "There was nothing else to do," he said. "We were out in the countryside, so I just drew people, places and things that I saw." When the revolution was over, he studied art at the Shanghai Drama Institute for three years, then taught for eight more years. In time, the artist's work came to the attention of Joe Cuomo, a professor at Queens College in New York. Cuomo not only invited Zhen-Huan Lu to exhibit his work at a gallery in New York but also offered to pay all his expenses as he had no money and didn't know anyone with whom to stay.

Zhen-Huan Lu emigrated to America in 1986. Although he spoke very little English, he had a New York show to his credit, an entrepreneurial spirit and the determination to make a living through painting. These earned him a contract with Hammer Galleries in New York City. In 1995, he became an American citizen. "There is no freedom in China like we have in America," he said. "In this country you can paint whatever you want, and that's what I love about it."

For him, creating a painting for the President and First Lady of the United States was a once-in-a-lifetime thrill. "It's a great honor to serve my country," he said. President Bush described the work as "spectacular!" As a double honor to the artist, when the Bushes hosted Chinese President Jiang Zemin at their ranch that October, they gave him the first copy of the White House Christmas gift print bearing Zhen-Huan Lu's art. The 13 1/4 by 17-inch print bore the blind embossed Seal of the President of the United States and the words "Best wishes for a happy holiday. 2002." Hallmark printed 6,600 of them. It was a gift the First Family was happy to give. Each year their gifts included, as well, a limited-edition Christmas ornament for commissioned officers, personal and political friends.

"All Creatures Great and Small"

The theme for the 2002 White House Christmas decorations was "All Creatures Great and Small." Focusing on those creatures that had resided at the White House over the years, the theme was one Mrs. Bush came up with herself after soliciting the staff for ideas. The decorations featured 25 papier-mâché replicas of Presidential pets, each of which was perched on a display table under the portrait of a former President or First Lady. Millie, the beloved springer spaniel, and her puppy Spot felt right at home beneath the portrait of Barbara Bush. The Fords' golden retriever, Liberty, stood below Betty Ford's portrait. Old Ike, the tobacco-chewing ram of Woodrow Wilson, was shown with Edith Boling Wilson. Rob Roy, one of Grace Coolidge's white collies, was paired with Rosalynn Carter. On the mantels in the East Room were Rebecca and Reuben, the pet raccoons of President and Mrs. Coolidge, and three of the sheep that grazed the lawn during the Wilson administration. Greeting visitors elsewhere were models of Macaroni and

Pushinka, pets of Caroline Kennedy; Warren Harding's Laddie Boy; the Johnson dogs, Him and Her; and even a squirrel representing the hundreds that became pets or pests of White House families over the years. The 18-foot tree in the Blue Room was covered with a flock of birds. Artists from every state in the union created an ornament representing a feathered friend native to their state.

Resident pets Barney, Spot and India were also on hand to greet visitors. Spot, born in the White House in 1989, was the only pet to live there during two Presidencies. India, also known as Willie, the shy black cat, had been a family pet since the early 1990s. Barney, the curious two-year-old Scottish terrier, was the President's birthday gift to Mrs. Bush in 2000. One of the most popular of all Presidential pets, Barney became a filmmaker in 2002. Allowed to wander through the White House with a tiny video camera attached to his collar, he conducted his own dog's-eye view tour of the house's decorations. Barney Cam was shown on the White House website, www.whitehouse.gov, doubling its traffic to 20 million hits a day.

While Christmas at the White House in 2001 was certainly somber because of September 11, spirits at Christmas 2002 continued to be guarded. "I think it makes it a very serious holiday," Mrs. Bush said. "This is true here at the White House and all over the United States. It makes it a holiday where we really want to be with our family and where we treasure again the freedoms that we're so fortunate to have as Americans."

2003: "Views of North America" From the Diplomatic Reception Room

The following year the Bushes chose watercolorist Barbara Ernst Prey, of Oyster Bay, New York, to paint the art for their Christmas card. It was at an art exhibit in Maine, while helping a cousin select a Prey painting for her home, that the First Lady met the artist, who is considered one of the foremost active landscape artists in the country. Mrs. Bush especially enjoyed the artist's vivid use of watercolors, as did the President.

When Andrea Ball popped the question by phone, Prey fumbled for words until she was able to say, "I would be honored to do the Christmas card for the President of the United States." After the call, the artist said she went numb. "It was overwhelming to realize that you are going to be working on a commission that will be sent to all the leaders of the free world."

Prey met with Mrs. Bush's Chief of Staff in the spring. "She was absolutely delightful to work with and the whole staff could not have been more helpful," recalled Prey. "They were excited about the prospects of the Christmas card, which means a lot to those who work there." Of the First

Lady, she said, "I have painted for over 30 years and have done many commissions in my life, but she was the easiest to work with. Mrs. Bush respects the creative process and gives the artist space."

A landscape was the First Lady's first idea for a subject. Prey described how together they walked around the North Lawn and South Lawn looking at different views. "It was very helpful to have met her before and to have established a relationship with her," said Prey. "I appreciated the time she took to go with me. Although she didn't tell me what to do, I could see what excited her. It was fun looking at the White House through her eyes."

It was a beautiful day when the artist finally got to sit on the lawn and sketch the White House from life. "That I will never forget," she says. "The dogs came and sat by me, the President's helicopter landed..... It was so wonderful it was practically like being in heaven." To top it off, her gracious hostess invited Prey to join her and the President for dinner to see how the White House looked after dark. A night scene was in the planning.

Only then did Mrs. Bush decide that with nighttime exterior scenes

A watercolor rendering of the Diplomatic Reception Room by Barbara Ernst Prey was the art for the 2003 Presidential card and gift print. HALLMARK CARDS appearing on several Christmas cards of previous administrations, it was time for a fresh approach. Switching back to the interior of the Executive Mansion, she selected five rooms from which to choose. Prey returned to the White House and walked these rooms with the First Lady and Andrea Ball. "Mrs. Bush was so accessible and I really appreciated her letting me see what resonated with her," said the artist. Prey sat and drew small detailed sketches of each of the rooms from life to finish at home in her studio. Although only preliminary works, Mrs. Bush used Prey's sketches of the Blue Room and the State Dining Room for party invitations later that year.

For the Christmas card, Mrs. Bush selected the sketch of the Diplomatic Reception Room, which serves as the family's entrance to the White House from the South Lawn. As its name implies, the room's official function is as the arrival point for diplomats presenting their credentials to the President. "She really chose the perfect setting," said Prey. "She wanted something unique that represented the United States after 9/11."

The beauty of the oval room and its strong colors inspired the artist. Removing chairs and a table, she focused on the simple elegance of fire burning in the fireplace near which Franklin D. Roosevelt used to deliver his fireside chats. A Federal-style wingback armchair in a rich golden fabric flanked each side of the hearth. A small tripod table held a bowl of apples. Adorning the wooden mantel was a fruit-studded holiday garland borrowed from the Christmas decorations.

The Gilbert Stuart painting of George Washington over the mantel presented an exciting challenge for the artist to reproduce. The 19th century panoramic "Views of North America" French wallpaper that was selected by Jacqueline Kennedy also fascinated Prey. "The details took a lot of time," she said, "but it was so much fun because I love color." She added, "The real treat was not just in doing the painting; for me it was being in this historical house in the midst of incredible furnishings and paintings that I had studied in college and that I knew as friends. Being a watercolorist, this room fit in perfectly with my gifts as an artist. It all came together as an amazing experience. One I will never forget."

Mrs. Bush summed up how both she and the President felt about the art Prey painted for their holiday card: "It really is a beautiful fireside that shows the friendliness and warmth of sitting with a friend or sitting in a chair reading by yourself." Another of Prey's paintings hangs in the White House and is part of the Bushes' personal collection.

On November 28, more than 1.5 million Christmas cards bearing a Crawford, Texas, postmark were mailed to the 2003 list of family, friends and all the requisite dignitaries. The Bushes' Scripture selection from Job 10:12 emphasized peace and thanksgiving: "You have granted me life and loving

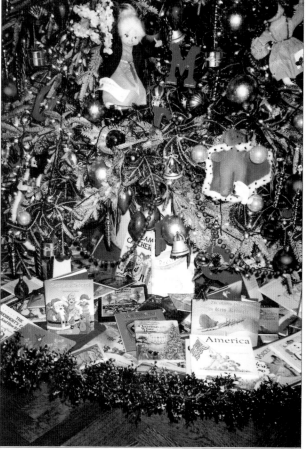

A Blue Room tree skirt of storybooks commemorated the "Season of Stories" holiday theme for 2003. LYNN TURPIN

kindness, and your care has preserved my spirit." Their holiday greeting read: "May you celebrate the joys of faith, family and friendship this holiday season and always. 2003." Prey's painting was reproduced on the card as a tip-on on elegant ecru stock and surrounded by a debossed border. An embossed gold-foil Presidential Seal graced the top of the 7 1/2 x 5 3/8-inch card, while facsimile signatures of George W. Bush and Laura Bush were printed across the bottom. More than 8,000 gift prints were reproduced by Hallmark.

"A Season of Stories"

Reading, always a passion of Mrs. Bush, became the key to her decorations that year as she chose "A Season of Stories" to be the holiday theme. For the Blue Room tree, Mrs. Bush borrowed 80 handmade storybook characters first introduced by Barbara Bush in 1989. Amid the literary ornaments were the likes of Little Red Riding Hood, Rumpelstiltskin, Mary Poppins, Pinocchio, the elephant Babar, Cinderella and Captain Hook. Under the 18-foot Fraser fir from Wisconsin, some 350 storybooks served as a magnificent tree skirt. The tour guide explained, "Santa has delivered piles of books because he knows that a good book is the perfect gift for readers of all ages."

Among the storybook characters selected by former librarian Laura Bush to adorn mantels and pier tables were Curious George; Clifford, the Big Red Dog; the Cat in the Hat; Little Women; Alice in Wonderland; Frog and Toad; the Three Billy Goats Gruff; Harry Potter; the Hardy Boys; and Nancy Drew. As amazing as was the State Dining Room's gingerbread house featuring the Three Little Pigs, the Very Hungry Caterpillar and *Goodnight Moon*, it was matched by the incredible centerpiece on the buffet table in the East Room. There, White House pastry chefs used 50 pounds of chocolate to create an elaborate vignette of *Charlie and the Chocolate Factory*.

After Thanksgiving, 45 volunteers ascended upon the White House to decorate the 19 Christmas trees, various mantels and pier tables. "The

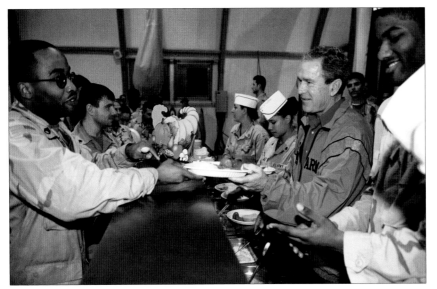

In Baghdad, Iraq, for Thanksgiving, the President mingles with troops to express his gratitude for their service to the country. WHITE HOUSE PHOTO BY TINA HAGER

decorations are spectacular," observed Mrs. Bush. "Every year I think that they are the prettiest, but this year they *are* the prettiest!"

A Dangerous Mission for the President

Thanksgiving 2003 was an anxious time for the Bush White House. Known only to privileged advisors and Mrs. Bush, the Commander-in-Chief had planned a surprise visit to Iraq, where Operation Iraqi Freedom had been in progress since mid-March. His purpose was to show support for America's troops and to share Thanksgiving dinner with them in Baghdad. He told them: "I was just looking for a warm meal somewhere. Thanks for inviting me to dinner." An astonished nation learned about President Bush's mission only after he had left Iraqi airspace and was safely headed home.

Back in Washington, those attending the lighting ceremony of the National Christmas Tree a few days later showed support for the President for his courage in this dangerous mission. Despite the cold, the audience remained standing throughout his entire speech, applauding more than usual and listening to his every word as he honored those serving far from home during the holidays. He said, "Our people in uniform can know that their families miss them and love them, that millions are praying for them and that America is grateful for the many men and women who serve and defend our country."

Within days, on December 13, U.S. military forces captured the fugitive former Iraqi leader Saddam Hussein alive. It was a Christmas present for the Iraqi people as well as all Americans. To the nation the President said: "We've come to this moment through patience and resolve and focused action. And that is our strategy moving forward. The war on terror is a different kind of war waged capture by capture, cell by cell, and victory by victory. Our security is assured by our perseverance and by our sure belief in the success of liberty. And the United States of America will not relent until this war is won."

2004: Red Room Revisited

Four years of an administration pass quickly, with 2004 being election year again—and a busy one for the incumbent President and First Lady. There were places to go and speeches to give. The President found his wife to be one of his best assets in the campaign, and the added responsibility of campaign travel and appearances had to be a real challenge to her already full schedule.

"We really start thinking about Christmas early in the year," admitted Mrs. Bush. "Nancy Clarke always appreciates having the theme for Christmas chosen by March." In 2004, it was a musical theme centering around what the First Lady described as "all those great Christmas songs that we all grew up with like 'Rudolph the Red-Nosed Reindeer,' 'Frosty the Snowman,' 'Rock Around the Christmas Tree,' 'I Saw Mommy Kissing Santa Claus,' songs that George and I loved when we were little and songs that we sang to our girls and which they loved too." The floral shop staff then spent the next seven months executing the 13 vignettes that illustrated the holiday theme. After Thanksgiving, volunteers decorated the 41 trees, various mantels and tables in the White House.

Since 2001, Cindi Holt was one the volunteers who helped decorate the Bush White House. A self-taught artist from Fort Worth, Texas, she started painting in the early '80s. In 1997, while George W. Bush was Governor of Texas, her artwork for the Fort Worth Van Cliburn Piano Competition caught the eye of the event's honorary chairperson, Laura Bush. In 1998, Holt participated in a Celebrity Art Auction for Diabetes and asked Mrs. Bush to be her celebrity. Working at the Governor's Mansion, Holt painted a series of 12 rooms, and her 12 paintings went on tour to five Texas museums. Said the artist: "The Library in particular called to me with its green walls, red chairs and fireplace. It also happened to be Mrs. Bush's favorite room, and she really liked the rendering." As a result, Governor and Mrs. Bush used that painting with slight modifications for their Christmas card in 1998. "I love it when things like this happen," said the artist.

Holt also had the opportunity to help decorate the Governor's Mansion at Christmas. After Governor Bush became President, the Texas volunteers asked if they could continue to do the Christmas decorations for the Bushes in their new home. Getting the nod, under high security and numerous threats, the volunteers set out for Washington two months after September 11. Each was assigned to a different team leader from the White House floral shop. Holt's team decorated the Red Room and Green Room. The following year, in December 2002, she asked if she could do some drawings of the Red Room while at the White House. By spring of 2003, using her fanciful style and lively colors, she had transformed her sketches into a 60 by

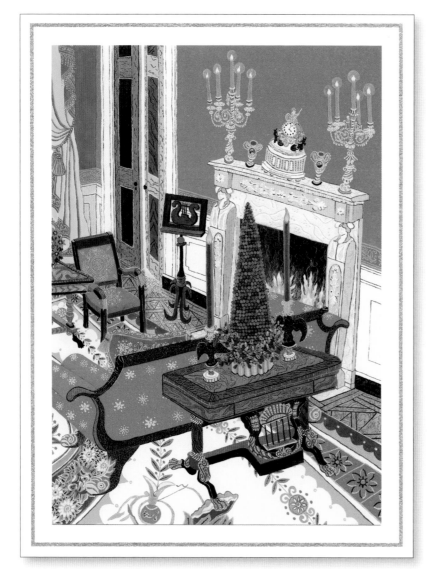

The Red Room, a popular subject of Christmas card art, was painted with an emphasis on light by Cindi Holt for the 2004 Presidential card and gift print. HALLMARK CARDS

50-inch oil painting of the Red Room. She then posted its image on her gallery's website.

After months of fruitless search for an artist to do the 2004 card art, Mrs. Bush viewed Holt's existing rendering of the Red Room online and thought it "the perfect room for a Christmas card. I know that it has been a subject of a lot of Christmas cards over the years because it *is* so perfect."

Working on a Short Deadline

It was June when Andrea Ball called Holt to ask if, in a month, she could execute a new painting with a few modifications. The request came as a surprise, and, because it usually takes the artist two to three months to complete a large-scale painting, the deadline represented a tough challenge. Realizing the importance of this opportunity, Holt agreed to paint a smaller version within the time frame.

The new work needed to be vertical rather than horizontal, however, and the doors to the room were to be left slightly ajar. In keeping with the musical theme of the decorations, Mrs. Bush requested that the artist add a music stand and, for a touch of Christmas, the Red Room's traditional cranberry tree. When Holt researched a music stand to add to the painting, she noticed it matched the carved lyre motif found on the 1825 oak card table in the foreground.

Unlike previous Red Room paintings for the Christmas cards of Presidents Kennedy, Reagan and Clinton, Holt's Matisse-like rendering emphasized the early 19th century French Savonnerie rug more than had the others. Attempting to capture the Grecian motif with her vibrant colors, she said, "I noticed that the lines in the foreground did not match up with the lines by the chair in the background. When I paint something, I try not to erase an 'oops'. I just leave it there. I think this makes for a lively painting, one that is action-packed, in which things are moving."

"The point of the painting," explained the artist, "is about letting your light shine." Inspired by Nelson Mandela's 1994 Inaugural Speech, she said, "As we let our light shine through, others will benefit from it. There is a lot of light in this painting." She hoped that "when people open the envelope and look at the painting on the card, they'll smile." Mrs. Bush said, "I think this is so exuberant and happy, and a really wonderful holiday card."

For their official holiday card, President and Mrs. Bush selected Scripture in keeping with their music theme. Taken from the New International Version, Psalm 95:2 read, "Let us come before Him with Thanksgiving and extol Him with music and song." Music was likewise included in their greeting: "May songs of joy fill your home with warmth and your heart with happiness this holiday season. 2004." A gold embossed Presidential Seal graced the top of the card, while facsimile signatures of George W. Bush and Laura Bush were printed across the bottom.

With the President's bid for reelection a success, more Christmas cards than ever were needed to express their heartfelt greetings to family, friends, campaign workers, supporters and foreign dignitaries around the world. Hallmark printed more than 2 million of the holiday cards bearing the title "'The Red Room, The White House 2004' by Cindi Holt, Oil on Canvas." In addition, Hallmark produced 11,000 of the gift prints.

A Much More Accessible White House

Of the holiday Mrs. Bush said, "Christmas is one of the happiest times at the White House. We get to show off how beautiful the White House looks at the holidays.... Visitors line up and come through. And then, of course, we have lots of parties. We have parties for a lot of people who work here–the White House staff and Secret Service. They get to bring their families, which is fun for us because it is one time of the year that we get to meet their families." About 6,500 guests were invited to receptions in 2004, for which the new executive pastry chef, Thaddeus R. DuBois, made about 24,000 cookies.

Since September 11, 2001, unfortunately, the White House had remained closed to public tours. According to Andrea Ball, "The White House is now much more accessible, but it is not open like it used to be–except to schools and the military. Now you have to contact your Congressman and set up a tour, but there are a lot more of them. For Christmas of 2004 we had a lot more people [an estimated 44,000]; our first Christmas no one came, except those who already had clearance. It was very sad," said Ball. "Now there are a lot of new rules and I have no idea if it will ever change again."

Andrea Ball, who retired after eight years as Mrs. Bush's Chief of Staff, was reflective. "A good thing that did come out of the situation is that there is media coverage of the White House decorations like never before. More people actually see the Executive Mansion at Christmas because of HGTV and all the networks that do segments on the decorations, knowing that people can't visit," she said. "Now everyone gets to see them. People I know can't wait for next year's *Christmas at the White House* special."

Mrs. Bush was pleased to be able to enjoy a few more Christmases at the White House. Before the election, she had wondered, "Is this our last Christmas here or just the first of several more? The whole idea," she said, "everything that goes along with decorating this beautiful house for the holidays is one of the most fun parts of my job, one of the things I really like to do."

Comparing the past to the future, Laura Bush was hopeful. "I think we are still aware of what happened on September 11th and what has happened since. But I think the mood of the country is good," she said. "I think people look at what has happened in Afghanistan.... Women not only can be a part of society now in Afghanistan, but also lined up to vote. And that's what we want to see in Iraq, and the elections that will come in January."

In the President's Christmas message on December 23, he encouraged everyone to especially remember the men and women serving in the military stationed far from home at Christmas. "In Afghanistan, Iraq and elsewhere," he said, "these courageous Americans are fighting the enemies of freedom and protecting our country from danger. By bringing liberty to the oppressed, our troops are defending the freedom and security of us all. They and their families are making many sacrifices for our nation, and all Americans are deeply grateful."

While spending Christmas at the Camp David Presidential retreat with family members, the President showed his own gratitude by placing telephone calls on Christmas Eve to 10 members of the Armed Forces, six of whom were serving in Iraq. He personally wanted to thank them for their sacrifice and service and to wish them a Merry Christmas.

His post-Christmas vacation at his Texas ranch was spent formulating goals for his second term, which included Social Security reforms and possible future nominations to the Supreme Court. The last week of 2004 was also devoted to thinking about what he wanted to tell the American peo-

For the 2005 Presidential Christmas card and gift print, Jamie Wyeth painted an angular view of the Truman Balcony and Andrew Jackson magnolia, with Bush Family pets in the snow. HALLMARK CARDS

ple on January 20 in his Inaugural Address as well as preparing for the State of the Union speech.

2005: Presidential Pets in the Painting

To do the painting for their Christmas card in 2005, the Bushes chose a popular contemporary artist who was no stranger to White House art. Jamie Wyeth had executed the South Portico of the White House for President and Mrs. Reagan in 1981. His focus at that time was on the single lighted window of the First Lady's dressing room in an otherwise darkened house on Christmas Eve. Three years later, when the Reagans repeated the invitation, Wyeth was inspired to paint a lone squirrel approaching the North Portico on Christmas morning. On both occasions, the artist incorporated the exterior of the Executive Mansion in his work.

Commenting on his White House experience, Wyeth told *The Phil Archives*, "I love the White House. To me, it's the nation's house. The White House never changes. What changes are the occupants and also their animals." Wyeth had observed that Ronald Reagan fed the White House squirrels and that George and Laura Bush had their own menagerie of four-legged friends. So, as a definable point of interest, he decided to incorporate in the 2005 Christmas card the Presidential pets: dogs Barney and Miss Beazley and the cat, India.

The backdrop for these frolicking White House pets was the artist's snowy winter scene on the South Lawn. Wyeth chose an angular perspective of the Truman Balcony flanked on the left by the magnolia tree planted by Andrew Jackson in memory of his wife. "I painted it right there on the White House lawn," Wyeth recalled. While the two Scottish terriers enjoyed playing together outside, he discovered that "the cat never leaves the house. I asked if they could just bring it out to the South Lawn. They did and it immediately began running toward the gates, with me and the Secret Service running after it. Thank God we caught it. I almost got it squished," he admitted.

Unlike the President's parents, who in 1991 had nixed a Mark Hampton painting of the Oval Office that was to show Millie, their springer spaniel, the younger Bushes loved Wyeth's composition with its inclusion of their beloved pets. His original art of mixed media covered a 10 1/8 by 15-inch board. Unveiling it to the media at the White House press preview, Laura Bush expressed her appreciation: "Jamie, thank you very, very much. It's absolutely beautiful."

Entitled "The Jackson Magnolia With Barney, Miss Beazley, and India Bush. The White House, 2005," the realistic work was reproduced by Hallmark Cards, Inc. The insert page carried the following message in gold script: "With best wishes for a holiday season of hope and happiness 2005." A gold embossed Presidential Seal appeared above what had become a Bush tradition, a verse from the Bible: "The Lord is my strength and my shield; In Him my heart trusts; So I am helped, and my heart exults, and with my song I give thanks to Him." (Psalm 28:7, RSV) Facsimile signatures of George W. Bush and Laura Bush in black ink completed the holiday greeting on the 5 1/4 x 7 1/2-inch card. The Republican National Committee confirmed the purchase of 1.28 million Presidential Christmas cards and 7,400 gift prints. President and Mrs. Bush proudly sent them to family and friends, supporters and dignitaries at home and in 200 countries abroad. This year, however, instead of spreading Christmas cheer, the President's card fueled a cultural dispute.

Christmas Card Controversy

Soon after its arrival in more than a million mailboxes, the card got caught in the cross fire of an ensuing battle between conservatives and corporations. The year 2005 was one when conservative groups pressured national chain stores to advertise "Christmas sales" rather than "holiday specials." Consumers were organized to boycott retailers who refused to recognize the day. Some viewed the omission of the word *Christmas* from the President's card as another blow to their efforts. Joseph Farah, editor of the conservative WorldNetDaily.com website, claims he discarded his White House card as soon as he received it. What was being called a "war on Christmas" escalated even more.

Consistent with his practice since being elected President, and even as Governor of Texas, George W. Bush had sent out an official card that extended holiday wishes instead of a "Merry Christmas" greeting. Now, however, he was accused of secularizing Christmas. The fact that he was the only U.S. President ever to incorporate a Bible verse on his Christmas card was not

The 18-foot Blue Room tree was decorated with fresh white lilies, garland and clear crystal ornaments. WHITE HOUSE PHOTO BY SHEALAH CRAIGHEAD

enough. The media frenzy spread the debate as far away as Australia.

Susan Whitson, Laura Bush's press secretary, responded, "Certainly President and Mrs. Bush, because of their faith, celebrate Christmas." She explained, "It's a time when we welcome all different faiths. The President has an obligation to acknowledge that.... Their cards in recent years have included best wishes for a holiday season, rather than Christmas wishes, because they were sent to people of all faiths." George and Barbara Bush were the last First Family to extend a "Merry Christmas" as part of the greeting on a Presidential Christmas card.

"All Things Bright and Beautiful"

Despite the controversy, the White House was made ready for its holiday guests. These included the 45,000 visitors who would come to see the Christmas decorations and the 9,500 people who were invited to one of the receptions during the holidays. Laura Bush chose to decorate the White House following the theme "All Things Bright and Beautiful." She told the press, "We wanted to use real and fresh flowers and garlands and fruits, and that's what we've done." Buffet tables were covered with 5-foot topiaries, made with layers of lemon leaves and tangerines. Hot-pink French tulips filled silver pedestal bowls accented by a collar of green pears. The mantels were decorated with rose topiaries and garlands of fresh boxwood. The centerpiece in the Blue Room was an 18-foot Christmas tree adorned with fresh white lilies, garland and clear crystal ornaments, all enhanced with white lights. The simple yet elegant decorations from nature awakened the senses of sight, taste and smell as a reminder that all God's creations are beautiful.

At the Pageant of Peace on December 1, the President applauded the annual ceremony with the words: "The lighting of the National Christmas Tree is one of the great traditions in our Nation's Capital. Each year, we gather here to celebrate the season of hope and joy—and to remember the story of one humble life that lifted the sights of humanity."

Over the next few weeks, the President delivered appropriate greetings to those who observed Hanukkah, to those who observed Kwanzaa and to those who celebrated Christmas. In his message on December 19, he revealed his heart, his hope and his faith in his country. He said:

More than 2,000 years ago, a virgin gave birth to a Son, and the God of Heaven came to Earth. Mankind had received its Savior, and to those who had dwelled in darkness, the light of hope had come. Each Christmas, we celebrate that first coming anew, and we rejoice in the knowledge that the God who came to Earth that night in Bethlehem is with us still and will remain with us forever.

Christmas is a season of hope and joy, a time to give thanks for the blessing of Christ's birth and for the blessings that surround us every day of the year. We have much to be thankful for in this country, and we have a responsibility to help those in need. Jesus calls us to help others, and acts of kindness toward the less fortunate fulfill the spirit of the Christmas season.

On Christmas, we pray for freedom, justice, and peace on Earth. We remember those who have made the ultimate sacrifice for our country and for our freedom, and we ask for God's blessing on their loved ones. We ask God to watch over all of our men and women in uniform. Many are serving in distant lands, helping to advance the cause of freedom and peace. Our entire Nation is grateful to them and prays for their safe return.

Laura and I send our best wishes for a blessed and merry Christmas.

2006: The Oval Office in December

The following year, President and Mrs. Bush chose a fellow Texan, James Blake, to create the art for their 2006 Christmas card. The artist was painting in Paris when he received the call from Fort Worth interior designer Ken Blasingame. Happy to oblige the First Family, Blake met Blasingame and Laura Bush in July for a tour of the White House. Mrs. Bush suggested that the art for the card feature the Oval Office.

Known for his still lifes and landscapes, Blake took photographs and made several drawings of the President's office and porch. Back in his studio in Fort Worth, the representational artist created a preliminary painting for the White House in which he portrayed the exterior of the Oval Office on a snowy day in December. The blue-gray sky, the gray cast on the house and the charcoal-colored limbs of the trees were a flash from his past. Having grown up in the Midwest, he remembered, "It was always a gray day when it snowed." He depicted the yellow walls in the Oval Office as "the sun shining

The Oval Office on a snowy December day was the subject of James Blake's 2006 Presidential card and gift print art. HALLMARK CARDS

through the gloom." The warm glow from the President's office was a cheerful invitation to "come in from the cold when the day is winding down," he said. Blake admitted that he took artistic license to create the kinds of trees he desired and reposition them and the shrubs strategically where he needed them. "I wanted the painting to be easygoing and loose," he said. "Normally my work tends to get tight, but I didn't want that for this picture."

The snowy scene originally included a 2-inch red border that both Mrs. Bush and Blasingame rejected. The blanket of snow was also an issue, but the artist could not imagine a winter landscape without it. "Snow was always a big part of Christmas when I was growing up," he said. While snow was not prominent in her original idea, the First Lady gave Blake freedom of expression in his work. She revealed her pleasure with "the beautiful Christmas card" in writing as well as at the press party in November. "Thank you so much, Jim," she said, "I appreciate it very much."

For the sixth consecutive year, the White House selected Hallmark Cards, Inc., to reproduce the Bushes' card. The exclusive design was entitled,

"The Oval Office in December. The White House, 2006." The 15 x 10-inch oil on canvas appeared as a tip-on on an elegant ecru card stock with a deckle edge. An embossed gold foil Presidential Seal highlighted the insert page. Under the seal were the words from Psalm 119:105: "Thy word is a lamp unto my feet, and a light unto my path." The traditional Bush Bible verse was followed by the greeting "May the light of the season shine bright in your heart now and in the new year." It was dated 2006 and bore facsimile signatures of George W. Bush and Laura Bush. The card measured 7 1/2 x 5 1/4 inches. While the return address on the envelope was The White House, Washington, D.C., the cards were postmarked in Crawford, Texas.

Hallmark printed 985,000 official cards and 7,600 of the 17 by 13-inch prints, which the First Family used as gifts to their White House staff. Whether or not bowing to the pressure of the previous year, the simple message on the gift print read: "Merry Christmas and Happy New Year 2006." Dan Stifter, Hallmark's project leader for the White House order, was thrilled to be able to be involved with it. For what was to be the 39th Christmas card Hallmark had produced for a President, his team began collaborating with President and Mrs. Bush in June. Said Stifter, "I am honored that Hallmark was once again chosen to help the Bush family continue the important annual tradition of sending holiday cards."

"Deck the Halls and Welcome All"

In March, Laura Bush started brainstorming with White House Chief Florist Nancy Clarke to determine the theme for the 2006 Christmas decorations. Inspired by the beautiful colors in the Red Room, the theme "Deck the Halls and Welcome All" was implemented through a predominant use of reds and greens. Red ornament balls, red carnations in vermeil containers, red poinsettias nestled into silvered pots as well as fashioned into trees provided a dramatic complement to the boughs of green, spiral evergreen trees, ivy topiaries and the forest of illuminated trees on the buffet tables.

Having decked the halls, the First Lady welcomed all to enjoy the splendor of her beautiful home beginning on November 30, which was to be a most busy day. It began with a showing of its holiday finery to America by way of the morning talk shows on ABC, CBS and NBC. Following that came her press preview of the sparkling White House decorations. At noon she held a reception for those who had decorated the house and designed the art for the card, the guidebook and their Christmas invitation. Meanwhile, Mrs. Bush was awaiting the return of the President from Jordan to help her host that evening's first party of the season. There would be a total of 24 parties over a period of 20 days. Considering the pressures placed upon President and Mrs. Bush, guests reported that both of them demonstrated "grace under fire."

With a growing rebellion among political factions at home over the war in Iraq, President Bush had flown to Amman, Jordan, to talk with Prime Minister Nouri al-Maliki in an effort to build and strengthen their recent rocky relationship. Their meeting came after 12 million Iraqis had cast their ballots in the country's first-ever free election. It was prior to the release of the Baker-Hamilton report that would call for accelerating the transition of responsibility for unity in the region into Iraq's hands. In view of the escalating violence in Baghdad, the President assured Maliki that he was committed to keeping U.S. troops in Iraq as long as the leaders mutually agreed that a U.S. military presence was needed for stability. Both understood that the future of Iraq rested with the Iraqi government.

Appreciation From the Commander-in-Chief

Children of deployed troops were the guests of President and Mrs. Bush at the Children's Christmas Party at the White House on December 4. The President said by way of welcome, "Thank you very much for supporting your mom and dad as they're on a very important mission for our country. I want you to know that they love you dearly, and the American people love and respect those who wear the uniform a lot." To entertain the children, Mrs. Bush introduced young actors from the Kennedy Center who performed scenes from the play *Willy Wonka and the Chocolate Factory*. She then encouraged her guests to go to the library, check out the book and read the whole story for themselves.

On December 18, the President expressed his deep appreciation to the men and women of the United States Armed Forces:

During this hopeful time of year, the hearts of Americans are filled with gratitude for the many blessings in our lives. We are especially thankful for the priceless gift of freedom that our armed forces help defend by serving the cause of peace and standing watch over our security. As courageous soldiers, sailors, airmen, marines, and coast guardsmen, you have set aside comfort and convenience to protect the rest of us, earning the respect of a grateful Nation and a proud Commander-in-Chief.

Many of you are confronting our adversaries abroad and observing the holidays in places far from home, but you are close to our hearts. You are serving at a time when our Nation needs you, and your fellow citizens appreciate the many sacrifices that you and your families are making every day. Over the holidays and throughout the New Year, we will continue to ask the Almighty to bestow His care on you and your loved ones.

Laura and I wish each of you a safe and joyous holiday season. May God bless and watch over you, and may God bless America.

President and Mrs. Bush participated in a service project at Walter Reed Army Medical Center on December 22 to express their gratitude to the volunteers who were there to help the families of troops injured in combat. On Christmas Eve, while celebrating Christmas with his family at Camp David, the President made phone calls to numerous members of the armed forces who were stationed overseas or who had recently returned from duty. Expressing that the men and women in uniform weighed heavily on his heart, he thanked them for their service and wished them a Merry Christmas.

2007: Sculpture in the First Lady's Garden

To paint the art for their 2007 Christmas card, the Bushes selected one of the Southwest's noted watercolorists, David Drummond, from Albuquerque, New Mexico. Widely known for his detailed and expressive paintings of water and rock around Glen Canyon's Lake Powell, he had had many of his paintings exhibited in his city's Arts in the Parks show. "Art is about communication and beauty," said Drummond. "I paint what I love to look at, hoping to bring that same emotion to the viewer."

As honorary chairperson of the National Park Foundation, Mrs. Bush became aware of his art when the foundation purchased one of his paintings. In May, Drummond received a phone call from the First Lady's Chief of Staff, Anita McBride, who asked if he would create a painting for the 2007 official Christmas card. The artist admitted that he was flattered to be chosen for the honor.

The Drummonds met Mrs. Bush at the White House in early July. "She spent quite a lot of time in the morning with my wife and me, showing us the pool and statue she wanted to be the subject of the painting," the artist reported. "She was very specific about the subject and I was very taken by the location. I took a lot of photos that day and asked for as many reference photos as possible of that area in winter. I had to create an image of the pool in winter, even though I had never seen it except in July."

Against the background of the East Wing Entrance Hall, Drummond focused on *The Little Gardener* originally commissioned by First Lady Jacqueline Kennedy and sculpted by Sylvia Shaw Judson. Noted McBride, "That particular year there was a Christmas tree in the position you see behind the statue. In other years, there were other large Christmas decorations."

Drummond's work was approved in mid-September. The proofs of *East Colonnade Depicting Sylvia Shaw Judson's Gardener in the Jacqueline Kennedy Garden* were given final approval by the artist at the Hallmark Cards offices in Kansas City and printed in Hallmark's plant in Lawrence, Kansas. It was

First Lady Jacqueline Kennedy commissioned *The Little Gardener* sculpture that was executed by Sylvia Shaw Judson. It became the subject of David Drummond's watercolor for the 2007 official Presidential card.

HALLMARK CARDS

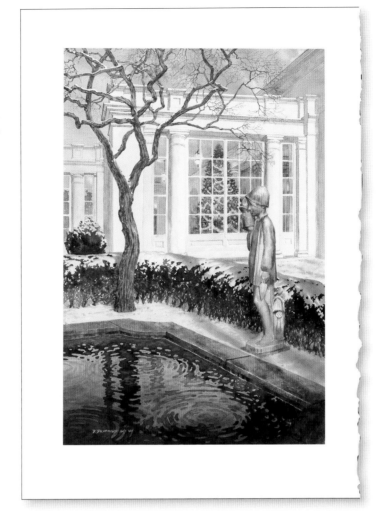

the 40th official card created for the White House by Hallmark, which also produced that year's Christmas card for Vice President and Mrs. Dick Cheney.

As a tip-on on elegant stock with a deckle edge, the 2007 card featured an embossed gold-foil Presidential Seal. Following their tradition, the Bushes chose a scripture verse for the insert page, this one from Nehemiah 9:6 (NIV): "You alone are the Lord. You made the heavens, even the highest heavens, and all their starry host, the earth and all that is on it, the seas and all that is in them. You give life to everything, and the multitudes of heaven worship you." The 5 1/4 x 7 1/2-inch card also included a brief personal message: "May the joy of all creation fill your heart this blessed season." According to a White House press release of November 29, the First Couple sent 895,000 official Christmas cards to their friends, family and foreign dignitaries.

East Colonnade was placed on display in the East Corridor of the White

House throughout the holidays, after which the artist donated the painting with all reproduction rights to the White House permanent collection. "Just to be in their collection is a tremendous honor," Drummond said.

"Holiday in the National Parks"

Early in the year, Laura Bush and White House Chief Florist Nancy Clarke had discussed plans for the holidays and agreed that it would be fun to celebrate the national parks. Most people do not know that the White House is a national park and that its lawns, gardens and façade are maintained by the National Park Service.

In her remarks at the media preview of the White House decorations, Mrs. Bush said:

> *This year we're celebrating America's national parks, in the lead-up to the National Park Centennial ... in 2016. We think that our national parks are more precious than gold to the United States. They're our major and most fabulous and magnificent landscapes, from Yosemite to Denali to the Everglades. But they are also our sacred historical sites.... The White House is a national park. All the White House grounds and the façade of the White House are taken care of by National Park employees. President's Park across the street, Lafayette Square, is also part of the national park—the White House National Park.*

Following up on that sentiment, the First Lady chose "Holiday in the National Parks" as the theme for her holiday decorations. She came up with the idea, she said, because "I hike in the national parks every year." In preparation for the 100th anniversary of the national parks in 2016, President Bush and Secretary of the Interior Dirk Kempthorne issued a challenge to the National Park Service to raise private funds as well as to the Congress to appropriate more money for the national parks prior to the centennial.

The theme was carried out by sending each of the 391 national parks a globe-shaped ornament with the request that an artist be selected to decorate it in a way that depicted that park. As a result, 347 national parks were represented on the White House Blue Room tree, among them ornaments from Fort McHenry National Site, where Francis Scott Key wrote the National Anthem; Crossroads National Battlefield; the Grand Tetons; Glacier National Park; and the San Antonio Missions National Park. The most recently established national park—Flight 93 National Memorial, near Shanksville, Pennsylvania—sent an ornament in keeping with its status as crash site of the ill-fated 9/11 flight.

In the Cross Hall were magnificent paintings depicting Angels Falls in

Zion National Park and the Grand Canyon from Hope Point. Both were created by the Bushes' 2001 card artist, Adrian Martinez, and displayed in the two niches. Greeting the 60,000 guests visiting the President's House during the holidays were models of Cape Hatteras Lighthouse in North Carolina, as well as Mount Rushmore and the Statue of Liberty.

The public toured the house by day, while invited guests attended one of 25 holiday receptions hosted by President and Mrs. Bush. Most Americans, however, viewed the decorations and ornaments on television when the major networks interviewed the First Lady. In addition, they got a peek at the 300-pound white chocolate gingerbread house featuring Presidential pets Barney, Miss Beazley and India hosting many animal residents of the national parks.

In his Christmas message to the American people on December 21, President Bush said:

At this special time of the year, we give thanks for Christ's message of love and mercy, and we are reminded of our responsibility to serve. America is blessed to have fine citizens who reach out with a compassionate hand to help brothers and sisters in need. We also remember our brave men and women in uniform who have volunteered to defend us in distant lands. Many of those who have answered the call of duty will spend Christmas far from home and separated from family. We honor their sacrifice, ask God to watch over them and their families, and pray for a safe return.

On Christmas Eve, the President spoke personally by telephone with 10 members of the Armed Forces who were stationed overseas. He wished them a Merry Christmas and thanked them for their service to the nation.

2008: "A Red, White and Blue Christmas"

For the President's eighth Christmas in office, George and Laura Bush chose to celebrate with "A Red, White and Blue Christmas." Mixing buntings with garland was a perfect fit for the 2008 election year and their final holiday season at the White House. Not only was it a theme that many Americans had suggested over the years but also one that was patriotic, all the way from the fife and drum corps marching across the lawn of the giant gingerbread house to the ornaments on the Blue Room tree.

Members of Congress each invited an artist from their districts to decorate an ornament in the American spirit to represent their community. North Carolina Congressman Robin Hayes selected Teresa Thibault to create his 8th District's ornament. Along with 368 others, her lighthouse-decorated ornament found a home on the Blue Room tree, a beautiful Fraser fir from Crumpler, North Carolina. Mrs. Bush was partial to the Texas ornaments featuring the state flag, the state butterfly and the armadillo. There was also one designed with a "jackalope that everyone in Texas says really exists—the jackrabbit with horns," she explained, but admitted to never having seen one. The youngest artist, 8-year-old Katie Schools, was selected by Congressman Eric Cantor of Virginia's 7th District. Though suffering from a brain tumor, she painted the state bird, a cardinal. To represent New York's 2nd District, Congressman Steve Israel selected 90-year-old Tom Deluca, the oldest artist, who painted Teddy Roosevelt of Sagamore Hill. The First Lady was delighted to meet all the artists at a White House reception she held later for them.

Although the holiday season was a very festive and happy time for the First Family, for Mrs. Bush, as her last one as First Lady, it was bittersweet. "It's fun to get to do this," she told Claire Shipman of ABC News. "No house decorates in a more beautiful way than the White House."

The White House also went "green" at Christmas in 2008. Chief Florist Nancy Clarke recycled nearly 400 red ornaments that had previously been used for holiday decorations. Because the President loved the outdoors, the tree in his Oval Office was adorned with 2007's ornaments showcasing the national parks. Returning to their respective mantels from 2001 were the miniature homes of former Presidents. For energy savings, LED lights were used on all 27 trees in the house.

In the booklet describing the decorations for visitors, the Bushes included the following greeting:

Thank you for joining us for "A Red, White and Blue Christmas" at the White House. This year's theme celebrates the patriotic spirit that unites us as Americans. During this hopeful season we are reminded of the blessings of freedom that we enjoy, and we renew our sense of what is important in our lives...

We are grateful to the White House Executive Residence staff, artists from around the country and many volunteers for decorating the White House red, white and blue! Thanks to their creativity and hard work, this year's holiday decorations reflect the best of the American spirit.

A View From the Truman Balcony
The Bushes' final White House Christmas card depicted a nostalgic view from the Truman Balcony by Tim Allen Lawson, a landscape painter from Rockport, Maine. As the son-in-law of historian David McCullough, Lawson had been to the White House before, but never to the family's residence, where he met Laura Bush. Before the First Lady's extensive tour of the

residence and the rest of the house, she showed the artist a favorite view from the Truman Balcony.

The scene of the Washington Monument and the Jefferson Memorial beyond the South Lawn was fabulous. Immediately everything clicked for the artist as he envisioned the whole panorama in a setting wintry sun. He asked Mrs. Bush if he could return to the balcony in the late afternoon to make some drawings, and she said it could be arranged.

After lunch, Sara Armstrong, the First Lady's Deputy Chief of Staff, accompanied Lawson back up to the residence with the materials he had brought with him. Propping his board against the back of a chair, he sat on the edge of the window and began sketching the railing and architectural details of the column. "I have a tendency to lose all sense of time when I am working," he recalled. "I did several compositions to give me a better sense of proportion as I waited for that early evening light to make some color compositions. As I concentrated on my drawing, I was struck by the detail and overall beauty of the White House. When you sit and study it for several hours, it was just breathtaking how beautiful the White House is as an architectural structure. I felt very blessed and privileged to sit there for over three hours and study it, particularly from that residential level."

Because the President and First Lady were expected to be leaving later by heli-

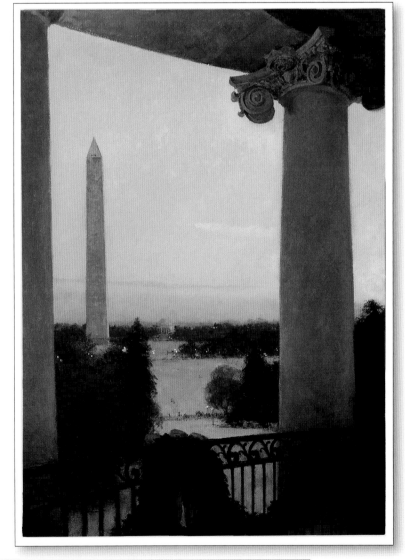

A late-day wintry view from the Truman Balcony was the subject of Tim Allen Lawson's oil painting for the 2008 official Presidential Christmas card, the last one President and Mrs. Bush would send.

copter from the South Lawn, the artist was instructed not to go near the railing, as it could be perceived as threatening. Totally absorbed in his task, he soon forgot about their departure until he suddenly heard a voice: "Who the hell is on my balcony?"

At first glance, Lawson didn't recognize the speaker. "Of course it is the President," he realized, surmising that no one had told him of the artist's presence. "I jumped up; my drawing toppled over and the pencils fell to the floor. As fast as I could, I tried to explain myself and who I was. I only got a few sentences out before he burst out laughing and said, 'Calm down, I know exactly who you are. I am the President and I just came in from my office to do a little paperwork before I leave this evening. I saw you blocking my view through the window.'"

The two stood on the balcony talking for quite a while about mutual acquaintances. "It was one of the most delightful conversations I have ever had," stated the artist. "I was slightly embarrassed about jumping up and making a fool of myself, but he had a wonderful sense of humor about the whole thing. He was dressed informally, with his tie loose about his neck and his sleeves rolled up.

"It was so pleasant; he made my whole day," concluded Lawson. "As I stood there talking with the President, I had a hard time believing it was happening. I wanted to pinch myself. I just wished that someone could have been with me to verify my dream. It was a day I will never forget."

Back in his studio in Maine, the artist painted the landscape in oil. There was no snow in Washington the day he visited the White House, so official photographers sent pictures of snow on the South Lawn. Although the trees had actually begun to leaf out, he made them dormant and moved others around to create abstract shapes. The monuments were in the right place to capture this view from the Truman Balcony. "I think they liked it," said Lawson. "It was an extreme honor to have the opportunity to paint for them."

Per instructions from the White House, Hallmark printed 1.25 million cards on recycled paper. Said Hallmark spokesperson Deidre Mize, "This is their effort to continue to go green, or make changes that will help the environment. I know it's an important issue for everybody, including the White House."

The 2008 Christmas card featured art as a tip-on on elegant stock with a debossed edge. The insert page featured an embossed gold-foil Presidential Seal, a Bible verse and a personal message. For the first time, the scripture was a New Testament verse, Matthew 5:16: "Let your light so shine before men, that they may see your good works, and glorify your Father which is in heaven." Their sentiment read, "May your heart and home be filled with the joys of the holiday season." The facsimile signatures of George and Laura Bush completed the page. The card measured 5 1/6 x 7 7/16 inches.

Speaking to the nation and a capacity D.C. crowd at his last official Pageant of Peace on December 4, the President remarked,

> *Today we celebrate the 85th anniversary of the National Christmas Tree lighting. In times of calm, and in times of challenge, Americans have gathered for this ceremony. The simple story we remember during the season speaks to every generation. It is the story of a humble birth in a quiet town, and the story of one life that changed millions more. For two millennia, the story of Christmas has brought joy to families, comfort to communities, and hope to hearts around the world. During Christmas we celebrate the blessings of the season, and the blessings that surround us every day. And the greatest of these blessings is freedom–the Almighty's gift to every man, woman, and child on the face of the Earth.*

Just nine months into his Presidency, the United States of America came under attack by terrorists the President described as "enemies of freedom."

"And today," he said, "we give thanks to the brave men and women who protect the American people by defending freedom around the world. Over the past eight years, my greatest honor as President has been serving as Commander-in-Chief of the finest military ever known."

Christmas of 2008 was a poignant one for the Bushes. They often found themselves talking wistfully about the First Families who had lived in the President's House before them and the national challenges and personal tragedies that each had faced. It was also nostalgic to conduct personal tours of their home for President-elect and Mrs. Obama. Said Mrs. Bush, "There's a great tradition of transition in the United States, welcoming the next family in and giving that tour and showing the next family what it's going to be like." From the life stories of all First Families, President and Mrs. Bush had the assurance that just as they had faced unique challenges in their eight years in the White House, America had the stability and security to face any new challenge that came its way.

THE OBAMAS
Christmas at the People's House

*T*raditions do not define the President. The President defines his own traditions. Every four or eight years a new family comes to the White House with a fresh personality and philosophy. In 2009 Barack Obama and his wife, Michelle, left Chicago to bring hope and change to Washington; they envisioned the White House as "the People's House."

To set their own tone for their administration, the Obamas brought in a close personal friend and corporate executive as the White House Social Secretary. Desirée Rogers was responsible for coordinating every event—from the Easter egg roll to Christmas parties and state dinners. Working closely in sync with the Obamas' philosophy of inclusiveness, Rogers' assignment was to carry out the persona of the President and First Lady and "to make their social events reflect their sensibilities." With the support of Mrs. Obama, she set out to open the doors of the People's House to all Americans.

2009: "Reflect, Rejoice and Renew"

Early in the year, former social secretaries hosted a luncheon to welcome Rogers to their group. According to Sheryl Gay Stolberg of the *New York Times*, Rogers surprised them by announcing that the Obamas were reaching out to all faiths with their plans for a "non-religious Christmas."

Facing page: The President and First Lady, posing before the 2009 Blue Room tree, prepare to launch their first Christmas season in the White House. WHITE HOUSE PHOTO BY LAWRENCE JACKSON

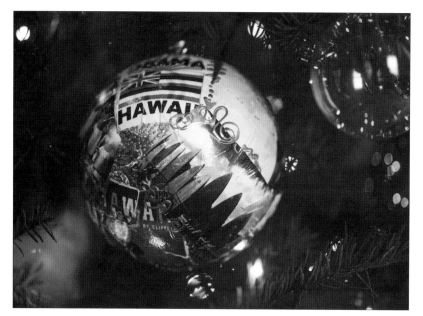

The President's home state of Hawaii was represented on the Blue Room tree by this ornament. WHITE HOUSE PHOTO BY CHUCK KENNEDY

When questioned about displaying the crèche in the East Room, she replied that "the Obamas did not intend to put the manger scene on display—a remark that drew an audible gasp from the tight-knit social secretary sister-hood," Stolberg wrote. Later, a spokesperson for the First Lady confirmed that the 18th century antique Baroque crèche acquired in 1967 would be on display in the East Room, in keeping with tradition.

Holiday planning began in the summer. At the holiday press preview on December 2, Mrs. Obama stated, "Our starting point was a very simple idea: that we include as many people, in as many places, in as many ways as we can." She explained how they chose the 2009 holiday theme, "Reflect, Rejoice and Renew."

"For the Obama family, Christmas and the New Year has always been a time to reflect on our many blessings," she said, "to rejoice in the pleasure of spending time with our family and our friends, and to renew our commit-ment to one another and to the causes that we believe in. And I wanted to continue that part of the tradition during our first holiday season here at the White House."

Mindful of the tight economic times, the First Lady's staff recycled about 800 ornaments from previous administrations and sent them to 60 community groups throughout the country. Individuals were requested to refurbish and decorate them with a favorite landmark and return them to the White House to be displayed on the Blue Room tree.

The 18 1/2-foot Fraser fir was decorated with nearly 700 repurposed ornaments amidst wide-ribbon garland, low-voltage LED lights and an organic tree skirt. Cherished Chicago landmarks, such as the Lincoln Park

Zoo, the Art Institute of Chicago, the DuSable Museum of African American History, and the old Chicago Theatre, had a strong showing.

Other landmark ornaments commemorated the Statue of Liberty, the Kennedy Space Center, Davy Crockett Park in Tennessee and the Ronald Reagan Presidential Library. Critics took issue with the inclusion on an American President's tree of Andy Warhol's *Mao Zedong*, the late Chinese Communist dictator, not to mention the Mount Rushmore landmark with the imaginative addition of President Obama's face.

Ninety-two volunteers from 24 states spent more than 3,400 hours decorating the White House. With the retirement of Chief White House Florist Nancy Clarke, the overall Christmas décor became the project of Creative Decorator Simon Doonan from Barney's of New York. Inspiration for the Obamas' maiden Christmas came from the Georgian style of the house itself. Traditional decorations reflected the scale, architecture and color of each room. Natural materials including hydrangea, magnolias, honeysuckle vine and pepper berries were integrated in the trees and wreaths throughout the State Rooms. The 390-pound gingerbread house came complete with Mrs. Obama's vegetable garden on the South Lawn; a strategically positioned cutout enabled visitors to see into the State Dining Room with its illuminated chandelier and dark chocolate furniture. The vegetables as well as First Dog Bo, the family's Portuguese water dog, were made of marzipan.

Katherine Skiba of the *Chicago Tribune* described the Obamas' first Christmas at the White House as "grand, glorious and green." They received 50,000 guests and hosted 27 parties and receptions requiring hundreds of thousands of cookies, candies, cakes and brownies for the holiday crowd. To accommodate even more people, the Obamas chose to dispense with formal receiving lines and individual photographs.

Hope and Happiness

For their first official Christmas card, President and Mrs. Obama chose a simple but elegant card featuring a gold-foil embossed Presidential Seal encircled by a gold-foil embossed wreath. The ecru card stock, selected by White House staff, bore the words "Season's Greetings 2009." A thin burgundy border framed the front of the 5 3/4 x 9 1/4-inch card. The design was likened to the simple style of the Christmas cards used by President and Mrs. Eisenhower throughout their eight years in the White House. Printed in gold ink, the Obamas' holiday message read: "May your family have a joyous holiday season and a new year blessed with hope and happiness." The signatures of Barack Obama and Michelle Obama were printed in black below the sentiment.

American Greetings Corp., the nation's largest publicly traded greeting card manufacturer, was selected to reproduce cards for the President and Vice President.

Although the Democratic National Committee (DNC) paid for the cards, a spokesperson declined to give details of quantity or cost. According to Associated Press reporter Nancy Benac, "Several hundred thousand have been mailed out," an unconfirmed number that paled in comparison with the 1.25 million sent by George and Laura Bush in 2008.

The holiday cards were mailed to members of Congress, the media, government officials, foreign dignitaries, family and friends. Ever since the Nixon administration, the official Christmas card of the President had traditionally been used as a thank you to political supporters. In the aftermath of the Obamas' first Christmas, the Politico website reported that a number of donors were upset because "some of the Obamas' biggest fund-raisers ... didn't even get a Christmas card." Even though a frameable keepsake had been given to the White House staff as a gift every year since President Hoover was in office, the traditional gift print based on the official Presidential card was passed up for Christmas of 2009.

On December 3, before a crowd of thousands, President Obama spoke at the 87th lighting of the National Christmas Tree. He began by recalling how the D.C. public schools were instrumental in starting the tree-lighting

The 2009 official Presidential card featured a text message in a simple but elegant setting. AMERICAN GREETINGS

Season's Greetings
2009

May your family have
a joyous holiday season
and a new year blessed
with hope and happiness.

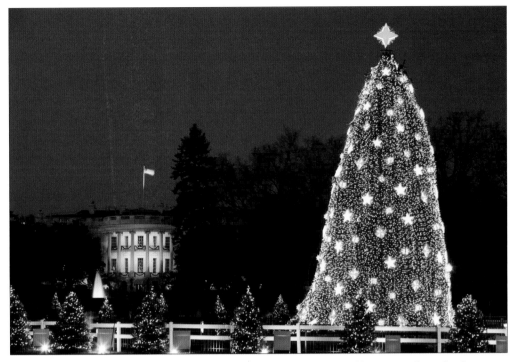

The White House and the National Christmas Tree are illuminated at dusk on the Ellipse in Washington, D.C. WHITE HOUSE PHOTO BY CHUCK KENNEDY

event on the Ellipse and recited the story of a child born to parents guided only by faith "who would ultimately spread a message that has endured for more than 2,000 years—that no matter who we are or where we are from, we are each called to love one another as brother and sister."

The Chief Executive also remembered the mothers and fathers, sons and daughters of the military who daily risked their lives to keep America free. Then he addressed his daughters, Malia and Sasha, and the First Lady.

"So, guys, come up here. I need some assistance. I'm technologically challenged and I might not get this right," he jested. "So we are going to do a countdown starting from five. Everybody has got to help me out here. Five, four, three, two, one—ho? [Applause] It worked!" The 40-foot Colorado blue spruce came to life with yellow lights sprinkled amidst gold stars.

Giving of Gifts

On December 13, President and Mrs. Obama welcomed Oprah Winfrey to the White House for an ABC prime-time special. "This was not about grilling the President," she said after trying to get an interview with him ever since his election. Instead, Winfrey "wanted to make sure the situation was 'comfortable'.... I wanted to be at the White House during Christmastime and to experience their first Christmas at the White House," she stated. In

At the Toys for Tots warehouse near the Marine Corps base at Quantico, Virginia, First Lady Michelle Obama helps deliver toys donated by the White House Executive Staff. WHITE HOUSE PHOTO BY CHUCK KENNEDY

the special, Michelle Obama escorted the well-known celebrity on a house tour that took in the grandeur of the 27 decorated trees. En route, they met the First Dog, Bo, who was wearing a red and white collar with bells and obviously on his best behavior, even giving a high-five to the First Lady and her TV host.

The hour-long program included a one-on-one conversation with the President in which she invited the First Couple to reflect on their childhood memories of Christmas. The President recalled getting a basketball from his father on a visit from Kenya. He also remembered his first 10-speed bike. Mrs. Obama's favorite gift was a metal dollhouse with plastic furniture. Winfrey then asked the President if there was more pressure to buy better gifts now that he was in the public eye. He admitted that he was the better gift giver in the family, noting the Garavelli brooch Mrs. Obama was wearing. "Here's the general rule," he said. "I give nicer stuff than I get."

The following day, the Chief Executive addressed the audience at the 28th Children's National Medical Center benefit celebration. On December 21, he visited the Boys and Girls Club facility in Northeast D.C., arriving with cookies in the shapes of Bo Obama, gingerbread men and Christmas trees. After reading *The Polar Express*, he related the Biblical story of the three wise men coming to pay respect to the baby Jesus. After asking what gifts his young audience wanted for Christmas, the President was challenged to a game of foosball. He accepted after the 7-year-old challenger agreed to let him win. "You know," he said, "I hate getting beat."

Michelle Obama visited the Toys for Tots warehouse close to the Marine Corps base at nearby Quantico, Virginia, and delivered a portion of the 500 toys that had been collected during a White House toy drive. Pledging to support the Toys for Tots program as long as she was First Lady, she helped sort toys for girls the ages of her own daughters. Noticing a shortage of toys for older children, she volunteered, "I'm going to go back shopping because we still have a couple of more days, and we are going to pick up some more toys." The First Family personally donated toys, with Malia, 11, and Sasha, 8, making selections for kids their age, all of which were distributed by the Marines to needy children in a nine-county area of Virginia.

After a whirlwind holiday season, the First Family left Washington to spend Christmas with family and friends in three houses they had rented on Kailua Beach in Hawaii. They decorated an 8-foot tree on Christmas Eve and exchanged gifts the following morning. After a traditional holiday dinner of roast beef, President and Mrs. Obama visited members of the Armed Forces at Marine Corps Base Hawaii in Kaneohe.

Each morning of his stay, the President returned to the base for an early workout, to play basketball or to address the nation concerning an attempted terrorist attack on Christmas Day. Vacation or not, the President was always on call.

2010: "Simple Gifts"

In her remarks at the holiday press preview on December 1, Mrs. Obama said, "The idea behind this year's theme is simple gifts, because in the end, the greatest blessings of all are the ones that don't cost a thing–the time that we spend with our loved ones, the freedoms we enjoy as Americans and the joy we feel when reaching out to those in need."

The First Lady thanked the 97 volunteers from 29 states who helped to decorate the 19 Christmas trees inside the house with the simple gifts of the season. To promote conservation, volunteers gathered dried oak leaves from their yards and neighborhood parks to create oak-leaf rosettes. They decorated the East Wing Lobby with treasures from the great outdoors, including magnolia garland and pinecone topiaries. In the Green Room, decorators created trees from six recycled magazines. In the East Colonnade, wreaths were made using 500 pomegranates, 450 artichokes and 1,900 gourds of various kinds and colors.

Within the overall theme, the Blue Room tree had a specific theme. "Gifts of the American Spirit" honored state and county fairs and featured prize ribbons from each state and territory. Another special tree was the Military Appreciation Tree. Visitors were encouraged to express their gratitude, on White House postcards, to troops who would be spending the holidays far from home.

This year Bo played a prominent role in the holiday décor. In addition to appearing in marzipan on the lawn of the 350-pound gingerbread house, a life-size sculpture of the Portuguese water dog greeted visitors along the tour route. Crafted out of 39,000 twisted pipe cleaners resembling his soft, curly coat, Bo was the star of the show. With each volunteer having been assigned a specific task in decking the halls of the White House, collectively they transformed it into a holiday showplace. Expressing her appreciation, the First Lady commented, "The house looks more beautiful than it did last year. It really is something special."

Mrs. Obama especially welcomed to the press preview many members of the military and their families. Besides the staff and volunteers, they were among the first to see the Christmas decorations. White House Pastry Chef Bill Yosses treated their children to holiday craft demonstrations in the State Dining Room, and he and Mrs. Obama helped the children decorate gingerbread cookies.

"In many ways, this is really what the White House is all about," the First Lady stated. "And I say this all the time. It's the 'People's House.' It's a place that is steeped in history, but it is a place where everyone should feel welcome. With the assistance of a new Social Secretary, Juliann Smoot,

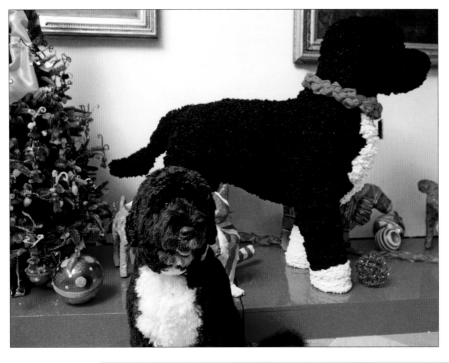

A life-size sculpture of Bo, the First Family's Portuguese water dog, was constructed out of 39,000 twisted pipe cleaners. WHITE HOUSE PHOTO BY LAWRENCE JACKSON

The First Family reacts to the grand spectacle of the newly lighted National Christmas Tree for 2010. WHITE HOUSE PHOTO BY CHUCK KENNEDY

preparations had been made to double the number of visitors who had come to the Obamas' first White House Christmas.

On December 2, President and Mrs. Obama took part in a Hanukkah candle-lighting ceremony in the East Room. On December 5, they hosted a reception for the Kennedy Center's Annual Celebration of the Arts recipients—among them Paul McCartney and Oprah Winfrey.

December 9 saw the First Family participating in the 88-year-old tradition of lighting the National Christmas Tree on the Ellipse. After the President's remarks, Mrs. Obama read "'Twas the Night Before Christmas" to a group of children on stage. B.B. King, as one of the performers, sang "Merry Christmas, Baby" to the local crowd and national TV audience.

White House Photo Card

The "Simple Gifts" theme was evidenced in President and Mrs. Obama's official Christmas card in 2010. The Chief White House Photographer, Pete Souza, captured a serene scene of the North Entry of the White House under a blanket of new-fallen snow. The black and white shot, with mere touches of color in the American flag waving over the mansion and a single light in an upper room of the residence, portrayed a peaceful day at the People's House. Titled simply "The White House," the 7 1/4 x 4 3/8-inch photograph was adhered to a maroon-ribbed cardstock. A thin white insert was adorned with a simple embossed Presidential Seal under which appeared the message in silver ink. It read: "May your holiday be filled with all the simple gifts of the season, and may your new year be blessed with health and happiness."

Positioned below it were facsimile signatures of Barack Obama and Michelle Obama and Malia and Sasha; Bo signed with a paw print. For the

Chief White House Photographer Pete Souza's photo of a wintry view of the White House's North Entry became the art for the official Presidential card in 2010. THE SEELEY COLLECTION OF PRESIDENTIAL MEMORABILIA

first time, the Obamas had a 16 x 12-inch frameable keepsake produced as a Christmas gift for the White House staff. It bore the same photo, mat, greetings and signatures as the official card, with the Presidential Seal embellishing the lower right side of the mat. Made with 30 percent recycled paper, the gift print was housed in a 17 x 13-inch commemorative folder of maroon-ribbed cardstock with a 3 1/2-inch embossed Presidential Seal on the front. On the back of both the card and print was an acknowledgment that it was "Paid for by the Democratic National Committee. www.democrats.org," also stating, "This communication is not authorized by any candidate or candidate's committee."

Salute to the Troops

For the second year in a row, the First Lady joined the President for his weekly radio address on December 25 to extend greetings to families across the country and to remind them of their debt to American service personnel around the world.

"Merry Christmas, everybody," the President began,
because this is the season when we celebrate the simplest yet most profound gift of all: the birth of a child who devoted his life to a message of peace, love

and redemption. A message that says no matter who we are, we are called to love one another—we are our brother's keeper, we are our sister's keeper, our separate stories in this big and busy world are really one.... That's the message I delivered when I visited our troops in Afghanistan a few weeks ago—that while you may be serving far from home, every American supports you and your families. We're with you.

He concluded by saying of the troops, "They've done everything they've been asked to do. They've been everything we've asked them to be."

Mrs. Obama added, "When our men and women in uniform answer the call to serve, their families serve, too. And they're proud and glad to do it. But as long as that service keeps the rest of us safe, their sacrifice should also be our own. Even heroes can use a hand, especially during the holidays."

On Christmas Day President and Mrs. Obama greeted service men and women and their families. The next day, the First Family attended services at St. Michael's Chapel at the Marine Corps Base Hawaii in Kailua.

2011: "Shine, Give, Share"

In 2011, Michelle Obama and new White House Social Secretary Jeremy Bernard, along with a team of volunteers and organizers, capitalized on the official theme, "Shine, Give, Share," to celebrate the contribution of the Armed Forces and honor their sacrifices. Even the decorators found creative ways to pay tribute to the troops and their families.

In the First Lady's remarks at the holiday preview, she said,

I have spoken with so many military spouses who are raising their kids alone while their loved one is stationed overseas for months at a time. I have heard from so many wonderful military children who pick up extra chores, and just step up and keep their grades going while mom or dad is away. And I've been inspired by the survivors of our fallen who keep giving back to the community day after day. But I also know that not every American hears these stories. Not every American knows what a Blue Star family is, or a Gold Star family is. We don't all understand what it's like to be in a military family. And that's one of the reasons why Jill [Biden] and I started our Joining Forces initiative because we wanted to rally all Americans to honor, recognize and support our military families.

On the Gold Star Family tree, at the East Landing, were photos of brave men and women who gave their lives in service to the country. Messages from their loved ones were a reminder that freedom is not free. The First

President Obama shows military officials the Blue Room tree decorated with medals, badges and patches from all the branches of the military. WHITE HOUSE PHOTO BY PETE SOUZA

Lady shared a poignant note from a Peoria, Illinois, wife, who wrote of her husband: "He never thought of himself as a hero, but he always was to me. It is still hard to know that he is gone. He was my soul mate." Gold Star Family visitors had the opportunity to inscribe a ceramic gold star with a name and personalized note to hang on the tree. Other visitors were supplied materials to share a holiday message with troops serving around the world.

The magnificent Blue Room tree, from Neshkoro, Wisconsin, recognized the dedication and service of Blue Star Families and was decorated with holiday cards from children who thoughtfully honored their parent in uniform. Five children from Medical Lake, Washington, were inspired to write: "No matter how many Christmases our Dad misses, he makes every Christmas special and we love him." Ornaments displaying emblems, medals, badges and patches from all the military branches hung on this tree as shining examples of support for military families. Ribbons inspired by the colors of the Armed Forces represented the brave men and women who were defending the nation's freedom.

While the official theme of the Obamas' third Christmas was "Shine, Give, Share," the unofficial emphasis was on the First Dog. "Where's Bo?",

Mrs. Obama asked the children of her military guests. "You got to find the Bo in every room, because he is hidden everywhere." A 4 1/2-foot likeness of the popular pet was fashioned out of 35 yards of wool felt; another Bo was created from 6,850 feet of trash bags; another Bo was constructed of 1,911 pieces of licorice and marshmallows; still another Bo, from 750 pom-poms. The littlest Bo—9 1/2 inches tall—was assembled from 318 buttons, beads and a few sequins. Bo sightings happened everywhere. The highlight of the day was when the real Bo made a surprise appearance, giving the children a chance to pet him.

Technology and the Times

When the Obamas decided to commission an artist to create their official Christmas card in 2011, they called on a man they knew and had worked with in the past. Mark Matuszak was a Los Angeles artist, illustrator and concept designer who had functioned as a concept artist in numerous fields throughout his career.

Social Secretary Bernard contacted Matuszak about creating the family's holiday card, which was to be an interior view, something home-related. Because Bo had played an important role in previous Christmases, the artist chose to focus again on the family's pet, this time in front of the fireplace in the Library.

According to David Ng of the *Los Angeles Times*, Matuszak described the Obamas' 2011 official Christmas card as the "first to be completely digitally designed." Compared to previous Presidential Christmas cards composed of photos or original paintings, this groundbreaking concept was a result of technology as well as the times.

By way of Adobe Photoshop, Matuszak combined a holiday scene of the library, including Georgia O'Keefe's painting *Mountain at Bear Lake– Taos,* with an image of Bo to create the setting. The finished product was a colorful rendering of the White House Library highlighted with reddish overtones stemming from the huge poinsettia placed on the pedestal table, the holiday garland on the mantel and the flames in the fireplace. The wood paneling and carpet reflected the lighting in the room. There, at rest before the fireplace, without a single family member in sight, was Bo Obama.

The 7 1/4 x 4 3/8-inch image was adhered to an 8 1/4 x 5 3/8-inch navy card stock framed by a gold-leaf line. The white insert featured a gold embossed Presidential Seal along with a message written in gold: "From our family to yours, may your holidays shine with the light of the season." It was signed Barack Obama, Michelle Obama, Malia and Sasha; Bo signed with a paw print. The reverse side of the unnamed scene simply read: "Art by Mark Matuszak." The Democratic National Committee paid for the card. For the

The White House Library was the subject of the 2011 official Presidential card art. Artist Mark Matuszak incorporated an image of Bo before the fireplace in this completely digitally designed card art. THE SEELEY COLLECTION OF PRESIDENTIAL MEMORABILIA

second year in a row, a 15 3/4 x 12-inch keepsake of the White House card was reproduced and given as Christmas gifts.

New Tree, New Tradition

On February 19, 2011, the majestic Colorado blue spruce on the Ellipse near the White House was felled by 50-mph winds. The 42-foot tree was 46 years old and had served as the National Christmas Tree since 1978. Knowing that it would eventually succumb to the elements, horticulturists had already selected a replacement. Stated Bill Line, National Park Service spokesperson, "We are sad, but we knew this would happen," as he noted that the previous two National Christmas Trees were also felled by winds. He added that unlike in the forest, this tree was fully exposed, with nothing to protect it.

The first replacement, a 26 1/2-foot Colorado blue spruce from New Jersey, was planted in March of 2011 but was declared dead 14 months later, due to "transport shock." Another Colorado blue spruce, this one from Virginia, was planted October 27, 2012. Even though Hurricane Sandy was scheduled to hit the area in less than 48 hours, the National Park Service thought the tree would have a better chance in the ground than in the container in which it had arrived. Cables were attached to the 28-foot tree to stabilize it; a special base surrounded the roots. As a standing practice, the National Park Service identified a successor tree so that a suitable backup would always be in place for December's tree-lighting ceremony.

On December 1, President Obama acknowledged the new tree in his remarks at the Lighting of the National Christmas Tree.

For 89 years, Presidents and Americans have come together to light the National Christmas Tree. And this year is a special one. This year, we have a brand-new tree. But we all know that this tradition is much larger than any single tree. And tonight, once again, we gather here not simply to light some decorations, but to honor a story that lights the world.

More than 2,000 years ago, a child was born to two faithful travelers who could find rest only in a stable, among the cattle and the sheep. But this was not just any child. Christ's birth made the angels rejoice and attracted shepherds and kings from afar. He was a manifestation of God's love for us. And He grew up to become a leader with a servant's heart who taught us a message as simple as it is powerful: that we should love God, and love our neigh-

The First Family, including daughters Malia and Sasha, poses for a Christmas photograph in the Oval Office in December 2011. WHITE HOUSE PHOTO BY PETE SOUZA *bor as ourselves. That teaching has come to encircle the globe. It has endured for generations. And today, it lies at the heart of my Christian faith and that of millions of Americans. No matter who we are, or where we come from, or how we worship, it's a message that can unite all of us in this holiday season.*

As in the previous two years, Mrs. Obama—assisted by Kermit the Frog—read "'Twas the Night Before Christmas," by now a new tradition. The First Family, along with the First Lady's mother, Marian Robinson, joined together to light the new National Christmas Tree.

Barbara Walters Interview

Just before President and Mrs. Obama left town to spend Christmas in Hawaii, they sat down for an exclusive interview with Barbara Walters, sharing personal insights for ABC's *20/20*. When asked about traits they deplored in themselves and others, the President admitted to laziness. "There is a deep-down, underneath all the work I do, there's a laziness in me. It's probably from, you know, growing up in Hawaii, and it's sunny outside and sitting on the beach. The thing actually that I most dislike is cruelty. I can't stand cruel people.... I tend not to be a mean person, you know, if I get lazy, then I get mad at myself."

Michelle Obama admitted that if she were to die and come back as another person or thing, it would be Bo. "I want to be Bo. He's got a great life. But only Bo, not just any dog. He's got it good!" The President agreed, "People do love Bo!"

For their holiday wish, the President urged "that people stay hopeful. Better days are coming ... they have a President who is thinking about them every day." The First Lady added, "The holidays are a time to reach out to family and friends with open hearts to find forgiveness where it is needed and caring for their health and the well-being of children of the next generation—that is the most important thing."

2012: "Joy to All"

Introducing her theme for their fourth Christmas in the White House, Mrs. Obama said, "'Joy to All' celebrates the many joys of the holiday seasons: the joy of giving and service to others, the joy of sharing our blessings with one another, and the joy of welcoming our friends and families as guests into our homes over the next several weeks." Eighty-five volunteers from 39 states decorated 54 trees and transformed the People's House into a holiday house for the anticipated 90,000 visitors.

The tradition of selecting a theme for the holidays began with Jacqueline Kennedy, who chose a nutcracker theme for her daughter,

Caroline. To honor the legacies of Christmases past, four trees in the Grand Foyer of 2012 were decorated with a collection of iconic ornaments. Said the First Lady: "We're bringing back some of the favorite ornaments of some of our most recent First Ladies, just to remember that the house never belongs to just one family."

Themed ornaments were selected from Lady Bird Johnson's "Early Americana," Pat Nixon's "Season of Gold," Betty Ford's "Homespun Christmas," Rosalynn Carter's "Classic American Christmas," Nancy Reagan's "Old-Fashioned Christmas," Barbara Bush's "Christmas Is a Storyland," Hillary Clinton's "Winter Wonderland" and Laura Bush's "Red, White and Blue Christmas."

In the China Room, the Truman china was set out to illustrate the joy of families sitting down to enjoy a holiday dinner. In the Red Room, lemon topiaries replaced the traditional cranberry tree as a tribute to First Lady Dolley Madison, who decorated with fabrics of sunflower yellow.

The official White House tree in the Blue Room was again dedicated to the courageous service of the troops, veterans and military families in uniform. The 18 1/2-foot Fraser fir was trimmed with handmade ornaments decorated by children living on U.S. military bases all over the world to honor their parents' commitment to service.

The East Garden Room became a children's wonderland full of bright colors and gingerbread wreaths, with a life-size topiary of Bo as the centerpiece. This one was fashioned from 20,000 mostly black one-inch pom-poms accented with a few white ones.

"We always find a way to incorporate Bo into our Christmas themes," admitted Mrs. Obama. "Bo is the most popular member of our family. The President is clear on it. There are times when people recognize Bo, and they don't even see *him*." A Bo statue made of marzipan sat on the lawn of the huge gingerbread house. Forty handmade "Bo-flake" ornaments hung from trees in eight rooms of the house. Holiday visitors received a Bo bookmark that encouraged them to join a scavenger hunt in search of Bo-themed decorations. "Where's Bo?" was the White House version of "Where's Waldo?"

A Bodacious Card

Not surprisingly, President and Mrs. Obama even chose an oil painting of their much-loved Bo romping in the snow on the South Lawn for their official 2012 Christmas card, the first one resulting from a nationwide art competition. About 80 artists were invited to create original art from either of two photographs—one of the President's House and the other, of the President's dog, with the winner's art being featured on the First Family's official Christmas card.

Bo was again the highlight of the 2012 official Presidential card, an oil painting of the South Lawn of the White House. For the first time, its artist, Larassa Kabel, was chosen in competition. THE SEELEY COLLECTION OF PRESIDENTIAL MEMORABILIA

Artist Larassa Kabel of Des Moines, Iowa, is known for her highly distinctive style of photorealism, as evidenced in a dramatic series of 8-foot "falling horses" hanging in a Des Moines gallery. She chose to do her interpretation of the adorable dog playing in the snow, but, she told ABC News' Sarah Parnass, she needed to make some changes. "Black animals are difficult to represent and have them read as three-dimensional," so Bo gained a scarf, and the artist used a toothbrush to make the snow look real, explaining, "It splatters so it looks like snow."

It wasn't long, though, before a caller from the White House informed her that Michelle Obama had chosen her work for the official Christmas card. "It was a very surreal moment," she said. "I don't know why she picked mine over others. The artist reported, happily, that once the First Lady had made the final decision, no changes to the painting were required. Her art, entitled *Bo in the Snow*, was framed and became part of the White House Collection.

The bodacious Presidential card was sent to members of Congress, government officials, governors, ambassadors and heads of state, political supporters, family and friends.

The painter's black and white illustration was adhered to 8 1/4 x 5 3/8-inch dark green card stock. The message on the card read, "This season, may your home be filled with family and friends, and the joy of the holidays." It bore the printed signatures of Barack Obama, Michelle Obama, Malia, Sasha, and the soon-to-be-world-famous Bo, by the print of one paw. Once again the traditional frameable gift print was not under the tree.

It's Christmas Time

At the 90th lighting of the National Christmas Tree on December 6, President Obama spoke about devastation and survival in the aftermath of Hurricane Sandy. Even the national tree was the second replacement in a little more than a year. "It just goes to show that nobody's job is safe here in Washington," he jested.

"I feel good about this one. It was planted just days before Hurricane Sandy and it made it through the storm in one piece. [But] ... some of our neighbors to the north saw a more ruthless and destructive Sandy," he said.

And this holiday season is especially difficult for families who lost everything in the storm. But it's also a time for us to be grateful for the heroism and perseverance of ordinary men and women in the storm's path who've shown us that Americans will always be stronger than the challenges that we face. And as I did before Thanksgiving, I can't help but tell a story of their enduring holiday spirit.

This evening, in Midland Beach, New York, on a street lined with houses and businesses devastated by the storm, a great big Christmas tree shines out of the darkness. Just a couple of weeks ago, as impacted families were still seeking some sense of getting back to normal, one local nursery donated the tree, another chipped in for the lights and a star, and 70-year-old Tom Killeen and his longtime buddies from the area planted it at the end of the street, overlooking the town beach. As Tom says, the tree has one message: "It's Christmas time, not disaster time."

And Tom is right. For centuries, the message of Christmas—of peace and goodwill to all—has guided millions of people around the world through good times but also through bad times. This year is no different. It's a chance for all of us to open our hearts to the least fortunate among us. It's a chance to remember what Christ taught us—that it is truly more blessed to give than to receive, and that the simplest gifts bring the greatest joy ... may every tree from Midland Beach to this Ellipse and all across the country shine as a beacon of hope for all Americans.

First Daughters Malia and Sasha, the First Lady and her mother, Marian Robinson, then helped the President flip the switch on the new tree.

Ablaze in the darkness, it was the focal point for the singing of "Santa Claus Is Coming to Town."

First Daughters in a TV Special

On December 20, NBC aired *A White House Christmas, First Families Remember*, with hosts Meredith Vieira and former First Daughter Jenna Bush Hager. As it turned out, displaying the themed ornaments of former First Ladies in the Grand Foyer in conjunction with the TV special was a perfect fit. The show brought together several members of former First Families to share their memories of White House holidays of the past.

Luci Baines Johnson, whose father ascended to the Presidency upon the assassination of John F. Kennedy just a little more than a month before Christmas, recalled: "Everywhere you went downstairs and in the public rooms, it was draped in black...there was a sense of respect for the unspeakable horror that our country had gone through." Then, after the 30 days of mourning, "All of a sudden, the black was gone, and the tree was up," she said. Her father lit the National Christmas Tree on December 22. "There was a sense there would be hope for tomorrow."

Tricia Nixon Cox, whose mother started the tradition of the edible White House gingerbread house, remembered her father always breaking off a piece of the home from where no one would notice. Unveiling the gingerbread house "was a high point because," she asked, "who doesn't feel young at heart in the presence of a charming old-fashioned gingerbread house?"

Recalling the first time she lit the National Christmas Tree, Chelsea Clinton said: "I remember thinking it might be anticlimactic to just hit a button. I don't know what I thought, but it was the furthest from anticlimactic. I mean, to watch the tree just burst into light, and to gasp along with the thousands of people that were watching on the Mall. It was a magical moment."

Jenna Bush Hager, who also served as executive producer of the segment, identified with the others as a First Daughter, but "that is not how we are known," she said. "We define ourselves as being of our careers, and our relationships and our children. But we are part of this club who's lived history, so it's amazing to hear everybody's perspective around something as nonpolitical as the holidays."

When asked by Hager, "What exactly is your role when it comes to the holidays every year?", the First Lady answered, "Well, I'm the hostess-in-chief. Welcome to the White House! Pretty cool, huh? One of the things that's really special for us is really being able to turn a spotlight onto our military families, which is something that we try to do every year through the holidays. I try to remember that this is the time when the White House is truly the People's House," she said. To the question of her daughters' favorite part of the holidays, Mrs. Obama replied, "Oh, gosh, I think they love the fact that the house is full of people and friends and music. You recall, whenever there are receptions downstairs, you hear the music just bubbling up."

Return to Hawaii

After a frenzied re-election campaign, the First Family once again returned to Hawaii to celebrate Christmas 5,000 miles away from the White House. For the President, it was a return to his roots, where he was born, grew up and went to high school. Mrs. Obama said, "We go out there, and we spend time with friends and family. That tends to be our gift to each other. We say, 'We're in Hawaii. Merry Christmas.'"

One of their traditions is a family talent show. "Everyone has to participate, whether it's singing or reading a poem. The kids will construct a play of some sort, or we'll sing Christmas carols," she shared. For Christmas dinner, they enjoy turkey, string beans and a little macaroni and cheese. "This is a time when I throw 'Let's Move' out the window for a moment and get that mac and cheese," she said. "Everybody deserves their mac and cheese."

On Christmas afternoon, the President and First Lady visited with Marines and their families at Marine Corps Base Hawaii at Kaneohe Bay. The practice of wishing the troops a Merry Christmas and thanking them for their extraordinary service had become another tradition of the Obamas.

After only five days in the Aloha State, the President returned to Washington to work with Congress in preventing the economy from going over the "fiscal cliff."

President and Mrs. Obama visit troops and their families at Marine Corps Base Hawaii at Kaneohe Bay on Christmas Day 2012.
WHITE HOUSE PHOTO BY PETE SOUZA

2013: *Gather Around*

As in the past, Michelle Obama invited military families to be the first to see the White House decorated for the holidays. In her remarks at the holiday press preview on December 4, she complimented them on their volunteerism. She quoted surveys that had shown the general public volunteering 27 percent of the time, while military families volunteer 81 percent regardless of the challenges they faced.

"So you guys really make us all look bad. [Laughter] But in short, your sacrifice and your service to this country, your families' stories are such an important part of our great American story—stories that remind us of the true meaning of the holiday season," she said. "And that actually brings me to this year's holiday theme, which is 'Gather Around the Stories of the Season.' This holiday season, we'll be focusing on the stories behind classic American holiday traditions—traditions celebrated here at the White House and across the country. Our goal is for every room and every tree to tell a story about who we are and how we gather around one another to mark the holidays," Mrs. Obama stated. In the Blue Room, the tree was "dedicated to gathering around the military."

Once again, the Blue Room tree was decorated with distinctive ornaments—2,000, in fact—many of them created by children on military bases. Some of the handmade greeting cards shared favorite holiday family traditions, while others celebrated joyous moments when families were united after a long separation. The tree at the East Entrance Landing was bedecked with ornaments memorializing a loved one as well as ornaments representing all five branches of the service.

Nearby in the East Garden Room, children were drawn to the ribbon topiaries of the Obama family dogs crafted from a thousand yards of black and white satin ribbon. Bo was depicted giving a high-five and new pet Sunny was portrayed as the playful pup; both sported tails that wagged. Mrs. Obama reported, "I was surprised last night; this year they actually move. They're mechanical.... We're stepping up in the world of Bo-and-Sunny honoring."

Chocolate versions of Bo and Sunny were also to be found in the State Dining Room on the front steps of the famous edible gingerbread house. Nearly 300 pounds of dough went into the 2013 version, complete this year with a lighted chandelier and a functioning water fountain on the North Lawn. More than 1,200 Springerie cookies served as a life-size hearth on which the house rested. The hearth's opening was made with sugar paste re-creations of tiles commissioned for FDR's old-fashioned fireplace of "fireside chats" fame.

A Pop-Up Christmas Card

Highlighting Bo on their official Christmas card had by this time become an Obama tradition, and 2013 did not disappoint. For the third year in a row, Bo was a central figure, but now there was a new dog in the house, Sunny. Also, very much a departure from the colorful though flat art of previous years, this holiday greeting was to be a pop-up replica of the White House with both dogs walking in front of 1600 Pennsylvania Avenue.

The pop-up card showcased the specialty of graphic artist Chris Hankinson, whose art was likened to Japanese "origamic architecture." In the previous year, 2012, the Grand Rapids, Michigan, artist had been approached by the White House to submit samples of his work and an outline of the process. "The reaction was positive," he said, "and I started negotiations with the DNC's marketing firm." These continued after submission of a series of prototypes, but then, unfortunately, "the negotiating took a long time, and we had to face the reality that if we did get the project, the time left just wasn't sufficient to deliver on time." At that point, the origami project got scrapped in favor of an open competition among traditional artists, and the 2012 card was awarded to Larassa Kabel. "It was a wonderful card," concluded Hankinson, "but I definitely came away with the feeling that I had lost the opportunity. So close, yet so far!"

In July of 2013, he was contacted again. "The White House still wanted to do the pop-up," a pleased Hankinson said. "This time around everyone was aware of the time frame we needed, and the negotiation went much smoother. After some minor tweaks to the design, we were off to the races."

The artist described his usual work flow: "I always start the old-fashioned way ... pencil and paper. I make preliminary drawings of how the card might look, which details might bog down production and which are too important to eliminate ... and try to find a happy medium. When I get something close, I cut out a prototype by hand. The process usually takes a few days."

After the White House had reviewed his original design, there came a request for Bo to be incorporated. Then, following the family's adoption of Sunny in August, a White House spokesman informed Hankinson that the second dog also had to be included. The artist expressed concern over the timing and feasibility of these additions but was informed that the President himself was specifically requesting both of the dogs.

From design to hand-fold, the most coveted Christmas card in America was proudly "Made in Michigan." The whole project took about three months to complete.

Hankinson reflected on the overall experience: "We certainly got a lot of press from it, and our website traffic doubled overnight, so the effect so far has been very positive." Once the President's card was in the mail, the artist and his wife attended a holiday reception at the White House.

"Seeing the card on display was hard to beat," he recalled. "It was fun to hear the comments of the people passing by." While refraining from telling how much he was paid or how many cards were printed, the artist did admit that creating the card for the President of the United States was a high-light of his career. "What could we possibly do to top this?"

The final version was a 6 3/4 x 4 3/4-inch stark white card with the White House popping open on the inside. The front was graced by a gold embossed Presidential Seal with the year, 2013. The message read: "As we

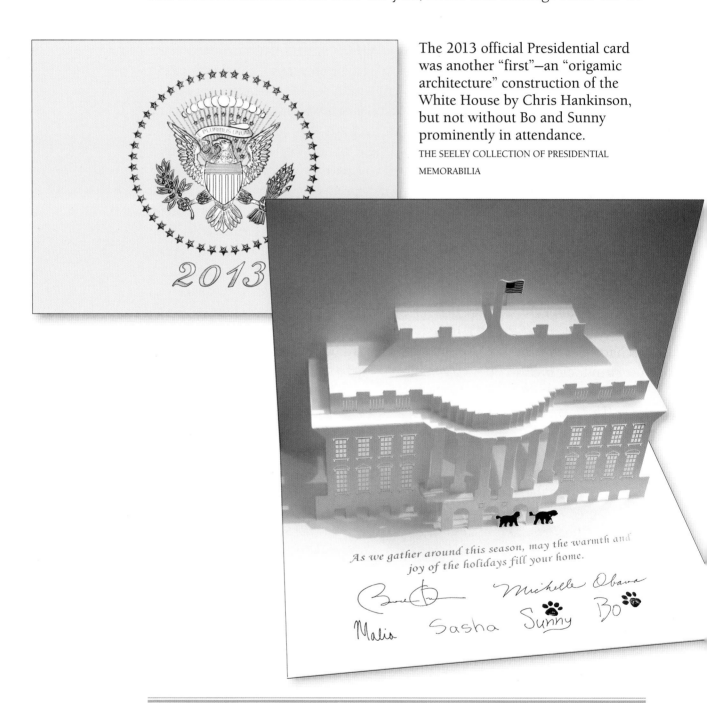

The 2013 official Presidential card was another "first"—an "origamic architecture" construction of the White House by Chris Hankinson, but not without Bo and Sunny prominently in attendance.

THE SEELEY COLLECTION OF PRESIDENTIAL MEMORABILIA

As we gather around this season, may the warmth and joy of the holidays fill your home.

Michelle Obama

Malia   Sasha   Sunny   Bo

gather around this season, may the warmth and joy of the holidays fill your home." The 3-D card bore facsimile signatures of Barack Obama, Michelle Obama, Sasha and Malia; Sunny and Bo each signed with a paw print.

On the back were the words "Design by Chris Hankinson." Again, the card creation did not lend itself as a large keepsake gift.

Many Traditions of Christmas

On December 6, the Obamas all took part in the annual lighting of the National Christmas Tree. Entertainers included Train, the Avett Brothers, Joshua Bell, Mariah Carey and Aretha Franklin, with host Jane Lynch. The weather was cold and rainy, but the spirit of those who attended was happy and bright.

A little-known tradition, dating back almost 60 years to Bess Truman, was the First Lady's visit to the Children's National Health System, located less than four miles from the White House. On December 16, Michelle Obama, accompanied by Bo and Sunny, visited patients and their families as well as doctors and nurses in the Medical Care Unit. In keeping with that tradition, the First Lady read the classic "'Twas the Night Before Christmas," asking the children questions as she went along. Chief Medical Officer David Wessel said, "Having a special visitor like Mrs. Obama is a wonderful treat for children in our medical unit who aren't able to go home for the holidays."

Five days before Christmas, the Obamas left the pressures of Washington for the relaxing beaches of Hawaii. In his year-end news conference, the President confessed that he was "eager to skip town" to get recharged for what he hoped would be a more productive 2014. Their schedule even took precedence over the Congressional Christmas party, where holiday photos were taken with stand-in hosts Vice President and Mrs. Joe Biden.

This would be the Obamas' fifth straight year of holiday time off in the oceanfront neighborhood of Kailua with family and friends. While the President would be receiving daily security briefings and updates on the deadlines of his affordable healthcare bill, he looked forward to days of rest and relaxation, hoping the change in scenery would help him rebound for the months ahead. He told reporters, "The end of the year is always a good time to reflect and see what we can do better next year. That's how I intend to approach it. I'm sure that I will have even better ideas after a couple of days of sleep and sun."

Douglas Brinkley, author of several Presidential biographies, offered this opinion. "The rebooting process is essential. He has got to get away to think. That is the most underrated attribute of what we need in a President— to think." In previous years, President Obama had spent a great deal of time on the golf course and on the white sandy beaches of Kailua. Basketball with the Marines and morning workouts with Mrs. Obama were also scheduled at Marine Corps Base Hawaii. On Christmas Day, he and the First Lady always visited with the troops and their families to wish them "Mele Kalikimaka"–Hawaiian for "Merry Christmas."

The Chief Executive and his daughters left Hawaii on January 4 to go back to work and school while the First Lady stayed behind. Both she and good friend Oprah Winfrey would soon be celebrating milestone birthdays. Together they would spend "girl time" at the TV celebrity's estate on the island of Maui. This surprise was part of the President's early birthday present to his wife, who would turn 50 on January 17. Again, it went to prove that when it came to exchanging gifts in the Obama family, the President gave better than he got!

2014: "A Children's Winter Wonderland"

Christmas decorations at the White House took a page from the digital age in 2014. In her remarks at the press preview that included military families, Mrs. Obama shared the latest on the fun technologies they were implementing that year. She began with a description of the interactive digital snowscape projected on a wall in the booksellers area that captured the movements of visitors amid falling snowflakes.

The First Lady encouraged the children to look for the robotic animations of First Dogs Bo and Sunny in the East Garden Room. "Sunny-bot's" eyes were programmed to move with infrared motion sensors in the direction of someone approaching. "I hope it's working," she added. Chief Floral Designer Laura Dowling admitted that the 2013 mechanical Bo had had a

First Lady Michelle Obama poses with the 2014 White House Christmas ornament in the Diplomatic Reception Room. WHITE HOUSE PHOTO BY CHUCK KENNEDY

mishap when its ribbon tail got caught in the motor and started to smoke. This year, an early version of "Bo-bot" was a "little creepy," causing designers to tone down the planned interaction of the Bo robot with guests.

In the Blue Room stood an 18-foot-tall by 12-foot-wide tree described as "huge" by the First Lady. "We've got a tree that was so big, we had to take the hinges off the front door and then take the doors off—literally—just to get this tree in. Can you imagine that? It's huge ... but it is beautiful because it has patriotic ornaments and ribbons that read 'America the Brave' as well as some wonderful cards created by children across the country to thank all of you [military families] for your service to our country. It's beautiful," she said of the tree and its 2,000 ornaments, many made by military children.

The theme for the White House decorations was "A Children's Winter Wonderland" to encourage visitors to rediscover the marvels of childhood. Scattered throughout the 26 Christmas trees in the house were ornaments resulting from a first-ever 3-D printed ornament challenge. The White House, in partnership with the Smithsonian, had announced the contest in October, after which students and artists all across the nation got busy and fashioned 300 whimsical, winter-inspired pieces. From the 26 finalists, five kinds of 3-D printed designs went on display in the White House.

Interactive Holiday Card

In keeping with their digital holiday twist, the Obamas released what they called their "first-ever interactive White House Holiday card," available to all in 2014 at whitehouse.gov. It was again the outcome of competition, this time open to artists participating in the State Department's Arts in Embassies program. Having worked with this program for eight years, Emily Buchanan, an artist known for her memorable landscapes of New England and the Hudson Valley, accepted the challenge without hesitation.

According to the First Lady's Press Office, "Ms. Buchanan was selected from among several applicants who submitted work over the course of the year." Most of her work is done out-of-doors, however, so when asked to paint an interior of the White House, everything was different, from the subject matter to the technique.

In an endeavor that took a year, the Connecticut-based artist designed a card displaying dual-fold white doors adorned with evergreen wreaths, red bows and berries. This opened like a triptych to reveal her painting of the festive Entrance Hall. The artist incorporated the official Blue Room tree in the center of the background, reserving front and center for the Obamas' two Portuguese water dogs on a checkered pattern of cream and brown Vermont marble floor. The *Architectural Digest* described them as "exquisitely rendered in watercolor."

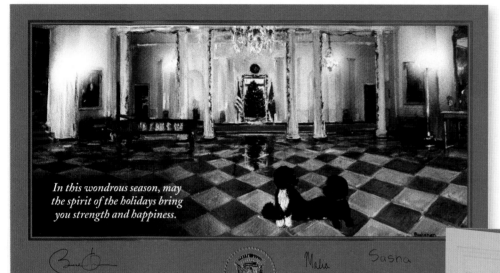

In this wondrous season, may the spirit of the holidays bring you strength and happiness.

Landscape artist Emily Buchanan created the water-color painting that adorned the three-panel rendition of the Entrance Hall with Bo and Sunny appearing front and center—almost. THE SEELEY COLLECTION OF PRESIDENTIAL MEMORABILIA

Following the tedious preliminaries, the actual painting took only 10 days, with the end result being "iconic Christmas," according to Kate Hartman at *Connecticut Magazine.* While Buchanan was initially a bit intimidated by the challenge, it was an incredible learning experience, with her touting the great lesson of "the importance of getting out of your comfort zone." When all was said and done, the Boston native was pleased with her work. "It's a huge honor," she said. "It's been fun through the whole process."

The sentiment of the card read, "In this wondrous season, may the spirit of the holiday bring you strength and happiness." Printed signatures of Barack Obama and Michelle Obama appeared to the left of the gold-embossed Presidential Seal beneath the painting. Malia's and Sasha's signatures were paired with Bo and Sunny paw prints on the lower right of the card. The 5 3/4 x 7-inch cards were printed by Allied Printing Trades Council, Washington, D.C., and paid for by the Democratic National Committee. A QR code appeared on the back with instructions to scan with a smart phone or tablet to view a special holiday greeting from the White House.

The First Family participated in the Lighting of the National Christmas Tree on the Ellipse on December 4. The President said, "Back in 1923, school kids here in Washington wrote a letter to the White House asking if they could put a Christmas tree on the South Lawn. And more than 90 years and a few different evergreens later, the National Christmas Tree still stands as a symbol of hope and holiday spirit, and we still gather as a country each year to light it. We still have school kids involved, too. But this year, they've given all the state and territory trees surrounding the National Christmas Tree their first digital upgrade. Young women from all 50 states used their computers—and their coding skills, to control the colors and patterns of the lights on the trees.... It's incredibly impressive."

On December 15, Michelle Obama went to the Children's National Health System to read "'Twas the Night Before Christmas" to the children while offering personal commentary. The presence of Bo and Sunny prompted numerous questions. They inquired about where the dogs were allowed to go in the White House and if they had their own Christmas stockings. Mrs. Obama was gracious in answering all the questions, even some unusual ones: Did she have Christmas pajamas? [No]; What was her favorite winter activity? [Skiing].

Christmas in Hawaii

The First Family left for their sixth annual Christmas holiday in Hawaii on December 16. On Christmas Eve, the President made phone calls to service members from every branch of the military to express appreciation for their service and sacrifice. Meanwhile, Mrs. Obama took calls from children asking where Santa was located as part of the annual NORAD Tracks Santa program operated by the North American Aerospace Defense Command.

To begin Christmas day, the First Family opened presents and sang carols. Meanwhile, the President and Mrs. Obama wished Americans a Merry Christmas and Happy Holidays in a joint message prerecorded at the White House. After three hours on the beach with the family, the President and First Lady visited members of the military and their families at the Marine Corps Base in Hawaii. Said the President: "So on a day when we celebrate the Prince of Peace and many of us count our blessings, one of the greatest blessings we have is the extraordinary dedication and sacrifices you all make. We could not be more thankful." He reassured the troops: "I know I speak for everyone in the entire country when I say, we salute you."

A military couple planning to get married in Hawaii invited the President to their wedding. On the day prior to the big event, he sent his regrets that he couldn't come, but wished them happiness on their wedding day. Then, within hours, the two Army captains were told they had to move their wedding, because the President was playing golf at the same venue that afternoon. Upon learning about the forced relocation of the wedding, the

President personally called the bride and her new husband to apologize and congratulate them. The *New York Daily News* reported, "The President saved the day." He then closed out 2014 the same way he had begun it—on the golf course with old friends.

2015: "A Timeless Tradition"

More than 68,000 guests were expected to visit the White House during the 2015 holidays. In preparation, the First Lady unveiled decorations showcasing the theme "A Timeless Tradition." The display included an expanded forest of 62 trees—compared with only 26 the previous year—70,000 ornaments and a huge, handcrafted 500-pound dark-chocolate gingerbread house. According to the press office, only 10 percent of the holiday décor used new products or materials; the remaining 90 percent were repurposed ornaments and embellishments already in inventory at the warehouse.

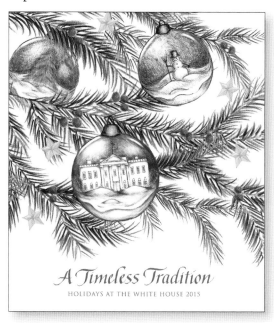

Via guide booklet, Barack and Michelle Obama invited visitors to join them on a tour of the White House's Timeless Traditions. THE SEELEY COLLECTION OF PRESIDENTIAL MEMORABILIA

Three of the rooms were designed by fashion designers the First Lady had enlisted. Humberto Leon and Carol Lim of Opening Ceremony along with KENZO transformed the White House Library into "a holiday forest of novels and manuscripts" highlighted by custom-made book ornaments and hand-painted marbleized globes. Decorated by Duro Olowu, the Vermeil Room featured two trees draped with vintage fabric and ribbons, and adorned with ornate toys and hanging balls. Carolina Herrera covered the central table in the China Room with classic navy plaid fabric topped with red gift boxes. Throughout the room ribbons of bright Kailua blue, reminiscent of the waters off the coast of the President's home state, represented the Obama family's china service, debuted the previous April at the Japan State Dinner.

The White House crèche, a long-standing holiday tradition, has remained the centerpiece of the East Room through nine administrations. In 2015, it was encircled by four magnificent trees, which were decked with iridescent pearls, glistening icicles and vintage jewels. The historic room also is home to two imposing paintings, one each of George and Martha Washington.

The Blue Room tree, an 18 1/2-foot Fraser fir, was wrapped with ribbon bearing messages to our troops from their families. As a token of appreciation for their service, each family would receive a copy of those messages at holidays' end. The patriotic symbols of red, white and blue and the garland of gold stars adorning the tree were inspired by the American flag. All the ornaments were chosen to honor the service members who protect our nation and preserve our personal liberties.

Returning again this year were the Obamas' popular Portuguese pooches. Larger-than-life replicas of Bo and Sunny were created out of nearly 55,000 feet of yarn fashioned into 7,000 pom-poms. Standing on a giant plaid doggie bed, the furry friends were flanked by two topiary trees made of yellow tennis balls. A third tree, filled with milk bones and more balls, catered to a canine's fantasy. A poem to all America from Bo and Sunny adorned the wall behind the display.

North Facade of the White House

To create their official holiday card in 2015, the Obamas turned to YiM Photography and Design in Washington, D.C. It was artist Meena Yi who designed a quad-fold card showcasing the North Facade of the White House among four major capital monuments: the Washington Monument, Jefferson Memorial and Lincoln Memorial appeared in red, with white representing the Capitol Building and White House. The artistically crafted 5 x 7-inch card was arranged so the monuments could be seen with the card either closed or open. The basically two-tone setting was decorated for the holidays with garlands of Christmas lights and snowflakes. Not to be overlooked, Bo and Sunny, out in the snow, made their final appearance on a holiday card.

On the last panel, printed in black under an official gold Presidential Seal, a bright holiday message read, "With gratitude and cheer, we send our warmest wishes for health and happiness this holiday season." Printed signatures of Barack Obama, Michelle Obama, Malia and Sasha, and paw prints of Sunny and Bo graced the bottom of the card. YiM reported that an average of more than 250,000 Obama holiday cards were mailed in 2015.

At the lighting of the National Christmas Tree on December 3, President Obama took time out of the festivities to remember the victims of the shooting the previous day in San Bernardino, California. He said, "Their loss is our loss, too, for we're all one American family. We look out for each other in good times and in bad. And they should know that all of us care about them this holiday season. They're in our thoughts, they're in our

Artist Meena Yi designed the 2015 quad-fold red and white holiday card displaying cutouts of four major capital monuments. THE SEELEY COLLECTION OF PRESIDENTIAL MEMORABILIA

prayers, and we send them our love." He also asked for prayer for those stationed far from home during the holidays. "Our men and women in uniform sacrifice so much for us. And it is because of them that we can celebrate freely, that we can worship as we please, that we can come together on a night like this—strong, and united, and free."

As always inspired by the Marines' Toys for Tots program, the First Lady arrived on December 9 at Joint Base Anacostia-Bolling with a bunch of toys—cars full of toys, all donated by the White House executive staff. Owing to the ages of her own children, she stressed the need for toys for teens. "We have to remember there are kids 13, 14, 15, 16, 17 who still need to have something under the tree. So let's not forget our teenagers." Mrs. Obama added, "Every day in every season is an opportunity to give more than you receive. It's an opportunity to sacrifice on behalf of others. So today, on behalf of myself and my husband, I want to once again thank you all for your extraordinary service to our communities and to our country."

A few days later, she again went to the Children's National Health System with "the most famous Obamas—we have Bo and Sunny Obama. Woo!" she cheered. After reading "'Twas the Night before Christmas," she fielded questions from the children about the dogs. "How can you tell them apart?", one asked. Another wondered, "Do they get presents?" Yet another asked, "Were Sunny and Bo naughty or nice this year?" Said the First Lady, "They have been very good dogs," but then confessed, "Sunny sometimes can be naughty.... She leaves the kitchen and she'll sneak, and she'll [leave a package] on the other end of the White House. But we're dealing with the problem." Other than that, the two Portuguese water dogs continued to serve as good ambassadors on behalf of the First Family.

Mrs. Obama enjoyed a personal question about the family. "If you could spend Christmas anywhere in the world, where would it be?" She replied:

"That's really good.... we have made a tradition of spending Christmas every single year in Hawaii. And that's where the President grew up, and that's where his family is. So we have been going to Hawaii now for more than 20 years, and that's like our family tradition. And because it is such an important tradition, I wouldn't want to be anywhere else in the world." And predictably, very soon thereafter, President and Mrs. Obama, Sasha, Malia, Bo and Sunny were on the plane bound for Hawaii and their Christmas holiday.

2016: "The Gift of the Holidays"

Joining Forces was an initiative begun in 2011 by the First Lady and Dr. Jill Biden, wife of Vice President Joe Biden, to give military families VIP treatment and raise public awareness and support. In keeping with that effort during the holiday observance at the White House, Mrs. Obama invited military spouses and children to be the first to see the decorations as one of her favorite traditions. She reminisced at her final holiday press preview, "As we celebrate my family's last holiday season at the White House, I'm thinking back to when we first came here to Washington and we promised to open up this house to as many people from as many backgrounds as possible. We truly wanted to make the White House the 'People's House,' particularly during the holiday season. And over the past eight years through the seasons we worked hard to achieve that goal."

The theme chosen for the 2016 decorations was "The Gift of the Holidays," reflecting the joys of giving and receiving along with the true gifts of service, friends and family, education and good health. The East Garden Room featured an American flag formed from images of brave military members; there was also the Gold Star Tree that honored men and women who had given the gift of service by sacrificing their lives for our country. Filled with a treasure trove of books and a collection of school supplies, the Library emphasized the gift of education for all. In the Green

In the East Garden Room, an attention-getting American flag flanked the tree featuring red, white and blue decorations.
OBAMAWHITEHOUSE.ARCHIVES.GOV

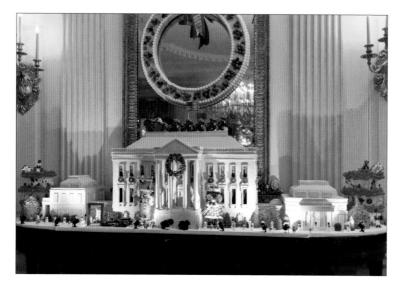

This year's White House gingerbread house was built from 150 pounds of gingerbread and 100 pounds of bread dough.

OBAMAWHITEHOUSE.ARCHIVES. GOV

Room, the decorations showcased vibrantly colored fruits and vegetables to signify the gift of good health.

Welcoming visitors "home for the holidays," the State Dining Room celebrated the gift of families. The year's traditional White House gingerbread house was constructed from 150 pounds of gingerbread and 100 pounds of bread dough. Giant gingerbread people stood guard at the entrance, and sugar versions of Bo and Sunny were stationed before the columns. Flanking the Lincoln fireplace, and displayed on two trees with circular shelves, were 56 gingerbread-like houses representing the American states and territories. A team of seven Lego Master Builders from Lego headquarters in Enfield, Connecticut, had incorporated 200,000 Legos into their construction of these one-of-kind houses unique to each state. A Mount Rushmore fashioned from Legos was even built into the roof of the South Dakota house.

The Blue Room tree celebrated "We the People." A ribbon garland emblazoned with the iconic words to the Preamble of the Constitution encircled the 17-foot, 6-inch tree. The guide booklet stated that "The tree's glimmering ornaments, with images of American families, farmers, and service members, reflect our country united by diversity and strengthened by a shared spirit of hope and optimism."

Finally, an Obama holiday White House would not have been complete without First Family members Bo and Sunny. Greeting visitors in the East Wing Hallway were larger-than-life likenesses made from more than 25,000 yarn pom-poms,

A Holiday Photo Card

For their final Presidential holiday card, the President and First Lady chose a photo of the First Family that had been taken by White House pho-

Meena Yi was recalled to design the 2016 holiday card featuring a family portrait by White House photographer Pete Souza. THE SEELEY COLLECTION OF PRESIDENTIAL MEMORABILIA

The White House 2016

tographer Pete Souza the previous March. The special occasion had been a formal State Dinner to honor Canada's Prime Minister Justin Trudeau. While the President wore black tie, Mrs. Obama chose a blue jacquard gown by Jason Wu. Daughters Malia, 18, and Sasha, 15, wore custom-embroidered Naeem Khan gowns.

To complete the card, for the second year in a row, the Obamas called on designer Meena Yi. The 3 1/4 x 4 1/2-inch Sousa photograph was adhered to a framed insert embellished by gold-foil snowflakes. The words "The White House 2016" were printed in gold below the design. The 5 1/2 x 8-inch ivory card was created to appeal in a minimalist fashion, with small accents of color.

A gold-embossed Seal of the President adorned the interior of the card above the greeting, "Happy Holidays." The sentiment in gold read: "As our family reflects on our many happy years spent in the White House, we are grateful for the friends we've made, the joy we've shared, and the gifts of kindness we've received. We wish you and your loved ones a joyous holiday season and a wonderful new year." Printed signatures of Barack Obama, Michelle Obama, Malia and Sasha appeared at the bottom in black. Absent from the photo, but present with their paw prints, were the First Dogs.

While the Obamas were the first to choose a photograph including their grown children on their holiday card, they followed the example of six previous Presidents who had featured themselves on their official holiday card or gift print. In 1932, Herbert and Lou Henry Hoover gave dual photos as a remembrance to their staff. Franklin and Eleanor Roosevelt were pictured seated for several of their Christmas cards and one gift print in 1941.

For Christmas of 1946, Harry and Bess Truman were photographed on the steps of their private plane, the *Sacred Cow*, and it became a gift to their staff. Dwight and Mamie Eisenhower gave dual portraits of themselves as gifts in 1956. For their official Christmas card in 1962, the Kennedys used a photo of Mrs. Kennedy on a sleigh ride on the South Lawn with her young children. A State Dining Room photograph of Bill and Hillary Clinton adorned their holiday card and gift print in 1993.

Lighting Their Last National Tree

A parade of celebrities joined President and Mrs. Obama at their last National Christmas Tree Lighting on December 1. Eva Longoria, Kelly Clarkson, Marc Anthony, The Lumineers, Garth Brooks and Trisha Yearwood were on hand to perform and celebrate with the First Family. Michelle Obama shared a reading of "A Visit From St. Nicholas."

In his closing remarks, the President delivered a message of unity, decency and hope:

> *Along with celebrations like these, the holidays also offer us a time for reflection and perspective. And over these next few weeks, as we celebrate the birth of our Savior, as we retell the story of weary travelers, a star, shepherds, Magi, I hope that we also focus ourselves on the message that this child brought to this Earth some 2,000 years ago–a message that says we have to be our brother's keepers, our sister's keepers; that we have to reach out to each other, to forgive each other. To let the light of our good deeds shine for all. To care for the sick, and the hungry, and the downtrodden. And of course, to love one another, even our enemies, and treat one another the way we would want to be treated ourselves.*
>
> *It's a message that grounds not just my family's Christian faith but that of Jewish Americans, Muslim Americans, non-believers–Americans of all backgrounds. It's a message of unity and a message of decency and a message of hope that never goes out of style. And it's one that we all need very much today.*

Toys for Tots

At the White House, Mrs. Obama led the drive for the staff to pitch in and give back through programs such as Toys for Tots. Finally, on December 7, at her last official Toys for Tots drive as First Lady, she invited special guests to help sort toys at Joint Base Anacostia-Bolling. From the Disney Channel came "Doc" McStuffins–a 6-year-old girl who cares for stuffed animals in her playhouse clinic; the stars of *Descendants 2*, Sofia and Cameron; Madison and Olivia from *Bizaardvark*; plus Radio Disney hosts Alex and Betsy.

Michelle and Barack Obama prerecorded a final holiday message before heading into the sunset for their Christmas holidays.OBAMAWHITEHOUSE. ARCHIVES.GOV

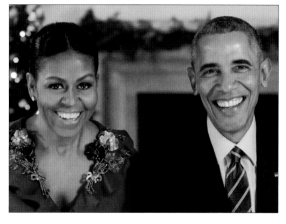

"They're our Santa's helpers!... And we are all here today to support the wonderful work that Toys for Tots has been doing year after year to make the holidays so much brighter for kids across this country," the First Lady said. "In fact, since Toys for Tots first started, they have sent more than 512 million toys to over 237 million children in all 50 states, Puerto Rico, Guam and the Virgin Islands. That's pretty cool!"

She concluded: "For eight years our staff has stepped up. And we came here today with cars filled with toys to contribute. So on behalf of myself and the President and my family, I just want to thank you all for the privilege to serve, and to thank everyone at Toys for Tots for everything you are doing."

Final Holiday Address

On Christmas Eve, the President and First Lady delivered their final prerecorded holiday message. As with all the previous messages, it was available online at youtube.com. Mixing nostalgia with humor, they shared the struggles they had faced while taping their first holiday address, when the President could not stop giggling. Tonight, with the giggles firmly under control, he wished everybody a Merry Christmas! In a four-minute address, the two of them took the opportunity to commemorate the holiday and reflect on the past eight years in Washington.

THE FIRST LADY: Celebrating the holidays in the White House over these past eight years has been a true privilege. We've been able to welcome over half a million guests ... our outstanding pastry chefs have baked 200,000 holiday cookies ... and Barack has treated the American people to countless dad jokes.

THE PRESIDENT: Although a few got a ... Frosty reception ... the greatest gift that Michelle and I have received over the last eight years has been the honor of serving as your President and First Lady. Together, we fought our way back from the worst recession in 80 years, and got unemployment to a nine-year low.... By so many measures, our country is stronger and more prosperous than it was when we first got here. And I'm hopeful we'll build on the progress we've made in the years to come.

Tomorrow, for the final time as the First Family, we will join our fellow Christians around the world to rejoice in the birth of our Savior. And as we retell His story from that Holy Night, we'll also remember His eternal message, one of boundless love, compassion and hope.

THE FIRST LADY: The idea that we are our brother's keeper and our sister's keeper. That we should treat others as we would want to be treated.... As always, many of our troops are far from home this time of year, and their families are serving and sacrificing right along with them. Their courage and dedication allow the rest of us to enjoy this season. That's why we've tried to serve them as well as they've served this country.

THE PRESIDENT: So as we look forward to the New Year, let's resolve to recommit ourselves to the values we share. And on behalf of all the Obamas—Michelle, Malia, Sasha, Bo, and that troublemaker Sunny—Merry Christmas, everybody.

THE FIRST LADY: And we wish you and your family a happy and healthy 2017... thanks, and God bless.

Aloha From Hawaii

This was to be the last time the Chief Executive would celebrate Christmas in Hawaii as President. He and his family had been coming to the islands for the holidays since before he was elected President. For the eight years after being elected to the high office, the Hawaii native kept up the tradition of returning "home for the holidays." Signaling their satisfaction with their previous stays in the Aloha State, the Obamas once again chose the same Kailua mansion on the island of Oahu for the holidays.

Barack Obama spent his final Christmas thanking troops and their families for their service at Marine Corps Base Hawaii, an activity that had become an annual Christmas Day tradition for him and the First Lady. "Although this will be my last time addressing you as President, I want you to know that, as a citizen, my gratitude will remain and our commitment to standing by you every step of the way—that won't stop," he told the service members.

On December 27, the President made a historic visit to the *USS Arizona* Memorial with Japanese Prime Minister Shinzo Abe, the first Japanese leader

Far from the pressures of office back in Washington, President Obama accepted the challenge to hike 1,200 feet up the grueling Koko Head Crater Trail to the crater's ridge overlooking his Aloha State. WHITE HOUSE PHOTO BY PETE SOUZA

to visit the site. Both paid tribute to the lives lost in the attack on Pearl Harbor 75 years earlier.

When not performing official duties, the President spent much of his time swimming and playing golf; the family went on hikes and dined at upscale restaurants including Alan Wong's and Nobu Waikiki. Malia and Sasha joined their father for their annual visit to Island Snow, a shave ice and surf shop in Kailua, where they opted for the shave ice, a frosty flavored Hawaiian house specialty. "Snowbama," a flavor especially created for the President, was a combination of lemon-lime, cherry and passion-guava.

Michelle Obama has said, "You can't really understand Barack until you understand Hawaii." According to Landess Kearns, senior editor at *HuffPost, Hawaii*, "You can't really understand Hawaii until you understand aloha. Aloha is a greeting, an expression of love, and a way of life. The aloha spirit ... permeates the lives of those who live and have lived in Hawaii, including the President. Once you know the meaning of aloha, Hawaii will hold a place in your heart, just as it does for the Obamas." President Obama admitted, "I am an island boy." Concluded Kearns, "There is nothing better than being home for Christmas."

Back in Washington, during the Obama years in office, the country had been witness to much change—in technology, in online achievements, in social media and instantaneous communication, as well as economic recovery. Despite all this, and amidst the vigorous partisan politics afoot in the nation's capital, the Obamas had set a goal of maintaining the White House as a place of inclusion, an institution belonging to all Americans. Especially at the holidays, it was to be enjoyed as the "People's House."

THE TRUMPS
Christmas Steeped in Tradition

One of Donald Trump's campaign promises was to bring back the holiday greeting "Merry Christmas." At a March 2016 news conference in Jupiter, Florida, the candidate announced that Americans were going to start using "Merry Christmas" again. "You know they don't say it anymore," he remarked, insisting that the celebration of Christmas was being threatened by efforts to make the holiday politically correct.

"I love Christmas," said Trump. "You go into stores and they have red walls and snow and even a sleigh, but it doesn't say Christmas. I tell my wife, don't go into those stores. I want to see Christmas. I want them to say 'Merry Christmas.' Remember the expression? If I am elected President, you are going to hear and see 'Merry Christmas' again." Tony Perkins of the Family Research Council asserted that "the President was talking about a lot more than the war on Christmas. He was speaking directly into the fight for religious liberty in America."

And, sure enough, as President, Donald Trump turned the holiday card back into a Christmas card. His official card read, "Merry Christmas and a Happy New Year." He retold the story of the Baby Jesus at the lighting of the National Christmas Tree. On Christmas Eve, the President tweeted, "People are proud to be saying 'Merry Christmas' again. I am proud to have led the

Facing page: President Donald J. Trump and First Lady Melania Trump pose in the Cross Hall for their 2017 official Christmas portrait. WHITE HOUSE PHOTO BY ANDREA HANKS charge against the assault of our cherished and beautiful phrase "MERRY CHRISTMAS!!!!!" And on Christmas morning of 2017, he and the First Lady wished the whole country "a very Merry Christmas" in a video message posted on Twitter. Declared Perkins: "To the people who elected Trump, this isn't just about putting Christ in a day. It's about putting faith back in American life."

2017: "Time-Honored Traditions"

In anticipation of 25,000 visitors to the Executive Mansion in 2017, the Trumps aimed to make the public tours meaningful and memorable. To set a tone for her holiday decorating, First Lady Melania Trump took a cue from her husband's desire for a traditional Christmas. Her vision for her family's first Christmas at the White House was traditional décor, which debuted in the classic colors of red, green and gold. She was involved in every detail of the decorations, envisioning traditional evergreen wreaths on each window of the White House and specifying traditional single-loop red bows on each wreath. According to the First Lady's spokeswoman, this addition made for a new Trump tradition that will continue to be seen during their tenure in the White House.

For her holiday theme, Melania Trump chose "Time-Honored Traditions," as documented in the 2017 Christmas tour booklet. Illustrator Jim Starr of Stewartstown, Pennsylvania, created the original artwork showcasing "the entire tour route and reception spaces...." Said the First Lady's spokeswoman, "Mrs. Trump wanted an accurate portrayal of the rooms so that attendees could gain not only historic context but also follow along with the thought process behind the décor elements." Working in tandem with the White House calligraphy team and using digital files, Starr could easily update his work in real time to match the evolving designs and décor throughout the house to capture the overall vision of the

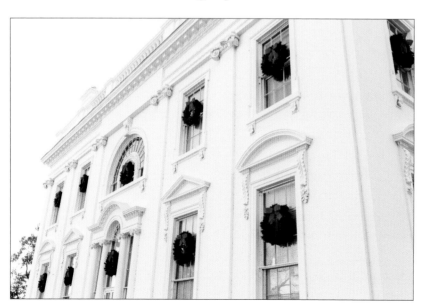

The First Lady's signature Christmas wreaths of evergreens and single-loop red bows, placed on 71 exterior windows for the first time ever, made White House history.
WHITE HOUSE PHOTO BY ANDREA HANKS

The First Family welcomed visitors via the White House Christmas tour booklet. THE SEELEY COLLECTION OF PRESIDENTIAL MEMORABILIA

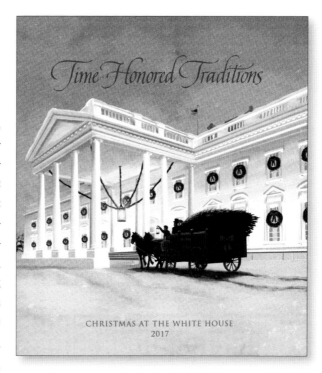

First Lady. All guests, whether members of the general public or personal invitees, received a copy of the booklet. It was also available for public download at whitehouse.gov, permitting anyone in the world with Internet access to learn about Christmas at the People's House. At a length of 20 pages, the 2017 publication was the most ambitious yet, with its copious descriptions of the decorations and traditions of the past. The project has evolved greatly since Rosalynn Carter initiated the practice in 1978 to welcome guests and describe her Victorian Christmas tree.

The booklet begins with a greeting from the First Family: "We are delighted to welcome you to the White House as we celebrate the time-honored traditions of the holiday season. We hope you enjoy exploring the festive grandeur of the 'People's House' during this very special time of year! More than 200 years ago, in December of 1800, President John Adams and First Lady Abigail Adams celebrated the first Christmas at the White House with their family and close friends. Since that time, each First Family has shared their cherished traditions as well as the wonder and excitement of the season with guests from our country and around the world." There are no less than 15 historical references to the traditions of former First Families.

The Trumps' 11-year-old son, Barron, wearing a red scarf over his navy blazer, was chosen by Mrs. Trump to represent the family in the booklet's pages. Pictured in the Library, he marveled at the "book tree" comprised of books with green dust jackets and marked with red ribbon bookmarks. Encased nearby was President Franklin Roosevelt's 1866 edition of Charles Dickens' *A Christmas Carol*—a story FDR traditionally read to his family during the holidays. Barron's amiable appearance throughout the booklet lends a personal family touch.

The booklet concludes with the reminder: "Presidents, patriots, and people from all backgrounds have walked these halls, through this very foyer.... Countless memories and over two centuries of history have taken place in this residence. We are all part of these time-honored traditions."

A Big Blue Room Tree

Three days before Thanksgiving, in keeping with a 51-year Blue Room tradition, the First Lady, escorted by Barron, accepted a 19 1/2-foot balsam fir from Jim, Diane and David Chapman, owners of Silent Night Evergreens in Endeavor, Wisconsin. According to standard practice, the official White House tree had to be between 18 and 19 feet tall. Because the Chapmans did not have a tree that size, they worked with Hanauer Christmas Tree Farms in Shawano, Wisconsin, to provide a suitable specimen for the Blue Room. The previous September 25, Dale Haney, White House Superintendent of Grounds, and Timothy Harleth, White House Chief Usher, had selected the tree after an on-site inspection.

The Chapmans were honored to deliver the tree to the North Portico entrance on a Clydesdale-drawn carriage. The family had also won the National Christmas Tree Association's National Tree Contest twice before, presenting a tree in 1998 as well as 2003. Mrs. Trump thanked the owners of Silent Night Evergreens for the beautiful tree. "We will decorate it very nicely; I hope you can come and visit with us," she said. "The President, Barron and I are very excited for our first Christmas in the White House. As with many families across the country, holiday traditions are very important to us. I hope when visiting the People's House this year, visitors will get a sense of being home for the holidays. On behalf of my husband and Barron, I want to wish everyone a Merry Christmas and joyous holiday season."

Preparation for the Trumps' first White House Christmas then began in the Blue Room

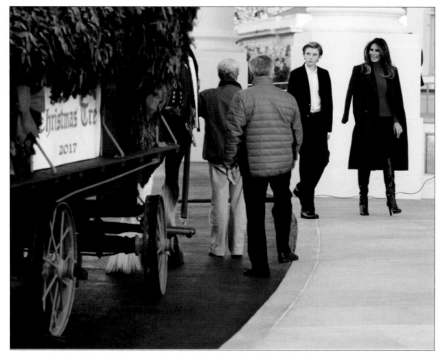

First Lady Melania Trump and son Barron welcome the official White House Christmas Tree at the North Portico entrance.
WHITE HOUSE PHOTO BY ANDREA HANKS

with the removal of the 19th century chandelier, which had to be taken down to make room for the tree. Other historical artifacts and antiques were also put in storage. With the tree finally set up, all was ready when the volunteers showed up to decorate it.

Traditional Christmas Decor

More than 150 florists, designers and volunteers arrived from 29 states to deck the halls of the Executive Mansion for Christmas. Starting before Thanksgiving, the decorating took 1,600 hours. The first 2 1/2 days were spent in a huge government warehouse in Maryland, where volunteers counted and sorted thousands of ornaments and prepared them for display. Some workers tied bows and wires to ornaments while others created pinecones and mistletoe out of brown paper to adorn the Green Room mantel. Among other preparatory tasks, gold lines had to be painted on glass stars to be hung on the Gold Star Tree honoring military members and their families. When finished, more than 12,000 ornaments, 18,000 feet of lights, 31,000 yards of ribbon, 1,000 feet of garland and 71 wreaths were transported to the White House. Volunteers were divided into decorating teams and assigned to different rooms.

Having seen the work of designer Nick Watts, the First Lady hired him to bring her very specific vision to life. She explained her ideas; he put them on paper and transformed them with color. His goal was to portray the theme of a traditional Christmas and let the beauty of the rooms compliment the decorations. Appearing later on an HGTV special, he was seen instructing the volunteers that no matter which room they were working on, they needed "to keep three things in mind: Ensure that all garlands are long and touch the floor, only tie bows in a classic shoestring style, and keep ornaments snug inside the trees throughout the house—all 53 of them."

Upon returning from Thanksgiving in Florida with the President, Mrs. Trump tweeted, "The decorations are up! @whitehouse is ready to celebrate! Wishing you a Merry Christmas & joyous holiday season!"

On Monday, November 27, the First Lady posted a behind-the-scenes video on Twitter, unveiling the White House decorations as a reflection of her personal style. The same day, her office previewed the decorations for journalists. Meanwhile, in a YouTube video, Mrs. Trump is seen checking that every detail was in place for Christmas. It captured her making a bow with velvet ribbon; examining crystal ornaments on the snow-covered trees; putting final touches on a green wreath; revealing the Trumps' official ornament featuring the Presidential Coat of Arms, and reviewing the White House tour booklet paying tribute to 200 years of "time-honored traditions" of former Presidents.

The gingerbread house featured green wreaths and red bows mirroring the exterior of the White House windows. WASHINGTONIAN MAGAZINE PHOTO BY DAN SWARTZ

In the White House kitchen, known as "Cookieville," Mrs. Trump is seen admiring samples of the 31,000 decorated cookies she would serve at more than 100 open houses and receptions between November 28 and December 21. There were more such events than in previous years, but "they were purposefully less crowded, making for a more impactful experience," according to the First Lady's spokeswoman.

Conferring with White House Executive Pastry Chef Susan Morrison and Pastry Assistant Brandon Blomquist, the First Lady commended them for their handiwork on the impressive 350-pound gingerbread White House complete with miniature wreaths in every window, mirroring the green wreaths and red bows attached to every window of the actual edifice. Nearly half a century earlier, Patricia Nixon had initiated this practice of displaying a gingerbread house in the State Dining Room at Christmas.

The video followed Mrs. Trump walking through the winter wonderland of the Grand Foyer, where nearly half of the 53 White House trees were displayed. Adorned with crystal ornaments of nutcrackers, ballerinas and icicles, the trees were dusted with faux snow. Lights projecting from floor to ceiling added to the ambiance of the wintry scene. In the Cross Hall, dancers from the Vivid Ballet Company of Hartford, Connecticut, performed for the First Lady. The Marine Band played excerpts from Tchaikovsky's *Nutcracker* ballet as a tribute to Jacqueline Kennedy's 1961 first themed Christmas featuring "The Nutcracker."

The seal of the District of Columbia is affixed to this gold ball on the Blue Room Tree. WHITE HOUSE PHOTO BY ANDREA HANKS

First Lady Melania Trump walks through the sparkle and glitter of dozens of trees in the Grand Foyer to view the Christmas decorations. WHITE HOUSE PHOTO BY ANDREA HANKS

Also captured on video was the 18th century crèche that has been a Christmas centerpiece of 10 administrations—spanning half a century in the White House. Displaying it at Christmas was a high priority for the President and Mrs. Trump. Back in 1967, during the Lyndon Johnson Administration, Mrs. Charles W. Engelhard had donated the Baroque-style crèche made in Naples, Italy, of terra-cotta and carved wood replete with 44 figures.

As the camera zoomed into the elegant Blue Room, the official White House tree was shown to be layered with a combination of blue and gold spider bows and Mrs. Trump's signature single-loop bows. Coordinated with the ornate walls of the oval room, blue and gold ornaments were incorporated into the tree. The original architect of the White House, James Hoban, had imagined an elliptical space to receive guests from all over the nation. In recognition of his vision, this year's Blue Room tree was decked with 500 gold glass balls—among them one each framed with a gold bow and bearing the seal of one of the states and U.S. territories.

Christmas Arts and Crafts

After showcasing the White House decorations on Twitter, Melania Trump hosted an event in her home by inviting schoolchildren from Joint Base Andrews in Maryland to the Executive Mansion to participate in holiday arts and crafts. Dressed in a winter-white dress with cape-like sleeves, she opened her arms to receive a group of small guests in the East Room. One boy asked, "Are you the First Lady?" He moved in for a hug; others joined in for a group hug. Another child remarked, "She looks like an angel." The First Lady's face lit up as she interacted easily with the children, chatting with them about their plans for Christmas and what they had asked Santa to bring them. Together they all decorated garlands with balls and bows and made wreaths.

Next door, in the Green Room, Mrs. Trump joined another group of children engaged in paper crafts. All the Christmas decorations in the room had been painstakingly made of paper by a number of the volunteers, who had also decorated the garland on the mantel with gold and green leaf mistletoe and gold pinecone. Nestled within the garland were framed gold silhouettes of former Presidents as a final flourish to the elaborate design gracing the room. One vignette depicted a family Christmas of President John Adams while another showed President Thomas Jefferson; each was

The First Lady participates in an arts and crafts project with schoolchildren from Joint Base Andrews during their visit to the White House Christmas preview event. WHITE HOUSE PHOTO BY ANDREA HANKS hung in a window to capture the spirit of the season. Inspired by these decorations and their historical references, the children, under the supervision of the First Lady, created silhouettes akin to those of the Presidents framed on the mantel.

The Red Room, sweetly transformed by peppermints, cookies and candy, was every child's dream. An evergreen tree in the center of the room was bedecked with red plaid and white bows. Real cookies were tied to the branches; the tree's stand was placed in a box made of gingerbread. Vases filled with candy canes, peppermints and lollipops were displayed on a side table. The First Lady had also displayed a real cranberry tree–the favorite decoration of Nancy Reagan and a traditional element in the Red Room since 1975.

"Surprise," said Mrs. Trump as she entered the room, where children were making red and green gumdrop trees. "So you want to show me how to do that?", she asked after sitting at a table with four students. One of the boys showed her how to get started. Chatting with the children, she admitted there was a lot of tempting sugar in the room.

For the final activity, Mrs. Trump strolled through the enchanted forest of glistening wintry branches to the East Garden Room. Here, the children were writing letters of appreciation to veterans and those currently serving in the military. Later that day, she tweeted, "Had a wonderful visit from @JBA_NAFW children today at the @whitehouse!"

Merry Christmas From the Trumps

The giving of Presidential Christmas cards began in the administration of Franklin D. Roosevelt, when Brewood Engravers of Washington, D.C., printed small one-sided cards for him to distribute to his White House staff, government officials, family and friends. The sending of official White House Christmas cards dates back to Dwight and Mamie Eisenhower, who began working with J.C. Hall of Hallmark Cards in 1953. To date, neither war nor death has interrupted this time-honored tradition.

To create their official White House Christmas card for 2017, the Trumps chose Artisan 2, Inc., a finishing company for the printing industry. Seasoned craftsmen at the Alexandria, Virginia, site produced a gold-foil embossed Presidential Seal encircled by 50 gold-foil embossed stars on Crane's crest 134# paper. A thin gold-foil embossed border framed the detailed design on the front of the 5 1/4 by 7 3/4-inch pearl white card. Engraved in a beautiful gold script, the message simply stated, "Merry Christmas and a Happy New Year." Gold engraved signatures of Donald Trump, Melania Trump and Barron Trump graced the interior below the sentiment. A gold insert lined the envelope, which was adorned with a small gold-foil embossed Presidential Seal on the flap and the words, "The White

Official 2017 White House Christmas card of President and Mrs. Trump.
THE SEELEY COLLECTION OF PRESIDENTIAL MEMORABILIA

House" in the upper left corner. The greeting was in keeping with Donald Trump's pledge during the campaign to say "Merry Christmas" again. On the back of the card was printed, "Paid for by the Republican National Committee. Not authorized by any candidate or candidate's committee. www.gop.com." The First Lady's office confirmed that 375,000 Christmas cards were printed for this holiday season.

While the image of the Presidential Seal was similar to Barack Obama's first holiday card in 2009, the distinction came in the messaging on the card. A greeting for the holiday season had been the preferred sentiment for the

The Trumps' 2017 commemorative Christmas card. THE SEELEY COLLECTION OF PRESIDENTIAL MEMORABILIA

Obamas, the Clintons and the George W. Bushes; not since George H.W. and Barbara Bush had a reference been made to "Christmas" in the official holiday cards.

The Trumps' Christmas card was mailed to members of the Cabinet, members of Congress, members of the media, staff, government officials, the Supreme Court, former Presidents, foreign dignitaries, the U.S. Secret Service, family and friends. The card also served as a thank-you to political supporters who had helped the President get elected and who undoubtedly viewed it as a treasured keepsake. For the first time, Christmas cards from the First Family were hand-delivered to staff and patients at Walter Reed Army Medical Center.

For the benefit of the visiting public, the 2017 official Christmas card was framed—showcasing the front and inside of the card—and displayed opposite a wall of other Presidential Christmas cards in what is known as the Bookseller's area of the White House.

Following the tradition of giving large frameable prints, President and Mrs. Trump invited Artisan 2, Inc., to also design a commemorative card incorporating the same elements as their official Christmas card. The result was a heavy 180# red card stock measuring 11 by 16 inches. On it they created an impressive image comprised of a 7-inch circle of gold-foil embossed stars surrounding the gold-foil embossed Seal of the President. Below the seal, they affixed what Trump described as the "cherished and beautiful phrase": "Merry Christmas" and added the year. The gold-foil embossed signatures of Donald Trump and Melania Trump appeared below. The commemorative card was housed in a natural white 100# certificate holder with a debossed and die-cut Presidential Seal in the center. A 4-inch red sash

The 2017 First Family official Christmas ornament.
THE SEELEY COLLECTION OF
PRESIDENTIAL MEMORABILIA

embellished with the same gold-embossed Presidential Seal slipped over the certificate holder, formalizing the presentation. This keepsake was placed in a large white envelope printed with nothing more than the words, "The White House," in the upper left corner.

Many of these 6,750 commemorative cards, paid for by the RNC, were hand-delivered to members of the Cabinet, members of Congress, government officials, staff and family. Others were mailed to political supporters and friends.

First Lady Lou Henry Hoover had started the tradition of giving gift prints at Christmas after her assistant came across some old black and white prints of Washington, D.C. The Hoovers then framed them to give as gifts to their staff at Christmas during the Depression. FDR and Harry Truman followed up with documents such as the D-Day Prayer and the V-E Day Proclamation as well as signed personal photographs for their staff. Dwight Eisenhower personally painted the original art that Hallmark reproduced for his gift prints. Presidents Gerald Ford and Jimmy Carter had early American prints reproduced and framed as gifts. More recent Presidents have commissioned artists to paint art reflecting features of the White House, which was then used for both their official Christmas card and commemorative gift print. Barack Obama interrupted this long-standing tradition by reproducing only two frameable gift prints during his eight years in office.

People who sent holiday greetings to the Trumps received an acknowledgement in the form of a one-sided reciprocal card stating, "Thank you for thinking of us during this very special time of year. Your thoughtfulness adds to the joy of the season. We send our best wishes to you and your family for good health, happiness, and prosperity in the coming year. God bless you." Facsimile signatures of Donald Trump and Melania Trump appeared below the message.

Another new Trump tradition, a First Family official Christmas ornament, was created to be given as a gift from the President and First Lady. The

4 1/2-inch, gold-finished brass piece was publicly displayed with large red bows on a tree in the East Garden Room. It featured a three-dimensional Coat of Arms of the President surrounded by a wreath comprised of traditional holly leaves and berries combined with oak leaves and acorns–the symbol of strength and longevity. The back of the ornament was signed in black by both the President and First Lady. A banner across the bottom read "Christmas at the White House 2017." The design and the title were hot-stamped in gold foil on the cover of the red gift box.

Vice President and Mrs. Pence followed in the footsteps of the First Family. Their official holiday photograph was taken in their home to showcase their holiday decor theme, "Make the Season Bright." Metallic ornaments in gold and silver on the Grand National Reserve Tree and candles on the mantel carried out this theme.

The Vice President's official Christmas card and a matching Christmas

Vice President Mike Pence and Second Lady Karen Pence are pictured in their official 2017 Christmas portrait, taken at the Vice President's residence at the Naval Observatory. WHITE HOUSE PHOTO BY D. MYLES CULLEN

The 2017 Vice Presidential Christmas card, painted by Second Lady Karen Pence.
THE SEELEY COLLECTION OF PRESIDENTIAL MEMORABILIA

President and Mrs. Trump wave to the crowd as they arrive at the 2017 National Christmas Tree Lighting Ceremony on the Ellipse.
WHITE HOUSE PHOTO BY JOYCE N. BOGHOSIAN

ornament had a unique personal touch. The original art, a watercolor of the Vice President's Residence at the Naval Observatory in Washington, D.C., had been painted by Second Lady Karen Pence. She and the Vice President welcomed more than 2,000 guests into their home over the holidays.

The 95th Annual National Christmas Tree Lighting on the Ellipse took place on the unseasonably warm evening of November 30, when the President and Mrs. Trump participated in a tradition dating back to 1923 and President Calvin Coolidge. In 2017, Kathie Lee Gifford and Dean Cain were cohosts at the star-studded event featuring the Beach Boys, Mannheim Steamroller, the Texas Tenors, Wynonna Judd and the "The World's Finest," the U.S. Navy Band. After their performances, the President spoke, saying in part:

Today's the day that I've been looking very much forward to all year long. It's one that we have heard and we speak about and we dream about and now as the President of the United States, it's my tremendous honor to finally wish America and the world a very Merry Christmas....

Melania and I are full of joy at the start of this very blessed season. We're thrilled to think of the people across the nation and all across the continent whose spirits are lifted by the miracle of Christmas....

Whatever our beliefs, we know that the birth of Jesus Christ and the story of this incredible life forever changed the course of human history. There's hardly an aspect of our lives today that His life has not touched: art, music, culture, law, and our respect for the sacred dignity of every person everywhere in the world.

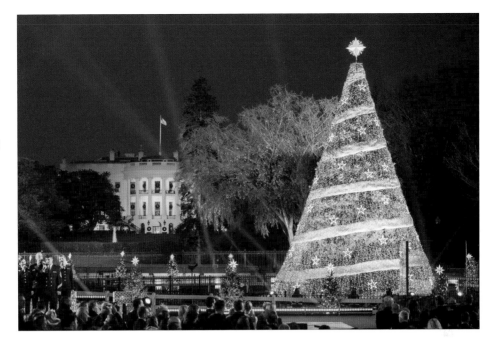

In 2017, the National Christmas Tree Lighting ceremony celebrated its 95th year. WHITE HOUSE PHOTO BY JOYCE N. BOGHOSIAN

Each and every year at Christmas time we recognize that the real spirit of Christmas is not what we have, it's about who we are—each one of us is a child of God. That is the true source of joy this time of the year.

And so, this Christmas we ask for God's blessings for our family, for our nation. And we pray that our country will be a place where every child knows a home filled with love, a community rich with hope, and a nation blest with faith.

The President led in the countdown from 10; the First Lady flipped the switch to light the National Christmas Tree—a Colorado blue spruce from a private home in Virginia. Permanently planted on the Ellipse on October 27, 2012, the tree stands as an internationally recognized symbol and a living testimony that Christmas has arrived in the nation's capital.

Reaching Out to Others

While the First Family hosted more than 100 Christmas open houses and receptions, hundreds of Americans were still suffering the effects of Hurricane Harvey. On December 6, First Lady Melania Trump and Second Lady Karen Pence returned to Houston to continue their efforts in supporting those affected by Texas' 2017 hurricane devastation. Arriving in Corpus Christi, they participated in a meet-and-greet with first responders who had been part of the recovery effort. Traveling to Rockport, they met a newly homeless family who were just seeing the new manufactured housing unit that would serve them temporarily until their permanet home was completed.

The two women also visited an elementary school where they spoke with students and teachers about the hurricane. To conclude their day, they visited a food bank to meet volunteers and help sort boxes of donations. In her remarks, Mrs. Trump said, "The effects of the hurricane season are still being felt throughout southern portions of the United States and in Puerto Rico, and residents still need our help. While I am heartened by the strength and resilience of those impacted by the storms, I will continue doing all I can to lend a voice and shine a spotlight on those who need assistance to rebuild and start new family traditions. As Christmas and the New Year approach, I encourage people to lend their time volunteering or providing financial support to those still reeling from the hurricanes."

Karen Pence added, "Our hearts are encouraged by the people of Texas and their continued enthusiasm to help each other pick up the pieces and rebuild after Hurricane Harvey. I am looking forward to the opportunity to accompany the First Lady of Texas and to visit with families and their children in the communities most impacted by the storm. Our thoughts and prayers remain with the people of Texas."

December 7 was a busy day for both the President and Mrs. Trump. At the White House, Donald Trump signed a proclamation designating the day as National Pearl Harbor Remembrance Day. To mark that occasion, several veterans of the attack on Pearl Harbor had gathered at the White House. In his remarks, the President said, "Today our entire nation pauses to remember Pearl Harbor and the brave warriors who on that day stood tall and fought for America. As I sign the proclamation making this National Pearl Harbor Remembrance Day," he went on, "I ask that God continue to bless and watch over each of you as very, very special people to our country. And God is watching over you."

According to S.A. Miller of the *Washington Times*, one of the veterans who survived the Japanese attack that day had described himself as "just a regular grunt in the service." The President disagreed: "A regular grunt, I don't think so. You're not a regular anything. You're a hero. All of you are heroes...," concluding, "Our surviving World War II veterans are a precious national treasure."

Meanwhile, in a tradition dating back to First Lady Bess Truman after World War II, Melania Trump visited the Children's National Hospital in Washington, D.C., where she read *The Polar Express*, handed out gift bags and visited with brave young patients. Sitting down with Santa, she answered personal questions the children had prepared.

One child inquired, "What is your favorite Christmas song?" She replied, "My favorite Christmas song is 'O Holy Night.' And what is yours?" He responded, "Mine is probably 'Jingle Bells.'"

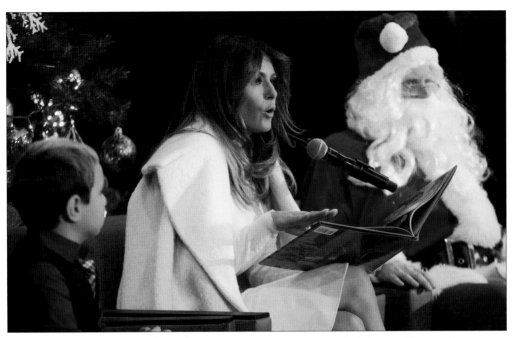

Melania Trump reads *The Polar Express* to patients at Children's National
Hospital. MICHAEL REYNOLDS/EPA-EFE/REX/SHUTTERSTOCK

Tara asked, "What is your favorite family Christmas tradition?" The
First Lady explained, "Our family tradition is to have dinner on Christmas
Eve and then go to midnight Mass or Christmas Day Mass the next day.
Then we have another dinner on the 25th; Santa comes, we open presents
and spend time together."

A 10-year-old named Andy asked, "If you could spend a holiday anywhere in the world, where would you go?" Her answer evoked laughter: "I
would spend my holidays on a deserted island, a tropical island, with my
family."

Olivia asked, "What is your favorite thing to eat for Christmas dinner?"
the First Lady answered, "My favorite thing to eat is some healthy food; you
feel very good afterwards. Not too much eating. We all enjoy it," adding, "the
most important part is to spend time with the family."

Lastly, a child inquired, "What did you ask Santa for Christmas?" Mrs.
Trump appreciated the question. "Very nice—I asked Santa for Peace in the
world, Health, Love and Kindness." It was obvious the First Lady endeared
herself to the children and she enjoyed being with them. The following day
she tweeted, "I was grateful at the opportunity to spend time with the children and their families yesterday, and want to thank the medical staff @chil-
drenshealth for their lifesaving work."

That evening, the President and First Lady hosted the annual
Hanukkah reception at the White House. The event came one day after the

Melania Trump helps children from Joint Base Anacostia-Bolling sort toys for the Marine Corps Reserves' Toys for Tots Drive. PLANETPIX/ALAMY LIVE NEWS

President's announcement recognizing Jerusalem as the capital of Israel and his decision to move the American Embassy from Tel Aviv to Jerusalem. Hundreds of guests gathered in the East Room for the reception, including daughter Ivanka Trump and son-in-law Jared Kushner, who are Jewish, Vice President and Mrs. Pence, Secretary of the Treasury Steven Mnuchin, Secretary of Veterans Affairs David Shulkin and Rabbi Meir Soloveichik. Menorahs were displayed from the First Jewish Congregation as well as a second menorah that had survived the Holocaust in the Tarnow Ghetto in southern Poland.

In his remarks at the event, the President said,

The miracle of Hanukkah is the miracle of Israel. The descendants of Abraham, Isaac and Jacob have endured unthinkable persecution and oppression. But no force has ever crushed your spirit and no evil has ever extinguished your faith. And that is why the Jewish people shine as a light to all nations.... We are deeply honored that Louise Lawrence-Israels is here to share the evening with us and to make a few remarks. Louise is a Holocaust survivor. The first three years of her life were spent hiding in the attic of a row house in Amsterdam.... Her family could not light the candles we are about to light this evening, but they lit them in their hearts. On my right is a lamp that survived the Tarnow Ghetto, a city in southern Poland that was ravaged by the Holocaust. It will remain unlit in memory of that darkest hour and in order to preserve this relic so that we never, ever, ever forget. We thank God that a woman that was born into that nightmare of oppression now lives in the land of the free and that she, along with everyone here tonight, can light the menorah for all the world to see. And the world is watching. Today our nation is stronger, and our world is more full of promise because of the Jewish people, the State of Israel, and the faith that burns brightly in your hearts.... May you all have a happy Hanukkah. God bless you and God bless America."

On December 13, Melania Trump visited about 40 children of military families at Joint Base Anacostia-Bolling. "Today I'm here to support the amazing work that Toys for Tots has been doing to make the holidays brighter for children across the country," she said. Praising the Marine Corps Reserves' annual toy drive, she reflected, "As my first year as First Lady comes to an end, I have been privileged to witness the spirit and resilience of so many people in our country.... I've seen people from all over our great nation pitch in to help those who lost everything, and I want to challenge people to continue with that giving spirit.... It is my hope that during this holiday season people will remember it is not about gifts. It is about family service and gratitude. We must continue to look out for and help each other."

With Christmas music playing in the background, Mrs. Trump and the children carried stuffed animals, action figures, dolls and games to oversize boxes marked "Boy," "Girl" and "Toddler." She bent down to assist some of the littlest helpers in sorting their toys, as one small boy carried a teddy bear bigger than himself to one of the bins.

Betsy Klein of CNN remarked that the First Lady "has made visits with children the hallmark of her public appearances during her tenure," noting that Mrs. Trump "animatedly exchanged hugs and high-fives and posed for photos with the children before moving to a card-decorating station. Dressed in a festive green coat, she lifted one little girl carrying a marker onto her lap as the children colored holiday cards, admiring their work."

According to Lt. General Rex McMillan, the campaign's 2017 goal was to collect 7 million toys for distribution to between three and four million children. Since the tradition started in 1947 during the Truman Administration, Toys for Tots had delivered 550 million toys to 250 million children across the country.

On December 21, continuing another long-standing tradition, President Trump visited wounded soldiers at Walter Reed National Military Medical Center, calling them "some of the bravest people anywhere in the world." He then bestowed the Purple Heart medal on 1st Lt. Victor Prato, who had been wounded on deployment to Afghanistan the previous month.

The 25-year-old suffered multiple injuries when his vehicle rolled over after being struck by an IED blast.

The President told reporters, "We'll be over there for a while, but we're just going to wish them a Merry Christmas." The previous day, Vice President Mike Pence had made a surprise visit to troops stationed in Afghanistan to personally thank them for their service. He also met with Afghan President Ashraf Ghani to discuss the country's ongoing security partnership with the United States.

A Great Christmas Gift

After a historic week for President Trump, House and Senate Republicans agreed on a tax-reform compromise that sent the bill to the President's desk for his signature. "We have a tremendous spirit for the tax reform. This is going to be one of the greatest Christmas gifts to middle-income people," said the President. "In addition to tax relief for individuals, the bill would help restore America's economic dominance by putting U.S. companies on a level playing field with foreign competitors. The bill will encourage companies to invest in growth," he added. "Companies are coming in, they are pouring into the country, they've already started. And this will be great for jobs," the President had remarked on December 16. "It will be fantastic for the middle-income people ... everybody's going to benefit."

On December 21, during his cabinet meeting, the President paused and called upon HUD Secretary Ben Carson to thank God for the new law's pending success. The Secretary thanked God for freedom and the opportunities we have as Americans. "In this time of discord, distrust and dishonesty," he asked God "for a spirit of gratitude, compassion and common sense. And give us the wisdom to be able to guide this great nation in the future."

The next day, before leaving to spend the Christmas holidays in Florida, Donald Trump signed the $1.5 trillion tax cut and reform bill into law in the Oval Office.

Since the birth of our nation, Presidents have prayed and called the nation to prayer "for such a time as this." Franklin Roosevelt's D-Day Prayer was so significant that the Government Printing Office printed copies of it for him to give to his senior staff and government officials as his Christmas gift.

Christmas in Florida

Donald Trump celebrated his first Christmas as President at the "Winter White House," his Mar-a-Lago estate in Palm Beach, where he was

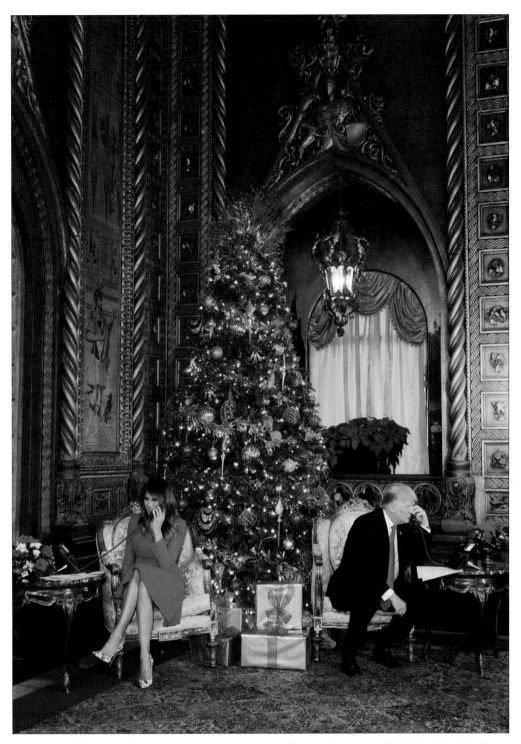

As part of the North American Aerospace Defense Command (NORAD) 62nd Santa Tracker tradition on Christmas Eve to keep watch on Santa's travels around the world, President and Mrs. Trump take phone calls in the library of Mar-a-Lago in Palm Beach. WHITE HOUSE PHOTO BY SHEALAH CRAIGHEAD surrounded by his wife, most of his children and grandchildren, and the First Lady's parents.

His Christmas Eve activity was participating in a video teleconference with five deployed units of the military. He began with a greeting to all the military: "I just want to wish everybody a very, very Merry Christmas. We say Christmas again, very proudly. Very, very Merry Christmas. We're going to have a great year. It's going to be an incredible year," the President said. "I'm thrilled to bring Season's Greetings on behalf of the First Lady and our entire family, and most importantly on behalf of the American people. Today and every day, we're incredibly thankful for you and your families. Your families have been tremendous. Always underappreciated–the military families–the greatest people on earth!"

The President welcomed and congratulated each branch of the Armed Forces starting with the Iron Brigade combat team under Colonel Chuck Lombardo, deployed to Kuwait. He recognized Colonel Chris Gideon and the Kuwait-based Marine Corps Air-Ground Task Force for providing more than 4,000 flight hours of support in the campaign against the Islamic State groups. He thanked Commander Tim Lebens and all the sailors aboard the *USS Sampson* for defending assets in the Strait of Hormuz. He singled out Colonel Paul Goossen and all the Knighthawks from the Air Force's 69th Expeditionary Bomb Squadron in Qatar for engaging more than 700 ISIS and Taliban targets in five countries. Finally, he showered great praise on the U.S. Coast Guard for their rescue efforts in Texas, Florida and Puerto Rico during the recent devastating hurricane season. "What a job you've done...," he said, "[you've] saved thousands and thousands of lives."

Also in his remarks, the President offered thanks. "As we celebrate the most precious holiday, we're grateful for each of you who spend this Christmas away from your families and defend all of our families, our freedoms and our flag. Every American heart is thankful to you, and we are asking God to watch over you and to watch over your families."

The second part of the teleconference video was an opportunity for service members in these units to ask questions of their Commander-in-Chief. At that point, the President asked the media to leave. "Enjoy yourselves.... Thank you very much for being here. If I don't see you during the day, have a great holiday and a great Christmas." After the teleconference, the Trump motorcade headed to Trump International Golf Club in West Palm Beach, where the President relaxed and played golf with friends.

Later in the day, the President and First Lady spoke with children who had called the North American Aerospace Defense Command (NORAD) to track Santa's Christmas Eve travels. The calls took place in the Mar-a-Lago Library.

President Trump asked children, "What would you like more than anything else?" One child wanted building blocks. "I always loved building blocks," replied the President.... "I predict Santa will bring you building blocks, so many you won't be able to use them all."

One young caller told the President that his family's wish was for their grandmother to get out of the hospital. "You want your grandma to get out of the hospital," he repeated. "That is great, that's better than asking for some toy or something." He told another young caller that his own Christmas wish was "peace for the country. We've got prosperity, now we want peace." The President took six calls and the First Lady took nine, according to the First Lady's office. They wished each child a very Merry Christmas.

After dinner and a few after-dinner tweets, the President's motorcade headed for a midnight Mass at the Bethesda-by-the-Sea Church, three miles north on Palm Beach Island. The historic church was the site of his 2005 wedding to Melania Knavs. The gothic stone building was filled with worshipers, who were politely asked to put away their cameras as the First Family entered. Some members of the congregation gave the Trumps a standing ovation; the President replied, "Merry Christmas."

Delivering his midnight homily, Church Rector James Harlan spoke about the need to make room for God in your life, putting aside resentments and hurts. "Your words can have as much destructive potential as they do healing. God's word is pure light."

The President and First Lady released a joint holiday video message to the American people they had prerecorded back at the White House and tweeted out by the President on Christmas Day. They said:

THE PRESIDENT: My fellow Americans, Melania and I are delighted to wish America and the entire world a very Merry Christmas.

THE FIRST LADY: At this time of the year we see the best of America and the soul of the American people. We see children packing boxes to brighten the Christmases of our brave men and women in uniform. We see families reaching out to neighbors in need, and we see communities coming together to serve one another.

THE PRESIDENT: In this season of joy, we spend time with our families; we renew the bonds of love and good will between our citizens, and most importantly we celebrate the miracle of Christmas. For Christians, we remember the story of Jesus, Mary and Joseph that began more than 2,000 years ago. As the book of Isaiah tells us, "For to us a child is born. To us a son is given. And the government will be on his shoulders, and he will be called wonderful counselor, mighty God, everlasting Father, Prince of Peace." This good news is the greatest Christmas gift of all, the reason for our joy and the true source of our hope.

THE FIRST LADY: This Christmas season, we celebrate our blessings as Americans, and we pray for peace all over the world.

THE PRESIDENT: On behalf of Melania, myself, Barron, and the entire Trump family, God bless you. God bless America. And have a very, very Merry Christmas and Happy New Year.

Although lasting less than two minutes, the video featured scenes showing the President and First Lady greeting troops and spending time with children. The footage also captured fragments of White House Christmas decorations, including a close-up of the Crèche in the East Room and a banner that read, "Merry Christmas."

The menu for Christmas Day dinner began with four salad or soup options, including Mr. Trump's signature wedge salad. For an entrée, choices were turkey, char-crusted filet mignon and seared foie gras, braised short ribs, pan-seared sea bass or diver scallops. Not skimping on sweets, among the five desserts offered was the famed three-layer chocolate cake served to President Xi of China on his visit to the Winter White House the previous April.

According to friends and advisers, Donald Trump has appeared most relaxed at Mar-a-Lago, where he has been going since the 1980's. He often socializes with members and uses them as a sounding board for his ideas. As expected, security for a President on vacation was tight, with police cars blocking traffic and the Coast Guard patrolling the waterways. In appreciation for their work, the President personally treated the law enforcement and military personnel to lunch.

President Trump had no public events scheduled on Christmas Day. But White House Press Secretary Sarah Huckabee Sanders said he had received a briefing on a deadly suicide bombing near an office of the Afghan intelligence service in the capital of Kabul, Afghanistan, that had killed at least six people. The Islamic State group (ISIS) claimed responsibility for the attack.

In his weekly address to the nation on December 30, the President marked the end of the year by saying,

It is truly incredible to think of how much we have accomplished on our jour-
ney together.... Since the election we have created more than 2 million jobs

for hard-working, wonderful families.... Unemployment is at a 17-year low; the stock market is at an all-time high.... We are rebuilding our nation, we are building our confidence and rebuilding our standing in the world.... We are facing all challenges with new solutions. We are seizing new opportunities with brimming confidence and boundless resolve.

Because of you and your patriotism, your devotion, your love for your family, we will be able to pass on the blessings of American liberties and prosperities to our children and our grandchildren. Together we are protecting our magnificent heritage and reaching for a glorious destiny.

Finally, Melania and I want to wish every American a very Happy New Year. Our country is great, our country is strong. We are doing things that no one thought possible. Thank you for giving me the opportunity to help. God bless you and God bless America.

In 2017, holiday greetings went out from the White House by word of mouth, through the mail, by the printed word and through social media. Despite the many uncertainties and unknowns that come with a changing culture, the tradition of celebrating Christmas in the White House through décor, hospitality and interaction with the American people continues.

Conforming to a pattern unbroken for almost a century, the President of the United States and the First Lady have extended to everyone across the nation and all around the world, Season's Greetings from the White House.

SELECTED TREE-LIGHTING SPEECHES
OF THE PRESIDENTS

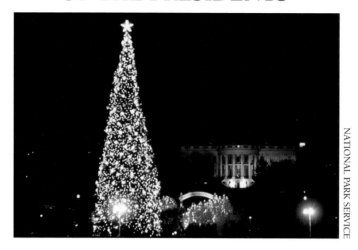

1928
Calvin Coolidge

Speaking at Sherman Square: In token of the good-will and happiness of the holiday season and as an expression of the best wishes of the people of the United States toward a Community Christmas Tree, in behalf of the city of Washington, I now turn on the current which will illuminate this tree.

1931
Herbert Hoover

Speaking at Sherman Square: Mr. Vice President, the people of Washington and of our whole country wide: This is the season and this is the occasion when the whole Nation unites in good cheer and good wishes. We dedicate it particularly to our children, and we give devotion to the faith from which it is inspired.

It gives me great pleasure to join in this ceremony of the lighting of this tree, which is indeed symbolic of that in every household in our country. I ardently wish to every home a Merry Christmas and a Happy New Year.

1933
Franklin D. Roosevelt

Speaking at Sherman Square: We in the Nation's capital are gathered around this symbolic tree celebrating the coming of Christmas. In spirit we join with millions of others, men and women and children, throughout our own land and in other countries and continents, in happy reverent observance of the spirit of Christmas.

For me and my family it is, I am sure, the happiest of Christmases. To the many thousands of you who have thought of me and have sent me greetings (and I hope all of you are hearing my voice), I want to tell you how profound-

ly grateful I am. If it were within my power so to do I would personally thank each and every one of you in every part of the land for your remembrances of me, but there are so many thousands of you that that happy task is impossible. But even more significant is the deep conviction that this year marks a greater national understanding of the significance in our modern life of the teachings of Him whose birth we are celebrating. To more and more of us the words "thou shalt love thy neighbor as thyself" have taken on a meaning that is showing itself and proving itself in our purposes and daily lives. May the practice of that high ideal grow in us all in the year to come, and so I give you and send you, one and all, old and young, a merry Christmas and a truly happy New Year. And so for now and for always, "God bless us every one."

1936
Franklin D. Roosevelt

Speaking at Lafayette Square: I have been reading the *Christmas Carol* to my family, in accordance with our old custom. On this eve of Christmas I want to quote to you the pledge of old Scrooge when, after many vicissitudes, he had come to understand in his heart the great lesson and the great opportunity of Christmastide.

"I will honor Christmas in my heart and try to keep it all the year. I will live in the Past, the Present and the Future. The Spirits of all Three shall strive within me. I will not shut out the lessons that they teach."

And at the end of the story is this glorious passage:

Scrooge was better than his word. He did it all and infinitely more; and to Tiny Tim, who did not die, he was a second father. He became as good a friend, as good a master and as good a man as the good old city knew, or any other good old city, town or borough in the good old world. Some people laughed to see the alteration in him, but he let them laugh and little heeded them; for he was wise enough to know that nothing ever happened on this globe for good, at which some people did not have their fill of laughter in the outset. His own heart laughed; and that was good enough for him.

The teaching of the Sermon on the Mount is as adequate to the needs of men and of Nations today as when it was first proclaimed among the hills above the Sea of Galilee. In such measure as its spirit is accepted men and nations may lay claim to be seekers after peace on earth.

We of the Western Hemisphere have this year rendered special tribute to the spirit of Christmas, for we have pledged anew our faith in the arbitrament of reason and the practice of friendship. To that faith we bear witness tonight. May that faith make us happy today and tomorrow and through all the coming year.

1938
Franklin D. Roosevelt

Speaking at Lafayette Square: Tonight is Christmas Eve. We are gathered again around our Community Tree here in Lafayette Park, across the street from the White House. Darkness has fallen over the Capital but all about us shine a myriad of brilliant lights. All our hearts, warmed by the eternal fire of Christmas, rejoice, because new life, new hope, new happiness are in them.

In this setting I wish my fellow countrymen everywhere a merry Christmas with peace, content and friendly cheer to all. I wish also to thank the thousands who have remembered me and my family this Christmas with individual greetings. We shall always treasure these friendly messages.

At this time let us hope that the boon of peace which we in this country and in the whole Western Hemisphere enjoy under the providence of God may likewise be vouchsafed to all nations and all peoples. We desire peace. We shall work for peace. We covet neither the lands nor the possessions of any other nation or people.

We of the western world, who have borne witness by works as well as words to our devotion to the cause of peace ought to take heart tonight from the atmosphere of hope and promise in which representatives of twenty-one free republics are now assembled in the Pan-American Conference at Lima, Peru.

I consider it a happy circumstance that these deliberations will be successfully concluded soon after the birthday of the Prince of Peace. It is indeed a holy season in which to work for good will among men. We derive new strength, new courage for our work from the spirit of Christmas.

We do not expect a new Heaven and a new Earth overnight, but in our own land, and other lands—wherever men of good will listen to our appeal, we shall work as best we can with the instruments at hand to banish hatred, greed and covetousness from the heart of mankind.

And so the pledge I have so often given to my own countrymen I renew before the whole world on this glad Christmas Eve, that I shall do whatever lies within my power

to hasten the day foretold by Isaiah, when men "shall beat their swords into ploughshares and their spears into pruning hooks; nation shall not lift up sword against nation, neither shall they learn war any more."

1939
Franklin D. Roosevelt

Speaking at the Ellipse: My neighbors of Washington and my neighbors in homes in every part of the nation:

The old year draws to a close. It began with dread of evil things to come and it ends with the horror of another war adding its toll of anguish to a world already bowed under the burden of suffering laid upon it by man's inhumanity to man. But, thank God for the interlude of Christmas.

This night is a night of joy and hope and happiness and promise of better things to come. And so in the happiness of this Eve of the most blessed day in the year I give to all my countrymen the old, old greeting—"Merry Christmas—Happy Christmas!"

A Christmas rite for me is always to re-read that immortal little story by Charles Dickens, *A Christmas Carol.* Reading between the lines and thinking as I always do of Bob Cratchit's humble home as a counterpart of millions of our own American homes, the story takes on a stirring significance for me.

Old Scrooge found that Christmas wasn't a humbug. He took unto himself the spirit of neighborliness. But today neighborliness no longer can be confined to one's own little neighborhood. Life has become much too complex for that. In our country neighborliness had gradually spread its boundaries—from home to town, to county, to State—and now at last to the whole nation.

For instance, who a generation ago would have thought that a week from tomorrow—January 1, 1940—tens of thousands of elderly men and women in every State and every county and every city of the nation will begin to receive checks every month for old age retirement insurance—and not only that but also insurance benefits for the wife, the widow, the orphan children and even dependent parents?

Who would have thought, a generation ago, that people who lost their jobs would, for an appreciable period, receive unemployment insurance and that the needy, the blind and the crippled children are receiving some measure of protection which will reach down to the millions of Bob Cratchits, the Marthas and the Tiny Tims of our own little four-room houses, in every part of the nation.

In these days of strife and sadness in many other lands, let us in this nation and in the other nations which still live at peace, forbear to give thanks not only for our good fortune in our peace. Let us rather pray that we may be given strength to live for others, to live more closely to the words of the Sermon on the Mount, and to pray that peoples in the nations which are at war may also read, learn and inwardly digest these deathless words. May their import reach into the hearts of all men and of all nations. And so I offer them as my Christmas message:

Blessed are the poor in spirit: for theirs is the Kingdom of Heaven.
Blessed are they that mourn: for they shall be comforted.
Blessed are the meek; for they shall inherit the earth.
Blessed are they which do hunger and thirst after righteousness: for they shall be filled.
Blessed are the merciful: for they shall obtain mercy.
Blessed are the pure in heart: for they shall see God.
Blessed are the peacemakers: for they shall be called the children of God.
Blessed are they which are persecuted for righteousness' sake: for theirs is the Kingdom of Heaven.

1941
Franklin D. Roosevelt
Speaking from the South Portico of the White House
With British Prime Minister Winston Churchill as guest

The President:

There are many men and women in America—sincere and faithful men and women—who ask themselves this Christmas: How can we light our trees? How can we give our gifts? How can we meet and worship with love and with uplifted hearts in a world at war, a world of fighting and suffering and death?

How can we pause, even for a day, even for Christmas Day, in our urgent labor of arming a decent humanity against the enemies which beset it?

How can we put the world aside, as men and women put the world aside in peaceful years, to rejoice in the birth of Christ?

These are natural—inevitable—questions in every part of the world which is resisting the evil thing.

Even as we ask those questions, we know the answer. There is another preparation demanded of this Nation beyond and beside the preparation of weapons and materials of war. There is demanded also of us the preparation of our hearts; the arming of our hearts. And when we make ready our hearts for the labor and the suffering and the ultimate victory which lie ahead, then we observe Christmas Day—with all of its memories and all of its meanings—as we should.

Looking into the days to come, I have set aside a Day of Prayer, and in that Proclamation I have said:

"The year 1941 has brought upon our Nation a war of aggression by powers dominated by arrogant rulers whose selfish purpose is to destroy free institutions. They would thereby take from the freedom-loving people of the earth the hard-won liberties gained over many centuries.

"The new year of 1942 calls for the courage and the resolution of old and young to help to win a world struggle in order that we may preserve all we hold dear.

"We are confident in our devotion to country, in our love of freedom, in our inheritance of courage. But our strength, as the strength of all men everywhere, is of greater avail as God upholds us.

"Therefore, I ... do hereby appoint the first day of the year 1942 as a day of prayer, of asking forgiveness for our shortcomings of the past, of consecration to the tasks of the present, of asking God's help in days to come.

"We need His guidance that this people may be humble in spirit but strong in the conviction of the right; steadfast to endure sacrifice, and brave to achieve a victory of liberty and peace."

Our strongest weapon in this war is that conviction of the dignity and brotherhood of man which Christmas Day signifies—more than any other day or any other symbol.

Against enemies who preach the principles of hate and practice them, we set our faith in human love and in God's care for us and all everywhere.

It is in that spirit, and with particular thoughtfulness of those, our sons and brothers, who serve in our armed forces on land and sea, near and far—those who serve for us and endure for us—that we light our Christmas candles now across the continent from one coast to the other on this Christmas Eve.

We have joined with many other Nations and peoples in a very great cause. Millions of them have been engaged in the task of defending good with their life-blood for months and years.

One of their great leaders stands beside me. He and his people in many parts of the world are having their Christmas trees with their little children around them, just as we do here. He and his people have pointed the way in courage and in sacrifice for the sake of little children everywhere.

And so I am asking my associate, my old and good friend, to say a word to the people of America, old and young, tonight—Winston Churchill, Prime Minister of Great Britain.

The Prime Minister:

Fellow workers in the cause of freedom.

I have the honor to add a pendant to the necklace of that Christmas goodwill and kindness with which my illustrious friend the President has encircled the homes and families of the United States by the message of Christmas Eve which he has just delivered.

I spend this anniversary and festival far from my country, far from my family, and yet I cannot truthfully say that I feel far from home. Whether it be the ties of blood on my mother's side, or the friendships I have developed here over many years of active life, or the commanding sentiment of comradeship in the common cause of great peoples who speak the same language, who kneel at the same altars, and who to a very large extent pursue the same ideals—whichever it may be—or all of them together—I cannot feel myself a stranger here in the center of the summit of these United States. I feel a sense of unity and fraternal association which through all your kindness convinces me that I have a right to sit at your fireside and share your Christmas joys.

Fellow workers, fellow soldiers in the cause, this is a strange Christmas Eve. Almost the whole world is locked in deadly struggle. Armed with the most terrible weapons which science can devise, the nations advance upon each other.

Ill would it be for us this Christmastide if we were not sure that no greed for the lands or wealth of any other people, no vulgar ambition, no morbid lust for material gain at the expense of others had led us to the field. Ill would be for us, if that were so.

Here in the midst of war, raging and roaring over all the lands and seas, creeping nearer to our hearts and homes—here, amid all these tumults, we have tonight the peace of the spirit in each cottage home and in every generous heart.

Therefore we may cast aside, for this night at least, the cares and dangers which beset us, and make for the children an evening of happiness in a world of storm.

Here then for one night only, each home throughout the English-speaking world should be a brightly lighted island of happiness and peace. Let the children have their night of fun and laughter—let the gifts of Father Christmas delight their play. Let us grownups share to the full in their unstained pleasures before we turn again to the stern tasks and formidable years that lie before us, resolved that by our sacrifice and daring these same children shall not be robbed of their inheritance or denied their right to live in a free and peaceful world.

And so in God's mercy, a happy Christmas to you all.

1945
Harry S. Truman

Speaking from the South Lawn of the White House: This is the Christmas that a war-weary world has prayed for through long and awful years. With peace come joy and gladness. The gloom of the war years fades as once more we light the National Community Christmas Tree. We meet in the spirit of the first Christmas, when the midnight choir sang the hymn of joy: "Glory to God in the highest, and on earth peace, good will toward men."

Let us not forget that the coming of the Savior brought a time of long peace to the Roman World. It is, therefore, fitting for us to remember that the spirit of Christmas is the spirit of peace, of love, of charity to all men. From the manger of Bethlehem came a new appeal to the minds and hearts of men: "A new commandment I give unto you, that ye love one another."

In love, which is the very essence of the message of the Prince of Peace, the world would find a solution for all its ills. I do not believe there is one problem in this country or in the world today which could not be settled if approached through the teaching of the Sermon on the Mount. The poet's dream, the lesson of priest and patriarch and the prophet's vision of a new heaven and a new earth, all are summed up in the message delivered in the Judean hills beside the Sea of Galilee. Would that the world would accept that message in this time of its greatest need!

This is a solemn hour. In the stillness of the Eve of the Nativity when the hopes of mankind hang on the peace that was offered to the world nineteen centuries ago, it is but natural, while we survey our destiny, that we give thought also to our past—to some of the things which have gone into the making of our Nation.

You will remember that Saint Paul, the Apostle of the Gentiles, and his companions, suffering shipwreck, "cast four anchors out of the stern and wished for the day." Happily for us, whenever the American Ship of State has been storm-tossed we have always had an anchor to the windward.

We are met [meeting] on the South Lawn of the White House. The setting is a reminder of Saint Paul's four anchors. To one side is the massive pile of the Washington Monument—fit symbol of our first anchor. On the opposite end of Potomac Park is the memorial to another of the anchors which we see when we look astern of the Ship of State—Abraham Lincoln, who preserved the Union that Washington wrought.

Between them is the memorial to Thomas Jefferson, the anchor of democracy. On the other side of the White House, in bronze, rides Andrew Jackson—fourth of our anchors—the pedestal of his monument bearing his immortal words: "Our Federal Union—it must be preserved."

It is well in this solemn hour that we bow to Washington, Jefferson, Jackson, and Lincoln as we face our destiny with its hopes and fears—its burdens and responsibilities. Out of the past we shall gather wisdom and inspiration to chart our future course.

With our enemies vanquished we must gird ourselves for the work that lies ahead. Peace has its victories no less hard won than success at arms. We must not fail or falter. We must strive without ceasing to make real the prophecy of Isaiah: "They shall beat their swords into plowshares and their spears into pruning hooks: nation shall not lift up sword against nation, neither shall they learn war any more."

In this day, whether it be far or near, the Kingdoms of this world shall become indeed the Kingdom of God and He will reign forever and ever, Lord of Lords and King of kings. With that message I wish my countrymen a Merry Christmas and joyous days in the New Year.

1947
Harry S. Truman

Speaking from the South Lawn of the White House: We are met on the south lawn of the White House. Above the barren treetops rises the towering shaft of the Washington Monument. The scene is peaceful and tranquil. The shadows deepen and the Holy Night falls gently over the National Capital as we gather around our Christmas tree.

Down the ages from the first Christmas through all the years of nineteen centuries, mankind in its weary pilgrimage through a changing world has been cheered and strengthened by the message of Christmas.

The angels sang for joy at the first Christmas in faraway Bethlehem. Their song has echoed through the corridors of time and will continue to sustain the heart of man through eternity.

Let us not forget that the first Christmas was a homeless one. A humble man and woman had gone up from Galilee out of the City of Nazareth to Bethlehem. There is a sense of desolation in St. Luke's brief chronicle of Mary "brought forth her firstborn son, wrapped Him in swaddling clothes, and laid Him in a manger; because there was no room for them in the inn."

For many of our brethren in Europe and Asia this too will be a homeless Christmas. There can be little happiness for those who will keep another Christmas in poverty and exile and in separation from their loved ones. As we prepare to celebrate our Christmas this year in a land of plenty, we would be heartless indeed if we were indifferent to the plight of less fortunate peoples overseas.

We must not forget that our Revolutionary fathers also knew a Christmas of suffering and desolation. Washington wrote from Valley Forge two days before Christmas in 1777: "We have this day no less that 2,873 men in camp unfit for duty because they are barefooted and otherwise naked."

We can be thankful that our people have risen today, as did our forefathers in Washington's time, to our obligation and our opportunity.

At this point in the world's history, the words of St. Paul have greater significance than ever before. He said:

"And now abideth faith, hope, charity these three; but the greatest of these is charity."

We believe this. We accept it as a basic principle of our lives. The great heart of the American people has been moved to compassion by the needs of those in other lands who are cold and hungry.

We have supplied a part of their needs and we shall do more. In this, we are maintaining the American tradition.

In extending aid to our less fortunate brothers we are developing in their hearts the return of "hope." Because of our efforts, the people of other lands see the advent of a new day in which they can lead lives free from the harrowing fear of starvation and want.

With the return of hope to these peoples will come renewed faith—faith in the dignity of the individual and the brotherhood of man.

The world grows old but the spirit of Christmas is ever young.

Happily for all mankind, the spirit of Christmas survives travail and suffering because it fills us with hope of better things to come. Let us then put our trust in the unerring Star which guided the Wise Men to the Manger of Bethlehem. Let us hearken again to the Angel Choir singing "Glory to God in the highest and on earth peace, good will toward men."

With hope for the future and with faith in God, I wish all my countrymen a very Merry Christmas.

1951
Harry S. Truman

Speaking from his home in Independence, Missouri: Christmas is the great home festival. It is the day in all the year which turns our thoughts toward home.

And so I am spending Christmas in my old home in Independence with my family and friends. As the Christmas tree is lighted on the White House grounds in Washington, I am glad to send this greeting to all of my countrymen.

Tonight we think of the birth of a Little Child in the City of David nineteen and a half centuries ago. In that humble birth God gave his message of love to the world. At this Christmas time the world is distracted by doubt and despair, torn by anger, envy and ill will. But our lesson should still be that same message of love, symbolized by the birth of the Redeemer of the World in a manger "because there was no room for them in the inn."

Our hearts are saddened on this Christmas Eve by the suffering and the sacrifice of our brave men and women in Korea. We miss our boys and girls who are out there. They are protecting us, and all free men, from aggression. They are trying to prevent another world war. We honor them for the great job they are doing. We pray to the Prince of Peace for their success and safety.

As we think of Korea, we should also think of another Christmas, 10 years ago, in 1941. That was just after Pearl Harbor, and the whole world was at war. Then almost every country. almost every home, was overshadowed by fear and sorrow.

The world is still in danger tonight, but a great change has come about. A new spirit has been born, and has grown up in the world, although perhaps we do not fully realize it. The struggle we are making today has a new and hopeful meaning.

Ten years ago total war was no longer a threat but a tragic reality. In those grim days, our Nation was straining all its efforts in a war of survival. It was not peace—not the prevention of war—but the stark reality of total war itself that filled our minds and overwhelmed our hearts and souls at Christmas 1941.

Tonight we have a different goal, and a higher hope. Despite difficulties, the free nations of the world have drawn together solidly for a great purpose; not solely to defend themselves; not merely to win a bloody war if it should come; but for the purpose of creating a real peace—a peace that shall be a positive reality and not an empty hope; a just and lasting peace.

When we look toward the battlefields of Korea, we see a conflict like no other in history. There the forces of the United Nations are fighting—not for territory, not for plunder, not to rule the lives of captive people. In Korea the free nations are proving, by deeds, that man is free and must remain free, that aggression must end, that nations must obey the law.

We still have a long struggle ahead of us before we can reach our goal of peace. In the words of the Bible, the day is not yet here when the bow shall be broken, and the lance cut off, and the chariot burned. But we have faith that that day will come.

We will be strong so long as we keep that faith—the faith that can move mountains, the faith which, as St. Paul says, is the substance of things hoped for, the evidence of things not seen.

Let us ask God to bless our efforts and redeem our faults. Let us resolve to follow his commandments—to carry the gospel to the poor; heal the brokenhearted; preach deliverance to the captive; give freedom to the slave. Let us try to do all things in that spirit of brotherly love that was revealed to mankind at Bethlehem on the first Christmas day.

The victory we seek is the victory of peace. That victory was promised to us long ago, in the words of the angel choir that sang over Bethlehem: "Glory to God in the highest, and on earth peace, good will toward men."

To all my countrymen: Merry Christmas.

1952
Harry S. Truman

Speaking from the White House Lawn: As we light the National Christmas tree tonight, here on the White House lawn—as all of us light our own Christmas trees in our own homes—we remember another night long ago. Then a Child was born in a stable. A star hovered over, drawing wise men from afar. Shepherds, in a field, heard angels singing: "Glory to God in the highest, and on earth peace, good will toward men." That was the first Christmas and it was God's greatest gift to us.

This is a wonderful story. Year after year it brings peace and tranquillity to troubled hearts in a troubled world. And tonight the earth seems hushed, as we turn the old, old story of how "God so loved the world, that He gave His only begotten Son, that whosoever believeth in Him should not perish, but have everlasting life."

Tonight, our hearts turn first of all to our brave men and women in Korea. They are fighting and suffering and even dying that we may preserve the chance of peace in the world. The struggle there has been long and bitter. But it has a hopeful meaning.

It has a hopeful meaning because it is the common struggle of many free nations which have joined together to seek a just and lasting peace. We know, all of us, that this is the only way we can bring about peace in the conditions of our time on this earth. Whether we shall succeed depends upon our patience and fortitude. We still have a long road ahead of us before we reach our goal. We must remain steadfast.

And as we go about our business of trying to achieve peace in the world, let us remember always to try to act and live in the spirit of the Prince of Peace. He bore in His heart no hate and no malice—nothing but love for all mankind. We should try as nearly as we can to follow His example.

Our efforts to establish law and order in the world are not directed against any nation or any people. We seek only a universal peace, where all nations shall be free and all peoples shall enjoy their inalienable human rights. We believe that all men are truly the children of God.

As we worship at this Christmastide, let us worship in this spirit. As we pray for our loved ones far from home—as we pray for our men and women in Korea, and all our service men and women wherever they are—let us also pray for our enemies. Let us pray that the spirit of God shall enter their lives and prevail in their lands. Let us pray for a fulfillment of the brotherhood of man.

Through Jesus Christ the world will yet be a better and a fairer place. This faith sustains us today as it has sustained mankind for centuries past. This is why the Christmas story, with the bright stars shining and the angels singing, moves us to wonder and stirs our hearts to praise.

Now, my fellow countrymen, I wish for all of you a Christmas filled with the joy of the Holy Spirit, and many years of future happiness with the peace of God reigning upon this earth.

1953
Dwight D. Eisenhower

Speaking from inside the White House: This evening's ceremony, here at the White House, is one of many thousands in America's traditional celebration of the birth, almost 2,000 years ago, of the Prince of Peace.

For us, this Christmas is truly a season of good will—and our first peaceful one since 1949. Our national and individual blessings are manifold. Our hopes are bright even though the world still stands divided in two antagonistic parts.

More precisely than in any other way, prayer places freedom and communism in opposition, one to the other. The Communist can find no reserve of strength in prayer because his doctrine of materialism and statism denies the dignity of man and consequently the existence of God. But in America, George Washington long ago rejected exclusive dependence upon mere materialistic values. In the bitter and critical winter at Valley Forge, when the cause of liberty was so near defeat, his recourse was sincere and earnest prayer. From it he received new hope and new strength of purpose out of which grew the freedom in which we celebrate this Christmas season.

As religious faith is the foundation of free government, so is prayer an indispensable part of that faith.

Tonight, richly endowed in the good things of the earth, in the fellowship of our neighbors and the love of our families, would it not be fitting for each of us to speak in prayer to the Father of all men and women on this earth, of whatever nation, and of every race and creed—to ask that He help us—and teach us—strengthen us—and receive our thanks.

Should we not pray that He help us? Help us to remember that the founders of this our country came first to these shores in search of freedom—freedom of man to walk in dignity; to live without fear; beyond the yoke of tyranny; ever to progress. Help us to cherish freedom for each of us and for all nations.

Might we not pray that He teach us? Teach us to shun the counsel of defeat and of despair of self-pride and self-deceit. Teach us and teach our leaders, to seek to understand the problems and the needs of all our people. Teach us how those problems may reach solution in wisdom and how best those needs may be met. But teach us, also, that where there may be special problems, there can be no special rights; and though there may be special needs, there can be no special privileges. Teach us to require of all those who seek to lead us, these things: integrity of purpose; the upright mind, selfless sacrifice, and the courage of the just. Teach us trust and hope and self-dependence. Teach us the security of faith.

And may we pray that He strengthen us. Strengthen us in understanding ourselves and others—in our homes, in our country, and in our world. Strengthen our concern for brotherhood. Strengthen our conviction that whatever we, as Americans, would bring to pass in the world must first come to pass in the heart of America. Strengthen our efforts to forge abroad those links of friendship which must one day encircle the world, if its people are to survive and live in peace.

Lastly, should we not pray that He receive our thanks? For certainly we are grateful for all the good we find about us; for the opportunity given us to use our strength and our faith to meet the problems of this hour. And on this Christmas Eve, all hearts in America are filled with special thanks to God that the blood of those we love no longer spills on battlefields abroad. May He receive the thanks of each of us for this, His greatest bounty and our supplication that peace on earth may live with us, always.

1956
Dwight D. Eisenhower

Speaking at the Pageant of Peace on the Ellipse: In this Nation's capital city we are joined tonight with millions in all our forty-eight States, and, indeed, throughout the world, in the happiness and in the hope that Christmas brings.

Not that everyone is filled with happiness and hope in this season of rejoicing. Far from it. There is weariness—there is suffering for multitudes. There is hunger as well as happiness, slavery as well as freedom in the world tonight. But in the myriads of Christmas candles we see the vision of a better world for all people.

In the light of Christmas, the dark curtains of the world are drawn aside for the moment. We see more clearly our neighbors next door; and our neighbors in other nations. We see ourselves and the responsibilities that belong to us. Inspired by the story of Christmas we seek to give of our happiness and abundance to others less fortunate. Even now the American people, on the farm and in the city, rallying through the Red Cross and other voluntary agencies to meet the needs of our neighbors in Hungary, are true to the spirit of Christmas.

Even more important, there are particularly manifested during this season those spiritual qualities of freedom and honor and neighborliness and good will—great virtues that

make all peoples one. Through them, and faith in them, we see how men can live together in peace; for one glorious moment we sense progress toward that aspiration of every religious faith—"Peace on earth, good will to men."

These are hallowed words; through ages they have heartened and moved mankind, even though their message of peace is far too often drowned by the strident voices of the fearful or the arrogant, who fill our minds with doubt and pessimism. They blur our vision with clouds of hate.

But the spirit of Christmas returns, yet again, to enable us to gain understanding of each other; to help each other; to obey the elemental precepts of justice; to practice good will toward all men of every tongue and color and creed; to remember that we are all identical in our aspirations for a peaceful, a decent, a rewarding life.

In the warm glow of the Christmas tree, it is easy to say these things, but when the trees come down and the lights are put away—as they always are—then we have a true testing of the spirit. That testing will be answered, throughout the year ahead, by the success each of us experiences in keeping alive the inspiration and exaltation of this moment.

We must proceed by faith, knowing the light of Christmas is eternal, though we cannot always see it.

We must believe that the truth of Christmas is constant; that men can live together in peace as Lincoln said, "with charity for all, with firmness in the right."

In this spirit, I now turn on the lights of the National Christmas Tree. [The lights are turned on.]

By the light of Christmas charity and Christmas truth, we enter the New Year with gratitude and strength. In this spirit, let us make sure that 1957 will add a memorable chapter to the story of mankind.

Now, on behalf of Mrs. Eisenhower and myself, may I wish for all of you in this audience—throughout our nation—throughout the world truly, Merry Christmas. And may the Father of us all bless all who dwell upon the earth.

Thank you very much.

1960
Dwight D. Eisenhower

Speaking at the Pageant of Peace on the Ellipse: Through the Ages men have felt the uplift of the spirit of Christmas. We commemorate the birth of the Christ Child by the giving of gifts, by joining in carols of celebration, by giving expression to our gratitude for the great things that His coming has brought about in the world. Such words as faith and hope and charity and compassion come naturally and gladly to our lips at this wondrous time of the year.

And Christmas inspires in us feelings even deeper than those of rejoicing. It impels us to test the sincerity of our own dedication to the ideals so beautifully expressed in the Christian ethic. We are led to self examination.

We are grateful for all the material comforts with which we have been blessed. We take great pride in our country's pre-eminent position in the family of nations. Yet as we look into the mirror of conscience, we see blots and blemishes that mar the picture of a nation of people who devoutly believe that they were created in the image of their Maker.

Too often we discern an apathy toward violations of law and standards of public and private integrity. When, through bitter prejudice and because of differences in skin pigmentation, individuals cannot enjoy equality of political and economic opportunity, we see another of these imperfections, one that is equally plain to those living beyond our borders. Whenever there is denied the right of anyone, because he dares to live by the moral code, to earn for himself and his family a living, this failure, too, is a blot on the brightness of America's image.

But one of America's imperishable virtues is her pride in the national ideals proclaimed at her birth. When danger to them threatens, America will fight for her spiritual heritage to the expenditure of the last atom of her material wealth; she will put justice above life itself. America will never cease in her striving to remove the blemishes on her own reflection.

Though we boast that ours is a government of laws, completeness in this work cannot be achieved by laws alone, necessary though these be. Law, to be truly effective, must command the respect and earnest support of public opinion, both generally and locally. And each of us helps form public opinion.

Before us, then, is a task that each must himself define and himself perform. Good it is that Christmas helps to make us aware of our imperfections. Better it is that we rededicate ourselves to the work of their eradication.

A year ago last night I returned from a trip that took me to the other side of the world, to eleven nations of wide variations in race, color, religion, and outlook. That homecoming had added meaning for me because I came back at this time of year, when we are unfailingly reminded that, under God, we are all brothers in one world.

In this season next year a new President will address you as I address you now. Each succeeding Christmas will, we pray, see ever greater striving by each of us to rekindle in our hearts and minds zeal for America's progress in fulfilling her own high purposes. In doing so, our veneration of Christmas and its meaning will be better understood throughout the world and we shall be true to ourselves, to our Nation, and to the Man whose birth, 2,000 years ago, we now celebrate.

And now, I ask Mrs. Eisenhower to join me. It is our privilege to turn on the lights of our National Christmas Tree.

1962
John F. Kennedy

Speaking at the Pageant of Peace on the Ellipse: With the lighting of this tree, which is an old ceremony in Washington and one which has been among the most important responsibilities of a good many Presidents of the United States, we initiate, in a formal way, the Christmas Season.

We mark the festival of Christmas which is the most

sacred and hopeful day in our civilization. For nearly 2,000 years the message of Christmas, the message of peace and good will towards all men, has been the guiding star of our endeavors. This morning I had a meeting at the White House which included some of our representatives from far-off countries in Africa and Asia. They were returning to their posts for the Christmas holidays. Talking with them afterwards, I was struck by the fact that in the far-off continents Moslems, Hindus, Buddhists, as well as Christians, pause from their labors on the 25th day of December to celebrate the birthday of the Prince of Peace. There could be no more striking proof that Christmas is truly the universal holiday of all men. It is the day when all of us dedicate our thoughts to others; when all are reminded that mercy and compassion are the enduring virtues; when all show, by small deeds and large and by acts, that it is more blessed to give than to receive.

It is the day when we remind ourselves that man can and must live in peace with his neighbors and that it is the peacemakers who are truly blessed. In this year of 1962 we greet each other at Christmas with some special sense of the blessings of peace. This has been a year of peril when the peace has been sorely threatened. But it has been a year when peril was faced and when reason ruled. As a result, we may talk at this Christmas, just a little bit more confidently of peace on earth, good will to men. As a result, the hopes of the American people are perhaps a little higher. We have much yet to do. We still need to ask that God bless everyone. But yet I think we can enter this season of good will with more than usual joy in our hearts.

And I think all of us extend a special word of gratitude and appreciation to those who serve the United States abroad; to the one million men in uniform who will celebrate this Christmas away from their homes; to those hundreds of young men and women and some older men and women who serve in far-off countries in our Peace Corps; to the members of the Foreign Service; to those who work in the various information services, A.I.D. agencies, and others who work for us abroad who will celebrate this December 25th thousands of miles from us at sea, on land, and in the air, but with us. It is to them that we offer the best of Christmases and to all of you I send my very best wishes for a blessed and happy Christmas and a peaceful and prosperous New Year. Thank you.

This [indicating the electric switch] was first pressed by President Coolidge in 1923 and succeedingly by President Hoover, Vice President Curtis, by President Franklin Roosevelt on many occasions, by President Harry Truman, by President Eisenhower, by Vice President Johnson. I am delighted to be in that illustrious company and we therefore light the tree.

1963
Lyndon B. Johnson

Speaking at the Pageant of Peace on the Ellipse: Tonight we come to the end of the season of great national sorrow, and the beginning of the season of great eternal joy. We mourn our great President, John F. Kennedy, but he would have us go on. While our spirits cannot be light, our hearts need not be heavy.

We were taught by Him whose birth we commemorate that after death there is life. We can believe, and we do believe, that from the death of our national leader will come a rebirth of the finest qualities of our national life.

On this same occasion 30 years ago, at the close of another troubled year in our Nation's history, a great President, Franklin D. Roosevelt, said to his countrymen, "To more and more of us the words 'Thou shalt love thy neighbor as thyself' have taken on a meaning that is showing itself and proving itself in our purposes and in our daily lives." I believe that this is no less true for all of us in all of our regions of our land today.

There is a turning away from things which are false and things which are small, and things which are shallow. There is a turning toward those things which are true, those things which are profound, and those things which are eternal. We can, we do, live tonight in a new hope and new confidence and new faith in ourselves and in what we can do together through the future.

Our need for such faith was never greater, for we are heirs of a great trust. In these last 200 years we have guided the building of our Nation and our society by those principles and precepts brought to earth nearly 2,000 years ago on that first Christmas.

We have our faults and we have our failings, as any mortal society must. But when sorrow befell us, we learned anew how great is the trust and how close is the kinship that mankind feels for us, and most of all, that we feel for each other. We must remember, and we must never forget, that the hopes and the fears of all the years rest with us, as with no other people in all history. We shall keep that trust working, as always we have worked, for peace on earth and good will among men.

On this occasion one year ago, our beloved President John F. Kennedy reminded us that Christmas is the day when all of us dedicate our thoughts to others, when we are all reminded that mercy and compassion are the really enduring virtues, when all of us show, by small deeds and by large, that it is more blessed to give than to receive.

So in that spirit tonight, let me express to you as your President the one wish that I have as we gather here. It is a wish that we not lose the closeness and the sense of sharing, and the spirit of mercy and compassion which these last few days have brought for us all.

Between tonight and Christmas Eve, let each American family, whatever their station, whatever their religion, whatever their race or their region—let each American family devote time to sharing with others something of themselves; yes, something of their very own. Let us, if we can do no more, lend a hand and share an hour, and say a prayer—and find some way with which to make this Christmas a prouder memory for what we gave instead of what we receive.

And now here, as we have done so many years, we turn on in your Capital City, the lights of our National Christmas Tree, and we say that we hope that the world will not narrow into a neighborhood before it has broadened into a brotherhood.

1965
Lyndon B. Johnson
Speaking at the Pageant of Peace on the Ellipse:
Guest: British Prime Minister Harold Wilson

Once again it is Christmas. Once again that time has come when the heart of man opens to the holiness of life. Once again we tell the ancient story of a baby, born into poverty and persecution, whose destiny it was to lift the iron burden of despair from his fellow men.

In the 20 centuries that have transpired since the sacred moment of His birth, mankind has never been wholly free of the scourge of war and the ravages of disease, illiteracy, and hunger. Yet the star of Bethlehem burns in our hearts on this December evening with a warmth that is not diminished by the years or discouraged by our failures. It reminds us that our first and most compelling task is peace.

As in other Christmas seasons in the past, our celebration this year is tempered by the absence of brave men from their homes and from their loved ones. We would not have it so. We have not sought the combat in which they are engaged. We have hungered for not one foot of another's territory, nor for the life of a single adversary. Our sons patrol the hills of Vietnam at this hour because we have learned that though men cry "Peace, peace," there is no peace to be gained ever by yielding to aggression. That lesson has been learned by a hundred generations. The guarantors of peace on earth have been those prepared to make sacrifices in its behalf.

On this platform with me this evening is the very distinguished and very great Prime Minister of Great Britain. He speaks for a people who have made such sacrifices in behalf of peace. On the battlefield and at the conference table, his countrymen have fought and have labored to create a just peace among the nations.

The distinguished Prime Minister, Harold Wilson, and I have spoken of this task this afternoon. We have spoken not only of the security of mankind, but of the countless opportunities for cooperation that are the true works of peace.

He has told me that his Government will renew the quest for peace as cochairman of the Geneva Conference. I have told him that any new way he can find to peace will have a ready response from the United States.

We know too that peace is not merely the absence of war. It is that climate in which man may be liberated from the hopelessness that imprisons his spirit.

In this strong and prosperous land, there are many that are still trapped in that prison where hope seems but a dream. We shall never rest until that dream becomes a reality.

But hope cannot be our province alone. For we shall never know peace in a world where a minority prospers and the vast majority is condemned to starvation and ignorance. This evening, inspired once more by Him who brought comfort and courage to the oppressed, we offer our hand to those who seek a new life for their people.

Above all things, we dedicate ourselves to the search for a just settlement of disputes between nations. We declare once more our desire to discuss an honorable peace in Vietnam. We know that nothing is to be gained by a further delay in talking. Our poet Emerson once said that "the god of victory is one-handed—but peace gives victory to both sides."

So in the name of a people who seek peace for their brothers on this earth—"that we may be the children of our Father which is in heaven; for He maketh His sun to rise on the evil and on the good, and sendeth rain on the just and on the unjust"—I turn on the lights of this tree, and pray that the Spirit that we revere this evening may illuminate the heart of every man on earth.

1970
Richard M. Nixon

Speaking at the Pageant of Peace on the Ellipse: I know we want to express our very grateful appreciation to the Mormon Choir and to the Friends University Symphonic Choir for their participation and particularly under the rather adverse weather conditions which I know are very hard for those of you in the audience.

As I was preparing my Christmas message to the Nation, it occurred to me that when we light the National Christmas tree, we do so not only as a Nation but really as a family, a family of more that 200 million members. This week and next week millions of trees all over America will be lighted just as we light this tree today. And all over America families will be gathering together.

At Christmas I think we all think of things like Currier and Ives prints, of snow and Santa Claus, of love and laughter and homecoming. For this is part of the spirit of Christmas. It speaks to something deep and eternal in the human spirit, a yearning for hope, a celebration of life, a wish to put aside all the care and the discord that press in upon us so much of the rest of the year, a wish to let 'the better angels of our nature' sing a little and to sing along with them. The spirit of Christmas is joyous, because it is the spirit of peace—a spirit of loving, of giving, of caring, and letting the light of life shine through.

I received a Christmas card the other day—and thousands of Christmas cards come to the President of the United States and his family—but this one particularly I remember from a lady in California. She wrote something on it. Let me read what she wrote:

"During this Christmas season and throughout the new year, all Americans would like to have peace in the world, peace in our homes, and especially peace in our hearts"—peace in the world, peace in our homes and peace in our hearts.

In the Christmas season, we do find peace in our hearts. We find it because this is a time for celebrating the simple things and the personal things, the things that mean so much to us in human terms. We celebrate the love that unites a family and the little acts of kindness, the touch of a hand, the words of comfort, the extra care that a mother takes as she bakes a Christmas pie.

And we think of the poor and the needy and the lonely, and we think of them not as problems, but as people with problems, and we try to help. And in the act of giving we discover once again how good it feels to give. We find peace in our hearts that way.

As families gather together and those who have been away come home, we discover once again the joys of sharing. We remember the past Christmases. We remember the little incidents of our childhood and how important the little things can be, the mending of a broken toy, the happiness of a grandfather at the sight of his grandchild's smile, and, together again, we find peace in our families.

And then in this larger family, this national family that we call America, of which all of us are a part, we find ourselves drawn together. We find that in the spirit of Christmas, in the spirit of peace, we can put aside what divides us and rediscover what really unites us—the concern for one another, the love of liberty and justice, the knowledge that we are a great Nation because we are a great and diverse people.

We are a national family of many different outlooks and many different hopes and many different problems. But what holds us together is that we respect one another, that we care about one another so that we draw strength from our differences as we address our problems.

Just the other evening when I opened the White House Conference on Children, I recalled something that Edmund Burke once said. What patriotism really means is love of country. And Burke reminded us that for us to love our country, our country must be lovely.

I want young Americans to learn to love America, not because it is the richest country in the world, and it is, and not because it is the strongest country in the world or merely because you happen to have been born here, but I want young Americans and all Americans to love America because this is a good country, and because we can, in our making it better, and because it therefore is truly a lovely country.

This, I think, is the spirit of the American family, knowing that there is much to be done, striving together to do it, and knowing that at heart, in the human sense of heart, this is a lovely country. In this spirit, we can find peace in our larger family.

And our greatest hope in this Christmas season and in all seasons is, of course, peace in the whole world. We can be grateful in this Christmas season that already we have been able to bring 200,000 men back from Vietnam, more coming home. We can look forward with assurance to an end of that war. And as we look around the world, we see that there are still many other danger spots. And there are also many other threats to the peace of the world.

But because of the progress that we have made over the past two years, as I stand here before you, the American people, in this Christmas season, I believe that I can confidently say that we now have the best chance since the end of World War II to build what we have not had in this whole century, a full generation of peace. As we look forward to that great hope of a generation of peace, we think especially of our children, and at Christmas we think especially of our children.

And as we light this great tree, and as millions of other trees are lighted in homes across the land, we do so in a spirit of peace and love and gathering together. And as the lights go on, we know that these lights will reflect the light in the eyes of millions of children and the light of hope that stirs in millions of hearts, for the true light of Christmas is not the light on the tree. It is the light in the eyes of a child.

And now we come to the big moment we have all been waiting for. We are going to light the tree, and because this is a very big tree, I understand that I am going to have some help to light it. And I am going to go down here in the audience and pick out one of the children to help me press the button to light the tree. I see we have lots of volunteers. Now, we picked this boy out. He is the smallest boy here. But he can do this, I know very well. And his name is Andre.

1973
Richard M. Nixon

Speaking at the Pageant of Peace on the Ellipse: Mr. Dixon, Mr. Secretary, all of the distinguished guests on the platform, all of the ladies and gentlemen, all of the children here in the audience, and our television and radio audience across this land: I think one of the greatest privileges that a President of the United States has is to light the Christmas tree, the Nation's Christmas tree, because it belongs to. all the Nation, here in the Nation's Capital.

This year, as the Secretary has already indicated, the tree is different. This year, Christmas will be different in terms of lights, perhaps, all across America. Instead of having many lights on the tree, as you will see over there in a few moments, there will be only one on it, the star at the top, and the other lights you see will simply be the glitter from the ground lights which are around the tree. And in a way, I suppose one could say with only one light on the tree, this will be a very dreary Christmas, but we know that isn't true, because the spirit of Christmas is not measured by the number of lights on a tree. The spirit of Christmas is measured by the love that each of us has in his heart for his family, for his friends, for his fellow Americans, and for people all over the world. And this year, while we have a problem, a problem the Secretary has alluded to, the problem of energy, I think that what we can all be thankful for is that it is a problem of peace and not a problem of war. That is what Americans can be thankful for.

This year we will drive a little slower. This year the thermostats will be a little lower. This year every American per-

haps will sacrifice a little, but no one will suffer. But we will do it for a great goal, the goal, first, of seeing to it that in a year when our energy supplies are not as high as we need, we can prepare for the future, and also a year in which America will make a great stride forward toward a new, great goal, and that is, by the year 1980 this Nation, which will celebrate its 200th anniversary of independence in 1976-by 1980 will celebrate Project Independence, when we are independent of any other country in the world where our energy supply is concerned. That we can do. As we consider these problems of peace, I think also we must be thankful, as the Secretary has already indicated, for the fact that this is the first Christmas in 12 years that a President has stood here at a time when America was at peace with every nation in the world.

It is the first Christmas in 8 years when no American prisoner of war is away from home at Christmas. And to all of these young people, and particularly to our very distinguished young people who participated in this program, it is also a Christmas for the first time in 20 years when no young American is being drafted for the armed services. That is what peace means to America. It would be well, of course, for us to stand simply on that achievement, but we know that there will always be threats to the peace of the world, and that is where we come in, and where each American comes in, looking to the future. Because as we look at the chances not just of getting peace, which we have now achieved, but of keeping peace, which we have not been able to do for a full generation, for a century, then what happens in America will decide it, whether America has the strength not just of its arms but more, of its spirit to provide the leadership that the world needs to keep the trouble spots in the world from blowing up into war and to build that permanent structure of peace that we all want. It is that to which we dedicate ourselves as we light the Nation's Christmas tree tonight. Let the year 1974 be one in which we make great progress toward the goal of a lasting peace, peace not only for America but for all nations, peace between peoples who have different forms of government, but who nevertheless can be friends.

A moment ago when the flowers were presented to Mrs. Nixon by Tyna, I remembered an occasion in 1959 when a little girl presented flowers to her in the Ural Mountains in Russia. We were driving through the mountains, and a group of schoolchildren stopped the cavalcade for a few moments and they presented flowers to Mrs. Nixon. And when they did so in this year 1959, when the cold war was still going on, they shouted out "Friendship, friendship" in English. When we got back into the car, our guide, Mr. Zhukov, said to me that the first word that a Russian child who learns English and studies English in a Russian school learns is the word "friendship." That is the first English word the Russian child learns.   Now, I do not mean to suggest by that that because a Russian child is taught, when he first studies English, the word "friendship" that it is inevitable that the Russian people and the American people are not going to have differences as far as their governments are concerned, but I do know this: We have had the great privilege, Mrs. Nixon and I, of traveling to most of the nations of the world, to the nations of Africa, to the nations of Asia, to China, to Russia, and I can tell you that the people of the world want peace, the people of the world want friendship, and every American, I know, wants his country and his Government to take the lead in building a world of peace.

As this Christmas season begins, let us just remember we do have some problems which we will overcome, but they are the problems of peace. And we also have a great challenge, the challenge of helping to build a structure of peace that all the 3 billion people in this world can enjoy. What a wonderful achievement that can be. There are times, of course, when we tire of the challenge. There are times when we would not like to accept that position of leadership, but let us remember that unless America, at this time in history, accepts the responsibility to lead for peace, we may not have it in the world. I think we can meet the challenge. I am sure we will. And on this particular day, in this year 1973, as we look at the beginning of the year 1974, let us so conduct ourselves as a people, let us so conduct ourselves as a nation in our leadership toward peace that in the years to come, people, not only in America but all over the world, will look back at what we have done, will look back and say "God bless America."

Thank you.

MR. JOHN W. DIXON (president, 1973 Christmas Pageant of Peace Committee). Thank you, Mr. President, and thank you, Mrs. Nixon, for being here. Mr. President, on behalf of the American people, I would like to ask you to do us the honor of lighting the National Community Christmas Tree.

THE PRESIDENT. Now I would like to suggest that this honor should be shared, and who better to share it with but young Americans, so if Tyna and Warren would join me here, we will press this button together and light the tree. There! We got it.

1976
Gerald R. Ford

Speaking at the Pageant of Peace on the Ellipse: As our Bicentennial Year comes to a close, it is especially appropriate to gather once more around the traditional symbol of family ties and friendly reunions, our Nation's Christmas tree. In doing so, we combine our year-long celebration of historical events with a personal rededication to timeless values.

The message of Christmas has not changed over the course of 20 centuries. Peace on Earth, good will toward men—that message is as inspiring today as it was when it was first proclaimed to the shepherds near Bethlehem. It was first proclaimed, as we all know, then.

In 1976 America has been blessed with peace and a significant restoration of domestic harmony. But true peace is more than an absence of battle. It is also the absence of prej-udice and the triumph of understanding. Brotherhood among all peoples must be the solid cornerstone of lasting peace. It has been a sustaining force for our Nation, and it remains a guiding light for our future.

The celebration of the birth of Jesus is observed on every continent. The customs and traditions are not always the same, but feelings that are generated between friends and family members are equally strong and equally warm.

In a few moments I will turn the switch that lights up our national Christmas tree. As beautiful as that tree is, it will be only a symbol if its light is not matched by the glow of love in our hearts. It is my personal prayer on this Christmas of 1976 that the tree which I light tonight is only the beginning, that each of you will also light a flame of love—love that is reflected in the eyes of all our brothers and sisters across the Nation, and around the world.

Now, Betty joins me in wishing you all a very, very Merry Christmas and a Happy New Year. Thank you and God bless you.

.

1978
Jimmy Carter

Speaking at the Pageant of Peace on the Ellipse: As you well know the theme of this year's Pageant of Peace is unity. There is much to divide us in this world. And sometimes we concentrate too much of our attention on those divisions among us. But Christmas is a good time to recall how much unites us as people and also as nations. We are united in our belief in human dignity, in our conviction that the most likely way to find truth is to silence people's voices and to try to make them deny what they really believe.

Our country is entering a period of healing and of hope. We are joining together as a people again, realizing the strength of a common purpose. We are blessed with warm fires and warm memories and the voices of children singing of joy in the night. I think that God in His great wisdom knew that we needed these things to help us face the cold and sometimes lonely times. We need the joy of children's voices to remind us that the only things that we can truly give to each other are the only things that we truly need—an ear to listen, a heart to care, a word of encouragement, and a hand to help.

At Christmas, we have not only this year's special moments but the rich store of all Christmases past to remember and to use.

When I was growing up, President Franklin Roosevelt was lighting the Nation's Christmas tree. During the difficult years of the Depression, and later during the Second World War, too many of our own Nation's Christmases have been shadowed by war. We are fortunate as we light this Christmas tree tonight that our Nation and most of the nations of the world are not at war.

This is always a matter of concern, the threat of violence in many corners of the globe. But this Christmas is a time of relative calm and also a time of great hope. Two ancient enemies are on the threshold of an agreement that could bring peace to the Middle East. It is my earnest prayer that the day will soon come when all children in the Middle East can play in the sunshine without fear, when their young men and women can turn their energies and talents away from war and death, to making the deserts fruitful and to building, instead of preparing to destroy.

The Prophet Isaiah, who wrote about ancient wars between Israel and her neighbors, tells us that the work of righteousness is peace. The United States has tried this year to help other nations find peace. We have succeeded in several troubled areas in getting people to talk to each other and to work out their differences without resorting to violence and to war.

I hope that the time has passed when people excuse the pain and destruction and death and see war in itself as a demonstration of national heroism. This generation, our generation has seen too much of war's desolation. We've seen what it can do spiritually, as well as physically, to a people. War is no longer the brave sound of parades and drums and trumpets. We've seen it as it is, the loss of the young in the full flower of their promise, the death of families and entire communities, and the threat of nuclear devastation for the world.

I think the world is more ready than ever before to understand the thrust of Ralph Waldo Emerson's words that peace is victory for both sides. I believe that nations may be ready now to accept the possibility that those whom they have called enemies might live undisturbed on Earth and that we might at last learn to call even enemies brothers and sisters.

Perhaps at last the same fervor and commitment and sense of high purpose with which we once sought victory in war can now be devoted to our search for peace. And then we will truly be able to say in our hearts, for the fulfillment of the ancient promise of peace on Earth, good will toward men.

The evergreen tree that we use at Christmas is a symbol of eternal life, and also of the perpetual renewal of life. As I light our Nation's Christmas tree, and whenever you see a glowing tree this Christmas, I hope that you will see it as a rekindling of our faith and hope and our dedication to the cause of unity and a great nation's influence throughout the world for peace on Earth.

Thank you very much. And now we'll proceed to wish all the world a happy Christmas by lighting the Christmas tree together.

1979
Jimmy Carter

Speaking at the Pageant of Peace on the Ellipse: Christmas means a lot of things. It means love. It means warmth. It means friendship. It means family. It means joy. It means light. But everyone this Christmas will not be experiencing those deep feelings. At this moment there are 50 Americans who don't have freedom, who don't have joy, and who don't have warmth, who don't have their families with them. And there are 50 American families in this Nation who also will not experience all the joys and the light and the happiness of Christmas.

I think it would be appropriate for all those in this audience and for all those listening to my voice or watching on television to pause just a few seconds in a silent prayer that American hostages will come home safe and come home soon—if you'd please join me just for a moment. [Pause for silent prayer.] Thank you very much.

Nineteen seventy-nine has not been a bad year. Many good things have happened to us individually and have also happened to our Nation. Not far from here, on the north side of the White House, we saw a remarkable ceremony, headed by a Jew, the leader of Israel, a Moslem, the President of Egypt, and myself, a Christian, the President of our country, signing a treaty of peace. This peace treaty was a historic development, and it was compatible with the commitment that we feel so deeply in the religious season now upon us.

Our Nation also opened up its arms of understanding, diplomatic relationships, and friendship—our Nation, the strongest on Earth, and China, the most populous nation on Earth. The establishment of new friendships is part of the Christmas season.

I went to Vienna and met with President Brezhnev. And he and I signed the SALT II treaty, which will help to limit and to reduce the spread of nuclear weapons, to bring about a better understanding between our two great countries, and to search for the kind of reduction of armaments that will lead, I think, to the realization of the true spirit of Christmas.

This fall we had a visit from a great spiritual leader, Pope John Paul II, who traveled throughout our country and who spoke in a quiet voice of understanding, of compassion, of love, of commitment, of morality, of ethics, of the unchanging things that are part of the spirit of Christmas. And I remember one thing in particular that he said on the White House lawn. He said, "Do not be afraid. Do not be afraid." And as you know that's the same message that the angels brought to the shepherds near Bethlehem the night that our Savior was born: "Fear not. Be not afraid." Many of the problems in our world derive from fear, from a lack of confidence in ourselves and, particularly, a lack of confidence in what we can do with God.

We hope we'll soon see peace in Zimbabwe-Rhodesia, a nation that has suffered much in the last few years. But we've also seen some needs for additional effort.

This is the Year of the Child, but it's possibly true that in Cambodia, or Kampuchea, the children will have suffered more in 1979 than in any other year in our lifetime—children so weak, so starved, that they don't even have the strength to cry. We've seen Vietnam refugees put to sea with very little hope of ever reaching land again. And our country has reached out its arms to help those starving children and those refugees adrift.

We've seen divisions among people because of religious beliefs. The recent events in Iran are an unfortunate example of that misguided application of belief in God. But I know that all Americans feel very deeply that the relationships between ourselves and the Moslem believers in the world of Islam is one of respect and care and brotherhood and good will and love.

So, we do have disappointments; we do have suffering; we do have divisions; we often have war. But in the midst of pain, we can still remember what Christmas is—a time of joy, a time of light, a time of warmth, a time of families, and a time of peace.

In our great country we have an awful lot for which we can be thankful: the birth of our Savior, the initiation of religious holidays tomorrow night for the Jews of America, and a realization that in our Nation we do have freedom to worship or not worship as we please. So let's remember our blessings, yes, but let's also remember the need for us to be more fervent in our belief in God and especially in sharing of our blessings with others.

Thank you very much. Merry Christmas to you all.

1982
Ronald Reagan

Speaking from the Rose Garden of the White House: My fellow Americans, the Christmas and Hanukkah decorations are up around the country, and in a moment we'll be lighting the National Christmas Tree here in the Nation's Capital.

In this holiday season, we celebrate the birthday of one who, for almost 2,000 years, has been a greater influence on humankind than all the rulers, all the scholars, all the armies, and all the navies that ever marched or sailed, all put together. He brought to the world, the simple message of peace on Earth, good will to all mankind.

Some celebrate the day as marking the birth of a great and good man, a wise teacher and prophet, and they do so sincerely. But for many of us it's also a holy day, the birthday of the Prince of Peace, a day when "God so loved the world that He sent us His only begotten Son" to assure forgiveness of our sins.

The Yuletide season is characterized in our country by the giving of gifts, a spirit of charity, and yes, good will, more so than at any other time of the year. Already traditional programs are underway, drives to collect food and clothing for those who are in need. The U. S. Marine Reserves have a toy collection drive to make sure that old St. Nicholas—Santa Claus—has enough to go around. And this is matched in countless American communities by firemen, policemen, churches, religious groups and service clubs.

Let me give you one specially moving example of what the Christmas spirit can do. I told this the other night. In Bridgeport, Connecticut, the Police Athletic League for years has maintained a kind of Christmas Center. It consists of a ranch type house, a manger and all the other things associated with Christmas. And during the holiday season it's manned by a Santa Claus, elves, and helpers. Thousands of children visit it every year, and thousands of toys are given to them.

This year, on Tuesday, December 7th, it was destroyed by fire set by a suspected arsonist. The mayor of Bridgeport called an emergency meeting. He asked for constructionists, carpenters, electricians, all the skills that are needed to help rebuild such a place. The answer to his call was instantaneous. More than 250 volunteers worked in shifts around the clock.

On Sunday, December 12th, five days later, at about 1:30 p.m. I phoned the mayor. He was officiating at the reopening of that Christmas Center to the cheers of hundreds and hundreds of citizens of Bridgeport. It had been rebuilt in only 4 days between the fire and the opening ceremony.

A recent initiative of Postmaster General William Bolger's will make it easier for all of us to do our part. He has instructed post offices across the country to display lists of the Christmas food, clothing and toy drives in their local areas, a guide to holiday giving open to all Americans.

This holiday season, as we work our way out of a recession, too many still find themselves without jobs, forced to cut back on things that they once thought of as their normal pattern of living. They aren't statistics; they're people. They're our neighbors, friends, and yes, family, and they make up that group that right now we call the unemployed. Their number's greater than it has been for some time past. Still, for every unemployed individual there are nine of us who do have jobs, and with that ratio of 1 out of 10 in mind, I'd like to make a suggestion. How about those of us who are employed making sure that those who aren't will nevertheless have a merry Christmas. This is something that needs doing at the community level—neighbor helping neighbor.

The people we're talking about may be members of your church, brothers and sisters in your local union, or that family across the street or down the block in your neighborhood. Surely between the nine of us, we can find a way to make Christmas merry for that one who temporarily can use our help. But remember, time is growing short, and Christmas is almost here, which brings us back to lighting the National Christmas Tree. This beloved tradition, which began nearly 60 years ago, has a special symbolism for our people. It's as if when we light this tree, we light something within ourselves as well. And during the Christmas season I think most Americans do feel a greater sense of family, friendship, giving, and joy. And there's a special joy in our children at this time of year. I've heard from many of them recently. I wish Nancy and I could personally thank all you children who've written in, but I want you to know how good your cards, letters and artwork make us feel.

Now, while Christmas is a time for children, it's also a time to think of those who are less fortunate than we are, and let us also remember the constant vigil of the families of our missing in action. As we light this Christmas tree, may it lift hope in the hearts of those who are lonely and needy.

In Ephesians we read that "Each of us has been given his gift, his portion of Christ's bounty." Well, let us share our bounty this Christmas season. Let us offer not only our hearts and prayers but a generous hand to those who need our help. And as we light this tree, let us brighten the lives of those here at home and around the world whose Christmas may not be as glowing and as cheerful as ours.

So, to all of you, God bless you and keep you during this cherished holiday season. And now let's turn on the National Christmas Tree.

And there it is. It's lighted.

1983
Ronald Reagan

Speaking from inside the White House: In just a moment we'll be lighting our National Christmas Tree, continuing a wonderful tradition that was started by President Coolidge 60 years ago. I know there's a special feeling that we share when we push the button lighting up that tree. It's as if each one of those twinkling lights sends a new spirit of love, hope, and joy through the heart of America. And of course, the brightest light of all is the Star of Peace, expressing our hopes and prayers for peace in our families, our communities, our nation, and the world.

On behalf of our fellow citizens, Nancy and I would like to thank all of you on the Ellipse who have given America such a beautiful Christmas present, the 1983 Pageant of Peace.

Christmas is a time for giving, and as we reach out to family and friends, I hope we'll also open our hearts to those who are lonely and in need, citizens less fortunate than ourselves, brave soldiers working to preserve peace from the tip of Alaska to the shores of Lebanon, to the DMZ in Korea, families maintaining a constant vigil for their missing in action, and millions forbidden the freedom to worship a God who so loved the world that He gave us the birth of the Christ Child so that we might learn to love each other. I know they would welcome your expressions of love and support.

Many stories have been written about Christmas. Charles Dickens' "Carol" is probably the most famous. Well, I'd like to read some lines from a favorite of mine called "One Solitary Life," which describes for me the meaning of Christmas. It's the story of a man born of Jewish parents who grew up in an obscure village working in a carpenter shop until he was 30 and then for three years as a preacher. And, as the story says, he never wrote a book, he never went to college, he never traveled 200 miles from the place where he was born. He never did one of the things that usually accompany greatness.

While still a young man, the tide of popular opinion turned against him. His friends ran away. One of them denied him. He was turned over to his enemies. He went through the mockery of a trial. He was nailed on a cross between two thieves. While he was dying, his executioners gambled for the only piece of property that he had on Earth. When he was dead he was taken down and laid in a borrowed grave.

Nineteen wide centuries have come and gone. And today

He's the centerpiece of much of the human race. All the armies that ever marched, all the navies that were ever built, and all the parliaments that ever sat, and all the kings that ever reigned, put together, have not affected life of man upon Earth as powerfully as this One Solitary Life.

I have always believed that the message of Jesus is one of hope and joy. I know there are those who recognize Christmas Day as the birthday of a great and good man, a wise teacher who gave us principles to live by. And then there are others of us who believe that he was the Son of God, that he was divine. If we live our lives for truth, for love, and for God, we never need be afraid. God will be with us and He will be part of something much larger, much more powerful and enduring than any force here on Earth.

Now tonight I have a very special person here with me to spread our Christmas joy. Her name is Amy Benham, and she comes all the way from Westport, Washington. Amy recently wrote the leaders of a public-spirited project named "Make a Wish" and said, "The Christmas tree that lights up for our country must be seen all the way to heaven. I would wish so much to help the President turn on those Christmas lights."

Well, Amy, the nicest Christmas present I could receive is helping make your wish come true. When you press the button over here—we're going over there—the whole world will know that Amy Benham lit up the skies, sending America's love, hope, and joy all the way to heaven and making the angels sing.

And now, you and I will walk over so you can light the tree. And then after that's done we'll all join in singing one of our favorite Christmas carols, "Joy to the World." So, let's go over here.

1985
Ronald Reagan

Speaking from the White House: My fellow Americans, thank you for joining Nancy and me on this festive evening. The menorah stands lighted in Lafayette Park, for this is also the time of Hanukkah, and this season is rich in the meaning of our Judeo-Christian tradition. In a moment we'll be lighting the National Christmas Tree, carrying forward what is now a 62-year tradition first begun by Calvin Coolidge.

Tonight we're drawn in warmth to one another as we reflect upon the deeply holy meaning of the miracle we shall soon celebrate. We know that Mary and Joseph reached the stable in Bethlehem sometime after sunset. We do not know the exact moment the Christ Child was born, only what we would have seen if we'd been standing there as we stand here now; Suddenly, a star from heaven shining with brilliant beauty across the skies, a star pointing toward eternity in the night, like a great ring of pure and endless light, and then all was calm, and all was bright. Such was the beginning of one solitary life that would shake the world as never before or since. When we speak of Jesus and of His life, we speak of a man revered as a prophet and teacher by people of all religions, and Christians speak of someone greater—a man who was and is divine. He brought forth a power that is infinite and a promise that is eternal, a power greater than all mankind's military might, for His power is Godly love, love that can lift our hearts and soothe our sorrows and heal our wounds and drive away our fears. He promised there will never be a long night that does not end. He promised to deliver us from dark torment and tragedy into the warming sunlight of human happiness, and beyond that, into paradise. He's never been a halfway giver; His generosity is pure and perfect and sure.

This, then expresses the true meaning of Christmas. If each of us could give but a fraction to one another of what He gave to the whole human family, how many hearts could heal, how much sorrow and pain could be driven away? There's still time for joy and gladness to touch a sad and lonely soul, still time to feed a hungry child, to wrap a present for a kind old man feeling forlorn and afraid, and to reach out to an abandoned mother raising children on her own. There's still time to remember our Armed Forces, to express our profound gratitude to those keeping watch on faraway frontiers of freedom, and to redouble our energies to account for our MIA's. They are not and never will be forgotten. And there's still time to remember the deepest truth of all: that there can be no prisons, no walls, no boundaries separating the members of God's family.

Let us reach out tonight to every person who is persecuted; let us embrace and comfort, support and love them. Let us come together as one family under the fatherhood of God, binding ourselves in a communion of hearts, for tonight and tomorrow and for all time. May we give thanks for an America abundantly blessed, for a nation united, free, and at peace. May we carry forward the happiness of the Christmas spirit as the guiding star of our endeavors 365 days a year. And as we light this magnificent tree, may all the youthful hope and joy of America light up the heavens and make the angels sing.

Merry Christmas, and God bless you all. And now we're going to light the tree.

1988
Ronald Reagan

Speaking from the South Balcony of the White House: Merry Christmas, Joe [Riley, Chairman of the Pageant of Peace} and a very Merry Christmas to all. Nancy and I are together with you in celebration and reflection—celebration of the great miracle nearly 2,000 years ago that brought the Christ child to us and reflection on the great gifts He has bestowed upon us.

Christmas casts its glow upon us, as it does every year. And it reminds us that we need not feel lonely because we are loved, loved with the greatest love there has ever been or ever will be. In the bustle and rush of daily life, we sometimes forget how very much we have and how much we have to thank God for providing—for things as beautiful as a winter snow or babies who will be seeing their first Christmas, seeing the wonder of its beauty in their eyes. And yes, from the poorest among us to the most fortunate, we are all

blessed.

Christmas reminds us, as well, that He taught us all we need to know about caring for our fellow man and to take responsibility for the very condition of the world. Thus we must reflect: We must ever reflect upon the love we have for others and the joy we take in giving of ourselves to those who are less fortunate. From those who must depend on charity to see that their children receive a Christmas present to the tragic victims of famine and earthquake worldwide, we know what it is we must do and how ennobling an experience it is to have done it.

We Americans live with bounties that those who lived at the time of the Christ child's birth could never have imagined. The bounties are material, yes, but chiefly they are spiritual. Those who would worship the birth of our Lord may do so in the church of their choosing. Those among us who do not so celebrate the birth are free to share with us in this, our time of joy. In this day, when our freedom to worship is most precious, let us redouble our efforts to bring this and other greatest freedoms to all peoples of the Earth.

May we give thanks for a free America, an America united in the wonder of a season that includes not only Christmas but Hanukkah as well. And as we light this glorious tree, may Nancy and I offer a final wish to all Americans: that every Christmas that follows will be as full of joy as we have these past years to work in your service. May God bless you all. And now Nancy will help me light the tree. And again, a very Merry Christmas!

1989
George Bush

Speaking at the Pageant of Peace on the Ellipse: Well, my special thanks to Santa Claus—that Santa mold will never be the same again. [Laughter] But to Loretta and—first Willard Scott, and then to Loretta and Peggy, Tommy Tune, Marilyn McCoo and Billy Davis, the great Air Force band and this marvelous team from Roanoke.

This is the Christmas that we've awaited for 50 years. And across Europe, East and West, 1989 is ending, bright with the prospect of a far better Christmastime than Europe has ever known—a far better future than the world dared to imagine. And 50 winters have come and gone since darkness closed over Europe in 1939—50 years. But last month, as Lech Walesa was coming to the White House, the wall in Berlin came tumbling down.

And another winter descended across Europe. Spring returned to Prague—an unconquerable people, unquenchable dreams. And today—there's a new sound at the wall. New sound rings out—not the hammer and sickle but the hammer and the chisel. The glad sound you hear is not only the bells of Christmas but also the bells of freedom. And in this new season of hope, the triumph looms. It's just like the joy of Christmas: not a triumph for one particular country or one particular religion but a triumph for all humankind. The holidays are—as we've seen here tonight—a time of laughter and children and counting our blessings, a time when songs fill the air and hope fills our hearts for peace on earth, good will to men.

And we've worked hard this year, all of us, all of you, to help build a better America, help someone else, help make this a kinder and gentler nation. But there remains a world of need all around us. In this holiday season, reach out to someone right where you live. Because from now on in America, "There's no room at the inn," that's simply not an acceptable answer.

From now on in America, any definition of a successful life must include serving others. For Christmas is measured not by what's beneath your tree but by what's inside your heart. And so this year, the spirit of the holidays is at long last matched by the spirit of the time. And it's the beginning of a new decade at the ending of an old century. And whatever your dream, whatever star you're following, the future is bright with possibility.

So, Barbara and I want to wish all of you a very Merry Christmas. And now, with simultaneous tree lightings from coast to coast, in Charleston and Santa Cruz, let's show our Thousand Points of Light—let's turn on the National Christmas Tree.

1990
George Bush

Speaking at the Pageant of Peace on the Ellipse: Thank you very much. Thank you, Joe Riley. And thank you, Jane Powell and Willard Scott and Ricky Van Shelton and Ruth Brown and the Army Band, the magnificent University of Wyoming Chorale and our members of the clergy, the California Raisins and, of course, Santa Claus. And may I give a special welcome to the American hostages just home from Kuwait and Iraq, who are with us here tonight. And my thanks to Secretary Lujan and the Department of the Interior, and a special thanks to the National Coal Association for this year's holiday gift: the 57 beautiful State and territorial trees lining our Pathway of Peace. It's a wonderful 1990's tale of careful stewardship and rebirth, for these trees were grown on mined land that has been reclaimed.

This Christmas tree lighting is always a very special moment. People talk of the magic of the season. Well, what is more magical than the way light dispels the darkness? And I've read that white light is actually made up of all the colors of the rainbow. So, that's what we see in the glow of this tree—red and blue and yellow bulbs mixing together to become something new—one light that represents both unity and diversity. And that's how I like to look at America: all of us, all different, all working together, giving the best of ourselves to make this country the strong, beautiful land that it is.

You know, there are so many emotions that we share tonight. We feel joy thinking of how freedom has at last illuminated the dark corners of Eastern Europe—and democracy coming to most of our own hemisphere. We feel pride

thinking of our young men and women standing strong in the harsh, distant deserts and on the waters of the Persian Gulf—and for their courage is the true eternal flames which will never be extinguished. And we think of their parents and their loved ones here at home who miss them very much. And we join them all in praying for the safe return of their soldier or their airman or their marine or their sailor. And let us also add a prayer for those Americans—for many years, but still held hostage against their will in the Middle East.

And here tonight we also feel determination that the bright warmth of this holiday season will stay with us all year and that we will be guided by our inner North Star, making family unity and community service and national pride the center of our lives. We're determined that our nation will become a constellation of hope made up of thousands of separate Points of Light, people helping those in need across our land. People like the more than 100 representatives of daily Points of Light here tonight—individuals like W.W. Johnson, and volunteers for groups like the Higher Achievement Program and the D.C. Central Kitchen and Mary's House. And following the lead of these Points of Light, let all of us echo that beautiful carol, "O, Little Town of Bethlehem" and like that long-ago star, let us shine in all "dark streets" and to all people in the "deep and dreamless sleep" of loneliness and despair.

For nearly 70 years Presidents have taken part in this tradition: flipping a switch to send thousands of lights sparkling into the chill night sky. As we gather here, we're doing what generations before us have done: watching our national Christmas tree become a brilliant symbol of hope, of peace, and of compassion for all the world. And so, let us pledge together that we will keep forever bright this shining legacy we celebrate here tonight. God bless the United States of America, and happy holidays to everybody. Merry Christmas! And now I will light the tree.

1991
George Bush

Speaking at the Pageant of Peace on the Ellipse: Well, thank you, Joe [Riley]. Please be seated, all of you, and it's good to see the Secretary of the Interior, so many other special guests here. And of course, a warm thank you to Marilyn Horne; this marvelous Tucson Boys Chorus; the Navy Band; Joe Williams; our favorites, the Gatlin Brothers over here; and all the performers who brought the Christmas spirit to Washington tonight.

And thanks to Santa. His big night is coming up. And we don't have to ask this particular Santa, Willard Scott, what the weather's going to be like on Christmas Eve. He's predicting it. And he is right every once in awhile.

This is a very special night. And I look over my shoulder here at the very special guests, the brave men who are with us here tonight. And on behalf of our loving country I say, finally, to Terry Anderson, to Tom Sutherland, Joseph

Cicippio and Alann Steen and Jesse Turner, and the others not here: Welcome home.

Welcome home, to this, the most generous and proud and free Nation on the face of the Earth. It is more than just appropriate, it is almost miraculous that we can celebrate with these five the lighting of our Nation's Christmas Tree. The idea is so moving because these men have come out of darkness into the bright light of liberty. And as you hear these remarkable men talk, you realize they were never lost in that darkness of sorrow, anguish and despair. Even at the worst moments, they were guided by a stubborn spark that cruelty could not extinguish, the spark of human spirit.

Their precious gift to us is to rekindle our Nation's belief in the light of faith and our belief in ourselves. And when Terry and Tom and Joseph and Alann and Jesse light our Nation's tree tonight, that act will be a reminder of what they and their companions living and gone, have already done to light our Nation's soul.

There have been special guests at these ceremonies before. Even Winston Churchill helped to light the tree during World War II, but this Nation has never been honored by the presence of men whose spirit meant more to all of us. Your fortitude, your humor, and generosity tell us the true meaning of this season. And at this time of year especially, these men remind us that the glitz and glamour of material things don't matter. The courage, the faith and the love of these men, that they embody, are all we need to recognize what's really important.

The way they've returned to their families and to us proves they live by the challenge of that beautiful prayer of St. Francis: "Grant that I may not so much seek to be consoled as to console; to be understood as to understand; to be loved as to love. Where there is despair, let us sow hope; where there is hatred, love; and where there is darkness, ever light."

When history remembers Christmas 1991, let it remember that tonight we gathered with men who show us that this is a season of spirit, not a celebration of plenty.

Let history remember that tonight we stood with these heroes and asked for God's blessing on this world. And finally, in the words of the carol we'll sing in a few minutes, let history remember that at Christmas 1991, this Nation united to give thanks to God and to ask God for peace on earth, good will to all. God bless these five men, this wonderful country, and now I'd like to ask them to join me as we light the Nation's Christmas Tree.

1994
William J. Clinton
Speaking at the Pageant of Peace on the Ellipse: Thank you John Betchkal [chairman of the Pageant of Peace], Mrs. Betchkal, Reverend Leon [pastor, St. John's Episcopal Church]. I want to thank especially our wonderful entertainment tonight: Willard Scott, who would make anybody

believe in Santa Claus; Trisha Yearwood, it's wonderful to see you again; Richard Leech, you are terrific. If I had a voice like you, I would have stayed out of politics [laughter]. And I want to say a word of thanks and congratulations to the magnificent Aretha Franklin, who was recently honored at the Kennedy Center Honors. We are glad to see all of you here tonight. Thank you. We congratulate the Cathedral Choir of Men and Boys for the wonderful job they did.

Let me say that Hillary and Chelsea and I are delighted to be back here for our second Pageant of Peace. I don't know how many of you were here last year, but it was a lot colder. And I still feel in the Christmas spirit and more comfortable doing so. I'm glad to be here tonight, and I appreciate this wonderful weather.

This year we have a lot to be grateful for. This is the first Christmas since the beginning of the cold war when our parents can tuck all of their children into bed on Christmas Eve knowing that there are no Russian missiles with nuclear warheads pointed at them.

In holy Bethlehem and throughout the Middle East, ancient enemies are taking giant steps toward peace and reconciliation. Peace is making progress in Northern Ireland, in South Africa, in Haiti, and Eastern and Central Europe, where people are making courageous steps to escape the shackles that have bound them.

Here at home, I appreciate what Willard Scott said about prosperity coming back. And we do have the strongest economy we've had in many years, but let us never forget that many of our people are living in poverty and others are working hard in insecurity, and that as we celebrate the birth of Jesus Christ, the Prince of Peace, let us not forget His lesson that one day we will be asked whether we lived out his love in ways that treated all of our brothers and sisters as we would have treated Him, even the least of them. He taught us all to seek peace and to treat all people with love.

In this holiday season as we gather our families and often go back to the places where we grew up, this is a time to rededicate ourselves to the things which matter most, to our responsibilities, to our families, our communities, and our country.

With all of our challenges in this holiday season, we can take great comfort in knowing that when we come together and seek God's help, we can come meet any challenge, At this holiday season, also my fellow Americans, let us extend our special gratitude and prayers for the men and women of our Armed Forces who protect the peace and stand sentry for our freedom. Many of them are very, very far from their families and friends; they must be close to our hearts.

Finally let me say, this wonderful evergreen Christmas tree, the "Tannenbaum" about which Aretha Franklin sang, is a symbol of the enduring values of our lives. As we light it, let it rekindle in our hearts faith and hope and love for one another. And now I wish God's blessings on you all this special season, and I'd like to ask Hillary and Chelsea to join me as we light the Christmas tree.

1995
William J. Clinton

Speaking at the Pageant of Peace on the Ellipse: Thank you so much. To John Betchkal, the Pageant of Peace chairman; Reverend John Tavlarides. To the Sherando High School Choir, congratulations. You guys were great tonight. To Brendan and Bridget Walsh, the Washington Ballet; to Denise Graves and Jack Jones and Kathy Lee Gifford, and the Navy Band; and of course, to Santa Claus. I would come here every year just to see Santa Claus.

We gather to begin our nation's celebration of the Christmas season with the lighting of this magnificent tree—a symbol, as evergreens have always been, of the infinite capacity of nature and people to renew themselves. We give gifts and we count our blessings.

My fellow Americans, I have just returned from a very moving trip to Europe—to England and to Northern Ireland and the Republic of Ireland; to Germany to see our troops, and to Spain. And I can tell you that among the things that I feel most grateful for at this Christmastime is the way people around the world look at our America. They see a nation graced by peace and prosperity; a land of freedom and fairness. And even though it imposes extra burdens on us, they trust us to work with them to share the blessings of peace.

This is my second Christmas tree lighting of the season, for just a few days ago I was in Belfast with the people of Northern Ireland, Protestant and Catholic alike, searching, yearning, longing for peace—celebrating their second Christmas of peace. I'm proud that I was introduced there by two children—a little Catholic girl named Catherine Hamill, and a young Protestant boy named David Sterrett, who joined hands and told the world of their hopes of the future; a future in which the only barriers they face are the limits of their dreams. That is the future we should want for our children and for all the children of the world.

I am pleased that Catherine Hamill, who touched the whole world with the story of suffering and her family's losses in Northern Ireland, and her family are here with us tonight to celebrate this lighting of the Christmas tree. And I'd like to ask her to stand up right down here and ask all of you to give her a fine hand. She has come all the way from Northern Ireland.

Remember at this Christmastime we celebrate the birth of a homeless child, whose only shelter was the straw of a manger, but who grew to become the Prince of Peace. The Prince of Peace said, "Blessed are the peacemakers." Let us bless the peacemakers at this Christmastime from the Middle East to Northern Ireland to our own troops in Bosnia. Let us pray especially for our peacemakers, those who will go to Bosnia and those who are soon to come home from Haiti.

And let us resolve, my fellow Americans, to be peacemakers. For just as many nations around the world and so many children around the world cry for peace, so do we need peace here at home in our toughest neighborhoods, where there are children, so many children who deserve to have their childhood and their future free and peaceful.

And let us remember from the example of the Prince of Peace how even the humblest of us can do [with] the acts of goodness and reconciliation extraordinary things. And as we light this wonderful Christmas tree, let us all remember that together a million small lights add up to make a great blaze of glory—not for ourselves, but for our families, our nation and the world, and for the future of our children.

Merry Christmas, and blessed are the peacemakers.

2000
William J. Clinton

Speaking at the Pageant of Peace on the Ellipse: Thank you very much, ladies and gentlemen. First, I'd like to thank Peter Nostrand and all the people who work on the Pageant of Peace every year. They give us a wonderful night, and I think we ought to give them all a big hand. Thank you very much. I'd love to thank these people who have come out in the cold to perform for us. I thank Kathy Mattea, Charlotte Church, Billy Gilman, the cast of "Fosse," the West Tennessee Youth Chorus, Al "Santa Claus" Roker. I also want to thank Anastasia Wroblewski and Kwami Dennis, our Camp Fire boy and Camp Fire girl. They did a great job up here; it's not so easy to remember those speeches. I thought they were terrific. And I'd like to thank Thomas Kinkade for his beautiful portrait that's on the cover of our program, and the United States Navy Band. Thank you very much.

On Christmas Eve, more than 75 years ago, President Calvin Coolidge lit the first National Christmas Tree. He later said, "Christmas is not a time or a season, but a state of mind, to cherish peace and goodwill, to be plenteous in mercy." Every President since President Coolidge has been part of that tradition, gathering around the Colorado spruce to rejoice in the spirit of Christmas—and to celebrate a new season of peace and goodwill.

Hillary, Chelsea and I always look forward to celebrating the Pageant of Peace with you, and the many traditions of the holiday season. Tonight, as we enjoy our last Christmas season in the White House, and the last time I'll have a chance to be here at the lighting of the Christmas tree, we are profoundly grateful for the gift you and all the American people have given us: the privilege to serve these last eight years, to live in this marvelous old house, and to participate in wonderful ceremonies like this. For Americans of many faiths, this is a season of renewal—of light returned from darkness, despair transformed to hope. A time to reflect on our lives, rejoice in our blessings, and give thanks.

Tonight, on this first Christmas of the new millennium, we celebrate an America blessed with unprecedented peace and prosperity, and a nation that through more than 220 years and even the toughest times has held together by the enduring values enshrined in our Constitution. This is a time for us to reflect, too, on that good fortune and a time to rededicate ourselves to the lessons of love and reconciliation taught by a child born in Bethlehem 2000 years ago. As we gather to decorate our trees and light our menorahs, let us remember the true meaning of the holidays by taking some time to give to those who need it most. And let us be thankful for the sacrifices of all those who serve us, especially those who serve us in the military who won't be home this year for Christmas. Let me say that when I leave you tonight, I'm going to Northern Ireland, to a small island where people were born that eventually came to America and gave us over 40 million of our citizens; a place where St. Patrick brought the spirit of Christmas almost 1,500 years ago. I hope that we can finish the business of peace there and help, again, America to give a gift to the rest of the world.

To all of you again, I say this has been a humbling and wondrous gift. We thank you, all of us in our family, for the chance to serve yours. God bless you and merry Christmas. And let's light the tree. Thank you very much.

2001
George W. Bush

Speaking at the Pageant of Peace on the Ellipse: Be seated, please—except for you all. (*Laughter.*) I want to thank you very much, and welcome you all to this year's Christmas Pageant of Peace. During this time of conflict and challenge, we once again celebrate the season of hope and the season of joy. We give thanks to our nation and to our families, and to our friends.

The First Lady and I are so honored to be here. I want to thank Peter Nostrand and the committee for putting this together, and I particularly want to thank the entertainment committee—the person in charge of getting these fantastic entertainers to come tonight. Thank you from the bottom of our hearts. I want to thank all the employees and sponsors who put on this magnificent event. I want to thank Fran Minella, the Director of the National Park Service, and all the Park Service employees who have worked hard to put this event on. I want to thank Santa Claus for being here tonight. I've been looking for you, Santa.

In a moment, we will light the National Christmas Tree, a tradition Americans have been celebrating since 1923. The history of this event has included some memorable moments, including 60 years ago, less than three weeks after the attack on Pearl Harbor, when Prime Minister Winston Churchill made an appearance with President Franklin Roosevelt to light the tree. Now, once again, we celebrate Christmas in a time of testing, with American troops far from home. This season finds our country with losses to mourn and great tasks to complete. In all those tasks, it is worth recalling the words from a beautiful Christmas hymn—in the third verse of "Oh Holy Night" we sing, "His law is love, and His gospel is peace. Chains ye shall break, for the slave is our brother. And in His name all oppression shall cease." America seeks peace, and believes in justice. We fight only when necessary. We fight so that oppression may cease. And even in the midst of war, we pray for peace on Earth and goodwill to men.

This is a time of the year for families and friends to gather together. Not simply to celebrate the season, but to renew the bonds of love and affection that give fulfillment to our lives. And this is a year we will not forget those who lost loved ones in the attacks on September the 11th and on the battlefield. They will remain in our prayers.

It is now my honor to invite Leon Patterson and Faith Elseth and Laura to join me up here as we light the National Christmas Tree. Leon and Faith's fathers, Major Clifford Patterson and Lt. Commander Robert Elseth, served in the United States military. Both of these good men were lost in the attack on the Pentagon. Leon and Faith, we thank you for helping us celebrate Christmas. You remind us of the comfort of Christmas that hope never fails, and love never ends. And now, would you please help Laura light up our beautiful tree.

2003
George W. Bush

Speaking at the Pageant of Peace on the Ellipse: Thank you all very much. Welcome to the Christmas Pageant of Peace. This evening, we continue a tradition in Washington as we gather to light the National Christmas Tree. Tonight, and throughout the Christmas season, our thoughts turn to a star in the east, seen 20 centuries ago, and to a light that can guide us still. Laura and I are so pleased to join you in this ceremony, and we thank you all for being here.

It's always good to see Santa. I know you've got a lot of commitments this time of year. [*Laughter*] We also know how Santa gets around: he travels in the dark of night, he arrives unannounced—[*laughter*]—and he's gone before you know he was there. [*Laughter*] Santa, I can assure you, it's a lot easier on a flying sled than it is on *Air Force One.* [*Laughter and applause*]

I want to thank Peter Nostrand, the chairman of the Christmas Pageant of Peace, and John Betchkal, the president. I want to thank very much Secretary of the Interior, Gale Norton, and her staff, for helping put this fine event on. I want to thank all the members of my Cabinet who are here. I appreciate Fran Mainella, who's the director of the National Park Service. I want to thank all the National Park Service employees, who work so hard on behalf of the American people. [*Applause*]

I want to thank Father Kleinwebber for his gracious offering of prayer. I appreciate the musicians—fantastic job tonight. Thank you all for coming. I want to thank the members of the board of the Christmas Pageant of Peace. I want to welcome all the children from the Boys and Girls Clubs from this region for being here.

Also with us this evening are military personnel—[*applause*]—including some who have recently returned from duty in Iraq and Afghanistan. [*Applause*] I know your families are glad to have you back. They're proud of your service, and so is our country. On behalf of all Americans, welcome home, and job well done. [*Applause*]

We also honor all of our fellow Americans serving far

away from home during the holidays. Separation from loved ones is especially difficult this time of year. Our people in uniform can know that their families miss them and love them, that millions are praying for them, and that America is grateful for the men and women who serve and defend our country.

The story of Christmas is familiar to us all, and it still holds a sense of wonder and surprise. When the good news came first to a young woman from Nazareth, her response was understandable. She asked, how can this be? The news would bring difficulty to her family and suspicion upon herself. Yet, Mary gave her reply, "Be it unto me according to Thy word." The wait for a new king had been long, and the manner of his arrival was not as many had expected. The king's first cries were heard by shepherds and cattle. He was raised by a carpenter's son.

Yet this one humble life lifted the sights of humanity forever. And in His words we hear a voice like no other. Across the generations, the poor have heard words of hope, the proud have heard words of challenge, and the weak and the dying have heard words of assurance. And mankind has been given a message first delivered by angels on a shepherd's field: "Fear not."

As we near Christmas in a time of war, these words bring comfort. We don't know all of God's ways, yet the Christmas story promises that God's purpose is justice, and His plan is peace. At times this belief is tested. During the Civil War, Longfellow wrote a poem that later became a part of a Christmas carol, "Hate is strong, and mocks the song of peace on earth, good will to men."

That poem also reminds us that hate is not the final word: "Then pealed the bells more loud and deep, 'God is not dead, nor doth He sleep, the wrong shall fail, the right prevail, with peace on earth, good will to men.'"

And now, as an expression of our own hope for peace in this Christmas season we light the national tree. Maggie Stuempfle and Andre Joyner are with us here. They're members of the Boys and Girls Clubs of America. Laura and I would like to ask Maggie and Andre to come up, and we'll turn on the lights. But I ask you all to join us in a national count down, starting with five, four, three, two, one. [*Applause*]

2008
George W. Bush

Speaking at the Pageant of Peace on the Ellipse: Thank you. Mr. Secretary, thank you for the introduction and thank you for the warm welcome. Laura and I are pleased to welcome all of you here for one of Washington's great traditions, the lighting of the National Christmas Tree.

Santa, thank you for finally showing up. [*Laughter*] I know you've come a long way. After all, you do live in the North Pole. You may have heard that Laura and I are going to have plenty of time next year. [*Laughter*] So we look forward to returning the favor. The problem is we're going to be short on an airplane. [*Laughter*] Have you got an extra sleigh?

[*Laughter*]

I welcome the members of my Cabinet; the administration and their families; members of Congress and their families; Vin Cipolla; Mary Bomar, the Director of the National Park Service-[*applause*]-Peggy O'Dell, Regional Director, National Capital Region of the National Park Service. [*Applause*] And all the National Park Service employees, we thank you for your dedication and work. [*Applause*]

Laura and I are thrilled to be here with our dear friend, Reverend Luis León. All the entertainers-thank you for being here. You were fabulous tonight. We appreciate your performance. [*Applause*] We especially welcome the folks from Enterprise, Alabama. [*Applause*] And we thank the School Choir for showing the determination and grit of some really fine people.

We want to thank all the volunteers who designed and created the ornaments for our state trees.

Today we celebrate the 85th anniversary of the National Christmas Tree lighting. In times of calm, and in times of challenge, Americans have gathered for this ceremony. The simple story we remember during the season speaks to every generation. It is the story of a humble birth in a quiet town, and the story of one life that changed millions more. For two millennia, the story of Christmas has brought joy to families, comfort to communities, and hope to hearts around the world.

During Christmas we celebrate the blessings of the season, and the blessings that surround us every day. And the greatest of these blessings is freedom-the Almighty's gift to every man, woman, and child on the face of the Earth. [*Applause*]

And today, we give thanks to the brave men and women who protect the American people by defending freedom around the world. [*Applause*] Over the past eight years, my greatest honor as President has been serving as Commander-in-Chief of the finest military ever known. [*Applause*]

Our men and women in uniform have stepped forward to defend our nation during a time of war. They serve with courage and with honor, and they've made incredible sacrifices. Many of them will spend this Christmas stationed in distant lands, far from the families they love. Yet they're never far from our thoughts, and they are always in our prayers. America honors their service, and we are grateful to the sacrifice of the families who stand by their side. [*Applause*]

Some of those families are with us tonight, and Laura and I are pleased to be joined by Kayleigh Kepler and Lindsey Van Horn. Lindsey's dad is in Baghdad. Kayleigh's dad will deploy to Iraq next year. Kayleigh and Lindsey, America is safer because of your dads, and moms and dads across America who have stepped forward to defend our country.

And now I'm going to ask Kayleigh and Lindsey to get up here with Laura-to please come up with Laura-[*laughter*]-and help us light this beautiful tree.

Everybody join-five, four, three, two, one! [*Applause*]

2009
Barack Obama

Speaking on the Ellipse: Thank you. Merry Christmas, happy holidays, Washington, DC. I want to, first of all, thank Secretary Salazar for not only the kind introduction but the extraordinary work he is doing in preserving the incredible bounty and natural resources of this country.

I want to thank all those involved in helping to organize this great event. Thank you to Randy Jackson and all the performers putting on an incredible show. I told Sasha just—we're not on "American Idol"–[*laughter*]–no singing. [*Laughter*]

I also want to thank Neil Mulholland, Jon Jarvis, and Peggy O'Dell from the National Park Service for being with us and all the Park Service employees who've worked so hard to put this event together. Give them a big round of applause. And I want to thank my outstanding Vice President and his gorgeous granddaughters–Joe Biden. Stand up, Joe.

In 1923, the Washington, DC, public schools wrote a letter to the White House asking if they could put up a Christmas tree on the South Lawn. And First Lady Grace Coolidge said they could use the Ellipse. [*Laughter*] And in the eight decades since, in times of war and peace, hardship and joy, Americans from every corner of this Nation have gathered here to share in the holiday spirit.

Tonight we celebrate a story that is as beautiful as it is simple. The story of a child born far from home to parents guided only by faith, but who would ultimately spread a message that has endured for more than 2,000 years, that no matter who we are or where we are from, we are each called to love one another as brother and sister.

While this story may be a Christian one, its lesson is universal. It speaks to the hope we share as a people, and it represents a tradition that we celebrate as a country, a tradition that has come to represent more than any one holiday or religion, but a season of brotherhood and generosity to our fellow citizens.

It's that spirit of unity that we must remember as we light the National Christmas Tree, a tree that will shine its light far beyond our city and our shores to every American around the world. And that's why tonight our thoughts and prayers are with the men and women who will be spending this holiday far away from home, the mothers and fathers, the sons and daughters of our military who risk their lives every day to keep us safe. We will be thinking of you and praying for you during this holiday season.

And let's also remember our neighbors who are struggling here at home, those who've lost a job or a home, a friend or a loved one, because even though it's easy to focus on receiving at this time of year, it's often in the simple act of giving that we find the greatest happiness.

So on behalf of Michelle and Malia and Sasha and my mother-in-law Mama Robinson, I want to wish all of you a very merry Christmas. May you go out with joy and be led forth in peace.

And now to the serious business of pressing the button and lighting this beautiful tree. So, guys, come up here. I need some assistance. I'm technologically challenged, and some–I might not get this right. So we're going to do a countdown, starting from five. Everybody got to help me out here. Five, four, three, two, one–ho! It worked!

2011
Barack Obama

Speaking on the Ellipse: It's nice having your own band. Please have a seat, everyone. Merry Christmas! Merry Christmas!

Thank you, Secretary Salazar, for that introduction and for your hard work to preserve and protect our land and our water and our wildlife. I also want to thank Minister Rogers for the beautiful invocation, as well as Neil Mulholland and everyone at the National Park Foundation and the National Park Service who helped put this outstanding event together. I'd like to thank Carson Daly and Big Time Rush, and all of tonight's performers for joining us to kick off the holiday season here at the White House.

For 89 years, Presidents and Americans have come together to light the National Christmas Tree. And this year is a special one. This year, we have a brand new tree. The last one stood here for more than 30 years — until we lost it in a storm earlier this year. But we all know that this tradition is much larger than any single tree. And tonight, once again, we gather here not simply to light some decorations, but to honor a story that lights the world.

More than 2,000 years ago, a child was born to two faithful travelers who could find rest only in a stable, among the cattle and the sheep. But this was not just any child. Christ's birth made the angels rejoice and attracted shepherds and kings from afar. He was a manifestation of God's love for us. And He grew up to become a leader with a servant's heart who taught us a message as simple as it is powerful: that we should love God, and love our neighbor as ourselves.

That teaching has come to encircle the globe. It has endured for generations. And today, it lies at the heart of my Christian faith and that of millions of Americans. No matter who we are, or where we come from, or how we worship, it's a message that can unite all of us on this holiday season.

So long as the gifts and the parties are happening, it's important for us to keep in mind the central message of this season, and keep Christ's words not only in our thoughts, but also in our deeds. In this season of hope, let's help those who need it most — the homeless, the hungry, the sick and shut in. In this season of plenty, let's reach out to those who struggle to find work or provide for their families. In this season of generosity, let's give thanks and honor to our troops and our veterans, and their families who've sacrificed so much for us. And let's welcome all those who are happily coming home. (*Applause.*)

And this holiday season, let us reaffirm our commitment to each other, as family members, as neighbors, as

Americans, regardless of our color or creed or faith. Let us remember that we are one, and we are a family.

So on behalf of Malia and Sasha and Michelle and our grandmother-in-chief, Marian – (*laughter*) – I wish you all the happiest holiday season, the merriest of Christmases. God bless you all, and may God bless the United States of America. (*Applause*.)

And with that, I'm going to invite the entire Obama clan up here to light the Christmas tree. I need some help, and there's a lot of technical aspects to this. (*Laughter.*) Come on, guys. (*Applause.*) All right.

Okay, we're going to start counting down here. We've got the switch right here.

MRS. OBAMA: All right, come on.

THE PRESIDENT: Everybody ready? And this is the new tree. I know it's not quite as big as the old tree, but it's going to take time to grow. But we're going to fill it up with some spirit and start a new tradition right now.

All right, everybody ready? We're going to start counting down. Five, four, three, two, one – (*Applause.*) There you go. That's a good-looking tree. Thank you, everyone

2016
Barack Obama

Speaking on the Ellipse: Merry Christmas, everybody! [*Applause*] Well, thank you, Dylan, for that introduction and for all that you do for our parks down in Texas. I also want to thank Reverend Haggins for her beautiful invocation. And as we continue to celebrate the centennial of our national parks, I want to recognize our tremendous Secretary of the Interior, Sally Jewell. [*Applause*] Our National Parks Service Director, Jonathan Jarvis. [*Applause*] And all the rangers and staff from the Park Service and the National Park Foundation–here's to another 100 years. [*Applause*]

Let's give it up for Eva Longoria and this star-studded group we have here performing tonight. [*Applause*] Gold medalist Simone Manuel. [*Applause*] Kelly Clarkson. Yolanda Adams. Garth Brooks and Trisha Yearwood. Chance the Rapper. [*Applause*] The Lumineers. Marc Anthony. James and Kim Taylor. [*Applause*] It's like a Christmas edition of Lollapalooza. [*Laughter*]

And this is just another example of why the holidays here at the White House are so special. Last week, I pardoned a turkey. [*Laughter*] Tonight, we're lighting the National Christmas Tree. This one is easier because a tree does not move. It does not gobble. [*Laughter*] You just push a button and it's electrified–which is exactly what you don't want to have happen at a turkey pardon. [*Laughter*] I thought that was funny, Michelle. [*Laughter*] Thankfully, both events have gone off without a hitch.

Along with celebrations like these, the holidays also offer us a time for reflection and perspective. And over these next few weeks, as we celebrate the birth of our Savior, as we retell the story of weary travelers, a star, shepherds, Magi, I hope that we also focus ourselves on the message that this child brought to this Earth some 2,000 years ago–a message that says we have to be our brother's keepers, our sister's keepers; that we have to reach out to each other, to forgive each other. To let the light of our good deeds shine for all. To care for the sick, and the hungry, and the downtrodden. And of course, to love one another, even our enemies, and treat one another the way we would want to be treated ourselves.

It's a message that grounds not just my family's Christian faith but that of Jewish Americans, Muslim Americans, non-believers–Americans of all backgrounds. It's a message of unity and a message of decency and a message of hope that never goes out of style. And it's one that we all need very much today.

After eight years as your President–[*Applause*]–I still believe that there's so much more that unites us than divides us. I've seen it in parents from every corner of this country just trying to give their kids a better shot. I've seen it in communities that come together and find common ground even in times of trial and times of tragedy. We see it in immigrants and refugees striving for that most American of ideals–to better ourselves and our families. We see it in our troops who serve far from home during this holiday season, these outstanding men and women who go into harm's way to protect the nation that we love and the freedoms that we hold dear–the freedom to vote and speak out, and practice our faith as we choose; the freedom to chart our own course as citizens and as a nation.

That is the America that I've seen as we've come back from the depths of an economic crisis to an economy on the move, as we've recovered from wars and natural tragedies. What I've seen is a big-hearted and hopeful and resilient people who look out for each other and who have each other's backs, and who find strength in our differences, and who keep moving forward knowing that we're all in this together.

Those are our values. That is who we are. That's who we will always be. And this is the 94th time that Americans have gathered to light our national tree. It's the eighth and final time for our family. Before we leave tonight, I just want to express what an incredible honor it has been to serve this nation–[*Applause*]–and to feel its warmth and to feel its generosity, and how our family has been awed by America's goodness. And, most of all, it has been so special to share these eight years with all of you.

So on behalf of Michelle and Malia, Sasha, Grandma, Bo and Sunny–Merry Christmas, everybody. Happy holidays. May God bless you all, and may God bless these United States of America. [*Applause*]

2017
Donald J. Trump

Speaking on the Ellipse: Today's the day that I've been looking very much forward to all year long. It's one that we have heard and we speak about and we dream about and now as the President of the United States, it's my tremendous honor to finally wish America and the world a very Merry Christmas.

I want to thank everyone who has come together here right in front of the White House, that beautiful, beautiful White House, and everyone watching from home to see the lighting of this incredible national Christmas tree.

For nearly a century, through good times and bad, every President has taken part in this wonderful tradition, first started by President Coolidge. But I was informed tonight that the weather we have is the best it's been in 25 years. In fact, I said, "Is it always like this?" And the secretary said, "Hasn't been like this for a long time." So, we are very lucky.

Finally, in 1870, President Ulysses S. Grant signed legislation making Christmas a Federal holiday. And I sort of feel we are doing that again. That's what's happening.

From the earliest days of our nation, Americans have known Christmas as a time for prayer and worship, for gratitude and good will, for peace and renewal.

Melania and I are full of joy at the start of this very blessed season. We're thrilled to think of the people across the nation and all across the continent whose spirits are lifted by the miracle of Christmas.

For Christians, this is a Holy season—the celebration of the birth of our Lord and Savior Jesus Christ. The Christmas story begins 2,000 years ago with a mother, a father, their baby son, and the most extraordinary gift of all, the gift of God's love for all of humanity.

Whatever our beliefs, we know that the birth of Jesus Christ and the story of this incredible life forever changed the course of human history. There's hardly an aspect of our lives today that His life has not touched: art, music, culture, law, and our respect for the sacred dignity of every person everywhere in the world.

Each and every year at Christmas time we recognize that the real spirit of Christmas is not what we have, it's about who we are—each one of us is a child of God.

That is the true source of joy this time of the year.

That is what makes every Christmas "merry."

And that is what we remember at today's beautiful ceremony, that we are called to serve one another, to love one another, and to pursue peace in our hearts and all throughout the world.

And so tonight, I thank the millions of Americans who light our lives and brighten our wonderful communities. I thank those who are serving the needy during the season and throughout the year. I thank our military men and women who are stationed around the world keeping us safe.

I thank our law enforcement officers who protect our streets and secure our homeland. I thank America's teachers, pastors, and all those religious, and those people that have taught us so much, for their leadership in our communities and our society.

And, especially tonight, I thank America's families. At Christmas, we are reminded more than ever that the family is the bedrock of American life.

And so, this Christmas we ask for God's blessings for our family, for our nation. And we pray that our country will be a place where every child knows a home filled with love, a community rich with hope, and a nation blest with faith.

SOURCES

THE COOLIDGES

"Calvin Coolidge Says," syndicated newspaper column, Dec. 24, 1930.

Coolidge, Calvin. *The Autobiography of Calvin Coolidge*. Plymouth, Vermont: The Calvin Coolidge Memorial Foundation, 1989.

Coolidge, John. Interview with author. Plymouth Notch, Vermont, June 13, 1994.

Coolidge, Mrs. Calvin. "What Christmas Means to Me," *Delineator Digest*, Dec. 1929.

Hoover, Irwin Hood. *Forty-Two Years in the White House*. Boston: Houghton Mifflin Company, 1934.

Library of Congress, Manuscript Division. Fish, H.J., letter to Sanders, E., Oct. 26, 1925; Moody, P., letter to President, Dec. 12, 1923; Sanders, E., telegram to Leach, Hon. George, Dec. 15, 1925.

National Archives. Records of the White House Files, 1900–35, Record Group 130: Hardy, L.W., letters to Slemp, C.B., Nov. 30, 1923, and Dec. 4, 1923; Hardy, L.W., letter to President, Dec. 20, 1923; Slemp, C.B., letter to Hardy, L.W., Dec. 21, 1923.

New York Herald Tribune, July 9, 1927.

New York Times, Dec. 25, 1924; Dec. 25, 1926; Dec. 25, 1928.

Parks, Lillian Rogers, in collaboration with Frances Spatz Leighton. *My Thirty Years Backstairs at the White House*. New York: Fleet Publishing Company, 1961.

Ross, Ishbel. *Grace Coolidge and Her Era*. New York: Dodd, Mead and Company, 1962.

Washington Herald, Dec. 23, 1923; Dec. 26, 1928.

Washington Post, Dec. 25, 1923; Dec. 25, 1924; Jan. 2, 1925; Dec. 25, 1925; Dec. 25, 1926; Dec. 24, 1928.

Washington Star, Dec. 12, 1923; Dec. 24, 1924; Dec. 25, 1924; Dec. 24, 1925; Dec. 25, 1926; Dec. 27, 1927; Dec. 25, 1928.

Williams, W.K. "The Presidents and Their Christmas Trees," *American Forests*, Dec. 1965.

THE HOOVERS

Amyx, Raleigh DeGeer. Interview with author. Warrenton, Virginia, March 1993.

Genn, Lillian G. "Herbert Hoover–Hero," *NPTA Journal*, Sept./Oct. 1979.

Herbert Hoover Library, West Branch, Iowa: Ruth Fesler File. Christmas 1929 card list and etching; photographs used as Christmas 1929 gifts; Christmas 1930 gift list and summary; Christmas 1931 gift inventory; Lipman, Ruth Fesler, transcribed interview with Mr. Henle.

Long, Ava, interview. *Ladies Home Journal*, Dec. 1935.

New York Times, Dec. 25, 1929; Jan. 2, 1930; Dec. 25, 1930; Dec. 24, 1930; Dec. 25, 1931.

Parks, Lillian Rogers, in collaboration with Frances Spatz Leighton. *My Thirty Years Backstairs at the White House*. New York: Fleet Publishing Company, 1961.

Public Papers of the Presidents of the United States: Herbert Hoover, 1929–33, 4 vols. Washington: GPO, 1974–77. Dec. 24, 1931.

"Twas the Night Before Christmas." *American Heritage*, Vol. 22, No. 1, 1970.

Washington Post, Dec. 17, 1929; Dec. 25, 1929; July 3, 1975.

Washington Star, Dec. 25, 1930.

THE ROOSEVELTS

Elsey, George. Interview with author by telephone, 1994.

Franklin D. Roosevelt Library. FDR Papers File 512: Early, S., letter to Eadie, H., Oct. 25, 1934; McIntyre, M.H., letter to Eadie, H., Oct. 8, 1934. President's Personal File 1051: Early, S., letter to Fisher, S., Oct. 21, 1937; Fisher, S., letter to Roosevelt, J., Oct. 19, 1937; Lowd, D., letter dated Jan. 2, 1934; President of Board of Commissioners, D.C., letter to President, Dec. 7, 1943. President's Secretary's File: Belmont Advertising, letter to Tully, G., Sept. 3, 1943; Christmas 1943; Cook, Nancy, letter to LeHand, M., July 30, 1937; D-Day Prayer of FDR; FDR memo to Tully, G., Oct. 18, 1943; Latta, M.C., memo to Summerlin; Scheider, M., letter to Marshall, A.E., at Brewood's, Sept. 7, 1937, 60.1, Box 575. Bills of Sale: The Forge: To President, Nov. 29, 1939, for letter holders; to Scheider, M., Dec. 15, 1937; to Mrs. Roosevelt, Dec. 5, 1938; to President, Dec. 17, 1938. Others: LeHand, M.A., letter to Cartier, Nov. 30, 1940, Dec. 6, 1940; LeHand, M., letter to Cook, N., Aug. 3, 1937; LeHand, M.A., letter to Fitch, F.A., Mark Cross Co., Nov. 30, 1940; Dec. 18, 1941; LeHand, M.A., letter to Hammacher Schlemmer Nov. 30, 1940, Jan. 6, 1941. Val-Kill Folder 2: Wright, Emily, "Eleanor Roosevelt and Val-Kill Industries 1925-1938," manuscript, Oct. 1978, Vertical File.

Nesbitt, Henrietta, *White House Diary*. New York: Doubleday & Co., 1948.

New York Times, Dec. 24, 1933; Dec. 25, 1935; Dec. 25, 1936; Dec. 7, 1937; Dec. 23, 1937; Dec. 25, 1938; Dec. 25, 1939; Dec. 25, 1940; Dec. 24, 1941; Dec. 25, 1941; Jan. 2, 1942; Nov. 27, 1942; Dec. 25, 1942; Dec. 14, 1943; Dec. 23, 1943; Dec. 25, 1943; June 7, 1944; Dec. 22, 1944; Dec. 25, 1944.

Public Papers and Addresses of FDR. New York: Random House. 1937–38.

Roosevelt, Eleanor, *Christmas 1940*. New York: St. Martin's Press.

———. *Eleanor Roosevelt's Christmas Book*. New York: Dodd, Mead & Company, 1963.

———. *On My Own*. New York: Harper & Brothers Publishers.

———, "The Right to Give," *Home Companion*, Dec. 1934.

———.*This I Remember*. Westport, Connecticut: Greenwood Press Publishers, 1949.

Roosevelt, James, and Shalett, Sidney, *Affectionately FDR, A Son's Story of a Lonely Man*. New York: Harcourt Brace & Co. 1959.

Washington Herald, Dec 31, 1933.

Washington Post, Dec. 25, 1934; Jan. 13,

1940; Dec. 25, 1940; Dec. 25, 1941; Dec. 25, 1942; Dec. 25, 1943.

Washington Star, Dec. 23, 1933; Dec. 25, 1933; Dec. 25, 1935; Dec. 25, 1936; Dec. 25, 1937; Dec. 25, 1941; Dec. 22, 1943.

THE TRUMANS

"Family Man, Truman Loved," *Arkansas Gazette*, Dec. 25, 1979.

Fields, Alonzo. *My Twenty-One Years in the White House.* New York: Coward-McCann, Inc. 1961.

Harry S. Truman Library. The President, letter to Deviny, J., of GPO, Jan. 5, 1951. Memorandum re: The President and Mrs. Truman's Christmas Gifts and cards. Oct. 18, 1947; memorandum re: President's Christmas Gift 1947, Eben, M.; Eben, M., memorandum for Barrows, Dec. 11, 1947; Eben, M., memorandum for Conway, Jan. 5, 1951; memorandum for Connelly, Nov. 6, 1951; Connelley, M.J., memorandum for M. Eben, PSF: Gifts and Greetings. Museum File Medals and Medallions: Bronze Casting of Presidential Seal, 1949.

New York Times, Dec. 24, 1945.

National Archives. R.M. Nixon Files: Fact Sheet on Harry S. Truman, Dec. 27, 1972.

Parks, Lillian Rogers, in collaboration with Frances Spatz Leighton. *My Thirty Years Backstairs at the White House.* New York: Fleet Publishing Company, 1961.

Public Papers of the Presidents of the United States: Harry S. Truman, 1945-53.

Truman, Harry, letter to Mama and Mary, May 8, 1945. The Seeley Collection.

Truman, Margaret. *Bess W. Truman.* New York: MacMillan Publishing Co., 1986.

———, "Dreaming of a White House Christmas," *Family Weekly*, Dec. 12, 1980.

Washington Post, Dec. 25, 1945; Dec. 25, 1952.

Washington Star, Dec. 22, 1945; Dec. 15, 1946; Dec. 25, 1951.

West, J.B., with Mary Lynn Kotz. *Upstairs at the White House.* New York: Coward, McCann and Geoghegan, Inc., 1973.

THE EISENHOWERS

Dwight D. Eisenhower Library. President's Personal File, Boxes 8, 11-18: Correspondence between Hall, J.C., and the President: Dec. 3, 1953;

Jan. 23, 1954; July 29, 1954; Dec. 6, 1954; Nov. 7, 1955; Dec. 10, 1955. President's letter to Brownell, H., Dec. 22, 1954; President's letter to Glew, D.H., Jr., Jan. 27, 1959; Rayburn, S., letter to the President, Jan. 4, 1960; McCaffree, Mary Jane, Papers, Boxes 1-4: McCaffree, M.J., letter to Hall, J.C., Oct. 27, 1954; Lee, J., letter to McCaffree, M.J., Oct. 21, 1958; Other Papers, Stewart, L., memorandum to Hall, J.C., Jan. 11, 1955; Hall, J.C., letter to Stephens, T.E., Feb. 18, 1954.

Dwight D. Eisenhower Museum, Abilene, Kansas.

Hall, J.C. *When You Care Enough.* Hallmark: Kansas City, Missouri, 1992.

Hallmark Archives, Kansas City, Missouri: Archenhold, Hans. Interview with Sharman Robertson; E 2E.7, A Request from the White House; *Ike's Art,* Wide World Photo.

Philadelphia Inquirer, Dec. 22, 1959.

Public Papers of the Presidents of the United States: Dwight D. Eisenhower, 1953-61.

Washington Post, Dec. 19, 1955.

Washington Star, Dec. 24, 1953; Dec. 11, 1958; Dec. 24, 1960.

West, J.B., with Mary Lynn Kotz. *Upstairs at the White House.* New York: Coward, McCann and Geoghegan, Inc., 1973.

THE KENNEDYS

Amyx, Raleigh DeGeer. Interview with author. Warrenton, Virginia, April 30, 1995.

Armentrout, Russell. Interview with author. July 1994.

Bethlehem Globe, Dec. 13, 1962.

"Bucks County Artist, Ed Lehman," Doylestown *Daily Intelligence*, 1990.

John F. Kennedy Library, President's Office File, Box 129, Folder: Christmas List. White House Social File, Box 120, Folder: Christmas Card List 1960: Baldrige, L., memorandum to O'Donnell, K., Nov. 16, 1961; Mrs. Kennedy letter to Hall, J.C., Dec. 7, 1962. Tuckerman, N., memorandum to White House staff, Dec. 1963. White House Central File, Box 351, H07 Invitations; Box 350, Hopkins, W.J., memorandum to O'Donnell, K., Nov. 30, 1961.

Hallmark Archives: Baldrige, L., letter to Hall, J.C., Dec. 13, 1961; Lee, J., letter to Clifton, T., Nov. 14, 1963; Lee, J.,

memorandum about President's Christmas Cards for 1970; Lee, J., telegram to Turnure, P., Nov. 22, 1963; Stewart, L. memorandum to Cutler, C., Nov. 1, 1963; Turnure, P., letter to Lee, J., Aug. 23, 1963, Sept. 20, 1963.

Kansas City Star, Sept. 11, 1963; Nov. 16, 1982.

Lee, Jeannette. Interview with author. Hallmark Archives, Kansas City, Missouri, July 27, 1993.

Lehman, Edward. Interview with author. Quakertown, Pennsylvania, Sept. 3, 1993.

———. personal files: Mrs. Kennedy letter to Lehman E., July 27, 1962; Turnure, P., letter to Lehman, E., Dec. 10, 1962; Feb. 12, 1963; Jan. 14, 1964.

Life, Sept. 1, 1961.

Look, Dec. 1963.

Newsweek, Feb. 26, 1962.

New York Times, Sept. 12, 1963.

Perbasie News Herald, Edward Lehman clipping.

Philadelphia Bulletin, Feb. 9, 1962.

Public Papers of the Presidents of the United States: John F. Kennedy, 1961-63.

Scouten, Rex. Interview with author. The White House, Nov. 3, 1993.

Stoughton, Cecil. Interview with author. Merritt Island, Florida, July 18, 1993.

Time, Feb. 23, 1962.

Washington Post, Nov. 22, 1960; Dec. 14, 1961; Dec. 21, 1961; Dec. 13, 1962.

Washington Star, Dec. 14, 1961; Dec. 24, 1961.

West, J.B., with Mary Lynn Kotz. *Upstairs at the White House.* New York: Coward, McCann and Geoghegan, Inc., 1973.

"The White House Christmas Tree Past and Present," *American Christmas Tree Journal*, Nov. 1981.

THE JOHNSONS

Abell, Bess. Interview with author. Potomac, Maryland, July 13, 1993.

American Greetings: Press Release, Presidential Greeting Cards: An Overview, Sept. 14, 1981; Pakish, E., letter to Abell, B., Feb. 15, 1965; memoranda to Stone, H, Nov. 15, 1966, Dec. 28, 1967, Jan. 3, 1969.

Cleveland *Plain Dealer*, Oct. 11, 1964.

Hallmark Archives: Presidential Christmas Cards Recap, Dave LeMoyne; Lee, J., memorandum to Fox, S., Dec. 17, 1963.

Johnson, Lady Bird., *A White House Diary.* New York: Holt, Rinehart and

Winston, 1970.

Johnson, Mrs. Lyndon, "Christmas Memories From the White House," *McCalls*, Dec. 1968.

Laessig, Robert. Interview with author. Cleveland, Ohio, October 21, 1993.

Lyndon B. Johnson Library, White House Central File, H07, #21: Christmas Card List, Dec. 16, 1993; Duke, A.B., memorandum to the President, Nov. 27, 1963. Clifton, memorandum to Abell, B., May 19, 1964; Sinclair, I., memorandum to Jenkins, W., Dec. 16, 1963.

White House Social File: Abell, B., letter to Stone, H., May 23, 1967; Johnson, Lady Bird, letter to Laessig, R., Dec. 28, 1965; Nathan, R., letter to Abell, B., May 8, 1964; Photographs and description of LBJ Christmas stocking; Poage, W.R., letter to President and Mrs. Johnson, Dec. 31, 1963; Stone, H., to Abell, B., June 4, 1965, Oct. 21, 1965, June 6, 1968.

New York Times, Dec. 16, 1966; Dec. 24, 1967.

Pakish, Ed. Interview with author. American Greetings, Cleveland, Ohio, Oct. 21, 1993.

Public Papers of the Presidents of the United States: Lyndon B. Johnson, 1963-69.

Robb, Lynda Bird Johnson. Interview with author. June 22, 1995.

Smith, Marie. *The President's Lady*. New York: Random House, New York, 1964.

Washington Post, Dec. 23, 1963; Dec. 24, 1963; Dec. 10, 1966; Dec. 19, 1966; Dec. 16, 1967.

West, J.B., with Mary Lynn Kotz. *Upstairs at the White House*. New York: Coward, McCann and Geoghegan, Inc., 1973.

The White House Gardens and Grounds, White House Historical Association.

The White House. Press Release, Dec. 22, 1967.

Williams, W.K., "The Presidents and Their Christmas Trees," *American Forests*, Dec. 1965.

THE NIXONS

Allen, Douglas and Allen, Douglas, Jr. *N.C. Wyeth*. New York: Bonanza Books, 1972.

"Christmas at the White House, With Julie Nixon Eisenhower and Charles Kuralt," CBS TV special, Dec. 25, 1969.

Conger, Clement E. Interview with author, the White House, Nov. 4, 1993.

Hallmark Archives. "Presidential Christmas Card Fact Sheet, 1990," news release; "President Nixon's Christmas Cards Are Unique Design," press release, Dec. 11, 1970; Guyton, S., memorandum to Fox, S., 1971.

"Mrs. Nixon's White House Restoration," unpublished summary from Helen Smith files.

National Archives. White House Central File, H012: Friedersdorf, M.L., letter to Kuykendall, D., Nov. 30, 1973; McGuire, K., letter to Woods, R.M., Dec. 30, 1970; the President's letter to Hall, J., Dec. 19, 1969; Stewart, S., letter to the President, Dec. 21, 1973; Winchester, L., memorandum to Hullin, T., Nov. 6, 1972; Winchester, L., memorandum to Mrs. Nixon, "Christmas Gift List, 1972"; Office of Staff Director: 1970 Christmas Display of White House Christmas Cards.

New York Times, Dec. 15, 1971.

Nixon, Mrs. Richard, "Christmas at the White House," *House and Garden*, Dec. 1971.

Nixon, Richard. *In the Arena*. New York: Pocket Books of Simon & Schuster, 1990.

"The Nixon Touch in the White House," *U.S. News and World Report*, Dec. 28, 1970.

"Pat Nixon Made a Quiet Contribution," *Providence Sunday Journal,* June 27, 1993.

Public Papers of the Presidents of the United States: Richard M. Nixon, 1969-1973.

Smith, Helen. Interview with author, Washington, D.C., July 14, 1993.

Washington Post, Dec. 16, 1969; Dec. 17, 1969; Nov. 26, 1970; Dec. 17, 1971; Dec. 17, 1972; Dec. 16, 1972; Dec. 14, 1973; Dec. 15, 1973.

Washington Star, Dec. 16, 1969.

THE FORDS

"Christmas at the New Winter White House," *Globe Democrat Sunday Magazine,* Dec. 8, 1974.

Conger, Clement E. Interview with author, Washington, D.C., Nov. 4, 1993.

———. *A Nation's Pride: Art in the White House*. Washington, D.C.: White House Historical Association, 1992.

Ford, Betty. Interview with author by telephone. February 15, 1996.

———. *The Times of My Life*. New York: Harper & Row Publishers, 1978.

Gerald R. Ford Library. National Park Service, news release, Dec. 18, 1975; Office of the Press Secretary memorandum to Mrs. Ford, Dec. 15, 1975; news release to Mrs. Ford Dec. 9, 1976.

Weidenfeld Files Boxes 35, 36: 1974 Christmas Card List; "Christmas 1975."

Hallmark Archives. "Presidential Christmas Card Fact Sheet, 1990," news release.

Nesle, A.R., letter to Conger, C.E., August 24, 1972. Unpublished; printed with permission of A.R. Nesle.

Public Papers of the Presidents of the United States: Gerald R. Ford, 1973-75.

U.S. News and World Report, Dec. 30, 1974.

Washington Star, Dec. 19, 1975.

Washington Post, Dec. 14, 1974; Dec. 15, 1974; Dec. 18, 1974.

Weidenfeld, Sheila. *First Lady's Lady*.

THE CARTERS

Administration of Jimmy Carter, 1977-81. Remarks on the Lighting of the National Christmas Tree.

American Greetings Overview.

Antique Monthly, Jan. 15, 1979.

Carter, Rosalynn. Interview with author by telephone, Nov. 9, 1995.

Conger, Clement E. Interview with author, Washington, D.C., Nov. 4, 1993.

Gamarekian, Barbara, "The Carter Favorites," *The New York Times Magazine*, Jan. 29, 1978.

Jimmy Carter Library. White House Central File HO16-1: Carter, H., memorandum to Weddington, S., re: Christmas cards, Sep. 6, 1979; Poston, G., memorandum to Jordan, H., Aug. 23, 1977; "Press Preview of Christmas Decorations," memorandum from Poston, G., to Mrs. Carter, Dec. 15, 1980; "Summary of Christmas Card Project, 1978, Recommendations for 1979," memorandum from Simpson, J., to Carter, H., Mar. 2, 1979; Torricelli memorandum to Berman, M., re: Use of appropriated funds for Christmas greeting cards. June 18, 1979.

National Park Service, news release, Nov. 1, 1977.

New York Times, Dec. 17, 1982.

U.S. News and World Report, Dec. 25, 1978; Dec. 24, 1979.

Washington Post, Dec. 6, 1977; Dec. 14, 1977; Dec. 23, 1977; Dec. 14, 1979; Dec. 21, 1980; Dec. 21, 1980; Dec. 25, 1985.

Washington Star, Dec. 13, 1978.

THE REAGANS

Administration of Ronald Reagan, 1981–89. Remarks on the Lighting of the National Christmas Tree.

Bailey, Patricia, "Thomas William Jones," *USArt*, Jan./Feb. 1990.

Cauble, Diane, "From a Quiet Place, *Focus/Santa Fe*, Jan.-Feb.-Mar 1994.

"Christmas Wish Comes True for Little Amy Benham," National Park Service news release, Dec. 15, 1983.

Hampton, Mark. Interview with author by telephone, Oct. 8, 1993.

Jones, Thomas William. Interview with author, Snohomish, Washington. Oct. 10, 1993.

Journal American, Dec. 5, 1986.

Los Angeles Times, Dec. 19, 1983.

Philadelphia Inquirer. Dec. 25, 1982.

Reagan, Nancy. Interview with author by telephone. Oct. 11, 1995.

———, "Christmas Memories," *Washington Home*, Dec. 16, 1982.

———. *My Turn, The Memoirs of Nancy Reagan*, New York: Random House, 1989.

Reagan, Ronald. *An American Life*. New York: Simon and Schuster, 1990.

Ronald Reagan Library. Office of the Press Secretary, Message by the President, "Christmas 1984." Dec. 21, 1984, "Christmas, 1988," Dec. 19, 1988; "Text of the Radio Address by the President to the Nation," Dec. 25, 1982; Memorandum: Recommended Telephone Call to Amy Benham, April 13, 1984; Staffing Memorandum, December 11, 1985; "Remarks, Christmas in Washington Concert"; "Christmas in Washington," videotape. White House Social Files: Brandon, M., letter to Roussel, C., Nov. 16, 1981; Shankman, S., Executive Director of Second Genesis, letter to Mrs. Reagan, Dec. 15, 1982; Sheila Tate Files: Weinraub, Judith, "Interview With the First Lady," Dec. 8, 1982 (draft).

Steinmeyer, James. Interview with author by telephone, May 10, 1994.

Wall Street Journal, Nov. 13, 1983.

Washington Post, Dec. 6, 1981; Nov. 30, 1984; Dec. 9, 1986.

Washington Times. Dec. 6, 1983.

Wyeth, Jamie. Interview with author by telephone, Nov. 3, 1995.

THE GEORGE BUSHES

Administration of George Bush. Remarks on the Lighting of the National Christmas Tree; Message on the Observance of Christmas; Christmas Message to American Troops.

Bush, Barbara. Interview with author by telephone. Nov. 22, 1995.

———. *A Memoir*. New York: Charles Scribner's Sons, 1994.

Gemmell, Bill. Interview with author, Washington, D.C., Dec. 10, 1993.

Hampton, Mark. Written interview for the author, Oct. 8, 1993.

Kubik, Kamil. Interview with author, North Bergen, New Jersey, Sept. 4, 1994.

Linden, Patricia, "I'm glad they elected you President, Darling–but really, that wallpaper in the Office has got to go." *Town & Country*, June 1992.

Lee, Jeannette, and Unverferth, Fayrol. Interview on tape at Hallmark Archives, Kansas City, Missouri, July 27, 1993.

"The People's House of Barbara Bush," *Washington Home*, Jan. 16, 1992.

Press Tour of the White House Christmas Decorations, Dec. 1989.

Town and Country, June 1991.

Washington Post, Dec. 14, 1989; Dec. 11. 1990; Dec. 10, 1991; Dec. 16, 1991; Dec. 2, 1992; Dec. 8, 1992.

THE CLINTONS

American Greetings. *Expressions*, Dec. 1, 1995; "Facts About the 1995 White House Christmas Card," booklet.

Anderson News of Lawrenceburg, Kentucky, Nov. 17, 1993.

AOL News @ aol.com, Dec. 7, 1998.

Arkansas Times, Dec. 2, 1993.

Chicago Tribune, Nov. 8, 1993.

Cleveland *Plain Dealer*, Nov. 23, 1993; Dec. 7, 1993, Nov. 29, 1996.

Clinton Family, "A Holiday Message From our Family to Yours," *Parade* Sunday supplement, Dec. 19, 1993.

Clinton, Hillary Rodham, "A White House Christmas," *Washington Times*, Dec. 1995.

———, press preview of White House decorations, taped interview, Dec 6, 1994.

Clinton White House. Christmas statement at author's request, May 28, 1996.

Davis, Susan. Interview with author, by telephone, May 9, 1995.

Detroit News, Dec. 7, 1994.

Ellis, Ray. Interview with author, by telephone, Mar. 2, 2002.

Greenwich Time, Dec. 1, 1995.

Hartford Courant, Dec. 1995.

"Holiday Treasures at The White House 1999," White House program book.

Jackson, Kay. Interview with author, Washington, D.C., Apr. 22, 1998.

Journal Messenger, Jan. 27, 1995.

Kansas City Star, Dec. 10, 1999.

Kotz, Mary Lynn, "Art in the White House," *ART News*, Sept. 1994.

Lawton Constitution, Dec. 4, 1994.

Lee, Jeannette. Interview with author. Hallmark Archives, Kansas City, Missouri, July 27, 1993.

Litchfield County Times, December 1995.

Lloyd, Nancy, "A White House Christmas," *Family Circle*, Dec. 21, 1993.

McCoy, Anne. Interview with author, by telephone, May 9, 1995.

McKnight, Thomas. Interview with author, by telephone, June 12, 1995, Dec. 13, 1995, Aug. 13, 1997.

———. *Voyage to Paradise*. San Francisco: Harper, 1993.

New York Times, Dec. 26, 1992; Dec. 7, 1993; Dec. 5, 1995.

Office of the Press Secretary, Remarks by the President at the Pageant of Peace; Remarks by the President in Christmas Eve Message to the Troops in Bosnia, Dec. 24, 1995.

Omaha World Herald, Jan. 3, 1999.

Palm Beach Daily News, Dec. 4, 1994; Dec. 6, 1995.

Palm Beach Post, Dec. 22, 1998.

Philadelphia Daily News, Dec. 7, 1993.

Richmond Times, Dec. 7, 1993.

State Journal of Frankfort, Kentucky, Nov. 18, 1993.

Stock, Ann. Interview with author, Washington, D.C., Jan. 7, 1994, Jan. 10, 1995.

Tampa Tribune, Feb. 13, 1999; Dec. 20, 1999.

Times Leader of Martins Ferry, Ohio, Dec. 4, 1994.

USA Today, Dec. 7, 1993; Dec. 1, 1994; Dec. 8, 1998.

Washington Post, Nov. 3, 1993; Nov. 4, 1993; Dec. 7, 1993; Dec. 25, 1993;

Dec. 9, 1994. Washington Home Section, Dec. 9, 1993; Dec. 19, 1998; Dec. 9, 1999; Dec. 26, 1999; Dec. 5, 2000; Mar. 6, 2002.

Washington Times, Dec. 7, 1993; Dec. 5, 1995; Dec. 25, 1995; Dec. 26, 1995; Dec. 20, 1998; Dec. 20, 1999; Dec. 25, 1999; Dec. 5, 2000; Dec. 12, 2000; Dec. 20, 2000; Dec. 25, 2000; Dec. 31, 2000.

Williams, Jeannie, "White House's Best Wishes," *USA Today*, Dec. 7, 1993.

THE GEORGE W. BUSHES

Albuquerque Journal, Nov. 30, 2007.

"All Creatures Great and Small," interview with Laura Bush by Bill Plante, CBS *Early Show*, Dec. 4, 2004.

Allman, William. Interview with author, by fax, March 8, 2008.

Anderson-Lee, Peg. Interview with author, by email, March 11, 2002

Ask the White House, georgewbush-whitehouse.archives.gov, Dec. 20, 2007.

Australian, Dec. 10, 2005.

Ball, Andrea. Interview with author, by telephone, March 7, 2005.

Blake, James R. Interview with author by telephone, March 21, 2007.

"Bush Declares Four-Day Holiday Weekend," www.FoxNewsChannel.com, Associated Press, Dec. 7, 2001.

Bush, Laura. Interviews with author, by telephone, March 27, 2002.

———. Interview on Larry King Live, transcript. www.CNN.com, Dec. 18, 2001.

Christian Science Monitor, Dec. 24, 2008.

"Christmas Pageant of Peace 2001," program book.

Downingtown Ledger, Dec. 20–26, 2001.

Drummond, David. Interview with author by email, March 26, 2014.

drummondart.com/news_whcc2007.htm.

Fineman, Howard, and Brant, Martha, "This Is Our Life Now," *Newsweek*, Dec. 3, 2001.

"First Lady Welcomes Holiday Season by Turning White House into Winter Wonderland," www.MSNBC.com, Dec. 4, 2001.

Fort Worth-Star Telegram, Jan. 1, 2007.

Hallmark Noon News, Dec. 3, 2001.

Hallmark press releases: "Hallmark Designs 2002 Presidential Holiday Card"; "Hallmark Designs 2003 Presidential Holiday Card"; "Hallmark Designs 2004 Presidential Holiday Card"; "Hallmark Designs 2005 Presidential Holiday Card"; "Hallmark Designs

2006 Presidential Holiday Card." Hallmark Press Room, Nov. 30, 2004.

Holt, Cindi. Interview with author, by telephone, Feb. 24, 2005.

"Home for the Holidays, The White House 2001," White House program book.

Lawrence Journal-World, Nov. 27, 2001; Feb. 10, 2002.

Lawson, Tim Allen. Interview with author by telephone, March 31, 2014.

Lilliefors, James., "Question and Answer: Jamie Wyeth," *The Phil Archives*, Philharmonic Center for the Arts, Naples, Fla., March-June 2006.

Marietta Daily Journal, Nov. 24, 2002.

Martinez, Adrian. Interview with author, by telephone, Feb. 19, 2002.

Milwaukee Journal Sentinel, Dec. 22, 2001.

Monkman, Betty. Interview with author, by telephone, March 19, 2002.

New York Times, Dec. 6, 2002; Dec. 9, 2002; Dec. 21, 2003.

New York Times National, Dec. 4, 2001.

Office of the First Lady, Remarks by Mrs. Bush at the White House Holiday Press Preview; Dec. 2, 2004; "Fact Sheet: White House Holiday Decorations," Dec. 2, 2004; "Fact Sheet: White House Holiday Decorations," Nov. 30, 2005; Remarks by Mrs. Bush at the White House Holiday Press Preview, Nov. 30, 2005; "Fact Sheet: White House Holiday Decorations," Nov. 30, 2006; Mrs. Bush's Remarks at a media preview, Nov. 29, 2007; Dec. 3, 2008. "Fact Sheet: White House Decorations," Dec. 3, 2008. Interview of Mrs. Bush by ABC's *Good Morning, America,* Nov. 29, 2007, Dec. 3, 2008. Interview of Mrs. Bush by CBS News' *The Early Show*, Nov. 29, 2007, Dec. 3, 2008. Interview of Mrs. Bush by CNN's *American Morning*, Nov. 29, 2007, Dec. 3, 2008. Interview of Mrs. Bush by Fox's *Fox and Friends*, Nov. 29, 2007, Dec. 3, 2008. Interview of Mrs. Bush by NBC's *Today Show*, Nov. 29, 2007, Dec. 3, 2008.

Office of the Press Secretary, Remarks by the President at Pageant of Peace Ceremony, Dec. 6, 2001; Remarks by the President in Honor of Eid Al-Fitr, Dec. 17, 2001; Christmas Radio Message by the President to the Nation, Dec. 25, 2001; "President Bush Meets with Troops in Iraq on Thanksgiving," Nov. 27, 2003;

"President Bush Lights the National Christmas Tree, Remarks by the President at the Pageant of Peace," Dec. 4, 2003; "President Bush Addresses Nation on the Capture of Saddam Hussein," Dec. 14, 2003; President's Christmas Message, Dec. 23, 2004; "President Bush Lights National Christmas Tree at Pageant of Peace," Dec. 19, 2005; President's Christmas Message, Dec. 19, 2005; "President and Mrs. Bush Host Children's Holiday Reception at the White House, Dec. 4, 2006; "President Bush Attends Lighting of the National Christmas Tree Ceremony," Dec. 6, 2007; "Presidential Message: Christmas 2007," Dec. 21, 2007; "President Bush Makes Christmas Eve Telephone Calls to Members of the Armed Forces," Dec. 24, 2007. "Presidential Message to the Men and Women of the United States Armed Forces, Dec. 18, 2006; "President and Mrs. Bush Participate in a Holiday Service Project," Dec. 22, 2006; "President Bush Makes Christmas Eve Telephone Calls to Members of the Armed Forces, Dec. 24, 2006.

Press briefing by National Security Advisor on President's meeting with Prime Minister Maliki, Nov. 30, 2006.

Prey, Barbara Ernst. Interview with author by telephone, March 1, 2005.

PRNewswire.com, Nov. 30, 2007. "Hallmark Designs 2007 Presidential Holiday Card."

"Q & A With First Lady Laura Bush, special presentation," Home and Garden Television, Dec. 5, 2004.

Stifter, Dan. Interview with author by telephone, March 10, 2005.

Tampa Tribune, Dec. 25, 2001.

USA Today, Dec. 20, 2001.

Washington Post, Dec. 7, 2001; Dec. 8, 2001; Dec. 10, 2001; Dec. 11, 2001; Dec. 21, 2001; Dec. 22, 2001; Dec. 7, 2005.

Washington Times, Nov. 21, 2001; Dec. 8, 2005.

"White House Cancels Holiday Tours," www.FoxNewsChannel.com, Nov. 21, 2001.

"White House Christmas 2001, White House Tour: Behind the Scenes With Laura Bush," hosted by Joy Philbin, Home and Garden Television, December 2001.

SOURCES

"White House Christmas 2002," hosted by Joan Steffend, Home and Garden Television, December 2002.

"White House Christmas 2003," hosted by Joan Steffend, Home and Garden Television, December 2003.

"White House Christmas 2004," hosted by Joan Steffend, Home and Garden Television, December 2004.

"White House Christmas Interview with President and Mrs. Bush," by Barbara Walters, transcript. www.ABC.com, Dec. 5, 2001.

"White House Christmas With Laura Bush," hosted by Jim Angle, Fox News Channel Television, December 2001.

White House Tour Guide Books: "A Season of Stories, Holidays at the White House 2003"; "A Season of Merriment and Melody, Holidays at the White House 2004."

White House Visitors' Booklet, 2008.

Ungaro, Susan Kelliher, "Why Traditions Matter," *Family Circle*, Dec. 18, 2001.

Zhen-Huan Lu. Interview with author, by telephone, Feb., 21, 2005.

THE OBAMAS

ABC.com, Dec. 15, 2011.

ABCNews.go.com, Dec. 6, 2012; Jan. 2, 2015.

American President's Blog, Dec. 18, 2011.

Biggovernment.com, Dec. 24, 2009.

Bloomberg News, Dec. 29, 2014.

CBSNews, Nov. 29, 2016.

Chicago Tribune, Dec. 3, 2009.

Childrensnational.org, Dec. 16, 2013.

Cleveland.com, Dec. 12, 2009; Jan. 2, 2010.

CNNPolitics.com, Dec. 26, 2016.

Connecticutmag.com, Dec. 10, 2014.

Dailycaller.com, Jan. 6, 2014.

Des Moines Register, Dec. 4, 2012.

Foxct.com, Dec. 24, 2014.

Foxnews.com, Dec. 24, 2009; Dec. 10, 2012; Dec. 16, 2013.

Hankinson, Chris. Interview with author by email, July 29, 2014.

Hawaiireporter.com, Dec. 16, 2013.

Holidays at the White House booklets: "Joy to All," 2012; "A Children's Winter Wonderland," 2014; "A Timeless Tradition," 2015; "The Gift of the Holidays," 2016.

Huffingtonpost.com, Dec. 18, 2009; Dec. 5, 2016, Dec. 20, 2016.

Kabel, Larassa. Interview with author by email, July 30, 2014.

Los Angeles Times, Dec. 15, 2011; Dec. 10, 2013.

Macomb Daily News, Jan. 7, 2014.

Meenayi.com, 2015, 2016 White House holiday cards.

MoodyontheMarket.com, Dec. 2013.

Monroe News, Dec. 21, 2013.

Mxschool.edu/news-events/articles, Dec. 14, 2014.

NBCNews.com, Dec. 19, 2012; Dec. 20, 2012.

New York Post, Dec. 12, 2016.

New York Times, Dec. 4, 2009.

Obama Foodorama, Dec. 4, 2013.

Office of the First Lady, Mrs. Obama's remarks at a Holiday Press Preview, Dec. 2, 2009; Dec. 1, 2010; Nov. 30, 2011; Nov. 28, 2012; Dec. 4, 2013; Dec. 3, 2014; Dec. 2, 2015; Dec. 7, 2016. Remarks by the First Lady at Annual Toys for Tots event, Dec. 9, 2015. Remarks by the First Lady at Children's National Health System, Dec. 15, 2014; Dec. 9, 2015.

Office of Media Affairs, "Information on White House Christmas," Dec. 4, 2013.

Office of the Press Secretary, Remarks by the President at the Lighting of the National Christmas Tree, Dec. 3, 2009; Dec. 9, 2010; Dec. 1, 2011; Dec. 6, 2012; Dec. 6, 2013; Dec. 4, 2014; Dec. 3, 2015; Dec. 1, 2016.

Politico.com, Mar. 16, 2010.

President Obama Blog, Dec. 25, 2012.

Refinery29.com, Dec. 11, 2016.

Seattle Times, Dec. 10, 2009.

USNews.com, Dec. 4, 2014.

Washington Post, Oct. 21, 2009; Feb. 19,2011; Dec. 21, 2013; Dec. 3, 2014; Dec. 4, 2014; Nov. 29, 2016.

Weekly address on YouTube: "The President and First Lady Extend Christmas Greetings," Dec. 25, 2010; Dec. 25, 2113; Dec. 25, 2016.

White House Blog, Dec. 1, 2010; Dec. 2, 2010; Dec. 10, 2010; Nov. 28, 2012; Dec. 4, 2012; Dec. 20, 2013.

THE TRUMPS

AOL Politics, Geobeats: Dec. 25, 2017.

AP News, Dec. 13, 2017.

Associated Press, Nov. 21, 2017; Nov. 27, 2017: "Decorations Are up for a Themed Christmas at the White House"; Nov. 27, 2017: "First Lady Goes With Classic, Traditional Christmas Décor"; Dec. 1, 2017.

BBC.com/news/world-us-canada, Dec. 3, 2017.

Business Insider, Nov. 28, 2017.

CNN, Dec. 13, 2017; Dec. 26, 2017.

Dailysignal.com, Nov. 29, 2017.

Family Research Council, Dec. 21, 2017.

Fox6now.com, Sept. 19, 2017.

FRC.org, Nov. 28, 2017.

Lifesite, Dec 1, 2017.

National Christmas Tree-Lighting program, 2017.

NYPost.com, Dec. 16, 2017.

TheHill.com, Dec. 13, 2017; Dec. 21, 2017; Dec. 24, 2017.

Washington Post, Reliable Source, Dec. 1, 2017.

Washington Post, Style, Nov. 27, 2017.

Washington Times, Dec. 7, 2017.

White House Tour Booklet, "Time-Honored Traditions: Christmas at the White House, 2017."

whitehouse.gov, Nov. 27, 2017: "First Lady Melania Trump Unveils Christmas at the White House"; Dec. 1, 2017: "Photos of the Week: Christmas at the White House"; Dec. 4, 2017: "Second Lady Karen Pence Unveils the Christmas Decorations at the Vice President's Residence"; Dec. 5, 2017: "First Lady Melania Trump and Second Lady Karen Pence to Visit Texas for Continued Hurricane Relief"; Dec. 12, 2017: "Christmas at the White House"; Dec. 14, 2017; "Merry Christmas From President Donald J. Trump and First Lady Melania Trump"; Dec. 24, 2017: "Christmas Eve Photo From President Donald J. Trump and First Lady Melania Trump."

TWITTER: Melania Trump @FLOTUS, Nov., Dec. 2017

Nov. 17: This year's @WhiteHouse Christmas booklet is in printing!

Nov. 20: Retweet, World News Tonight: FL Melania Trump, son Barron welcomed the White House tree.

Nov. 20: Thank you, Silent Night Evergreens in Wisconsin: Video.

Nov. 22: Preparations are underway to celebrate the holidays at the @WhiteHouse!

Nov. 27: The decorations are up! @whitehouse is ready to celebrate! Video.

Nov. 27: Had a wonderful visit from @JBA_NAFW children today @whitehouse!

Nov. 28: So important to thank our service members for their service especially those away.

Nov. 29: Thank you to the talented performers from Vivid Ballet Company who helped us unveil decorations.

Nov. 30: Retweet, World News Tonight: President Trump and FL Melania Trump Participate in LNCT.

Dec. 6: Thoughts and prayers to those affected by wildfires in CA.

Dec. 6: Thank you #Texas.

Dec. 7: Today we honor Pearl Harbor heroes. Thank you to all military for your courage.

Dec. 7: Wonderful to spend time with @secondlady Mrs. Pence @TexasFLCA Mrs. Abbott.

Dec. 7: Fun questions from the kids @childrenshealth with NBC News video @NBCNEWS.

Dec. 8: I was so grateful at the opportunity to spend time with the children and families yesterday.

Dec. 10: The effects of the hurricane season are still being felt and residents still need our help.

Dec. 12: Enjoyed last week's visit to @childrenshealth in DC. Wonderful to meet brave patients.

Dec. 13: Great day with military families @ JBABdc as we sorted toys for children.

Dec .14: Merry Christmas from President and First Lady Melania Trump in official portrait.

Dec. 24: Looking forward to helping kids track Santa today.

Dec. 25: Retweet, Merry Christmas Video.

YouTube Videos, Nov., Dec. 2017

Nov. 27: First Lady Melania Trump Unveils White House Christmas Decorations, Channel 90. youtube.com/watch?v=w5qcfsZUSxg.

Nov. 30: President Trump's Christmas Speech 2017.

Dec. 1: Trump Worries That Americans Don't Say "Merry Christmas."

Dec. 1: We're Saying "Merry Christmas" Again.

Dec. 7: First Lady Melania Trump Reads a Christmas Story to Children at Children's National Hospital.

Dec. 7: Remarks: Donald Trump Hosts a Chanukah Party at the White House.

Dec. 13: Melania Trump Visits Kids, Helps With Toys for Tots Campaign.

Dec. 24: Trump Participates in Christmas Eve Video to Military.

Dec. 24: President Trump's Christmas at Mar-a-Lago.

Dec. 24: President Trump and First Lady Attend Midnight Mass.

Dec. 25: President Trump and First Lady Melania Trump's 2017 Christmas Message.

Dec. 26: President Marks First Christmas in Office.

Dec. 30: Weekly Message.

PERMISSIONS

The Seeley Collection of
Presidential Christmas Memorabilia

Recognized nationally, the Seeley Collection has been the holiday centerpiece of 10 Presidential libraries and numerous other museums from coast to coast. As one of the most extensive collections of its kind—comprised of hundreds of rare and unique items—it documents and details Christmas at the White House. Often, however, the stories behind the artifacts are of equal significance to the collector.

The earliest item is a handwritten letter by President **James Madison** thanking a gentleman for his Christmas gift of 1829. On Christmas Day, 1880, President-elect **James Garfield** signed daughter Mollie's velvet autograph book. Then there's an original hand-painted and calligraphy rendition of **Calvin Coolidge**'s 1927 Christmas message, once rescued from a garage sale.

Favorite artifacts: an original military telegram from the War Department to a prison camp dated December 24, 1863, in which **A. Lincoln** requests the release of two boy soldier "Rebel POWS"; a rare Autographed Letter Signed by President **Chester Arthur** expressing Christmas greetings to his friend R.G. Dun of D&B; and a signed D-Day Prayer written by **FDR**, with four sons in the war, to his Secretary of War.

Perhaps the rarest part of the Seeley Collection documents the shortened administration of John F. Kennedy: two of only 30 Crèche cards signed by both **President and Mrs. Kennedy** just prior to the President's death in 1963; the only 1963 Green Room gift print that Jacqueline Kennedy inscribed—with 50 words to artist Edward Lehman in appreciation of the art he had painted for them; and the original 1964 Blue Room painting that Lehman created for what was to have been the Kennedys' 1964 Christmas gift print. President Kennedy actually held the art in his hands and said the Blue Room was his favorite of the three state rooms.

Another one-of-a-kind collectible is a Hallmark prototype of what was planned to be **Richard Nixon**'s 1974 gift print, in a velour folder, featuring President Woodrow Wilson. A true treasure, indeed, is Thomas William Jones' original art of the North Entry Hall that he painted for **President and Mrs. Reagan**'s final Christmas. Dr. Seeley purchased it as a gift for his wife in recognition of the work she had done to preserve America's heritage.

Ronald Seeley, the inveterate collector, continues to keep the collection current through each administration. Due to his exuberance, select historical pieces are available for purchase.

**For more information about the Seeley Collection of
Presidential Christmas Memorabilia,
contact Ronald and Mary Seeley:
MLS42@aol.com or whitehouseholidays.com.**